The World of William Glackens

VOLUME III

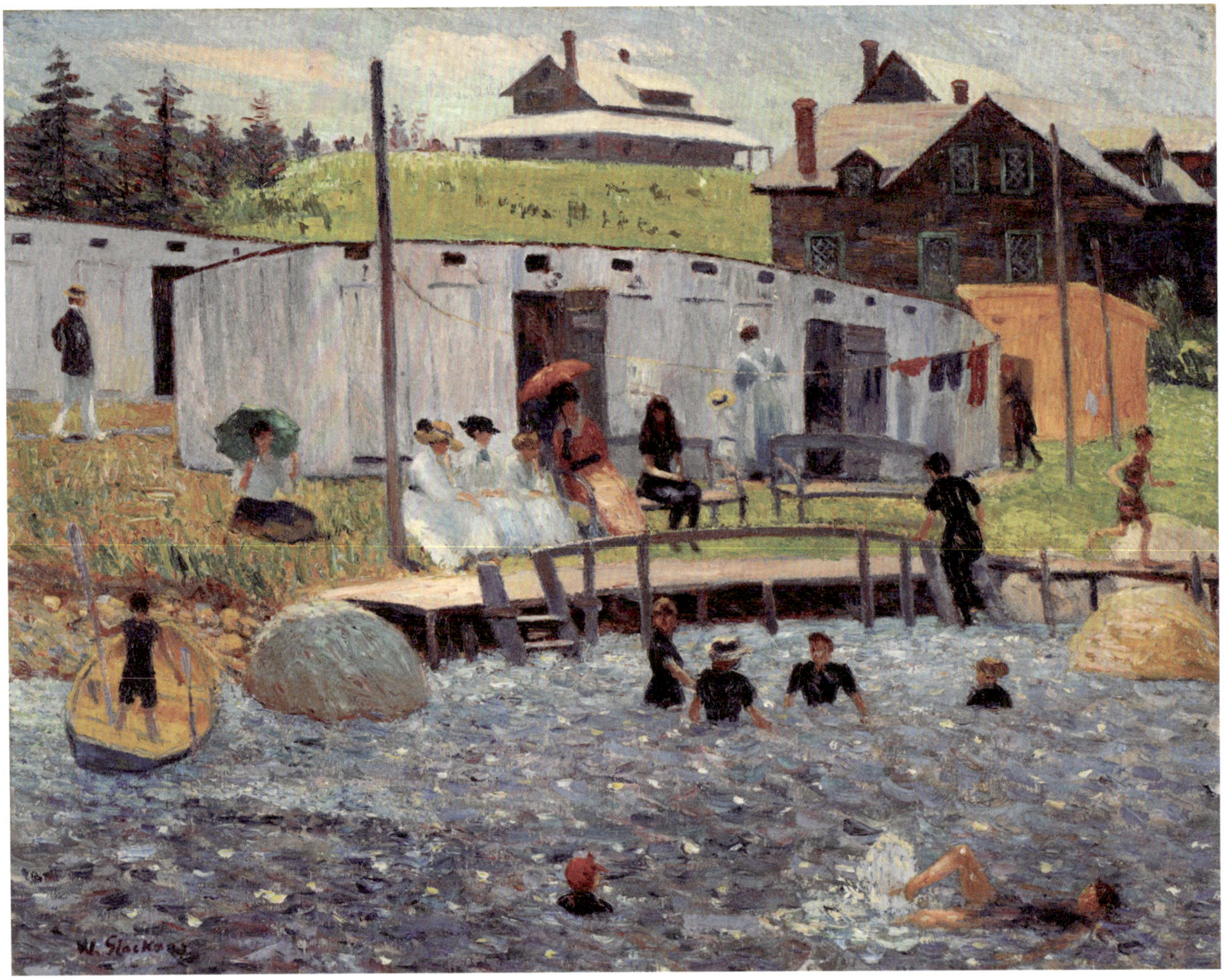
W. Glackens

THE WORLD OF
William Glackens

VOLUME III

The C. Richard Hilker Art Lectures

Essays by

Avis Berman

Heather Campbell Coyle

David B. Dearinger

Kathleen A. Foster

Carol Troyen

The Sansom Foundation, Inc.

Stephanie Salomon, *Project Manager and Editor*
Sarah Wolberg, *Copy Editor*
Jacob Horn, *Proofreader*
Anita Duquette, *Picture Researcher, Rights, and Permissions*
Barbara Smith, *Indexer*

Tina Henderson and Rita Jules, Miko McGinty Inc., *Design and Typesetting based on previous volumes in this series*

Printed by GHP Media
East Haven, Connecticut
Stock: 100 lb. Mohawk Superfine Ultrawhite

ISBN: 979-8-218-52877-5

FRONTISPIECE
William Glackens
The Bathing Hour, Chester, Nova Scotia, 1910
Oil on canvas
26 × 32 in. (66 × 81.3 cm)
The Barnes Foundation, Philadelphia; BF149

Contents

Preface and Acknowledgments

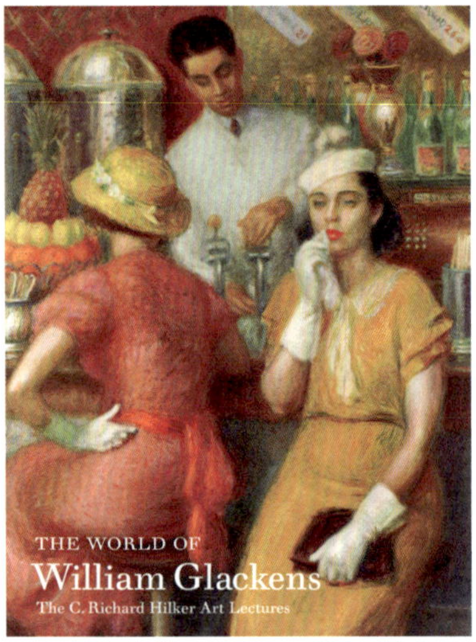

The World of William Glackens,
Volume I, cover.

Volume III of *The World of William Glackens: The C. Richard Hilker Art Lectures* marks the conclusion of a series of publications that began more than two decades ago. It has been my privilege to introduce the two previous volumes on behalf of the Board of Directors of The Sansom Foundation. It is indeed a pleasure to present this third volume.

The lectures and their publication would not have been possible without the foresight of Ira and Nancy Glackens who established The Sansom Foundation in 1956. This endowment continues to permit the Foundation to make significant contributions to American art and culture.

Avis Berman, Heather Campbell Coyle, David B. Dearinger, Kathleen A. Foster, and Carol Troyen have our gratitude for their groundbreaking contributions brought to life in each of the five lectures—given from 2017 to 2022—and in this volume as splendidly illustrated essays. These essays provide both the expert and the general reader with a wealth of information that the Foundation hopes will foster further interest in, and research focused on, nineteenth- and early twentieth-century American art.

In the first essay, "The Butterfly and the Ashcan: The Impact of Whistler on The Eight and Their Circle," writer and art historian Avis Berman delves into works by James McNeill Whistler and their influence on William Glackens, Robert Henri, Ernest Lawson, Maurice Prendergast, Joan Sloan, Alfred Maurer, and George Bellows.

Carol Troyen, the Roger Servison Curator Emerita of American Paintings, at the Museum of Fine Arts, Boston, examines the work that Glackens, Frederic Remington, and Howard Chandler Christy made at a turbulent time in Cuba in "Images and Imperialisms: American Artists and Cuba at the Turn of the Twentieth Century."

"Was the Medium the Message? American Artists Rediscover Pastel at the Turn of the Twentieth Century," by Kathleen A. Foster, Robert L. McNeil Jr., Senior Curator of American Art and Director, Center for American Art at the Philadelphia Museum of Art, takes a

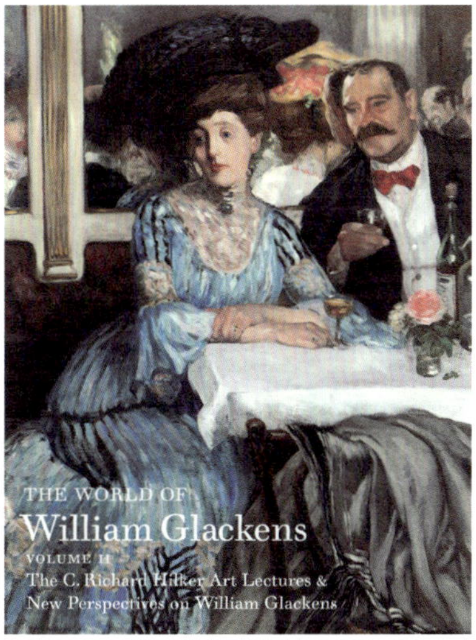

The World of William Glackens, Volume II, cover.

striking look at the employment of this intimate medium by Whistler, Glackens, Everett Shinn, Mary Cassatt, Arthur B. Davies, Arthur Dove, Joseph Stella, and Georgia O'Keeffe.

Art historian and museum curator David B. Dearinger's "What a Relief! Innovations in American Sculpture, 1875–1910" focuses on the work of Augustus Saint-Gaudens and Daniel Chester French.

The final essay, "Fishing Lure: George Luks in Nova Scotia," by Heather Campbell Coyle, Curator of American Art at the Delaware Art Museum, examines the urban realist painter's very personal forays into the natural artistry of the Canadian wilderness.

The Sansom Foundation is particularly indebted to our dear friend and colleague Doris Palca, whose vision, discerning judgment, and unerring eye are reflected in all three volumes of *The World of William Glackens* and to whom this third volume is gratefully dedicated. We also thank Emily Russell, who provided invaluable advice concerning the publications.

As the Foundation brings the C. Richard Hilker Art Lectures series to a close, it is the Board's hope that readers will find this volume as enlightening and engrossing as the previous two volumes. Going forward, we have no doubt that The Sansom Foundation will continue to support various worthwhile projects concerning American art, and the arts generally, in ongoing fulfillment of the wishes of our Founders.

Frank Buscaglia
PRESIDENT
THE SANSOM FOUNDATION, INC.
DECEMBER 2024

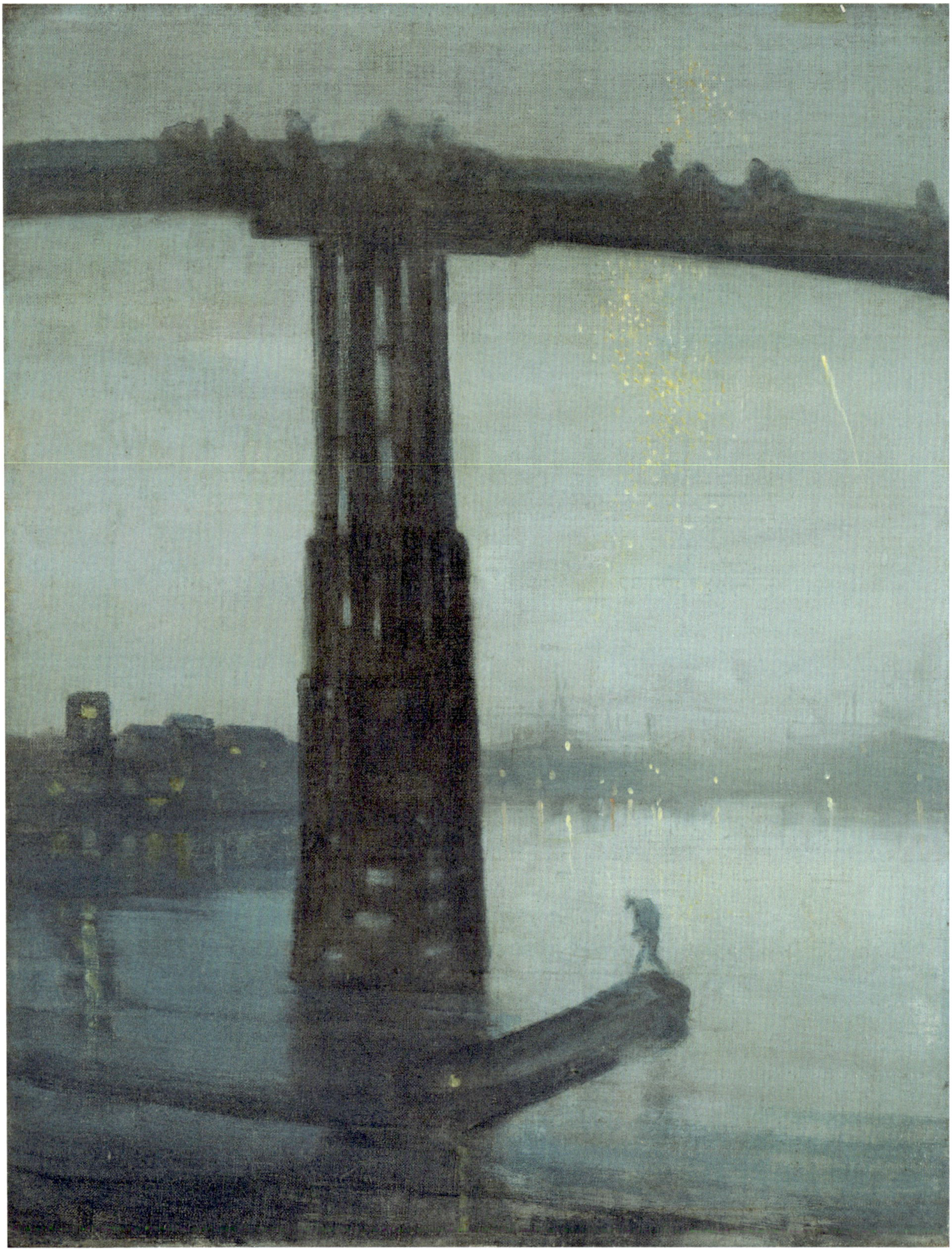

Compliments of The Sansom Foundation, Inc.

Lecture given on
May 4, 2017

Museum of the
City of New York

New York City

The Butterfly and the Ashcan: The Impact of Whistler on The Eight and Their Circle

AVIS BERMAN

The most famous American artist of the late nineteenth and early twentieth centuries, James McNeill Whistler (Fig. 2), an expatriate Yankee who shuttled between studios in London and Paris, was an avatar of modernism for his peers who stayed at home. By the mid-1880s, with *Arrangement in Grey and Black No. 1* (1871; Musée D'Orsay, Paris), the iconic portrait of the artist's mother, earning triumphant reviews in exhibitions in Philadelphia and New York, along with the publication of his "Ten O'Clock" lecture, Whistler's most sustained proclamation of the art-for-art's-sake philosophy, his status as a celebrity as well as a serious artist was assured. His monogram signature of the butterfly, which he began using as a design element in the 1860s, became a nickname and a shorthand for the fastidious aestheticism that he embodied, although Whistler, whose wit lacerated his critics, was a butterfly armed with a whiplash sting.

The affectations belied a lasting record of innovation. Whistler's art paralleled and sometimes predated Impressionism in the modernity of its subject matter and in its use of color and light, and he was a pioneer in extending the imagery and spatial premises of Asian art into Western painting. In his distinctly nonnarrative and atmospheric night paintings of London, or "Nocturnes," as he so immortally titled them, Whistler not only claimed the subject of the urban night but also took painting to the brink of abstraction. He was critical to the nineteenth-century revivals of etching and pastel, which were then neglected media. Whistler was not the greatest painter of his age, but he was one of the most meaningful for other artists; for Americans in particular, he was one of the few of their own who had prevailed on an international stage. As Linda Merrill has pointed out, Whistler's aesthetic philosophy, his "radically original style," and the audacity of his public persona "exercised a decisive influence" on turn-of-the-century American painting and printmaking.[1]

Among those artists who profited deeply from Whistler's work and example were five members of The Eight: William Glackens, Robert

Fig. 1
James McNeill Whistler
Nocturne: Blue and Gold—Old Battersea Bridge, c. 1872–75
Oil on canvas
26⅞ × 20⅛ in. (68.3 × 51.2 cm)
Tate Britain, London; Presented by the Art Fund 1905 N01959

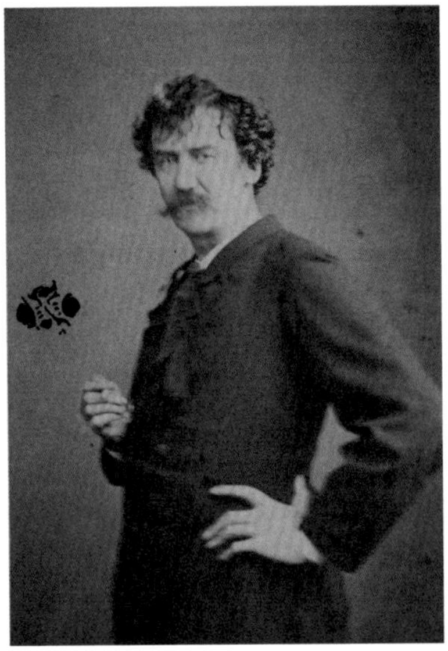

Fig. 2
James McNeill Whistler with butterfly monogram
Photograph published by London Stereoscopic Co., 1878
Library of Congress Prints and Photographs Division, Washington, DC

Henri, Ernest Lawson, Maurice Prendergast, and John Sloan.[2] They all studied Whistler closely, as did their peers and early co-exhibitors Alfred Maurer and George Bellows. Given the preceding calibration of the magnitude of Whistler's star power, this may not appear to be a startling or profound insight. But unlike the legions of self-proclaimed disciples—such as the young Americans who knew Whistler in Venice in 1879–80, like Frank Duveneck and Robert Blum, or Whistler's friend, admirer, and indefatigable advocate William Merritt Chase, or the Tonalists John Henry Twachtman, Henry Ossawa Tanner, and Thomas Wilmer Dewing, who produced their own nocturnes, gray-green landscapes, and vignettes of ethereal women in misty interiors—the realist painters allied with the Ashcan School or with The Eight are almost never characterized as succumbing to Whistler. Sloan, Henri, Glackens, Everett Shinn, and George Luks were key members of both groups, but it is necessary to differentiate between them. Rather than a true movement or school, the Ashcan rubric encompassed a loose coalition of artists, beginning with the Henri circle, who painted lively and sympathetic scenes of New York life with an approach that was new to American art; the results, on canvas and in drawings and prints, were buoyed by a democratic verisimilitude and unafraid of the harsher side of the urban milieu—they portrayed bums, tenements, and ashcans. Rather than the Four Hundred, the elite who populated the canvases of genteel painters of the Gilded Age, the Ashcan artists focused on the equivalent of O. Henry's Four Million, whose experiences were underrepresented in art.

The artists of the first generation of the Ashcan School were Henri, Sloan, Glackens, Shinn, Luks, and their friend Jerome Myers. The second generation consisted of some of Henri's most important students, including George Bellows, Glenn O. Coleman, and the early Stuart Davis. The Eight solely consisted of artists who exhibited together just once, in the historic exhibition at Macbeth Galleries in 1908. Joining Sloan, Henri, Glackens, Luks, and Shinn as members of The Eight were three painters who eschewed the yeastiness of Ashcan representation—Arthur B. Davies, Lawson, and Prendergast.

The Eight and the Ashcan painters are typically branded as opposing the doctrine of exquisiteness articulated by Whistler, but that assumption is questionable. As H. Barbara Weinberg has noted, dichotomies between groups and schools of artists are often "deceptive" and "exaggerated."[3] Past scholarship has reflexively emphasized the realists' "art for life's sake" credo, which exalted the rough and the uncouth at the expense of a Whistler-inspired "art for art's sake" viewpoint that was deemed too removed from the actualities of existence.[4] They were promoted as muscular and virile,[5] because they took their subjects from low-down precincts. However, what appeared to be defined as the art-for-art's-sake ethos was either a saccharine academic idealism that was often photographic in detail or similarly escapist nods to prevailing good taste.[6] Such grotesque misinterpretations of intent may have been true of Whistler's more pedestrian acolytes, but not of the man himself. Long on record as an enemy of anecdotal and moralistic art, Whistler despised literalism as an imaginative work's raison d'être and agitated for the artist's right to render appearances as he or she wished. Whistler did deal with the facts of life, but he noted them in a spare, elliptical manner. The painter and critic Guy Pène du Bois, who saw The Eight show and knew all the artists in it, commented, "Whistler, through the old masters, influenced the tone of the exhibition."[7]

The young American realists admired and learned from Whistler. They quietly but regularly turned to him for artistic solutions. Even Bellows stated that Whistler was one of the American artists who influenced him the most. And, after all, if the principle of making art for life's sake is taken literally, if the inchoateness of life is not modified by a more conscious shaping into a whole, then no lasting work of art will be created. Sloan himself theorized, "In nature we see a tangled document of form and color... out of which the mind identifies form. The mind takes hold of the phenomena of color and turns them into things."[8] This seems nothing less than a call-and-response to Whistler's formulation, "To say to the painter, that Nature is to be taken as she is, is to say to the player, that he may sit on the piano."[9] Glackens later observed that Whistler was a "young painter's" attraction,[10] and none of the infatuations with him were permanent, but their existence suggests that the catalysts of modernism are more various than one might think. The ubiquity of Whistler's presence challenges the standard pedigree of early twentieth-century American realism. Along with Rembrandt, Velázquez, Frans Hals, Édouard Manet, and Thomas Eakins, he should be accepted as a consistent and co-equal precursor by tracing "the Whistlerian moment" of these seven artists, when the butterfly alighted on the ashcan.

What did our seven artists know of Whistler, and when did they know it? And why was this strain of influence largely ignored? Part of the difficulty lies in untangling the intricacies of art history, especially as they pertain to the artistic heroes of the mid-nineteenth century. A well-rehearsed trope of modern art is that its French masters, most notably Gustave Courbet and Manet, discovered and emulated the work of the great Spanish painters El Greco, Goya, and especially Velázquez. Furthermore, the transmission of Hispanic (and Dutch) painting via the French avant-garde as an ongoing artistic legacy was handed down by Chase and Henri, the leading late nineteenth-century professional instructors of American artists, but they always acknowledged Whistler in the classroom and on the easel. Only in later retellings was Whistler dropped from the story and Manet left as the leading protagonist.

However, to Chase and Henri, Whistler and Manet were contemporaries who enriched their own work by identifying with the seventeenth-century Spanish and Dutch artists' sensitivity to the medium of paint. Manet was born in 1832 and Whistler in 1834, and since Whistler lived in Paris in the 1850s and went back and forth frequently after he moved to London in 1859, he knew what the strongest artists in France were doing. As a young man, Whistler was close to Courbet, the leader of the new modern movement, and he met Manet in the summer of 1861, well after he had painted *At the Piano* (1858–59; Taft Museum of Art, Cincinnati), *The Thames in Ice* (1860; Freer Gallery of Art, Smithsonian Institution, Washington, DC), and *Wapping* (1860–64; National Gallery of Art, Washington, DC). All three canvases demonstrate that he had already grasped the new realism and understood its motifs and sources. Whistler's *Symphony in White, No. 1: The White Girl* (1862; National Gallery of Art, Washington, DC) and Manet's *Luncheon on the Grass* (1863; Musée d'Orsay) were the most controversial and execrated pictures in the Salon des Refusés of 1863. The two men were on such parallel tracks that Whistler was accepted as a core member of the French avant-garde, as Henri Fantin-Latour documented in *Homage to Delacroix* (1864; Musée d'Orsay), in which he made Whistler and Manet the central figures in his composition. For many years, the two men were brother innovators and touchstones of the modern, not an either-or choice.

The most significant distinction between Manet and Whistler for the American artists under discussion was the difference between an immediate versus a secondhand experience of their work, particularly at a time when black-and-white engravings and occasional photographs were all that were available as reproductions. For those who could not go abroad, Whistler was exhibited in the United States far more than Manet, especially in Philadelphia, where five of The Eight first lived; they were too young to have seen the huge 1886 Impressionist exhibitions in New York, filled with works by Manet. Moreover, Manet died in 1883, whereas Whistler was professionally active and very much alive, producing new work, including portraits for Philadelphia clients,[11] and constantly in the press. There was more opportunity for the Philadelphians to learn about Whistler and see his work before they moved to Manhattan, where Manet was in the collection of the Metropolitan Museum of Art and exhibited in the New York branch of the Durand-Ruel Galleries.

In October 1886, twenty-one-year-old Robert Henri, an art student from Atlantic City, arrived in Philadelphia to enroll in the Pennsylvania Academy of the Fine Arts, the oldest art school in the country. Thomas Anshutz and Thomas Hovenden, his principal professors, grounded him in realist fundamentals; whether or not he heard about Whistler

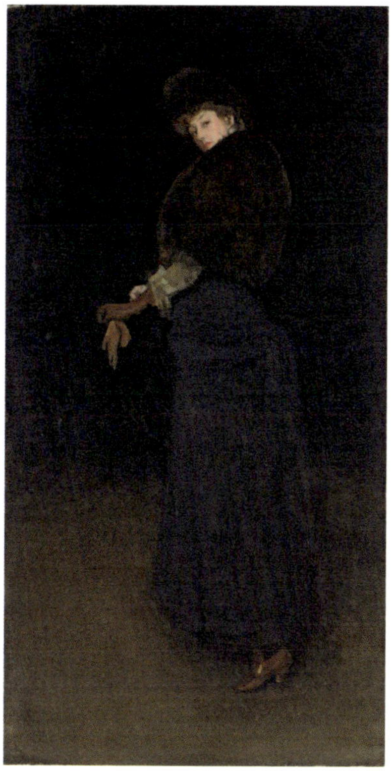

Fig. 3
James McNeill Whistler
Arrangement in Black (The Lady in the Yellow Buskin), c. 1883
Oil on canvas
7 ft. 2 in. × 43½ in. (218.4 × 110.5 cm)
Philadelphia Museum of Art; Purchased with the W. P. Wilstach Fund, 1895 (W1895-1-1)

in class, he certainly would have read about him in the newspapers. In September 1888, Henri embarked on his first trip to Europe, which lasted for three years. He visited the Exposition Universelle, the fair commemorating the hundredth anniversary of the French Revolution, which was open from May to November 1889 and marked by the completion of the Eiffel Tower. This may well have been Henri's first in-person exposure to paintings by Whistler, who was represented by *Variations in Flesh Colour and Green: The Balcony* (1864–70; Freer Gallery of Art) and *Arrangement in Black (The Lady in the Yellow Buskin)* (Fig. 3).[12] Given that Henri preferred the Barbizon School paintings in the exhibition, and his favorite work there was Jules Bastien-Lepage's *Joan of Arc* (1879; Metropolitan Museum of Art, New York),[13] it is doubtful that he was ready for Whistler's elliptical approach to figure painting.

Henri also attended the Salon of 1890, where Whistler exhibited two important Nocturnes: *Nocturne in Blue and Gold: Valparaiso Bay* (1866; Freer Gallery of Art) and *Nocturne: Black and Gold—The Fire Wheel* (1875; Tate Britain, London). In 1891, Whistler sent *Crepuscule in Flesh Colour and Green: Valparaiso* (1866; Tate Britain) and *Arrangement in Brown and Black: Portrait of Miss Rosa Corder* (1876–78; Frick Collection, New York)[14] to the first exhibition of more modern Salon artists, held at the Champ de Mars, which Henri also visited.[15] Henri sailed for Philadelphia in September 1891, and two months later, *Arrangement in Grey and Black No. 1* was bought by the French government for the Musée du Luxembourg, the contemporary art museum that served as a waystation for the Louvre. Whistler was the first American to be honored this way, and the event made headlines in the United States.

In 1892, Henri began teaching art in Philadelphia, and he made friends with Sloan, Glackens, Luks, and Shinn, all a little younger than he was. Sloan, Glackens, and Shinn were taking classes at the Pennsylvania Academy, and they and Luks were artist-reporters on local newspapers. Henri, who had an exhibition history and had lived abroad, emerged as their mentor, sophisticated and charismatic. Sloan, Shinn, and Glackens had not yet tried painting in oils, but Henri guided them toward it. Holding weekly get-togethers at his studio, he declared that any subject was fit for art and spoke of Rembrandt, Hals, Goya, Velázquez, Manet—all the exponents of black painting—and Whistler. Now familiar with Manet and Whistler from seeing their work in Paris, Henri characterized them as the contemporary artists who were heirs to this great tradition. He celebrated iconoclasm and read aloud from *The Gentle Art of Making Enemies*, Whistler's compilation of ripostes, skirmishes, and scores settled that became a financial and literary smash when it was published in 1890. No insurgent artist would have missed its debut, and the book was critical to Henri's conviction that artists like Whistler and Manet gave their peers a

Fig. 4
William Glackens in his studio, 1894
Archival photograph
NSU Art Museum Fort Lauderdale, FL;
William Glackens Archives Collection
(ARC2021.306)

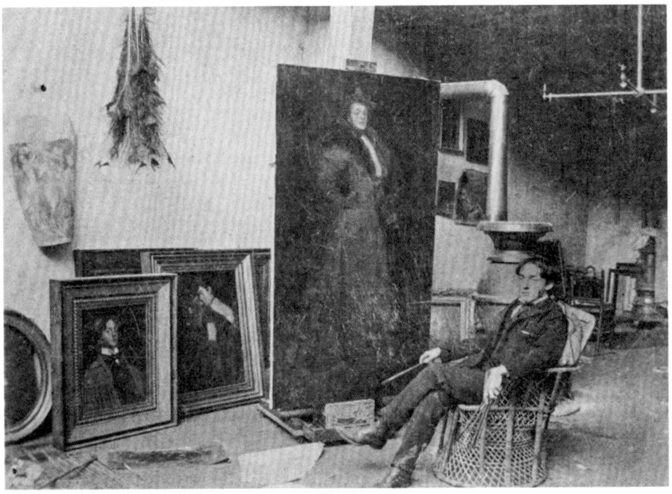

license to rebel and persevere, in spite of being despised. He cited "Walt Whitman, whose book of poems Whittier cast into the fire... Degas, Manet and Whistler and their academy of the neglected."[16]

In Philadelphia, however, an even more effective proponent for Whistler emerged when the Pennsylvania Academy hired Harrison Morris as its managing director in 1892. Morris was a man of vision, and he wanted to make the Academy an active hub of contemporary art. In 1893, in preparation for his first Academy annual, he went to the World's Columbian Exposition in Chicago to see its art exhibition. Morris selected ninety-four paintings by Eakins, Whistler, Chase, Robert Vonnoh, Winslow Homer, George Inness, Eastman Johnson, and John Singer Sargent, among other artists, for a show opening at the Academy in December 1893.[17] Whistler exhibited six paintings in Chicago, and five of them traveled to Philadelphia. Four were female figures: *La Princesse du pays de la porcelaine* (1863–65; Freer Gallery of Art), *Arrangement in Black and Brown: The Fur Jacket* (1877; Worcester Art Museum), *The Chelsea Girl* (1884; Crystal Bridges Museum of American Art, Bentonville, AR), and *Arrangement in Black (The Lady in the Yellow Buskin)* (see Fig. 3). The fifth was *Nocturne in Blue and Gold: Valparaiso Bay*. In his installation of the galleries, Morris showcased Whistler's paintings (Fig. 5), which Henri, Glackens, Shinn, Sloan, and Luks viewed. Indeed, Whistler's canvases, along with Sargent's portrait of *Ellen Terry as Lady Macbeth* (1889; Tate Britain) garnered the lion's share of public attention.[18] In 1894, when the Academy students organized their first show of caricatures that burlesqued canvases in the concomitant annuals, eight of the thirty-two identified works travestied Whistler. Sloan was a particularly busy contestant—he parodied *The Lady in the Yellow Buskin* and *Nocturne in Blue and Gold*, and he won first prize for *Ellen Terrified*, which satirized Sargent's portrait. Glackens earned an honorable mention for *Jimmie*, a portrait of Whistler dressed as his *Chelsea Girl*.[19]

During the run of the Academy's exhibition, Morris pleaded with its trustees to buy *The Fur Jacket* or *The Lady in the Yellow Buskin*, but in vain. He had better luck with the Philadelphia lawyer and collector John G. Johnson, whom he persuaded to purchase the latter work for the Philadelphia Museum of Art, which thus became the first American museum to acquire an oil by Whistler when the painting was accepted in 1895.[20] As for the Academy, between 1893 and 1907, Whistler was exhibited every year but one,[21] and Henri, Glackens, and Sloan consistently attended those Academy annuals, even after they moved to New York.

Henri and Glackens went to New York in late March of 1894 to make the rounds of the exhibitions, which included a visit to the Metropolitan Museum of Art, where Manet's *Boy with a Sword* (1861) and *Young Lady in 1866* (1866), both recent acquisitions, were on view. Whistler too was a topic of conversation. After visiting the National Academy of Design, Henri remarked, "Many painters, many pictures, few artists and few works of art. Vive the Japanese, Whistler, Puvis de Chevannes [*sic*]!"[22] In November 1894, Glackens returned to the museum because *Symphony in White, No. 1: The White Girl* was on loan for several months. In a letter to a friend, he repeated his praise for *Boy with a Sword*, linking it to Velázquez, and found that it as well as *Young Lady in 1866* (also known as *Lady with a Parakeet*) had "a family resemblance" to *The White Girl*. "The intention of both men is identical, and their theory of drawing the same," Glackens continued. "We gloated over these three pictures all afternoon, and we came back the next day and gloated over them until it grew dark, and then we went back home to Philadelphia."[23]

The Whistler paintings that Glackens saw in Philadelphia and New York considerably affected his development. Before then, in 1893, Glackens had painted a few landscapes. In a photograph taken of Glackens in his studio in early 1894 (Fig. 4), visible on the easel is a full-length portrait of a woman that is clearly indebted to his exposure

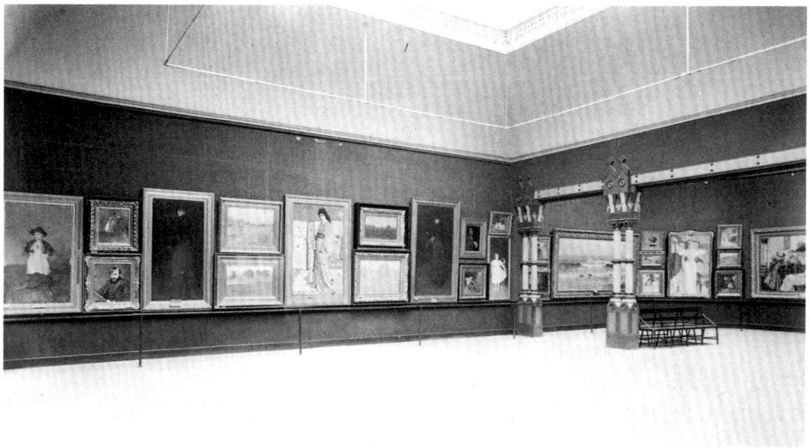

Fig. 5
Installation view of 63rd Annual Exhibition at the Pennsylvania Academy of the Fine Arts, showing Whistler's paintings on the walls, 1893
Archival photograph
Pennsylvania Academy of the Fine Arts, Philadelphia; Dorothy and Kenneth Woodcock Archives (PC0104_1893_005)

Fig. 6
William Glackens, with *Girl in White* in the background, in the studio he shared with Robert Henri, 1894
Archival photograph
NSU Art Museum Fort Lauderdale, FL; William Glackens Archives Collection (ARC2021.9.E)

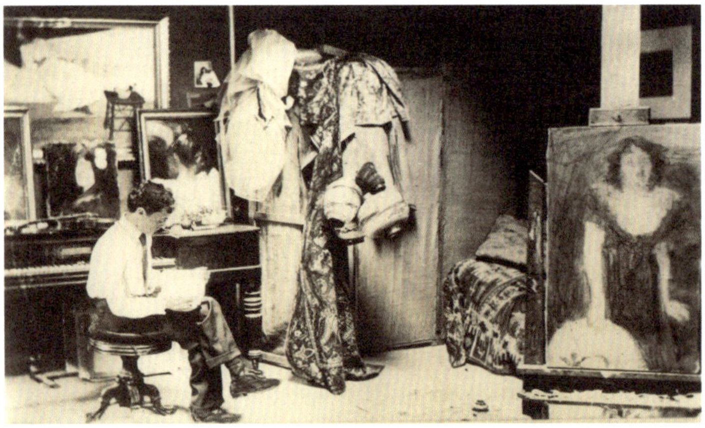

to *The Fur Jacket* and *The Lady in the Yellow Buskin.* In November 1894, Glackens started sharing a studio with Henri on Chestnut Street, and a photograph of Glackens working there (Fig. 6) shows that Whistlerian Japonisme has taken hold. Japanese lanterns are available as props, and *Girl in White* (Fig. 7) is on the wall. Glackens was experimenting with the task of orchestrating a symphony of whites of his own, with a female figure in a cloistered environment, flattening forms as Whistler did.

Whistler was so much a part of Pennsylvania Academy culture that he figured in its amateur theatricals. In 1894, first as a magazine serial and then as a novel, the *Punch* cartoonist George du Maurier (who had been an art student with Whistler in Paris in the 1850s) published *Trilby*, a Victorian melodrama of sex and mesmerism that is chiefly known today for the name of its villain, Svengali. But at the time, it was a publishing sensation, selling over 200,000 copies in its first six months. Du Maurier illustrated as well as wrote his story about Trilby O'Ferrall, an artist's model in the clutches of the evil impresario Svengali. One of the students besotted by Trilby was a lazy, foppish American immediately recognizable on the page as Whistler, who threatened to sue the publishers for defamation, which promptly increased publicity and sales.[24]

The *Trilby* craze was especially fervid in Philadelphia, where several ministers had denounced the book as immoral from their pulpits, and it was a must-read for art students. The Henri crowd decided to put on what turned out to be the first dramatic production anywhere of the book, a burlesque called *Twillbe*, which was performed at the Academy on December 29, 1894. Fittingly, Henri was Svengali, the hypnotic leader; Sloan was Twillbe because he could sing falsetto; Glackens was Gecko, "a fiddling genius in love with Twillbe"; and Shinn played both Taffy, "a Welsh Apollo in Love with Twillbe," and "James McNails Whiskers, with a chip on his shoulder."[25] The *Philadelphia Inquirer* gave *Twillbe* a splendid review, and the performance was repeated by popular demand.[26]

Fig. 7
William Glackens
Girl in White, 1894
Oil on canvas
28¼ × 35 in. (71.8 × 88.9 cm)
Private collection

In June 1895, Henri, Glackens, and several other Philadelphia artists sailed for Paris. Glackens immersed himself in French painting, but he also maintained his dialogue with Whistler. He wrote to a friend, "At the Luxembourg, [the only paintings] I care to see are Whistler's mother, Sargent's Carmencita, Manet's Olympia, and Chavanne's Poor Fisherman."[27] One of Glackens's most bewitching Paris paintings was *La Villette* (Fig. 8) It features a high arched footbridge with a parade of dark silhouetted figures below it, in a composition reminiscent of *Nocturne: Blue and Gold—Old Battersea Bridge* (Fig. 1). Glackens chose to portray the scene before him at twilight, Whistler's favorite time, when forms become indistinct. La Villette was an industrial neighborhood in northeastern Paris, where the unlovely dominated—the livestock markets and abbatoirs were located there. Yet, like Whistler, Glackens could tease out unexpected beauty in banal urban areas, especially when they were cloaked by fading light. Indeed, Glackens's canvas is an uncanny evocation of a famous passage from Whistler's "Ten O'Clock" lecture:

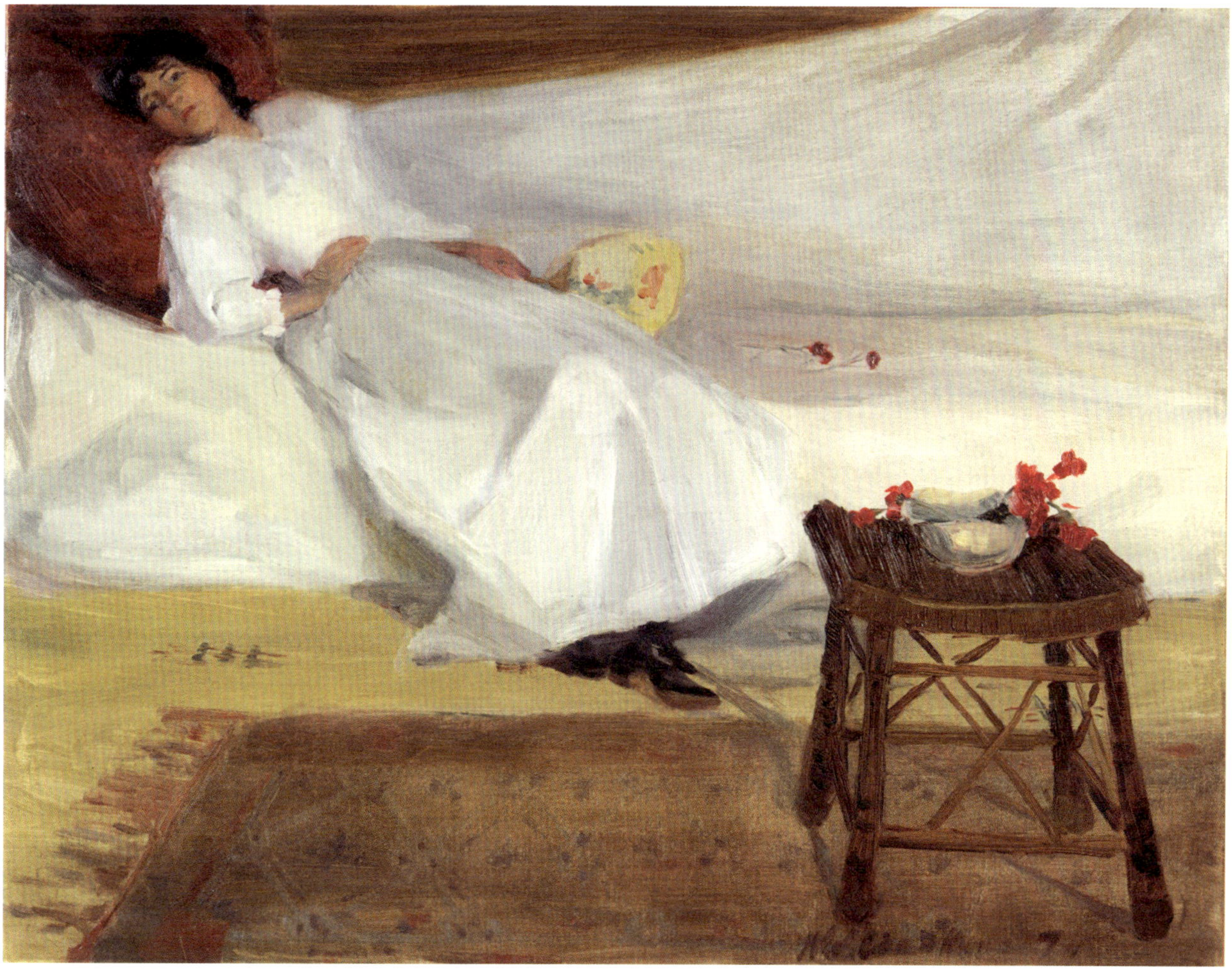

Fig. 8
William Glackens
La Villette, c. 1895
Oil on canvas
24 × 29 in. (61 × 73.7 cm)
Carnegie Museum of Art, Pittsburgh; Patrons Art Fund, 56.13

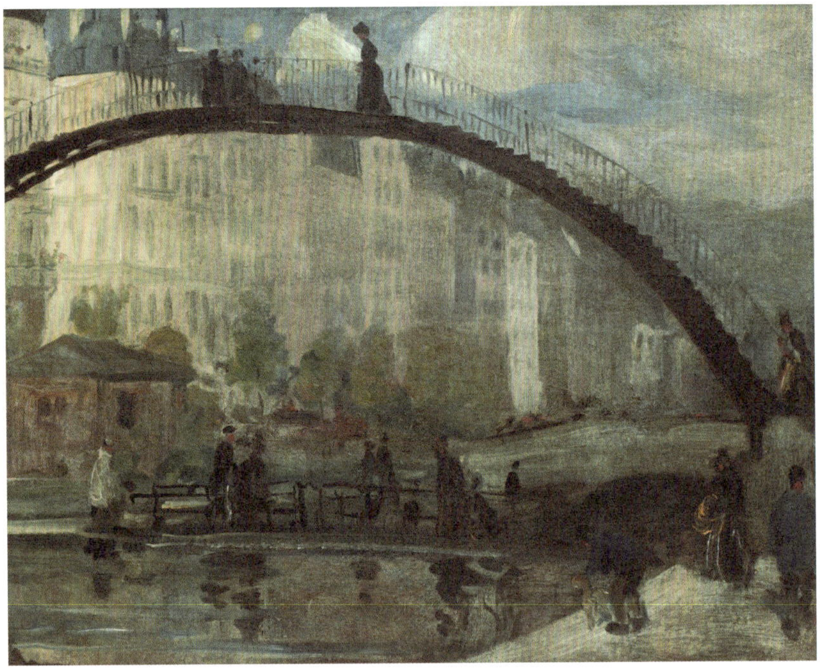

> And when the evening mist clothes the riverside with poetry, as with a veil, and the poor buildings lose themselves in the dim sky, and the tall chimneys become campanili, and the warehouses are palaces in the night, and the whole city hangs in the heavens . . . then the wayfarer hastens home.[28]

Glackens hastened home to Philadelphia in October 1896, but moved permanently to New York before the year was out. To a critic there, Glackens twice asserted that Whistler and Manet were "the great black and white artists of this century."[29]

Henri married Linda Craige, one of his students, in June 1898 in Philadelphia, and the two moved to Paris that September. Confronting Whistler and his energetic influence was no longer oblique. It was direct: directly exciting and directly frustrating. Henri had planned to support himself by teaching American students in Paris, some of whom had been pupils in Philadelphia. However, in October 1898, Whistler and Carmen Rossi, who had modeled for him as a child, opened an art school called the Académie Carmen, and, as Henri found out, the new school lured away his prospective students.[30] Whistler did not appear at the school much, but his name was motivation enough for young Britons and Americans to enroll. As a result, the Henris were on the point of impoverishment because their expected source of income went elsewhere. Henri was curious enough about his competition to visit the school, although he sniffed at it. He wrote to his parents:

> It was a great many flights of stairs and not [a] very big studio—very small in fact for a class although I hear other rooms are to be opened

shortly, as fast as they fill up. A homely, ugly Italian woman was posing nude and among the shafts of easels I saw the serious faces of about a dozen Americans, men and women—but recognized none of them.[31]

This irritating situation did nothing to change Henri's belief that Whistler was "a very great artist,"[32] and Whistler did shape Henri's style and technique in several Paris cityscapes, made with a palette of browns and grays. Rather than laying on slashing Impressionist brushwork, Henri used Whistler's method of applying one tone to the entire surface of the canvas and then working the forms into it.[33] *La Neige* (1899 ; Musée d'Orsay), a nocturne composed of broad uniform tones of reduced color, is such a picture, although the figures and structures are more fully described than in a typical Whistler canvas. It was accepted for the Champ de Mars Salon of 1899 and then bought by the Luxembourg. Henri's first reaction was to write to his parents in astonishment: "I can hardly believe what I'm going to tell you. La Neige . . . has been bought for the Luxembourg. . . . [It] will hang in the same room with Whistler's portrait of his mother."[34] The Henris returned to the United States in September 1900 and settled in New York, where the artist continued to explore Whistlerian themes and techniques, painting moody views of the East River from the window of his apartment on East 58th Street (Fig. 9).

Whereas Henri and Glackens were accepting of Whistler, Sloan's response was ambivalent. The further away he moved from his formative years, the more likely he was to grant Whistler's impact. In

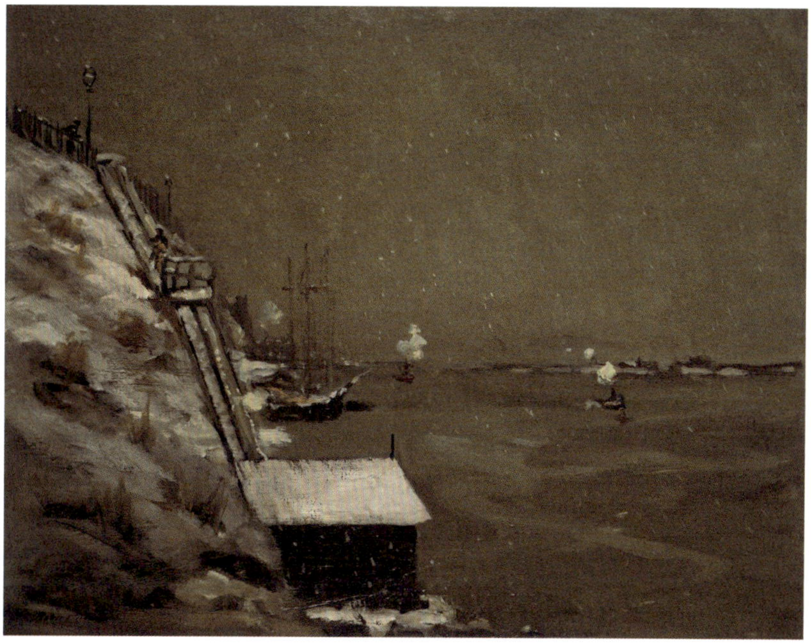

Fig. 9
Robert Henri
East River Embankment, Winter, 1900
Oil on canvas
25¾ × 32 in. (65.4 × 81.3 cm)
Hirshhorn Museum and Sculpture Garden, Smithsonian Institution, Washington, DC; Gift of the Joseph H. Hirshhorn Foundation, 1966.66.2435

1938, Sloan reminisced, "Back in the Nineties our gods were Whistler, Velasquez [*sic*], and Frans Hals."[35] In 1950, when he could be even more detached, he revised himself again, explaining,

> Our palette [then] consisted of earth colors with occasional use of blue and green and yellow to "kick up" neutral tones. This was a simple palette to control and sufficient for our purposes. . . . There can be seen a relationship with Whistler in Glackens' and my early work, which came via Velasquez [*sic*]. Our pictures were tonal. . . .[36]

But in his youth, without a substantial career behind him, Sloan was antagonistic, deriding Whistler as the exemplar of a narrow little cult of the beautiful.[37]

Sloan could be accused of creative misprision—the deliberate concealment of one's knowledge or a purposely erroneous judgment, especially in estimating the value of something (Figs. 10, 11). The archaic word "misprision" was brilliantly revived by Harold Bloom in his classic study *The Anxiety of Influence.* In that book, Bloom argues that artists purposely misread or denounce each other "in order to clear imaginative space for themselves."[38] Artists with their own adamant core are often anxious about influence because they do not want to face the fact that they were not alone in inventing themselves.

How does one artist quarry another? Logically, the devotion to etching would be the bond between Whistler, the most important American etcher of his time, and Sloan, born in 1871, the first significant American etcher to emerge after Whistler's death.[39] But the latter was resistant to owning that connection. Some easy continuities of form and subject matter can be discerned, which mainly remind us that Whistler's early etchings were viable ancestors of Ashcan realism. They chronicle ramshackle urban dwellings and their ragged inhabitants, but Sloan never acknowledged that body of work, although he studied the history of etching and would have known about Whistler's depictions of the poor. When he was young and influenced by Rembrandt, Whistler also drew character studies, as Sloan would in his New York etchings but not in his Philadelphia oils. But this was a blindness useful to Sloan's aesthetic struggles, as was a belief that artists like Whistler were insufficiently tough-minded.[40]

Whistler, the consummate aesthete, was too finicky and radiated preciosity, whereas Sloan was against anything "arty." "All my life I have been in rebellion against the orthodox," Sloan declared, and since it became accepted for the artist to be "a misfit and eccentric," he was "against that too."[41] Whistler was preeminently the American artist who went to Europe and evaded calls to return, while Sloan was someone who insisted that he had to stay home, meet obligations, and support his parents and sisters. Whistler represented the threatening notions of artistic selfishness and emotional freedom that were out of the question for Sloan, and in his personal writings Sloan was always

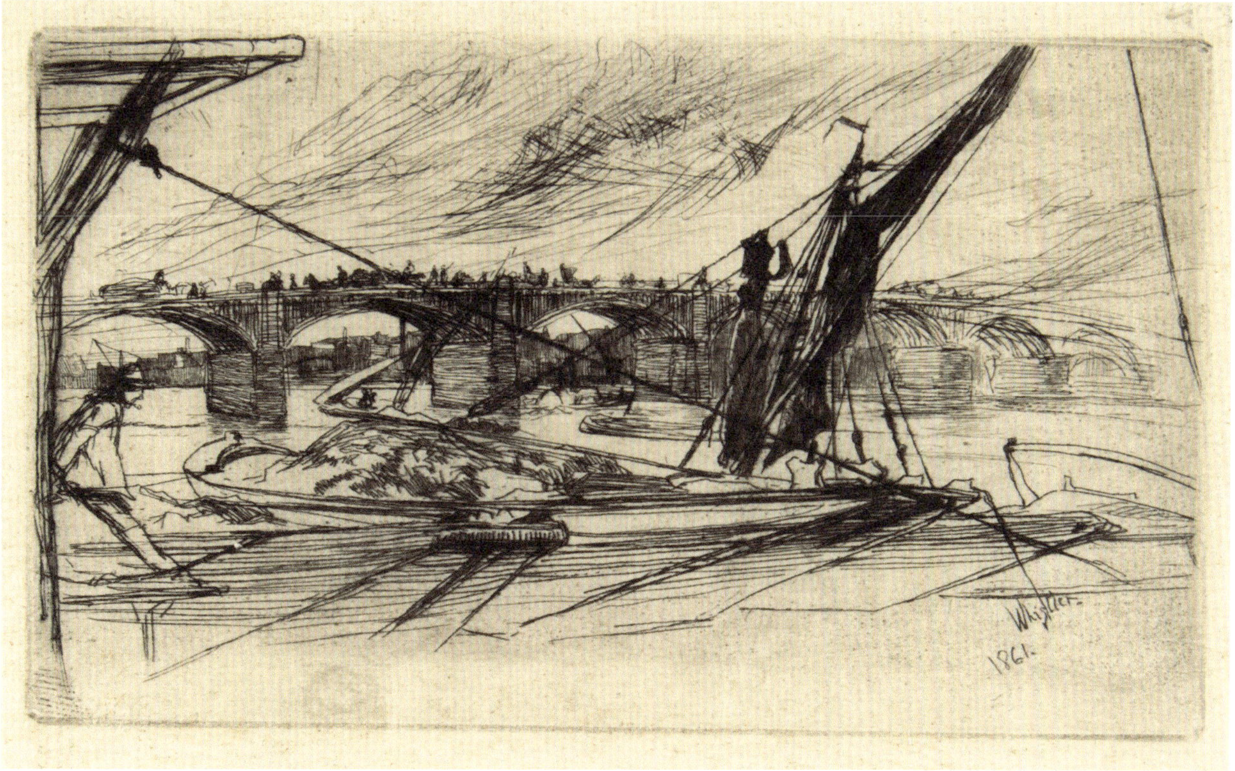

Fig. 10
James McNeill Whistler
Vauxhall Bridge, 1861
Etching and drypoint, printed in black ink on fine buff fibrous laid Japan, second state of two (Glasgow)
Sheet: $8\frac{3}{4} \times 10\frac{7}{16}$ in. (22.2 × 26.5 cm)
The Metropolitan Museum of Art, New York; Gift of William Loring Andrews, 1883, transferred from the Library (83.1.29)

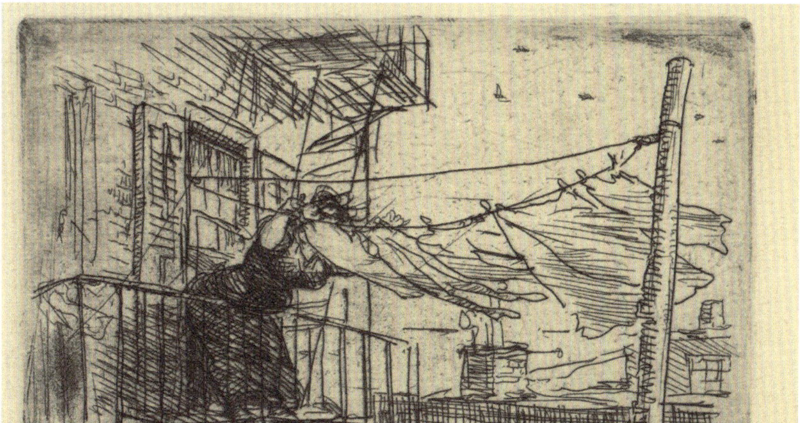

Fig. 11
John Sloan
Hanging Clothes, 1912
Etching
Plate: $2\frac{11}{16} \times 3\frac{3}{4}$ in. (6.8 × 9.5 cm)
Sheet: $4\frac{1}{8} \times 6$ in. (10.4 × 15.2 cm)
The Metropolitan Museum of Art, New York; Gift of Mrs. Harry Payne Whitney, 1926 (26.30.37)

Fig. 12
John Sloan
Schuylkill River, 1894
Etching
Plate: 8⅛ × 5⅛ in. (20.6 × 13 cm)
Sheet: 10%⁄16 × 8¹¹⁄16 in. (26.8 × 22 cm)
The Metropolitan Museum of Art, New York; Gift of Mrs. Harry Payne Whitney, 1926 (26.30.5)

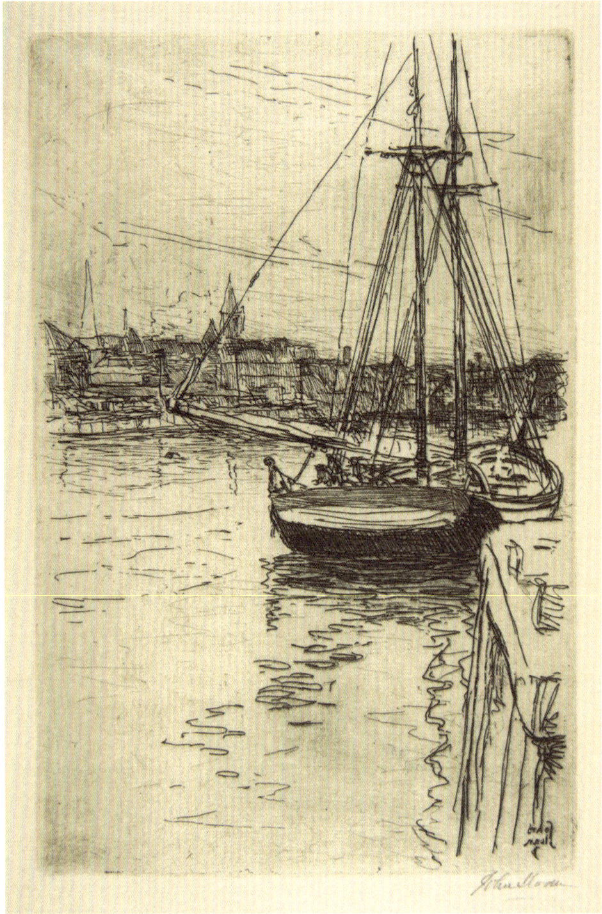

on the defensive as to why he had not gone to Paris, which he framed as a siren tempting him into an unsavory, unproductive, bohemian life.[42] That had plainly not happened to his friends Henri and Glackens, but staying put was a stratagem for self-preservation in a society ready to ensnare and distract him. Europe, with its connotations of sensual experience, was the Svengali to Sloan's Trilby.[43] On a deeper level, Sloan correctly intuited that influence means not merely a transmission of images or ideas but a transfer of personality that is assimilated and thus becomes an echo of someone else. He first expressed this discomfort in commenting on his early etching *Schuylkill River* (Fig. 12).

Sloan made the plate for *Schuylkill River* in the spring of 1894, when he was teaching Glackens how to etch. They went to the docks together and drew from nature.[44] Sloan as an etcher did not persevere with busy river scenes, presumably because Whistler had long taken imaginative possession of the Thames and industrial London. Sloan remarked that *Schuylkill River* was "one of my few plates that looks like an etching from the connoisseur's point of view" because "it catered to the 'white space' point of view. . . . Had I pursued the direction here suggested my etchings might have become quite popular."[45] Sloan abhorred commercial

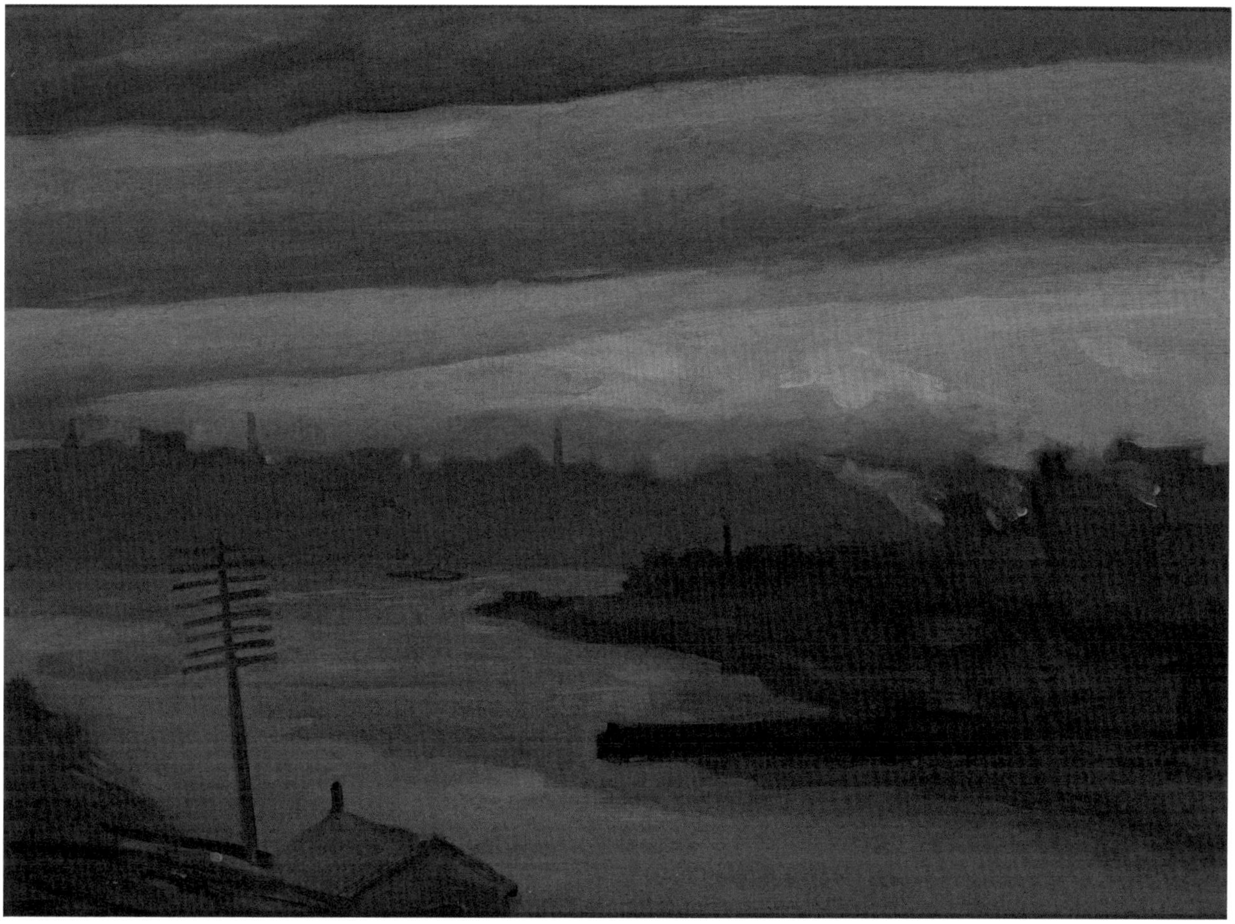

Fig. 13
John Sloan
Schuylkill River, 1900–2
Oil on canvas
24 × 32 in. (61 × 81.3 cm)
Delaware Art Museum, Wilmington; Gift of the John Sloan Trust, 2006-63

success, equating it with artistic failure. And since Whistler was lionized in the 1890s, Sloan wanted to distance himself from him. But in a tortuous way, Sloan was acknowledging his precursor's importance to printmaking, because it was Whistler who drove the revival of etching as an artistic, expressive medium in England and the United States. Even Sloan could not wish away that achievement. And the honored Whistler of the 1890s had always broken the rules. For example, the expansive white foreground that Sloan fretted about was castigated as lazy and unfinished when Whistler had introduced it in his etchings of the 1860s.

Six years later after etching *Schuylkill River*, Sloan reconsidered his resistance to Whistler's work and ideas. By then, he had seen Whistler's oils, including the Nocturnes, exhibited at the Pennsylvania Academy annually, and Sloan returned to the river, this time accepting it as a motif applicable to painting (Fig. 13). Whistler's Nocturnes of the Thames were a starting point for Sloan's river scenes in their color, tone, horizontal composition, time of day, inclusion of an industrial background, elimination of figures, and overall sense of emptiness. Rowland Elzea, the author of Sloan's catalogue raisonné and always a careful thinker about the artist, wrote that although it was "tempting to see Whistler's influence" in Sloan's muted tonalities, he cautioned against linking the two. Instead, he posited a likelier tie to Henri, who had moved to New York from Paris in late 1900 and was painting gray scenes of the East River.[46] However, since Sloan remained a Philadelphia resident until 1904, he would have had infrequent opportunities to examine Henri's work in New York. And, as we have seen, Henri himself, coming directly off his success with *La Neige*, had continued to appropriate Whistlerian themes and processes, and thus the common origin of the river scenes both Sloan and Henri made in about 1900 was Whistler. In addition, Whistler's *Nocturne: Blue and Gold—Southampton Water* (1872; Art Institute of Chicago) was shown at the Pennsylvania Academy from January 14 to February 23, 1901; Sloan certainly saw it, because his work was also in that exhibition.

Ernest Lawson, an American Impressionist landscapist, was drawn to Whistler's subjects, palette, and compositional devices, despite pronounced differences in technique. Schooled in the Impressionism of Monet and Sisley, rather than that of Manet, Lawson used a palette knife and brush and applied his paint thickly to obtain impastoed and often rugged surfaces. He developed an interest in painting snowstorms and snow-covered countrysides, a theme that met the Whistlerian challenge of delineating gradations of whites and grays amid hazy backgrounds (Fig. 14). Lawson later essayed nocturnes, which are some of his most accomplished canvases. Both the snow scenes and the night pictures of necessity employed the restricted palette that Whistler had demonstrated could be exploited to such great effect. When Glackens observed that young painters were attracted to Whistler, he recognized that beginners could better control a limited, often monochromatic palette, and Whistler exemplified how much could be achieved with it. When Whistler was involved with the Académie Carmen, he explained how a student should approach color: "My idea is to give them three or four colours—let them learn to model and paint the form and line first until they are strong enough to use others."[47] As Glackens and his peers began to expand their chromatic range and venture into more complex color relationships, Whistler's hold faded. Lawson started with a muted palette to unify his earlier compositions and moved into bolder colors as he matured.

Lawson was born in 1873 in Halifax, Nova Scotia, and grew up in the Midwest, but he claimed that his birthplace was San Francisco, which allowed him to exhibit and be identified as an American artist. In 1891, he moved to New York where he studied with Julian Alden Weir and John Henry Twachtman, whose own delicate winter scenes were inflected by Whistler and Japanese art. From 1893 to 1895, Lawson lived in Paris; in his letters home, he singled out works he had seen by Whistler as being of interest to him.[48] During the time Lawson was in Paris, Whistler exhibited several recent seascapes at the fourth Champ

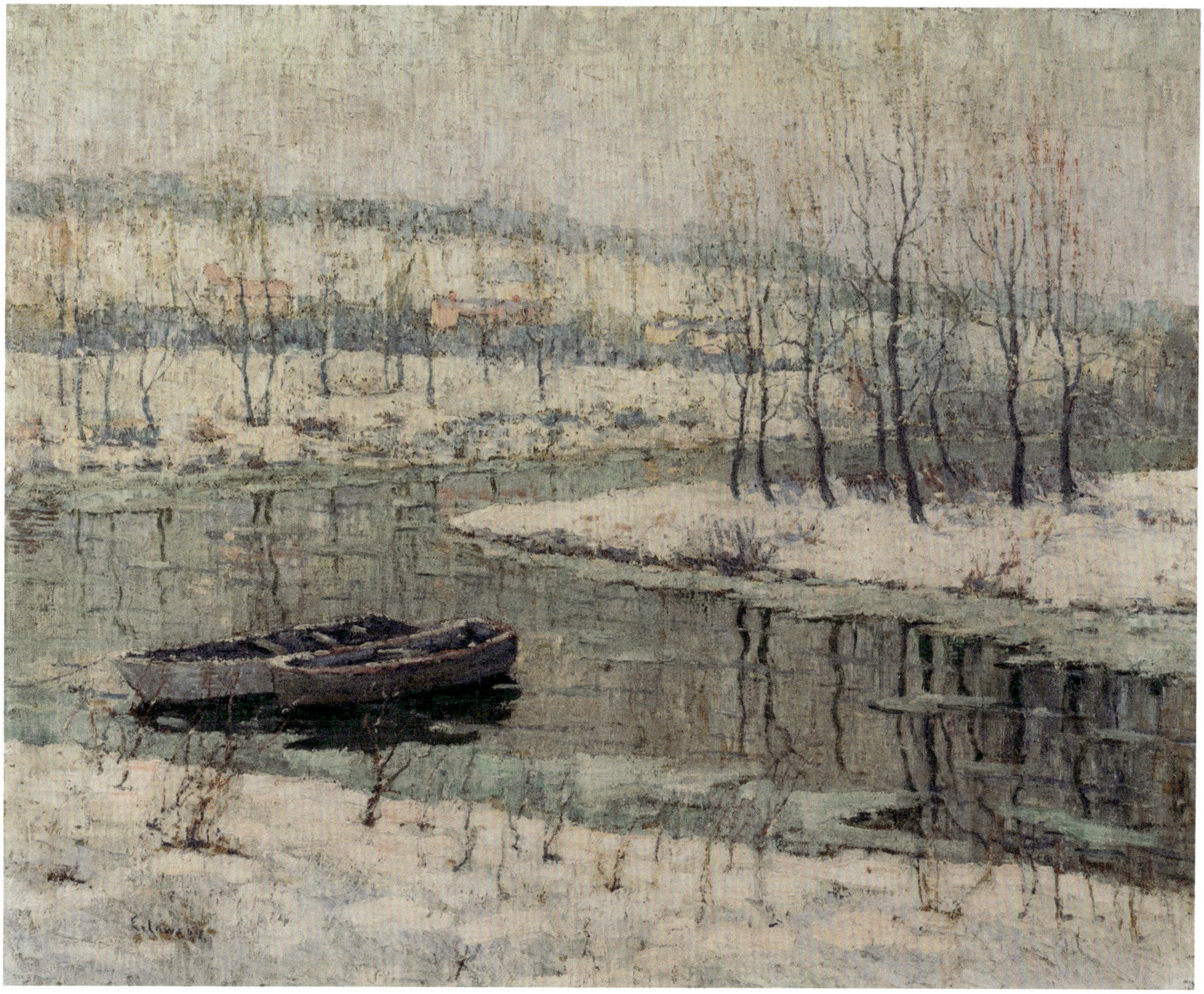

Fig. 14
Ernest Lawson
Spring Thaw, c. 1910
Oil on canvas
25¼ × 30⅛ in. (64.1 × 76.5 cm)
Terra Foundation for American Art, Chicago; Daniel J. Terra Collection, 1999.85

de Mars Salon in the spring of 1894: *Violet and Silver—The Deep Sea* (1893; Art Institute of Chicago), *Violet and Blue: Among the Rollers* (c. 1893; Detroit Institute of Arts), and *Symphony in Violet and Blue* (1893; Hill-Stead Museum, Farmington, CT).[49] Perhaps the freedom of the paint handling engaged him, because he was dissatisfied with the orthodox teachings he was receiving at the Académie Julian.[50]

In 1898, Lawson moved to Washington Heights in Upper Manhattan. There he found terrain that could unite form and content: the Harlem River and its bridges and embankments. What the Thames was to Whistler, the Harlem River was to Lawson, and he painted it and its environs in different seasons and times of day. Even when he relocated to West 23rd Street in 1906 and Greenwich Village a year later, Upper Manhattan remained a favorite subject. In 1903, Lawson met Henri, Sloan, Glackens, and Luks when they all exhibited together.[51] His solidity as a landscapist earned the esteem of the New York realists, and these friendships might have precipitated his move downtown.

The commercial hurly-burly of New York did not mesh with Lawson's temperament but being in the middle of the city, with its glaring lights and looming buildings, must have awakened him to the transformative power of night, when a drab environment can be reborn as an atmospheric and mysterious place. The nocturne also represented a technical experiment: successful ones are extremely hard to achieve because the artist must render subtle gradations of light and shade, allowing certain areas to be discerned, while adjacent passages are plunged into deep darkness.

When Lawson turned to night scenes, the comparisons with Whistler were not merely inevitable but justifiable. Like Whistler (see Fig. 1), Lawson commandeered the forceful architecture of a bridge, with its bulky horizontals and verticals, as a means to anchor forms, set off the atmospheric blending of sky and water, and juxtapose the manmade with the natural. Duncan Phillips, the purchaser of *Spring Night, Harlem River* (Fig. 15), pinpointed another similarity between the two artists—that Lawson could convert the prosaic into the poetic. As Phillips explained in some rather flowery language of his own, "Lawson can make a suburban wilderness enchanting. His *Moonlight—Harlem River*... with its home lights and bridge lamps glimmering in a tremulous turquoise air [is like] some garden of romance."[52]

Lawson continued with nocturnes, seeking other bridges as subjects. This later work, wrote Valerie Ann Leeds in an essay on the artist, is "an amalgam of Impressionism and Realism."[53] His forms are monumental and more clearly defined, but he has not abandoned the Whistlerian panoramic format nor the flowing, tapestrylike arrangement of tones. Whistler, who employed such terms as "Notes," "Harmonies," and "Arrangements" as titles, consistently emphasized correspondences between music and painting, as in this well-known proposition from the "Ten O'Clock" lecture:

> Nature contains the elements, in colour and form, of all pictures, as the keyboard contains the notes of all music.
>
> But the artist is born to pick and choose... these elements, that the result may be beautiful—as the musician gathers his notes, and forms his chords, until he brings forth from chaos glorious harmony.[54]

As late as the 1930s, when interviewed about his use of color, Lawson echoed the master when he replied, "It affects me like music affects some persons... emotionally.... I like to play with colors... like a composer playing with counterpoint in music."[55]

As with Lawson, Paris was the incubator for Maurice Prendergast's Whistlerian interlude. Prendergast was born in 1858 in Newfoundland, but he, his parents, and his younger brother Charles moved to

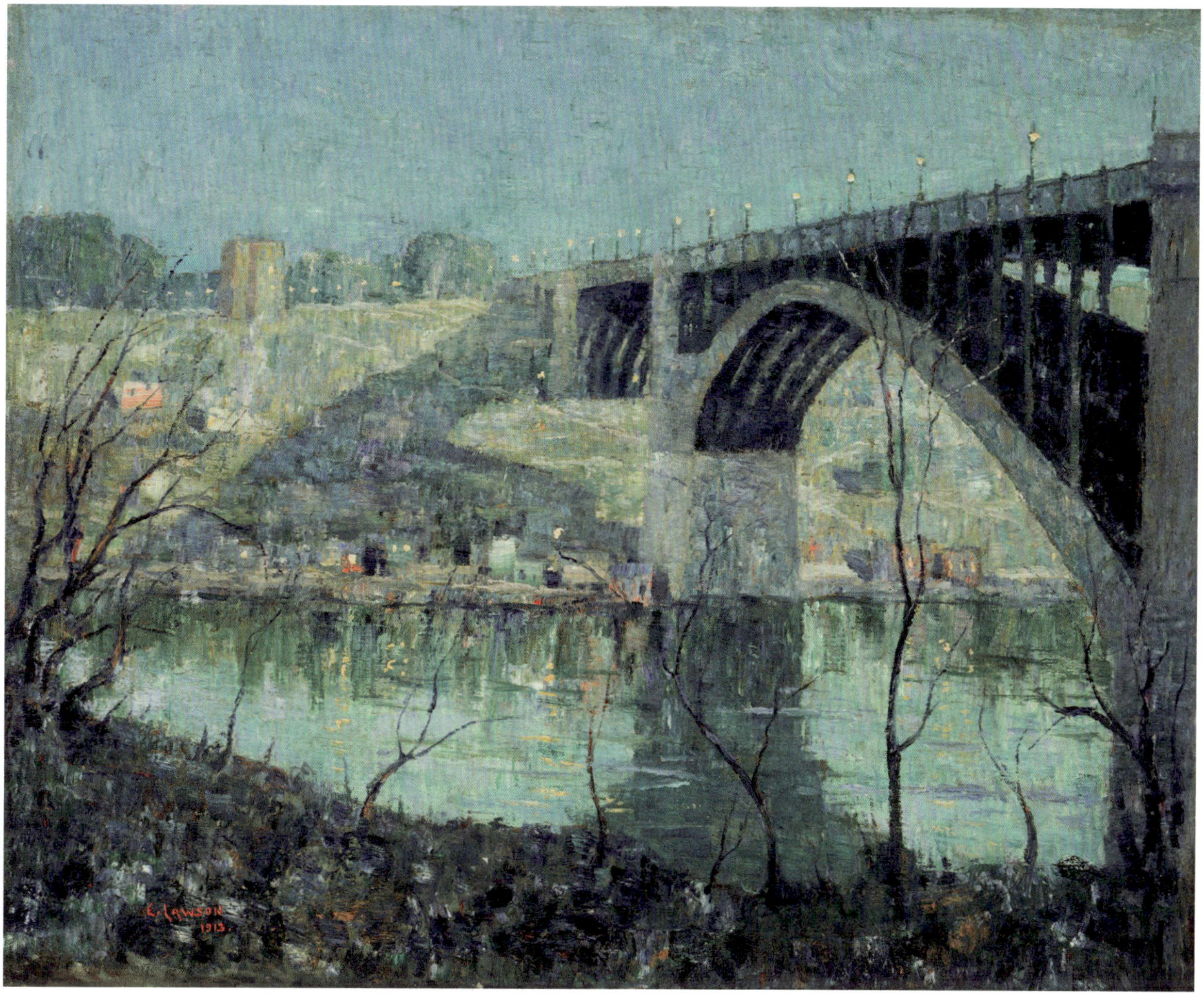

Fig. 15
Ernest Lawson
Spring Night, Harlem River, 1913
Oil on canvas mounted on panel
25⅛ × 30⅛ in. (63.8 × 76.5 cm)
The Phillips Collection, Washington, DC; Acquired 1920 (1191)

Boston in 1868 in search of a better life. The boys went to grammar school until they were fourteen and then were sent out to work. Maurice Prendergast became a commercial artist and painted signs and advertisements. The Prendergasts would have known about Whistler through magazines, newspapers, and the talk of other artists, but any firsthand experience of his work was unlikely. The Boston collector Isabella Stewart Gardner was one of Whistler's most sympathetic patrons: she met him in 1879 and started buying paintings, drawings, and etchings in the mid-1880s. But at that time, her collection was private. As for public opportunities, Boston galleries showed Impressionist paintings and Japanese prints, but nothing by Whistler. Unless Prendergast were steadily journeying to New York, he could not have seen Whistler's paintings, drawings, or prints in person. It is doubtful that he traveled much at all, because both brothers were saving up to live in Paris; it took them five years to accumulate $1,000, so every cent had to be justified. Moreover, in the Prendergast catalogue

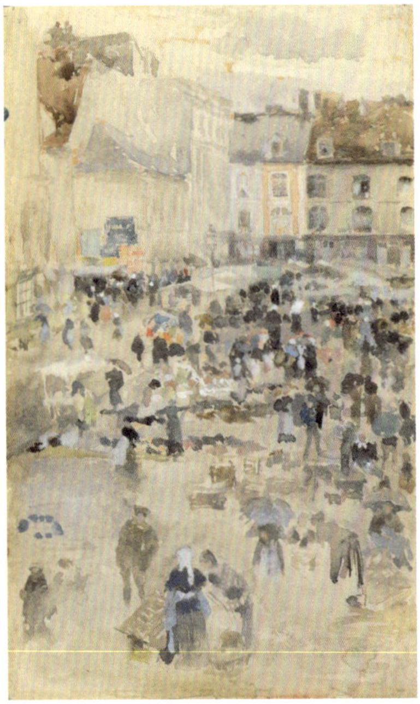

Fig. 16
James McNeill Whistler
Variations in Violet and Grey—Market Place, Dieppe, 1885
Gouache and watercolor on off-white wove paper mounted on academy board
7 15⁄16 × 5 in. (20.2 × 12.7 cm)
The Metropolitan Museum of Art, New York; Gift of Douglass Campbell, Richard Strachan, and Stephen M. Strachan, in memory of Mrs. Douglass Campbell and Mrs. William Lyman Campbell, 2000 (2000.512)

raisonné, the pre-Paris watercolors and sketches give no hint of any ability beyond routine skill. They betray no sign of any modern artist, let alone Whistler. Only in the liberating milieu of France did Prendergast's art dramatically change.

The Prendergasts arrived in Paris by January 1891; Charles left about a year later, and Maurice stayed until September 1894. The latter enrolled in the Julian and Colarossi academies, but drawing from casts did not interest him in the way that street life and modern expression did. He made friends with the British artist Charles Conder and with James Wilson Morrice, the Canadian painter and incorrigible bon vivant, who knew Whistler.[56] Another acquaintance was Hermann Dudley Murphy, a fellow transplant from Boston, who embraced a career as a Whistler epigone and later went into the frame-making business with Charles Prendergast.[57]

In 1893, Maurice Prendergast came to Whistler's notice, but anonymously. An Englishman named Michael Dignam, who was visiting one of Prendergast's studio mates, picked up a sketchbook of Prendergast's and made off with it. Dignam took the sketchbook to *The Studio* magazine in London, passing it off as his own. Whistler saw the drawings and was struck by the artist's talent, which led to six sketches being published in the magazine,[58] but they were credited to the thief.[59] Prendergast learned what happened but did not correct the injustice. Perhaps it was enough to know that the master thought so highly of his work. By then, Prendergast would have seen *Crepuscule in Flesh Colour and Green: Valparaiso* and *Arrangement in Brown and Black: Portrait of Miss Rosa Corder*, which Whistler chose for the first Champ de Mars exhibition in May 1891; later in the year, the portrait of Whistler's mother entered the Luxembourg. In the 1892 Champ de Mars show, Whistler exhibited six paintings and six graphic works of Venice, including the important oils *Nocturne: Trafalgar Snow, Chelsea—Snow* (c. 1875–77; Freer Gallery of Art), *Nocturne in Grey and Gold: Chelsea Snow* (1876; Harvard Art Museums, Cambridge, MA), and *Harmony in Pink and Grey: Portrait of Lady Meux* (1881–82; Frick Collection).[60]

During his first years in Paris, Prendergast produced Whistlerian oils and watercolors of deserted beaches and distant women. His work progressed as he refined his adoption of Whistler's muted palette, penchant for working on small canvases and sheets of paper, and delicacy in organizing and overlapping his figures (Figs. 16, 17). In comparing Whistler's lithographs of the 1890s with Prendergast's quicksilver watercolors from about the same time, Trevor Fairbrother observed, "Following a judicious and presumably additive approach, each artist constructed a composition that feels casual, momentary, and pleasantly incomplete. Through careful editing, their pictures convey the sensation of an unhurried glimpse."[61]

Whistler encouraged his younger contemporaries to pursue so-called minor and overlooked media, such as watercolor and monotype.

Among the first known American monotypes was a portrait of Whistler, produced in 1880 by Charles Abel Corwin when they were both in Venice.[62] Prendergast was the first American artist to assimilate the monotype into his practice on a consistent basis: it was not a side diversion to him but a process entwined in image and effect with his oils and watercolors. Prendergast created memorable monotypes of Paris at night, and in other works he achieved Whistlerian mistiness and subdued color harmonies by fading and blurring. He printed an image not once, as is customary with a monotype, which is by definition a single-impression print, but several times. The exuberance of surface pattern so visible in *Bastille Day* (Fig. 18), Prendergast's nocturnal celebration of the French holiday, was his artistic future, as were a looser paint treatment and the addition of notes of pure and sparkling color. In Paris, Prendergast also became aware of the Nabis, and their ideas infused his own work by 1895, when he returned to Boston. Three years later, he was a fully modern artist and a virtuoso of vibrant and luminous watercolors.

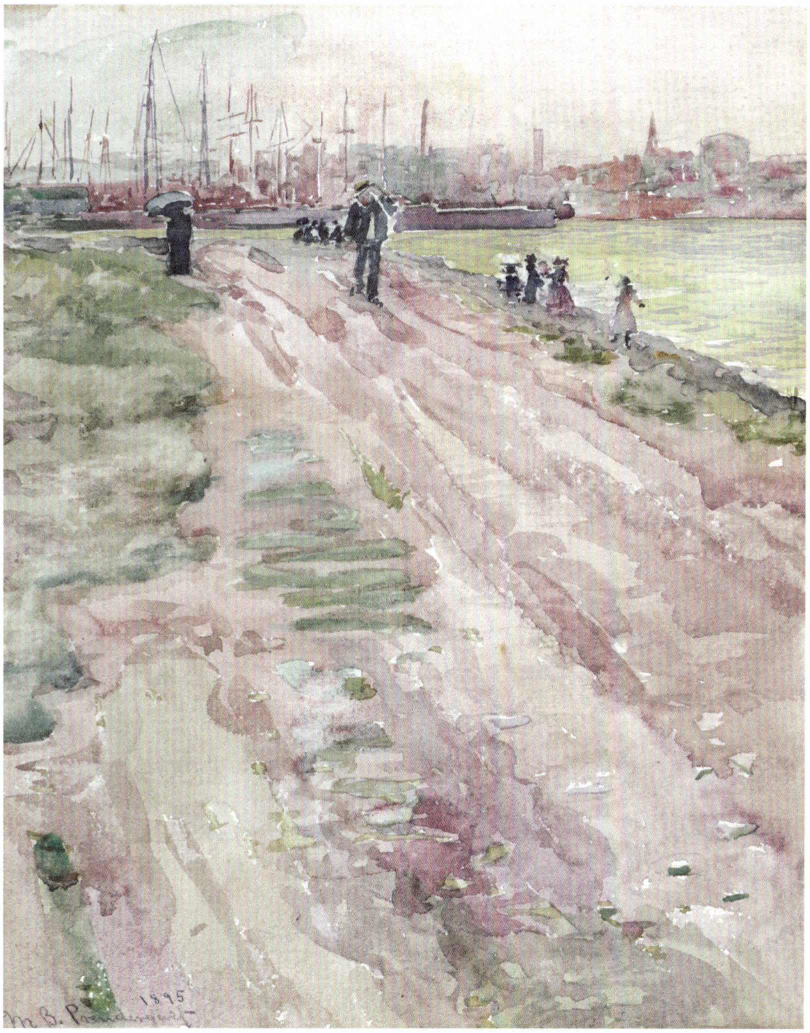

Fig. 17
Maurice Prendergast
The Harbor from City Point (*New England Shore and Harbor Scene*), 1895
Watercolor over graphite on wove paper
Sheet: 14 × 10 in. (35.6 × 25.4 cm)
Hood Museum of Art, Dartmouth College, Hanover, NH; Bequest of Warren F. Upham, Class of 1916 (W.976.136)

Henri's last glimpse of Whistler in Paris was at the 1900 Exposition Universelle, where Whistler showed *Symphony in White, No. 2: The Little White Girl* (1864; Tate Britain), *Mother of Pearl and Silver: The Andalusian* (Fig. 19), and the self-portrait *Brown and Gold* (c. 1895–1900; Hunterian Museum and Art Gallery, University of Glasgow). The first two canvases, images of women, were an apposite artistic send-off for Henri, who relocated to Manhattan in August of that year because he concluded that opportunities would be greater there than in Philadelphia. Although Henri painted several winter cityscapes in New York, his last urban view was created in 1902. Those paintings did not sell, and he determined to support himself by teaching and by portraiture. Henri was eminently aware of the commercially and artistically successful full-length portraits by Chase and Sargent and their own emulations of Velázquez, but in the early 1900s, Henri's thoughtful depictions of women reflected the quietude, introspection, and restraint of Whistler's portraits (Figs. 20, 21). The compositions, all of single figures, depict women in black, women in white, women in profile or angled away from the viewer, and women subtly emerging from monochromatic backgrounds. Henri purposely reinforced this influence in 1902, when the Pennsylvania Academy showed *The Andalusian* in its annual exhibition. He and Glackens went to see the

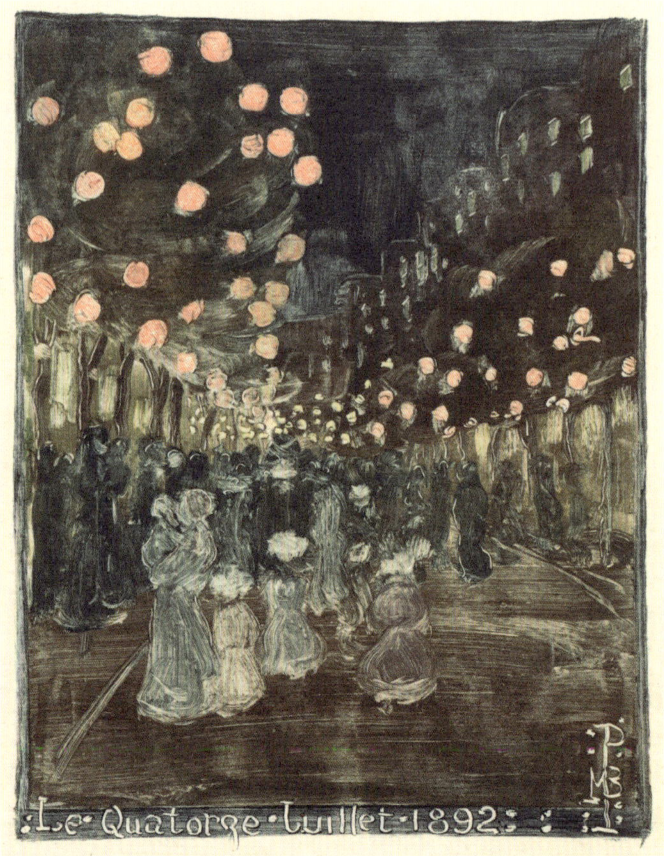

Fig. 18
Maurice Prendergast
Bastille Day, 1892
Color monotype on cream laid paper
6 7/8 × 5 3/16 in. (17.4 × 13.1 cm)
Plate: 10 1/16 × 7 7/8 in. (25.5 × 20 cm).
Sheet: 12 × 9 3/4 in. (30.5 × 24.8 cm)
Cleveland Museum of Art; Gift of The Print Club of Cleveland (1954.337)

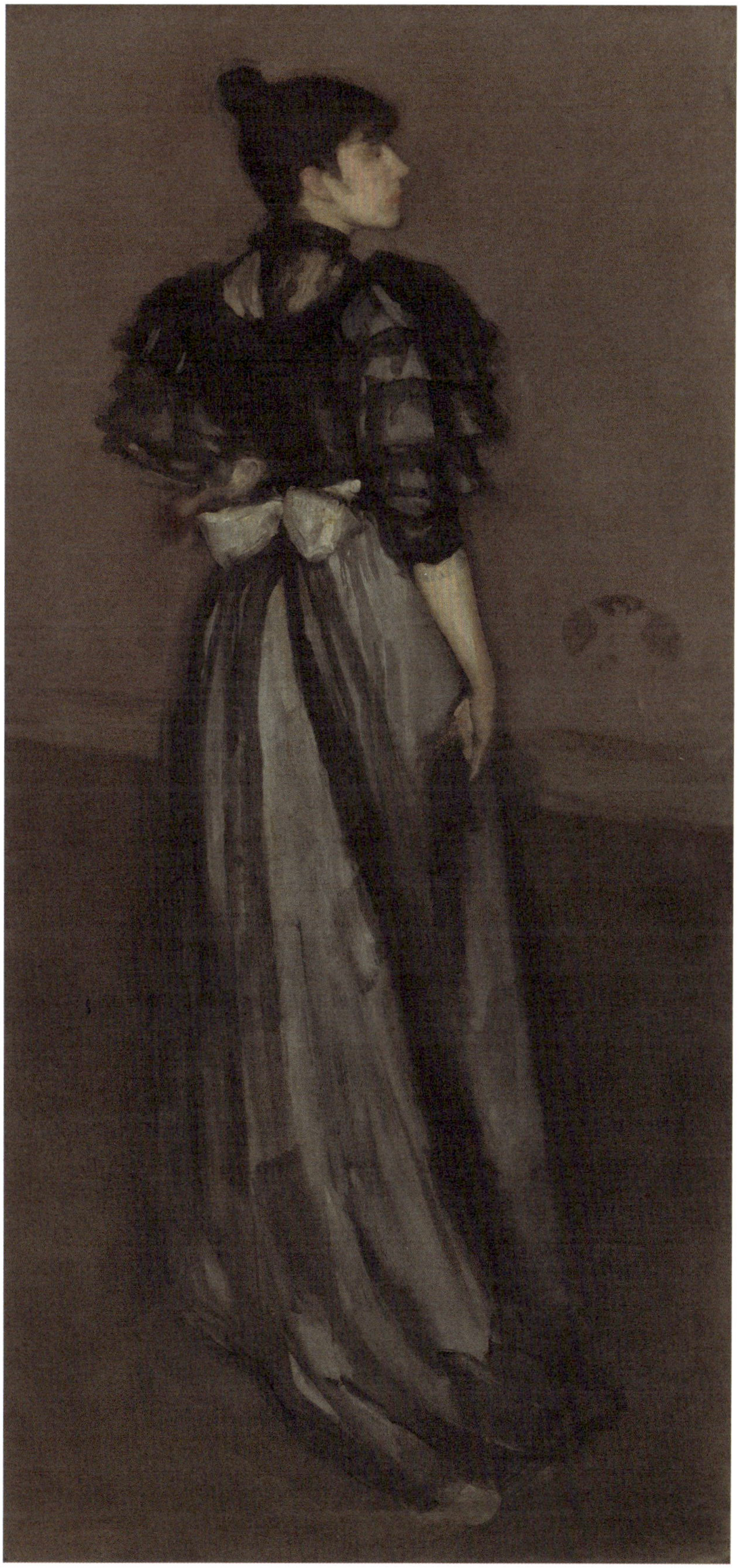

Fig. 19
James McNeill Whistler
Mother of Pearl and Silver: The Andalusian, 1888(?)–1900
Oil on canvas
75⅜ × 35⅜ in. (191.5 × 89.8 cm)
National Gallery of Art, Washington, DC; Harris Whittemore Collection (1943.6.1)

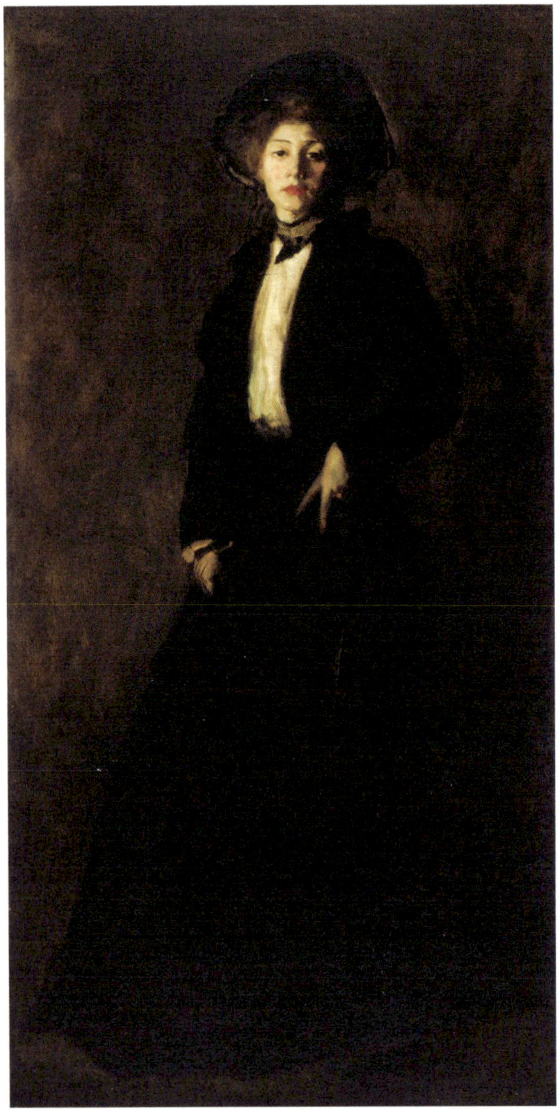

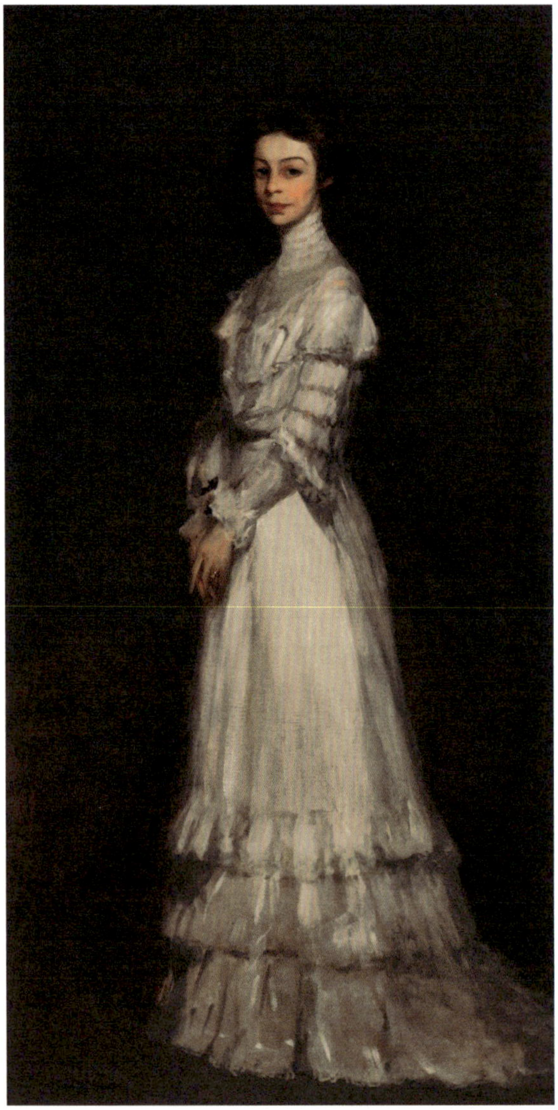

Fig. 20
Robert Henri
Young Woman in Black, 1902
Oil on canvas
77 × 38½ in. (195.6 × 97.8 cm)
The Art Institute of Chicago; Friends of American Art Collection (1910.317)

Fig. 21
Robert Henri
Edith Dimock Glackens, 1902–4
Oil on canvas
77¼ × 38⅝ in. (196.2 × 98.1 cm)
Sheldon Museum of Art, Nebraska Art Association, Lincoln; Gift of Miss Alice Abel, Mr. and Mrs. Gene H. Tallman, The Abel Foundation, and Mrs. Olga N. Sheldon (N-245.1970)

show and visit the picture. (Sloan, still in Philadelphia, would have seen it too.) Henri recorded in his diary on January 4, 1902, that they looked at "Whistlers [*sic*] portrait which was also at Paris Expo. 1900. Great picture—elemental, etc."[63]

During the early years of the twentieth century, Glackens made one important portrait in the Whistlerian mode, that of his friend, the art critic Charles FitzGerald (Fig. 22), whom he met about 1901. Along with giving him a positive review that year, FitzGerald introduced Glackens to Maurice Prendergast, which led to the latter's becoming a member of The Eight. FitzGerald sat for Glackens in 1903, and the canvas constitutes one of his last major meditations on Whistler. The somber palette of blacks, whites, and grays; the fluid paint handling; and the elegant, elongated figure gazing into the distance, melded with its soft, dark background, are all hallmarks of a classic Whistler

Fig. 22
William Glackens
Portrait of Charles FitzGerald, 1903
Oil on canvas
74⅝ × 39½ in. (189.6 × 100.3 cm)
NSU Art Museum, Fort Lauderdale, FL; Gift of The Sansom Foundation, Inc. 92.45

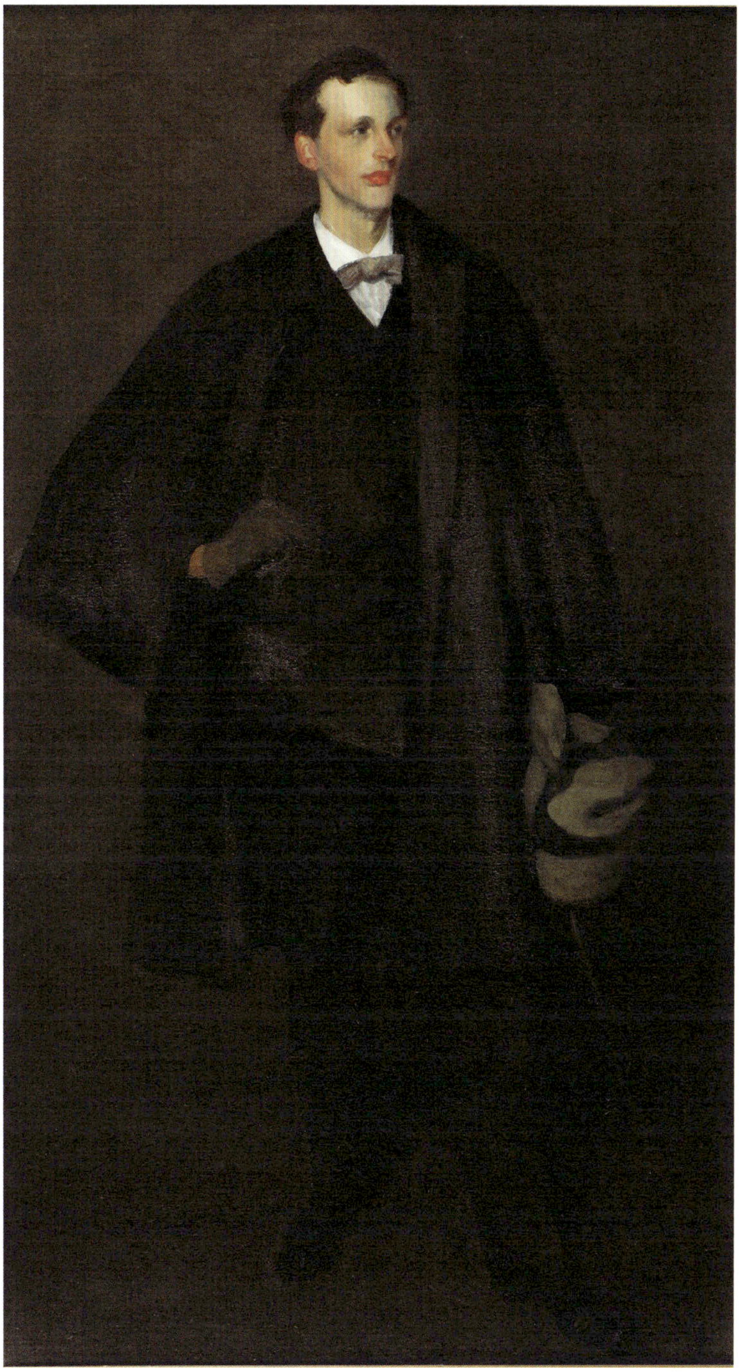

portrait. It is tantalizing to think that Glackens created his homage in late 1903, in memory of Whistler, who died in July of that year. His passing was commemorated in every leading newspaper and art journal, and FitzGerald wrote a tribute in his own paper, the *Sun*.

Sloan too tried his hand at Whistlerian women in white, and the results may have helped sour him on the artist as an influence, at least judging from some of his early public comments. *Girl in White (Full*

Fig. 23
John Sloan's painting *Girl in White (Full Length)* photographed in 1906
John Sloan Catalogue Raisonné files, Helen Farr Sloan Library & Archives, Delaware Art Museum, Wilmington

Fig. 24
John Sloan
Stein and Press, 1906
Oil on canvas
32 × 26¹⁄₁₀ in. (81.3 × 66.3 cm)
Art Gallery of Hamilton, Ontario; Gift of Mr. and Mrs. J.A. McCuaig in memory of her father, H.B. Hall, Esq., 1964, 64.111.5

Length), painted in 1905, only survives as a photograph (Fig. 23); Sloan destroyed the original canvas many years later because it bothered him as "an anomaly" in his work.[64] *Girl in White* and *Stein and Press* (Fig. 24) are souvenirs of a contest with a vexing ghost—the Whistlerian conception of womanhood. Neither of these paintings works inordinately well, because Whistler's female figures reside in spheres of their own, whereas even in a studio setting, Sloan wanted his women to inhabit an animated, real world, and these two are existing uneasily in between.

Stein and Press was rejected by the National Academy of Design for its 1906 annual exhibition, but it was accepted a year later by the Pennsylvania Academy. The Academy's annual was written up in the *New York Times*, and the reviewer recognized the painting's lineage, because he lapsed into Whistlerian language to describe it:

> "Girl and the Etching Press" by John Sloan . . . is one of the very finest things in the whole show. It is a harmony in delicate grays, subdued browns and blue-greens, in which the figure of the girl, robed in warm gray, is the lightest note. There is a suavity and calm restraint in the brushwork, a refinement of color, and, unlike so much of his work, it has a feeling of space and atmosphere, which makes this a notable achievement.[65]

Sloan was at his best when he could perceive an incident on which to build a picture. Once he realized how felicitous the incident could be

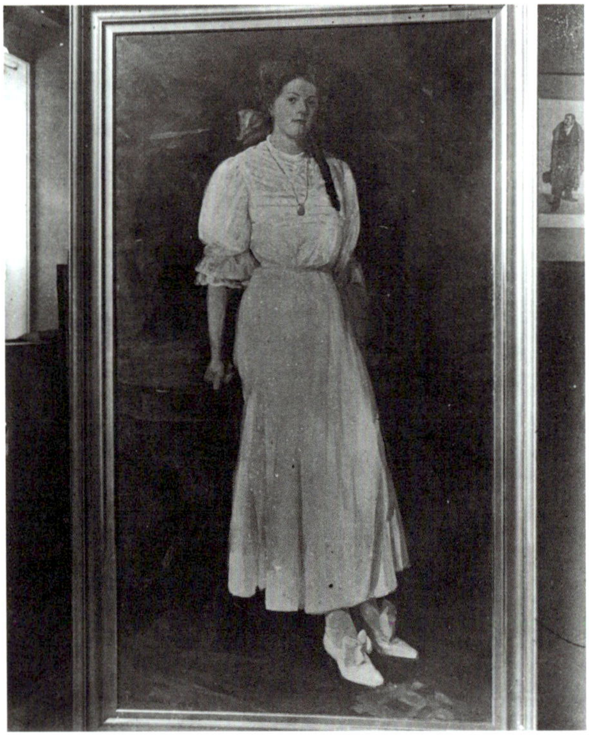

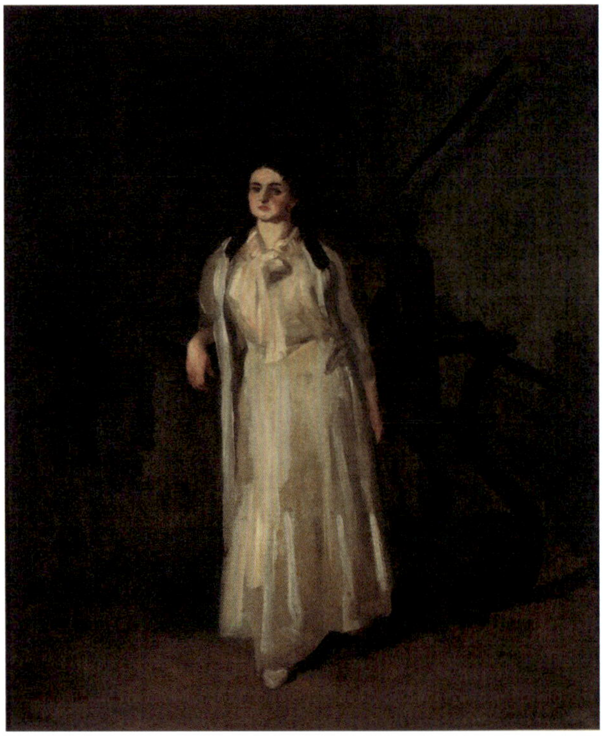

Fig. 25
John Sloan
The Cot, 1907
Oil on canvas
36¼ × 30¼ in. (92.1 × 76.8 cm)
Bowdoin College Museum of Art, Brunswick, ME; Museum Purchase, Bequest of George Otis Hamlin

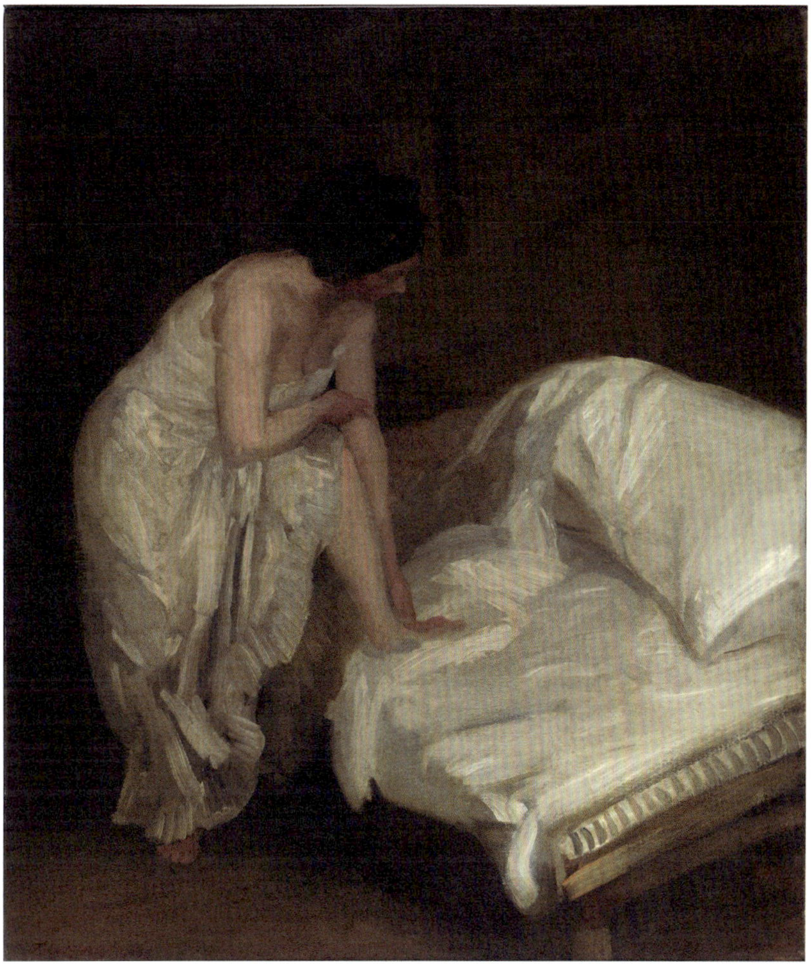

for him, he could liberate himself from Whistler's unsuitable qualities and appropriate the useful aspects. Subtle tonal relationships, especially a sparkling range of whites, were put in service of fresh urban encounters and interactions among strong and purposeful women who navigated a tough material world. Whistler's women are silent, whereas a Sloan woman is often ebullient, either speaking or on the point of it. Sloan glories in an unidealized vision of the female body. All women are beautiful to him, no matter the size or shape, as long as they are active and independent. Thus, when he decided to portray white-clad women in real settings—women with avid facial expressions who were at home with the sensual—the outcome (Fig. 25) was marvelously different from *Girl in White (Full Length)* and *Stein and Press.*

Sloan kept expressing his disdain of the imitative and being foolishly influenced, especially when he had the chance to deflate a rather dim art writer who dared tell him what to do. When a visiting critic suggested that Sloan rename his paintings à la Whistler—she proposed "Nocturne in Green and Gold"—he offered to rename a canvas provisionally titled "Girl in Studio" to "Effect of Light on Stout Healthy

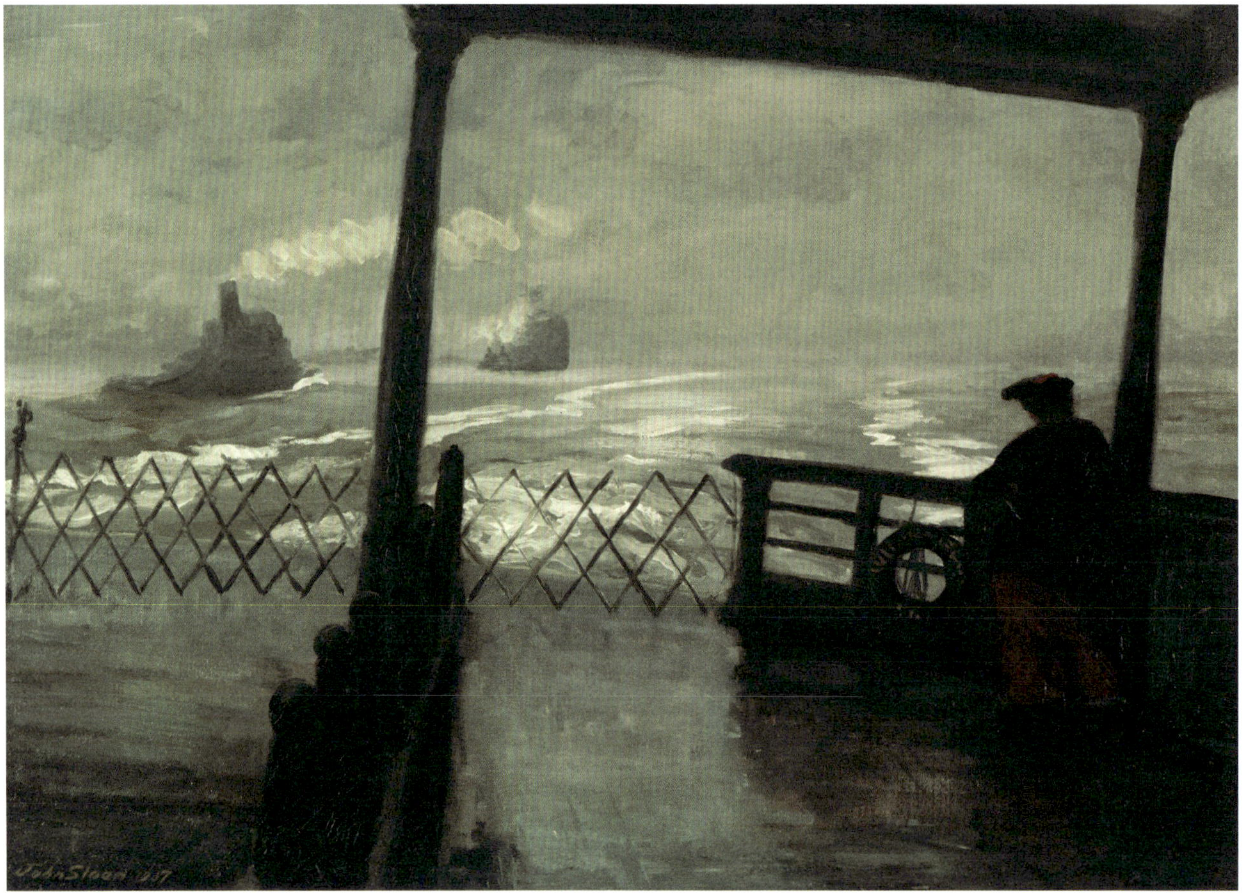

Fig. 26
John Sloan
The Wake of the Ferry II, 1907
Oil on canvas
26 × 32 in. (66 × 81.3 cm)
The Phillips Collection, Washington, DC; Acquired 1922 (1761)

Wench."[66] But to himself, Sloan's response was more bemused. In his diary in 1908, he noted, "Whistler's a great man for himself but not a very good influence. Am I wrong? I don't know."[67]

Not everything that Whistler stood for was alien to Sloan, and he was honest enough to recognize it. Viewing *The Fur Jacket* in 1910, he wrote, "It is a splendid picture, . . . a beautiful conception of a woman."[68] And when an episode was not primary, Whistler was a potent force. *The Coffee Line* (1905; Carnegie Museum of Art, Pittsburgh), the first major oil Sloan completed in New York, is a night painting that makes use of a Whistlerian compositional format and palette and conveys unusual stillness. Undertaking something so thematically uncharacteristic may well have been a purposeful break from the rowdier images populating the etchings of New York life that Sloan was working on at the time. *The Wake of the Ferry II* (Fig. 26) is a Whistlerian hymn to disciplined indeterminacy. The extreme editing of human activity allows the ambiguous melding of the boat and ambient water and the myriad gradations of pigment constituting the sky and river to be seen in higher relief. In its organization of space and elision of detail, *The Wake of the Ferry II* remains one of Sloan's most modern pictures.

Henri, Sloan, and Glackens spent around a decade experimenting with Whistlerian themes and techniques with varying degrees of aptitude, but the apprenticeship of Alfred Maurer to the master was short, swift, and spectacular, without tentativeness or misstep. It is astonishing how quickly Maurer integrated, understood, and individualized Whistler to strengthen his own growth as a modern artist. Stacey B. Epstein, the author of two authoritative monographs on Maurer, has stated that he was "superbly skilled" at "elegant and ambitious pictures built on the Whistlerian and realist esthetics then revered."[69] His quick grasp of surface appearances and modernist simplifications would ultimately lead to his becoming a pioneer of color abstraction. Whistler understood that subject matter was always subsumed by formal concerns, and Maurer grasped the full implications of that principle. From Whistler, "Maurer ultimately learned how to . . . think about space in abstract terms," wrote Epstein.[70]

Maurer was born in 1868 in New York, the son of Louis Maurer, a lithographer for Currier & Ives. Alfred Maurer is the only one of the seven artists under consideration who grew up in New York and with an art background. He could have seen Whistler's work as early as 1882, when Whistler made his New York debut with a loan of the portrait of his mother. More feasibly, at the age of twenty-one, Maurer could have visited Whistler's first one-person show in America, which took place in New York in 1889. At sixteen, Maurer left school to work in the family lithography business, and in 1894, he joined another commercial firm, designing calendars, showcards, and booklets, while taking art classes at night. He studied at the National Academy of Design from 1885 to 1892 and again from 1893 to 1895. In the late 1890s, Maurer joined the Country Sketch Club, a group that went to rural New Jersey on weekends to draw and paint landscapes. One of the members was Glackens, freshly back from Paris and full of Manet and Whistler. The two men were sympathetic spirits, and they became firm friends.

In November 1897, Maurer made his first visit to Paris. He enrolled at the Académie Julian, but only attended classes for a few weeks, preferring to study in the Louvre. He met and became friends with Henri when the latter was in France between 1898 and 1900. Like Henri, Maurer saw *Symphony in White, No. 2: The Little White Girl*, *The Andalusian*, and *Brown and Gold*—Whistler's contributions to the Exposition Universelle of 1900—because he too was in the exhibition, with an anguished female figure seen from the back. Painted in 1899–1900, *At the Window* (Hirshhorn Museum and Sculpture Garden, Smithsonian Institution, Washington, DC) demonstrated a familiarity with Degas, Toulouse-Lautrec, and the Symbolists. By 1901, Maurer, who was concentrating on images of solitary women in spare backgrounds, had fallen under Whistler's spell, but with a difference. There is often a clarity and a solidity to Maurer's female figures, as in *Gabrielle* (c. 1901; Montana Museum of Art and Culture,

Fig. 27
Alfred Maurer
An Arrangement, 1901
Oil on paperboard
36³⁄₁₆ × 32⅛ in. (91.9 × 81.6 cm)
Whitney Museum of American Art, New York; Gift of Mr. and Mrs. Hudson D. Walker 50.13

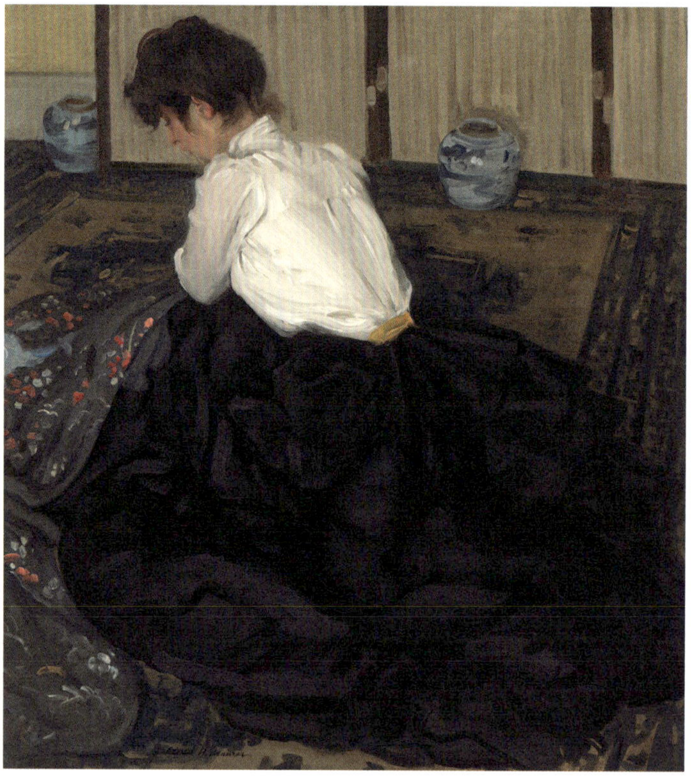

Missoula), that combine a Whistlerian pose with more substantial, almost sculptural treatment of the body and clothing. In his friend Maurice Sterne's words, Maurer was in those days "keenly alive to reality, . . . sensitive to character."[71]

Maurer traveled back to New York in 1901, and soon after he was settled, he created *An Arrangement* (Fig. 27), which was painted on a piece of cardboard given to him by Sterne. *An Arrangement* is Maurer's best-known early painting: it has a perfectly Whistlerian title, matched by an equally masterly deployment of the motif of a partially revealed woman in an aestheticized interior with Asian accents. Just as expert was Maurer's manipulation of form, color, value, texture, and pattern. In New York, Maurer reunited with Glackens and Henri, and Henri invited him to join a group exhibition that he was assembling at the Allan Gallery in April 1901. This was the first gathering of the New York realists—Sloan was included as well—and it contained the germ of all the later exhibitions that Henri arranged for him and his friends to advance their art directly before the public. As an inveterate organizer of and participant in artist-run shows for "greater freedom of exhibitions," Henri followed the call of Courbet, the Impressionists, and Whistler. In his pronouncements and broadsides against the art establishment, Whistler had steadily demanded a culture in which "artists, as opposed to critics, patrons, or politicians, were sovereign."[72]

An Arrangement was shown at the Allan Gallery, and Maurer went on to enter it in the Carnegie Museum of Art's annual exhibition, which

Fig. 28
Alfred Maurer
Jeanne, c. 1904
Oil on canvas
74¾ × 39⅜ in. (190 × 100 cm)
Courtesy of Crystal Bridges Museum of American Art, Bentonville, AR

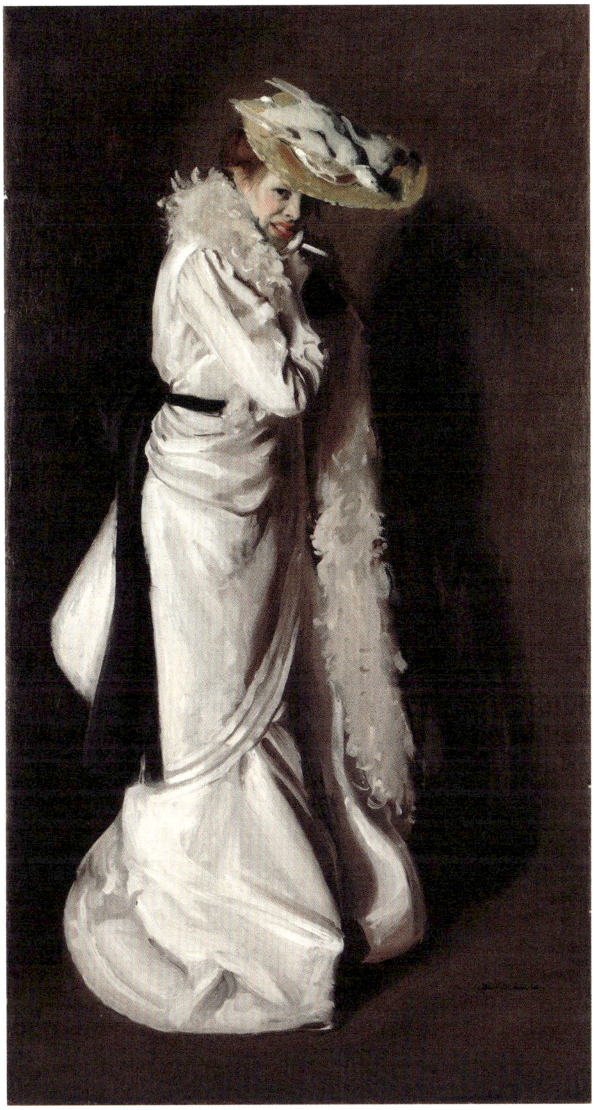

opened in November 1901. The painting won first prize and established Maurer as a rising talent; the money allowed him to go back to Paris in 1902.[73] Ensconced in France again, Maurer continued to paint images of women but added scenes of city life—vignettes of cafés and parks that evinced the lively realism that Sterne so admired—and even nocturnes. His female figures, while still inflected by Whistler, grew more assertive, less withdrawn, and more substantial. They have more in common with the true-to-life women that Sloan and Luks were soon to portray, but they were more audacious in approach. Dentures, revealed by the slight but unmistakable set of the jaw in Maurer's *Woman in Black* (c. 1904; Hirshhorn Museum and Sculpture Garden, Smithsonian Institution, Washington, DC) do not seem to be noticeable in earlier depictions of women in American art. But these canvases were merely preamble to *Jeanne* (Fig. 28), a spellbinding performance that exploits the tensions between Whistlerian aestheticism and Ashcan verisimilitude and speeds them to a dramatic resolution.

With *Jeanne*, Maurer proves that he can compose a female figure in white as splendid as any by a grand-manner painter. Sensuous passages of feathers, plumes, and folds of cloth are highlighted against a shadowed background as their wearer bursts forth from a pool of dark tones. Yet *Jeanne* upends everything to do with the genteel tradition of the remote woman in white. Her gaze is the boldest we have seen since Lady Archie Campbell's, and it is as direct in intent as Manet's *Olympia*. The model poses as a woman of the streets—a woman smoking, a woman coarsely made up, a contemporary woman who magnetizes and confronts us. She laughs at conventional audiences through her stance, expression, and attitude. Maurer sheds euphemism, leaping beyond any full-length American portrait of his time. He aligns himself with the caustic reality of Toulouse-Lautrec and Degas and their exposés of actresses, models, and prostitutes. *Jeanne* is the apogee of his early work and from it, Maurer, who was increasingly attracted to pure prismatic color, became the first American to respond to Henri Matisse and Fauvism in his work.

George Bellows was born in 1882, and by the time he was an art student, Whistler was not only iconic but inescapable. Yet other than in the perceptive writings of David Park Curry,[74] Bellows has not been associated with Whistler, because he is so extravagantly celebrated for his visceral urban realism. However, he tackled many subjects besides high-oxygen boxing matches. When he wanted a quietistic or contemplative effect or, frankly, when he sought to learn restraint, Bellows looked to Whistler. But in truth, there are never one-to-one correspondences between artists and those whom they venerate. Whistler was one of Bellows's heroes, and the latter had no trouble acknowledging it. In reply to a letter asking him to comment on artists in 1924, the year before his death and the same year he painted *Dempsey and Firpo* (Whitney Museum of American Art, New York), his last boxing picture, Bellows wrote, "[Of the great artists], Winslow Homer is my particular pet. And one other American or better, two, stand on the same pedestal with him, in my mind, neither of whom you mentioned: Thomas Eakins and Whistler."[75] And when Bellows evoked Whistler, he was not an old man reminiscing in a rosy twilight blur about long-ago thoughts; when he died of appendicitis on January 8, 1925, Bellows was forty-two years old.

Bellows was born and raised in Ohio. As a student at Ohio State University, he made a name as an athlete and turned down a contract to play professional baseball in favor of studying art. He arrived in New York in September 1904 and enrolled in the New York School of Art, where he got a full dose of Whistler because his teachers were Chase and Henri. Chase always told his students about his experiences

Fig. 29
George Bellows
Little Girl in White (Queenie Burnett), 1907
Oil on canvas
62³⁄₁₆ × 34¼ in. (158 × 87 cm)
National Gallery of Art, Washington, DC; Gift of Mr. and Mrs. Paul Mellon
1983.1.2

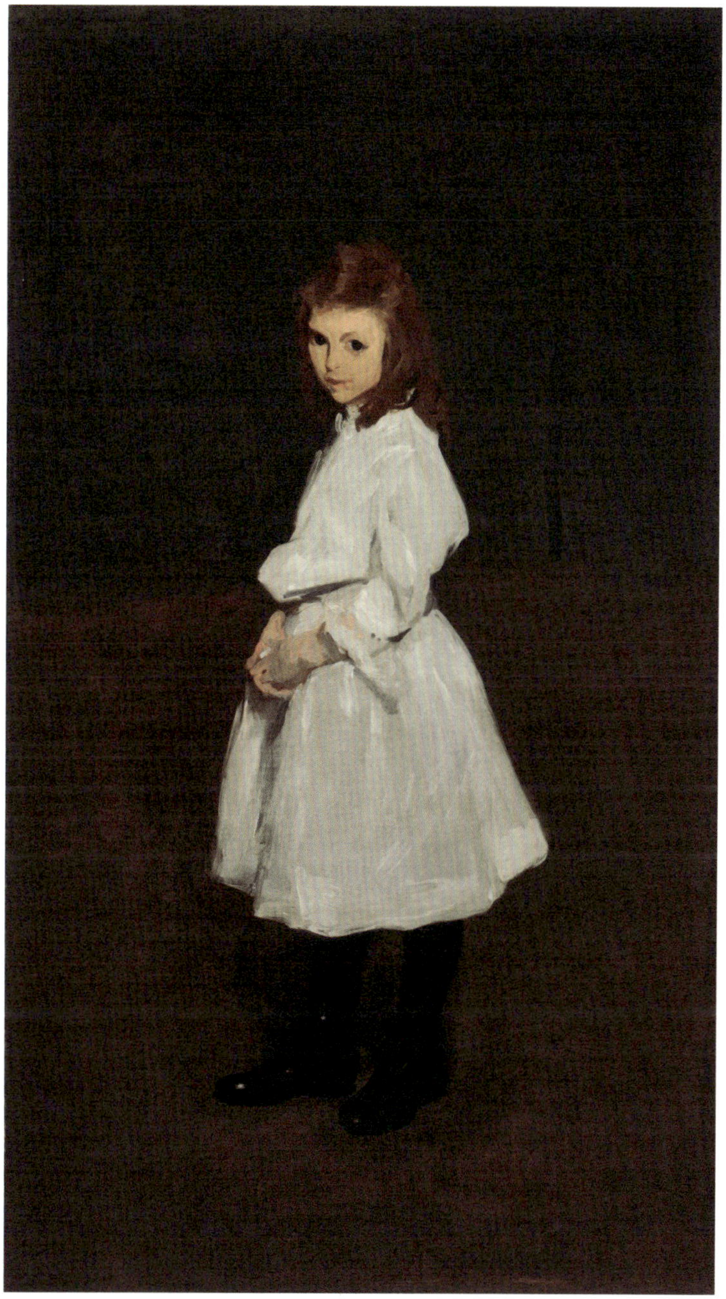

with Whistler. Henri not only was proselytizing about Velázquez, Hals, Manet, and Whistler as supreme masters but was also engrossed in producing the full-length portraits of women that were indebted to Whistler and Manet. Bellows wrote of the Henri class, "My life begins at this point."[76] Bellows emerged as a prodigy, but even the most gifted students have to find an individual style through their predecessors, and it is natural that he would begin with artists touted by Henri.

In 1907, Bellows was able to compose *Little Girl in White (Queenie Burnett)* (Fig. 29), a much more accomplished portrait. Despite the artist's choice to clothe her in a pristine and elegant dress, the little girl worked at a laundry. Her pinched face reveals that her childhood was not comfortable, in marked opposition to Bellows's source of inspiration—Whistler's incomparable portrait of the aristocratic Cicely Alexander (Fig. 30). Bellows registers compassion for someone who appears to be intimidated by the prospect of being painted by a professional artist, as opposed to the composed and pouting Miss Alexander, who was confident enough to express some pique. The canvas was originally titled "Little Laundry Girl," but Bellows changed it to "Little Girl in White," and under this highly Whistlerian title, it was first exhibited in 1910.[77]

Nocturne in Black and Gold, the Falling Rocket (1875; Detroit Institute of Arts), Whistler's most notorious Nocturne and "the pot of paint" that had been the subject of the infamous Whistler-Ruskin libel suit of 1878, was shown at the Metropolitan Museum of Art in 1907. The year before, his *Nocturne in Green and Gold* was donated to the museum. Bellows would not have missed seeing either canvas, which may have suggested to him that incidents were not required to shape a genre painting. They may also have buttressed his inclination toward a palette of greater dark-light contrasts, although he was already familiar with such oppositions in Manet and Henri. In the nocturnes that Bellows essayed after *The Falling Rocket* was exhibited in New York, his darkness is even murkier than Whistler's. In *Excavation at Night* (1908; Crystal Bridges Museum of American Art), an oil from his series charting the construction of the Pennsylvania Railroad Station, Bellows harnessed Whistler's idea of veiling industrial areas in deep shadow and propelled it to a dynamic new level with the choice of a bruising Ashcan subject.

After triumphing as an artist of urban genre, sport, and the sea, Bellows launched himself as a portraitist. He had created unconventional depictions of slum children and members of his own family, but in each case, he could take risks because his sitters would not refuse or censure his work. But when he sought commissions from people in society and business who would be paying for their likenesses and imposing the demands of fashion, he, like Whistler, experienced resistance and rejection. It was no wonder that the younger artist imitated Whistler in his concept of arriving at what a cosmopolitan portrait of a woman was expected to look like; throughout his career, Bellows frequently studied the art of the past for guidance, and it was a natural behavior for him.

In 1912, Bellows returned to Ohio as a hero, for his first big exhibition there.[78] The local worthies ordered portraits done by the brilliant native son, and Bellows was to immortalize two Columbus socialites, neither of whom are recognizable as being painted by George Bellows. In his portrait of Mrs. Albert Miller, Bellows labors intractably. The woman's face seems drained of animation, and the energy and brio that he could summon was inappropriate for a run-of-the-mill offering of a placid woman in white. The artist did find a better compositional formula for his portrait of Mrs. Harold B. Arnold (Fig. 31), although

Fig. 30
James McNeill Whistler
Harmony in Grey and Green: Miss Cicely Alexander, 1903
Oil on canvas
74⅞ × 38½ in. (190.2 × 97.8 cm)
Tate Britain, London; Bequeathed by W.C. Alexander 1932 (N04622)

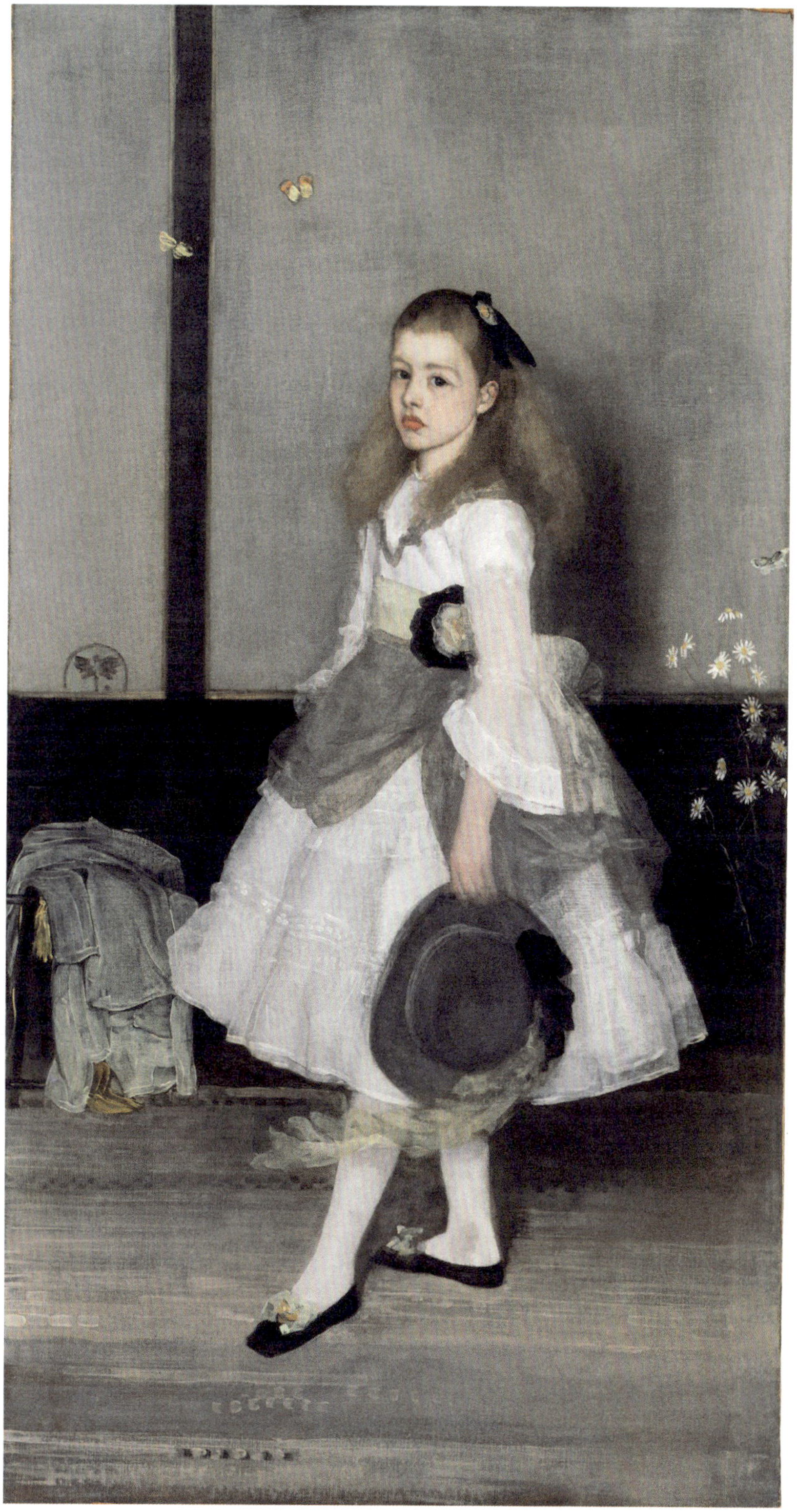

Fig. 31
George Bellows
Mrs. H. B. Arnold, 1913
Oil on canvas
77½ × 37 in. (196.9 × 94 cm)
Columbus Museum of Art, Columbus, OH; Gift of H. Bartley Arnold, Jr. (1955.058)

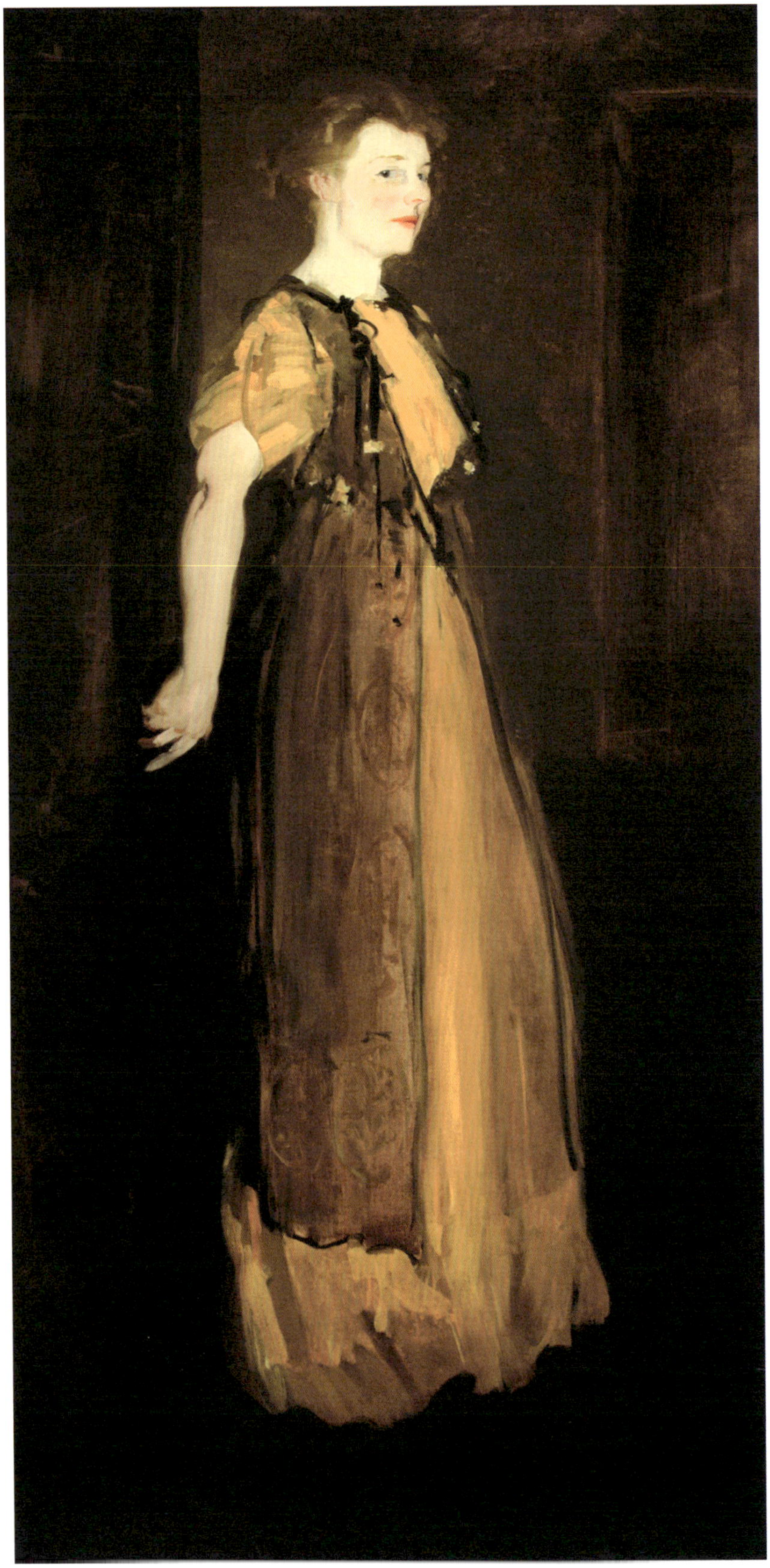

not a Bellows of the first rank. Following Whistler, Bellows elected to pose his subject at an angle at that showed off her diaphanous gown and presented the woman herself as the stylishly central actor in a harmonious aesthetic cocoon. Nonetheless, the Arnolds rejected the portrait, and it was still in the artist's estate when he died.[79]

In the 1910s, Bellows was moderating and moving away from the thick, active application of paint, pulling that knockout punch of his in favor of a more considered power of restraint. The evolution of his approach may well be what Bellows meant by "reserve" in the following passage from an important letter. In 1915, he wrote to one of his former professors at Ohio State,

> Wish you could see my things for the past two years. I have been trying to discover dignity in powerful colors. I have been painting with the pure stuff and arriving at a richer statement with more reserve than before. This sounds paradoxical. But great, dignified masses can just as well or better often be made with powerful colors as with grays. Would you like to see Whistler's reserve in pure Orange and Blue? It can be done.[80]

Affinities in theme, composition, and palette can be fairly simple to discern among artists related in time and place, but the less straightforward conclusion to be drawn from them lies in the variety of ways that emulation could be transfigured into something distinctive and individual as our artists went down roads that the master could not travel. Those possibilities confirm, as Henry James said, that "an achievement in art or in letters grows more interesting when we perceive its connections."[81]

NOTES

1. Linda Merrill, "Preface," in Linda Merrill et al., *After Whistler: The Artist and His Influence on American Painting* (New Haven, CT: Yale University Press, in association with the High Museum of Art, 2003), 7.
2. I found no significant connection or pattern of influence between Whistler and Arthur B. Davies or George Luks. Everett Shinn had a working awareness of Whistler, but he was influenced more generally than deeply. Because his work reflects a cursory dialogue with Whistler, I have not included it here.
3. H. Barbara Weinberg, "Introduction," in H. Barbara Weinberg, Doreen Bolger, and David Park Curry, *American Impressionism and Realism: The Painting of Modern Life, 1885–1915* (New York: Metropolitan Museum of Art, 1994), 3.
4. See Weinberg, "Introduction," in *American Impressionism and Realism*, 3, 14.
5. Mary Fanton Roberts, an editor of *The Craftsman* magazine from 1906 to 1916, was a loyal supporter of The Eight, and her journal was a platform for these artists. She published three articles by Henri, including his manifesto, "Progress in Our National Art Must Spring from the Development of Individuality of Expression: A Suggestion for a New School," *The Craftsman* 15 (January 1909): 387–401, in which he wrote, "The men who become the artists must... express... the virile ideas of their country" (391). In his autobiography, *Artists Say the Silliest Things* (New York: American Artists Group, 1940), Guy Pène du Bois, who studied with Henri, wrote that his former teacher saw "men as men instead of puppets moving with carefully mincing steps in a fantastically emasculated society" (82). See also Robert W. Snyder and Rebecca Zurier, "Picturing the City," in Rebecca Zurier, Robert W. Snyder, and Virginia M. Mecklenburg, *Metropolitan Lives: The Ashcan Artists and Their New York* (Washington, DC: National Museum of American Art, in association with W. W. Norton, 1995), 182 and 187, in which the authors document the preoccupation with asserting Bellows's American virility and red-bloodedness. Valerie Ann Leeds in *Ernest Lawson* (New York: Gerald Peters Gallery, 2000), lists contemporaneous articles that call attention to the "virile quality" of Lawson's work (14, 39–40).
6. Du Bois, *Artists Say the Silliest Things*, 82–88; John Sloan, verbatim notes, 1944–50, John Sloan Archives, Delaware Art Museum, Wilmington (hereafter JSA), 102. I am grateful to Heather Campbell Coyle for providing me with a copy of this manuscript.
7. Guy Pène du Bois, *Ernest Lawson* (New York: Whitney Museum of American Art, 1932), 9.
8. Sloan, verbatim notes, JSA, 302.
9. James McNeill Whistler, "Mr. Whistler's 'Ten O'Clock,'" in *The Gentle Art of Making Enemies* (New York: Dover, 1967 [repr. of 2nd ed., 1892]), 143.
10. William Glackens, "The American Section: The National Art," *Arts and Decoration* 3, no. 5 (March 1913): 162.
11. For example, in 1883 Whistler began painting a full-length portrait of Lois Cassatt, the wife of the Philadelphian Alexander J. Cassatt, president of the Pennsylvania Railroad and the brother of Mary Cassatt.
12. Andrew McLaren Young et al., *The Paintings of James McNeill Whistler*, vol. 2 (New Haven, CT: Yale University Press, 1980), 31, 134.
13. Bennard B. Perlman, *Robert Henri: His Life and Art* (New York: Dover, 1991), 15.
14. Young et al., *Paintings of James McNeill Whistler*, 44, 96, 43, 117.
15. Perlman, *Robert Henri: His Life and Art*, 18.
16. Quoted in Bennard B. Perlman, *The Immortal Eight: American Painting from Eakins to the Armory Show, 1870–1913* (Westport, CT: North Light Publishers, 1979), 148.

17. Harrison S. Morris, *Confessions in Art* (New York: Sears Publishing Co., 1930), 17–20; see also Sylvia Yount, "Whistler and Philadelphia: A Question of Character," in Merrill et al., *After Whistler*, 50–63, for fundamental documentation of the Pennsylvania Academy of Art's support of Whistler, and Avis Berman, "Glackens and Whistler: A Young Man's Attraction," *The Magazine Antiques* 181, no. 1 (January–February 2014): 206–15.
18. Yount, "Whistler and Philadelphia," 56.
19. Heather Campbell Coyle, "Laughing Matters: Art Caricature in America, 1878–1918" (PhD diss., University of Delaware, 2011), 201; "Great Paintings Caricatured: A Unique Exhibit by the Students at the Academy of Fine Arts," *Philadelphia Inquirer*, March 4, 1894, 9.
20. Morris, *Confessions in Art*, 45–46.
21. Peter Hastings Falk, comp. and ed., *The Exhibition Record of the Pennsylvania Academy of Fine Arts, 1876–1913, Vol. II* (Madison, CT: Sound View Press, 1989), 515–16.
22. Robert Henri, journal, April 4, 1894, box 20, folder 471, Yale Collection of American Literature, Beinecke Rare Book and Manuscript Library, Yale University, New Haven, CT (hereafter YCAL).
23. William Glackens, letter to Miss Smith, November 25, 1894, Kraushaar Galleries Archives, New York.
24. Avis Berman, "George du Maurier's *Trilby* Whipped Up a Worldwide Storm," *Smithsonian Magazine* 24, no. 9 (December 1993): 118–19, 121.
25. Playbill for *Twillbe*, December 29, 1894, box 31, JSA.
26. "Science and Inventions," *Philadelphia Inquirer*, December 30, 1894, 20.
27. William Glackens, letter to Miss Smith, September 7, 1895, Kraushaar Galleries Archives.
28. Whistler, "Mr. Whistler's 'Ten O'Clock,'" 144.
29. See Regina Armstrong, "Representative Young Illustrators," *The Art Interchange* 43, no. 5 (November 1899): 109; and "The New Leaders in American Illustration IV: The Typists: McCarter, Yohn, Glackens, Shinn and Luks," *Bookman* 11 (May 1900): 247.
30. See Robert Henri, letter to John Sloan, November 5, 1899, in Bennard B. Perlman, ed., *Revolutionaries of Realism: The Letters of John Sloan and Robert Henri* (Princeton, NJ: Princeton University Press, 1997), 36.
31. Robert Henri, letter to Richard and Theresa Lee, October 10, 1898, quoted in Perlman, *Robert Henri: His Life and Art*, 40.
32. Robert Henri, letter to Richard and Theresa Lee, February 18, 1897, quoted in William Innes Homer and Violet Organ, *Robert Henri and His Circle* (Ithaca, NY: Cornell University Press, 1969), 87.
33. See Bennard B. Perlman, *Robert Henri: Painter* (Wilmington: Delaware Art Museum, 1984), 47.
34. Robert Henri, letter to Richard and Theresa Lee, June 1899, quoted in Perlman, *Robert Henri: His Life and Art*, 43.
35. John Sloan, *Gist of Art: Principles and Practise Expanded in the Classroom and Studio* (New York: Dover, 1977 [repr. of 1939 ed.]), 15.
36. Sloan, verbatim notes, JSA, 139.
37. Sloan, verbatim notes, JSA, 192.
38. Harold Bloom, *The Anxiety of Influence: A Theory of Poetry* (New York: Oxford University Press, 1975), 5.
39. Jacob Kainen, "Foreword," in Peter Morse, *John Sloan's Prints: A Catalogue Raisonné of the Etchings, Lithographs, and Posters* (New Haven, CT: Yale University Press, 1969), viii.
40. Bloom, *Anxiety of Influence*, 69.

41. Sloan, verbatim notes, JSA, 114.
42. Sloan, verbatim notes, JSA, 108, 128.
43. This comparison was articulated for American artists in general by Sarah Burns in *Inventing the Modern Artist: Art and Culture in Gilded Age America* (New Haven, CT: Yale University Press, 1996), 60.
44. Glackens's etching from this outing also had a Whistlerian motif. It is a panoramic view of boats docked along the Schuylkill River, in the collection of the National Museum of American History, Smithsonian Institution, Washington, DC.
45. Quoted in Morse, *John Sloan's Prints*, 62, 383.
46. Rowland Elzea, *John Sloan's Oil Paintings: A Catalogue Raisonné, Part I* (Newark, DE: University of Delaware Press, 1991), 54.
47. Quoted in E. R. and J. Pennell, *The Life of James McNeill Whistler*, vol. 2 (New York: AMS Press, 1973 [repr. of 1908 ed.]), 240.
48. Henry and Sidney Berry-Hill, *Ernest Lawson: American Impressionist, 1873–1939* (Leigh-on-Sea, England: F. Lewis, 1968), 20.
49. Young et al., *Paintings of James McNeill Whistler*, 183–85.
50. Barbara O'Neal, "Introduction," in *Ernest Lawson, 1873–1939* (Ottawa: National Gallery of Canada, 1967), 8.
51. Leeds, *Ernest Lawson*, 15.
52. Duncan Phillips, "Ernest Lawson," in *A Collection in the Making; A Survey of the Problems Involved in Collecting Pictures, Together with Brief Estimates of the Painters in the Phillips Memorial Gallery* (New York: E. Weyhe, 1926), 57.
53. Leeds, *Ernest Lawson*, 111.
54. Whistler, "Mr. Whistler's 'Ten O'Clock,'" 142–43.
55. Quoted in Lacey Taylor, entry for *Spring Night, Harlem River*, in Merrill et al., *After Whistler*, 204.
56. See Cecily Langdale, *Charles Conder, Robert Henri, James Morrice, Maurice Prendergast: The Formative Years, Paris 1890s* (New York: Davis & Long, 1975); and Nicole Cloutier, *James Wilson Morrice, 1865–1924* (Montreal: Montreal Museum of Fine Arts, 1986).
57. Nancy Mowll Mathews, *Maurice Prendergast* (Williamstown, MA: Williams College Museum of Art and Prestel-Verlag, 1990), 12–13.
58. Carol Clark et al., *Maurice Brazil Prendergast, Charles Prendergast: A Catalogue Raisonné* (Williamstown, MA: Williams College Museum of Art and Prestel-Verlag, 1990), 636–37, and Mathews, *Maurice Prendergast*, 12.
59. Van Wyck Brooks, "Anecdotes of Maurice Prendergast," in *The Prendergasts* (Andover, MA: Addison Gallery of American Art, Phillips Academy, 1938), 35–36.
60. Young et al., *Paintings of James McNeill Whistler*, 100, 129.
61. Trevor J. Fairbrother, "'Audacities': Maurice Prendergast and the Culture of Fin-de-Siècle Boston," in Joachim Homann et al., *Maurice Prendergast: By the Sea* (New York: Bowdoin College Museum of Art and DelMonico Books, 2013), 76.
62. David W. Kiehl, "'A Means of Entertainment,'" *ARTnews* 79, no. 3 (March 1980): 90–91.
63. Robert Henri, diary entry, January 4, 1902, Robert Henri Papers, reel 885, Archives of American Art, Smithsonian Institution, Washington DC.
64. Elzea, *John Sloan's Oil Paintings: A Catalogue Raisonné, Part I*, 66.
65. "Younger Painters to the Fore," *New York Times*, November 11, 1907, 6.
66. Quoted in Avis Berman, "Artist as Rebel: John Sloan Versus the Status Quo," *Smithsonian Magazine* 19, no. 1 (April 1988): 82.
67. John Sloan, diary entry, March 25, 1908, quoted in Bruce St. John, ed., *John Sloan's New York Scene: From the Diaries, Notes and Correspondence, 1906–1913* (New York: Harper and Row, 1965), 208.
68. Sloan, diary entry, February 25, 1910, quoted in *John Sloan's New York Scene*, 391.

69. Stacey B. Epstein, *Alfred Maurer: At the Vanguard of Modernism* (Andover, MA: Addison Gallery of American Art, Phillips Academy, 2015), 13. Unless otherwise stated, all biographical information on Maurer is drawn from this publication. See also Stacey B. Epstein, *Alfred H. Maurer: Aestheticism to Modernism* (New York: Hollis Taggart Galleries, 1999), for an earlier discussion of Maurer and Whistler.
70. Epstein, *Alfred Maurer: At the Vanguard of Modernism*, 24.
71. Maurice Sterne, undated, unpublished reminiscences, Maurice Sterne papers, box 6, YCAL MSS 39.
72. Charles Brock, "George Bellows: An Unfinished Life," in Charles Brock et al., *George Bellows* (Washington, DC: National Gallery of Art, 2012), 12.
73. Sterne, undated, unpublished reminiscences of Alfred Maurer, Maurice Sterne papers, box 6, YCAL MSS 39.
74. See, for example, David Park Curry, "Life of Leisure: Polo, Parks, and Tennis, 1910–1920," in Brock et al., *George Bellows*, 132–34.
75. Quoted in Charles H. Morgan, *George Bellows: Painter of America* (New York: Reynal, 1965), 272; see also "Notes," in Brock et al., *George Bellows*, 318 n23.
76. Morgan, *George Bellows: Painter of America*, 37.
77. Jane Myers, "'The Most Searching Place in the World': Bellows and Portraiture," in *The Paintings of George Bellows* (Fort Worth, TX: Amon Carter Museum, 1992), 231n23.
78. Morgan, *George Bellows*, 159–60.
79. Myers, "'The Most Searching Place in the World,'" 189.
80. Quoted in Morgan, *George Bellows*, 190–91.
81. Quoted in Miranda Seymour, "The Unbuttoned Henry James," *New York Times Book Review*, November 22, 1992, 12.

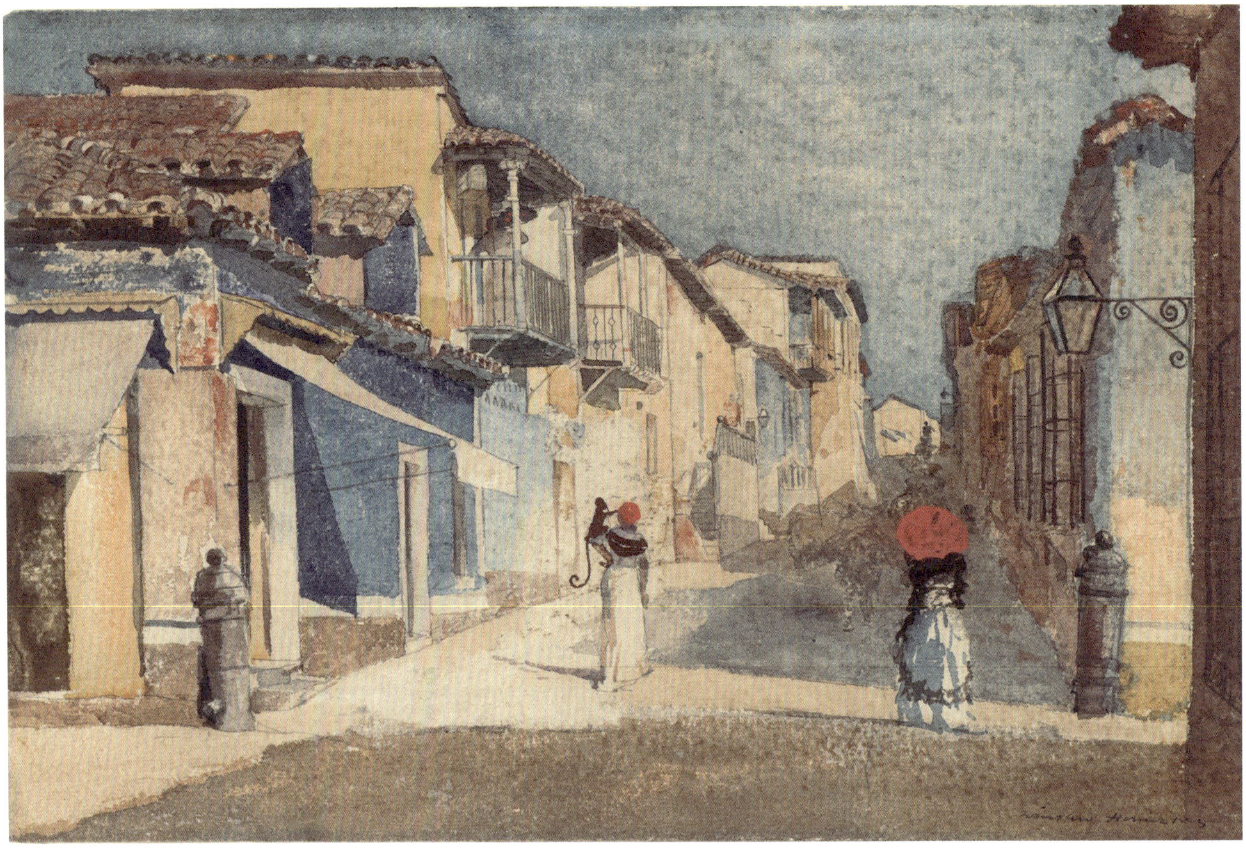

Lecture given on
May 3, 2018

New-York
Historical Society

New York City

Images and Imperialisms: American Artists and Cuba at the Turn of the Twentieth Century

CAROL TROYEN

The story of artists from the United States working in Cuba begins not with a painter but with a publisher. In January 1897, William Randolph Hearst, the owner of the *New York Journal and Advertiser*, sent Frederic Remington to Havana to cover the rising tensions between native Cubans and the colonial Spanish government. According to legend, Remington got there, looked around, and found things surprisingly calm. He cabled Hearst, "Everything is quiet. There is no trouble. There will be no war. I wish to return." Hearst cabled back, "Please remain. You furnish the pictures and I'll furnish the war." The fact that this exchange probably never took place makes it no less striking a metaphor for the role that manipulation and propaganda played in the United States' seizing agency in the conflict between the Cubans and the Spanish.[1]

Hearst was not the only publisher to hire an artist to "furnish the pictures." His rival, Joseph Pulitzer, publisher of the *New York World*, was one of numerous other newspaper and magazine owners who sent journalists to cover the turmoil in the Caribbean. Among the artists dispatched to Cuba were Remington, William Glackens, George Luks, and Howard Chandler Christy; the reporters included Richard Harding Davis and novelist-journalists Frank Norris and Stephen Crane (Fig. 33). Crane calculated that by the time the United States and Spain declared war on one another in April 1898, there were some 250 correspondents milling around Key West, Florida, waiting for a dispatch tug to carry them the short distance across the sea to Cuba.[2]

The War of 1898 was a key element in the ongoing rivalry between Hearst's *Journal* and Pulitzer's *World*, a rivalry that began well before Spanish and US forces began firing on one another in Cuba.[3] The drama of the Cuban struggle for independence, unfolding so close to America's shores, presented a great opportunity to sell papers, and in their competition for readership, the *World* and the *Journal* sought to outdo one another in reporting stories of political intrigue, poignancy, and violence (Fig. 34). This was the era of "yellow" journalism, in

Fig. 32
Winslow Homer
Street Scene, Santiago de Cuba, 1885
Watercolor on paper
12 × 17¾ in. (30.5 × 45.1 cm)
Philadelphia Museum of Art; Gift of Dr. and Mrs. George Woodward 1939, 1939-7-15

Fig. 33
"Richard Harding Davis and Frederic Remington in Cuba for the *Journal*"
Published on front page of *New York Journal and Advertiser*, January 17, 1897
Library of Congress, Washington, DC

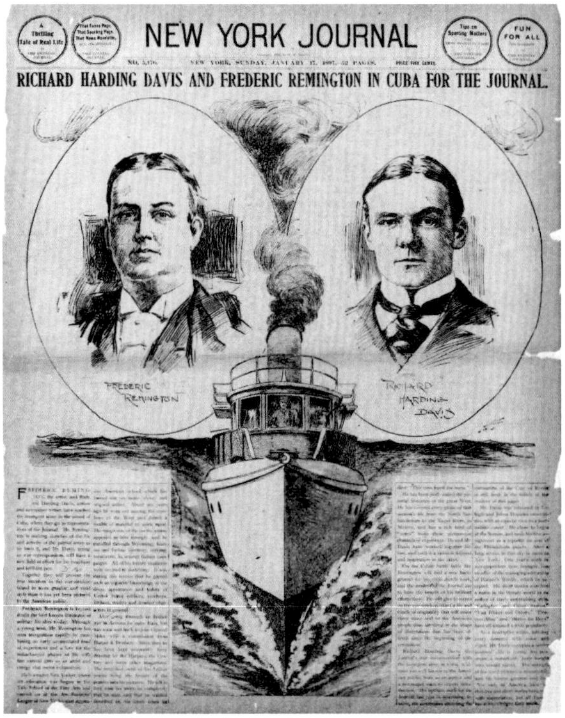
NEW YORK JOURNAL

RICHARD HARDING DAVIS AND FREDERIC REMINGTON IN CUBA FOR THE JOURNAL.

which standards of accuracy and verification were set aside for the kind of sensationalism that could entice readers to buy a paper every day over a long period of time.

Although the Cuban insurgency began in 1895 (and the Philippine Revolution against Spain the following year), the war between the United States and Spain in those territories lasted only four months, from April 25, 1898, when the United States issued a declaration of war, until August 12, when Spain signed a protocol of peace. The final treaty signed by the two nations on December 10, 1898, marked the end of the Spanish empire and the emergence of the United States as an international power. The treaty required Spain to turn over sovereignty of Puerto Rico and Guam to the US and sell the Philippines for $20 million. Cuba was declared independent from Spain, but the continued presence of American troops and the imposition of other controls made it in essence a US protectorate.[4]

Cuba had been under Spanish dominion since 1492, when Christopher Columbus landed in the Bahamas and claimed the nearby islands for Spain. The indigenous peoples of Cuba were subjugated through massacre, and their population was further decimated by smallpox, transmitted by the Spanish. For the next four centuries, the island would be ruled by a Spanish governor in Havana and would become a crucial part of Spain's colonial empire. Strategically located in the heart of the Caribbean, Cuba provided numerous sources of revenue, and the island was becoming more and more prosperous and populous. By about 1800, Havana was the third-largest city in the Americas.

During the late eighteenth century, inspired by revolutions in the American colonies and France and the slave revolt in Haiti, Cubans began pressing for independence from Spain. Spain, in turn, became more repressive. Responding to Spain's increasingly aggressive behavior—and with an eye to its own commercial and territorial interests—in 1823 the United States issued the Monroe Doctrine, opposing European colonialism in the Americas. This did little to ease internal tensions, however, and in 1868 Cubans began a war for independence from the Spanish colonial government that lasted ten years. The Cubans were defeated, and the repressions continued.

Still, by the third quarter of the nineteenth century, Cuba offered Americans many opportunities, both commercial and recreational. American businessmen began investing heavily in Cuba, notably in sugar and tobacco, as well as in cruise ships and hotels, as more and more Americans were attracted by the island's balmy winters, lush vegetation, and elegant Hispano-Moorish architecture.[5] Winslow Homer was one of those Americans, visiting Cuba in 1885.

Homer traveled there from the Bahamas, where he had spent two months working on a project for *Century* magazine. He had painted thirty-three dazzling watercolors in the Bahamas, each one a testament to the beauty and the tourist appeal of the place. After finishing his assignment in February 1885, Homer was eager to travel elsewhere in the Caribbean. Cuba was close by, and he may well have been encouraged to visit by its reputation as a tropical paradise and by the enthusiasm of fellow artists, such as this encomium by Thomas Moran, who had been there for a few days in 1883: "[Havana] is I think the most picturesque place I ever saw. Everywhere it is a picture. The color is something indescribably beautiful. The people, the vehicles, churches, plaza, everything is pictorial."[6]

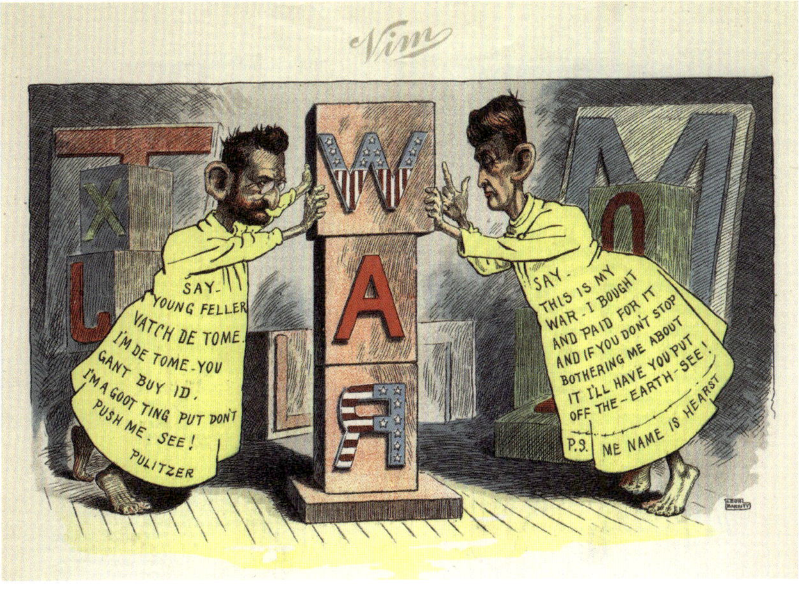

Fig. 34
Leon Barritt
The Big Type War of the Yellow Kids
Lithograph depicting rival publishers Joseph Pulitzer and William Randolph Hearst
Published in *Vim* 1, no. 2, June 29, 1898
Library of Congress Prints and Photographs Division, Washington, DC

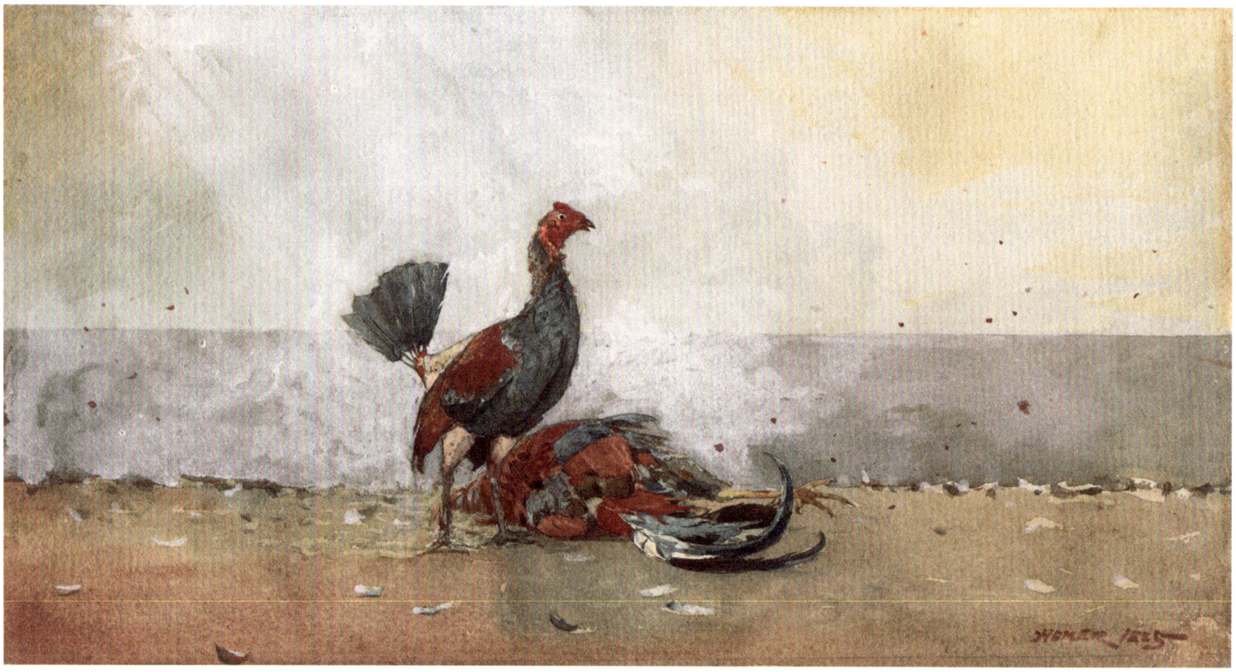

Fig. 35
Winslow Homer
The Cock Fight, 1885
Watercolor on paper
10¼ × 19 in. (26 × 48.3 cm)
The Art Institute of Chicago; George F. Harding Collection, 1982.1579

Homer was extremely optimistic about his trip to Cuba, as he wrote to his brother Charles: "I expect some fine things—it is certainly the richest field for an Artist that I have seen." His actual experience proved to be quite disappointing. He complained of his accommodations—bad smells, scorpions on the floor—as well as the heat, humidity, and unsanitary conditions. He also seemed aware of the political tensions in Cuba. He called Santiago, where he spent his entire visit, a "red hot place full of soldiers" and told his brother about a recent execution of arms smugglers. Frictions between the government and the citizenry made it hard for him to work. The first time he tried to paint outdoors, he attracted so many onlookers that "I was ordered to move on until the crowd dispersed."[7]

Nonetheless, Homer was nearly as productive in Cuba as he had been in the Bahamas, producing about twenty watercolors and several drawings during his five weeks there. He was attracted to the local architecture[8]—not to Santiago's grand monuments and plazas, but rather to its old residential buildings with crumbling, faded stucco walls that lined the side streets, sometimes with a view down to the sea; see, for example, *Street Corner, Santiago de Cuba* (1885; Museum of Fine Arts, Boston). In these watercolors, the streets are relatively empty, the figures small. Homer used a blue and yellow palette, enlivened with bits of red. His command of watercolor techniques—scraping out, layering washes, sponging—enabled him to evoke the dustiness of the streets and the air shimmering in the heat.

Homer portrayed Santiago as elegant but also exotic, and he was sensitive to the cultural divisions between its people. In *Spanish Club,*

Santiago de Cuba (1885; Peabody Essex Museum, Salem, MA), he showed a fashionably dressed woman of Spanish descent walking along the street, while her servant, a more simply dressed local woman, follows along, several paces behind. In *Street Scene, Santiago de Cuba* (Fig. 32), he focused on a woman strolling with her pet monkey on her shoulder. He makes us aware, by his scrupulous attention to costume, that she is of a different race and social standing than the woman with the red parasol, a member of the colonizing class.

Unlike Homer's watercolors of the Bahamas, the Cuban watercolors are not idyllic. Skies are often stormy, and there are no crystalline views of the sea or orange trees laden with fruit or charming children walking along sandy pink paths. A vague sense of unease marks many of his Cuban pictures, which becomes more focused in the images of cockfights.[9] Homer did not shy away from rendering impending violence or its aftermath, but *The Cock Fight* (Fig. 35) is a rare instance of a close-up, graphic description of cruelty. The victor, despite having lost much of his back plumage (Homer shows spots of blood at the base of his tail feathers), stands triumphantly over the limp body of his adversary. The contest has just ended: there are ripped feathers scattered all about, and flecks of red paint representing the blood of the birds still fly through the air.

Cockfighting had long been popular in Cuba. It was often depicted in tourist albums, where the gore was de-emphasized (Fig. 36). Instead, the sport was portrayed as an amusing local custom. The focus was on the crowd, shown laughing, drinking, arguing, and placing bets, rather than on the combatants. Homer's rendering, however, does not attempt to show the charms of Cuban "local color." The birds, with their glorious plumage, one living, the other dead, are isolated against a bare stucco wall. The brutality of the sport is inescapable—Homer gives the viewer nothing else to look at. The image is darkly beautiful and unsettling, as Homer's time in Cuba seems to have been.

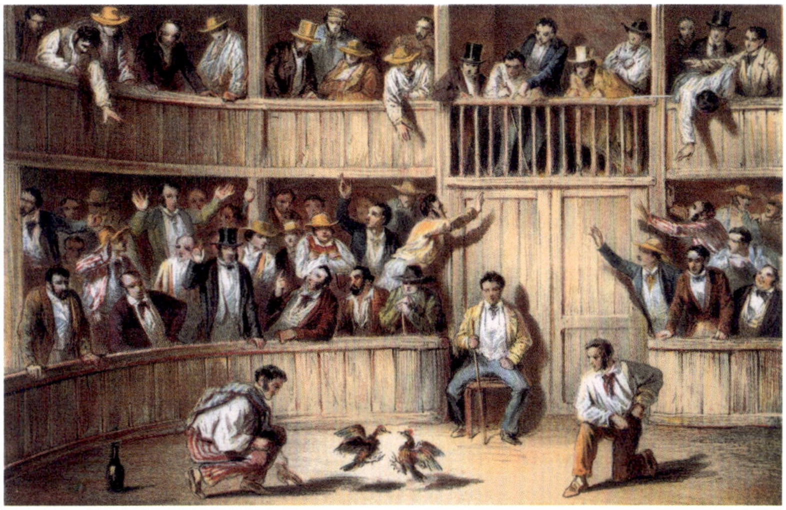

Fig. 36
Pierre Toussaint Frederic Mialhe
Valla de Gallos (Cockfight), 1855
Chromolithograph from *Album pintoresco de la isla de Cuba*, 1855
(Berlin: B[ernado]. May y Ca., 1855)
Approximately 9½ × 13½ in.
(24.1 × 34.3 cm)
Private collection

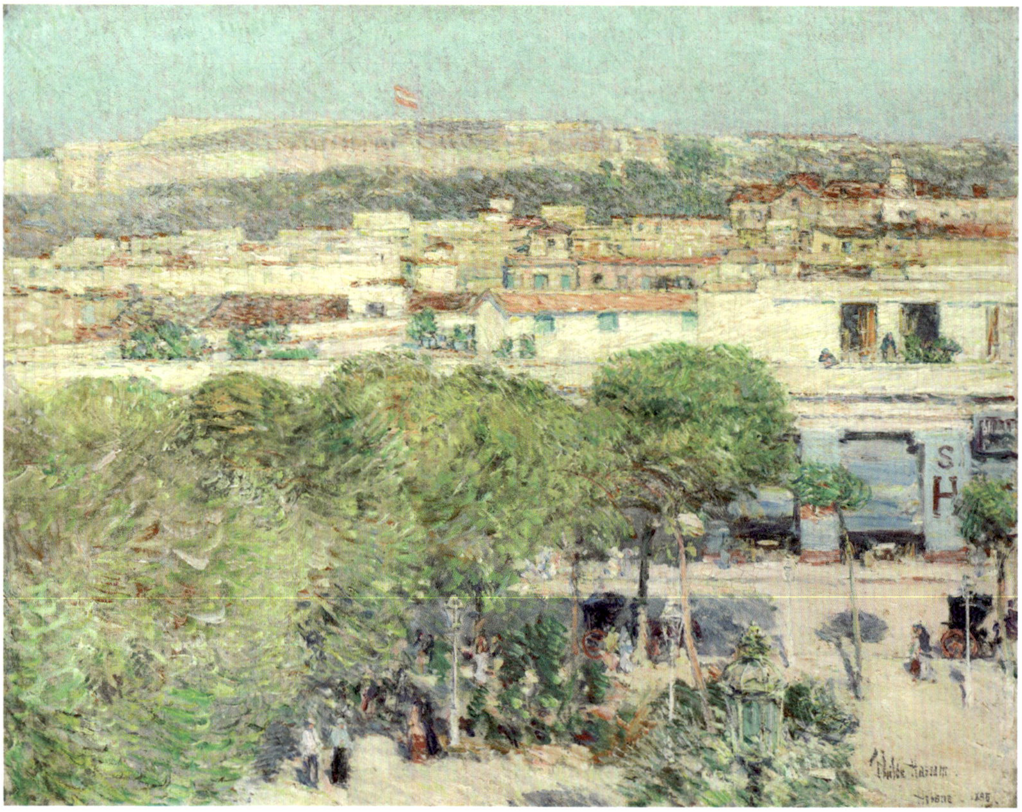

Fig. 37
Childe Hassam
Place Centrale and Fort Cabanas, Havana, 1895
Oil on canvas
21¼ × 26¼ in. (54 × 66.7 cm)
Detroit Institute of Arts; American Art before 1950, City of Detroit Purchase 11.5

The next major American artist to visit Cuba chose to focus on the country's more welcoming aspects. Childe Hassam traveled there in January 1895, in the company of a friend who had lucrative contracts with the Cuban electric company. By this time, American businessmen had over $50 million worth of investments in Cuba. In order to protect those investments, the US government was determined to preserve stability there and to maintain good relationships with the island's commercial elite, namely wealthy white Cubans and the Spanish governing community. While Hassam's traveling companion visited Cuba for business, the artist, like Homer and Moran before him, was attracted by the reports of sunshine, handsome architecture, and lush scenery—by Cuba's reputation as a tropical paradise.

Hassam was on the island for about a month, during which time he painted a handful of modest-sized canvases in his appealing Impressionist style. These pictures capture the kinds of sights he saw from his hotel on the main square in the most prosperous, most elegant part of town. In several of his paintings, such as *Vista del Paseo del Prado* (1895; Museo Nacional de Bellas Artes de la Habana), *Havana* (1895; private collection), and *Place Centrale and Fort Cabanas, Havana* (Fig. 37), Hassam used a bird's-eye perspective—a favorite vantage point to which he would return in such New York scenes as *Union Square, Spring* (1896; Smith College Museum of Art, Northampton,

MA). In fact, the sites he sought out in Cuba are often compared to New York: the Place Centrale is Havana's Central Park; the Paseo del Prado is its Fifth Avenue.[10]

The wide visual angle and deep perspective of *Vista del Paseo del Prado* are compositional devices familiar from Hassam's previous cityscapes (see, for example, *Boston Common at Twilight*, 1885; Museum of Fine Arts, Boston). Here the view is especially dramatic, as impressive rows of buildings lead the eye along an elegant promenade from a broad, sunlit foreground space to the sea. Hassam portrayed the city as handsome and modern. At the same time, the aerial viewpoint allowed him to convey a sense of bustle and energy and elegance—he shows plazas filled with carriages and small, orderly pedestrians—while avoiding some of the less comfortable particulars that a street-level view of these spaces might have revealed (Fig. 38).[11]

The poverty of some of Cuba's citizens, the racial and economic tensions in the country, and the increasing, and increasingly ominous, presence of the Spanish military would not have been of particular interest to Hassam. He was not especially sensitive to social and political inequities and almost never portrayed distressing aspects of urban life. Yet he was not unaware. Looking back on the Cuba trip, he noted that he left just before the insurrection broke out, in February 1895. It was, he said, a significant moment: "the last time that the Spanish flag flew in the Eastern [*sic*] Hemisphere over a Spanish possession."[12]

When he returned to New York, Hassam sold several sketches to *Harper's Weekly*, which the magazine used to accompany a story about current events in Cuba. Hassam portrayed Havana as charming, picturesque, and sophisticated. His views of Santiago, where the insurgency was centered, presented a less attractive place (Fig. 39). Santiago was Cuba's second most important city, a major port, and quite cosmopolitan. A contemporary writer described it as "sparkling in the sun," and

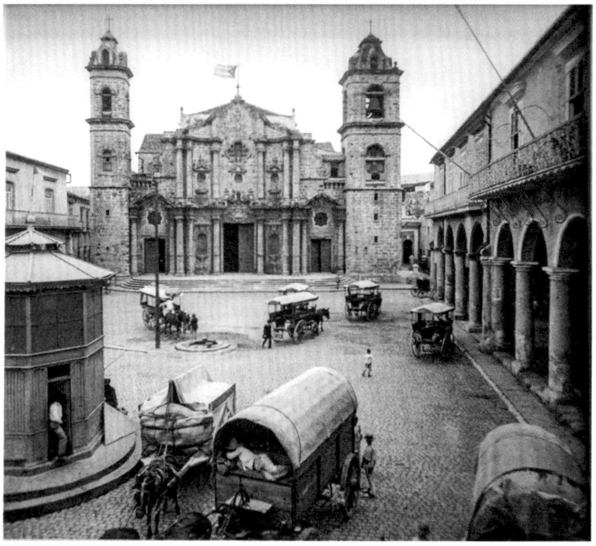

Fig. 38
Unidentified photographer
Cathedral, Havana., n.d.
Stereoscopic photograph
California Museum of Photography
at University of California—Riverside
ARTSblock; Keystone-Mast Collection
(In Michael Lesy, *Looking Backward: A Photographic Portrait of the World at the Beginning of the Twentieth Century* [New York and London: W. W. Norton, 2017], 30)

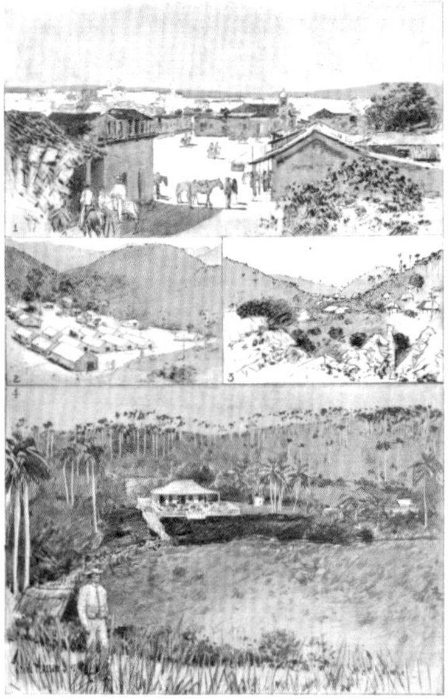

Fig. 39
Childe Hassam
Scenes in Eastern Cuba, the Seat of the Present Rebellion, 1895
Published in *Harper's Weekly* 39, no. 2004 (May 18, 1895): 458

the nearby countryside, "a perfect Eden of tropical growth."[13] But Hassam showed it as surrounded by unpromising, unpicturesque scenery, scarred by iron mines, and represented the city itself as dusty, quiet, and provincial. At the same time, his sketches provided no evidence of the political unrest or the Spanish military presence. They implied that the political situation in Cuba was not a source of concern. The accompanying unsigned *Harper's Weekly* article, "The Insurrection in Cuba," was equally dismissive. It characterized the revolution as a "cigar-maker's revolt," led largely by "mulattos and negroes," and concluded that the rebels' chances for success were small and their efforts ultimately unimportant.[14]

Hassam's Santiago sketches and the article on the "cigar-makers' revolt" appeared in *Harper's Weekly* on May 18, 1895. A day later, the great rebel leader José Martí was killed in a skirmish with the Spanish. By the end of the year, the insurgency, pressing for independence, had spread across the island, and Cuba was an armed camp.

The American press quickly realized that the situation in Cuba was becoming more and more urgent. By the end of the year, many newspapers and magazines began sending correspondents to Cuba. Among the first to arrive were the up-and-coming young sketch artist George Luks and reporter Maurice M. O'Leary, whom the *Philadelphia Evening Bulletin* dispatched to Havana in mid-December 1895. Luks was in Cuba for about two months and produced more than thirty drawings. Some of these—such as his sketch of Spanish troops lined up on the Prado in Havana (*Morning Review of Volunteers*)—were based on events he could have observed. There were other events that he undoubtedly did not witness, such as the insurgents' attack on the town of Jaruco, near Havana, on February 18, 1896 (Fig. 40). However, the latter was the kind of subject Luks's editors wanted. Showing troops on horseback dashing through the town, tearing down the gates of a prison where many dissenters had been held, it was a dramatic, even shocking scene and served as a call to action. Luks's drawing may have been an "artful fabrication," as one critic put it,[15] but it provided a stirring visual counterpart to the inflammatory prose reporters were sending back:

> No man's life, no man's property is safe [in Cuba]. American citizens are imprisoned or slain without cause. American property is destroyed.... The horrors of a barbarous struggle for the extermination of the native population are witnessed in all parts of the country. Blood on the roadsides, blood in the field, blood on the doorsteps, blood blood blood!... Is there no nation wise enough, brave enough to aid this blood-smitten land?[16]

Luks has often been accused of having experienced the war in Cuba from a bar. That is, he is thought to have based his images almost entirely on reports from those who, unlike him, had actually been on the front lines. (He claimed, of course, that he had been an eyewitness

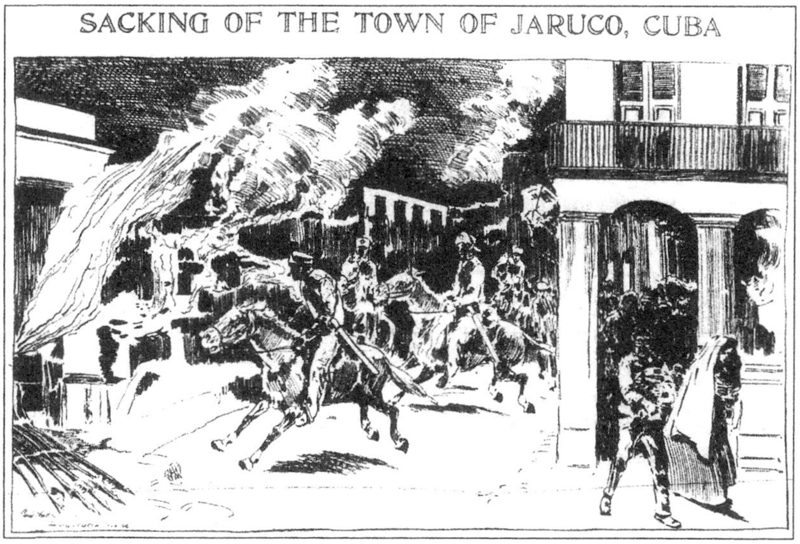

Fig. 40
George Luks
Sacking of the Town of Jaruco, Cuba, 1896
Published in *Philadelphia Evening Bulletin*, March 2, 1896, 1 (from Robert L. Gambone, *Life on the Press: The Popular Art and Illustrations of George Benjamin Luks* [Jackson, MI: University Press of Mississippi], 98)

to the action. He noted on one of his drawings for the *Bulletin*, "An insurgent scout [was] . . . overtaken by Spanish troops . . . [who] fire[d] upon him, and *The Bulletin* artist . . . sketche[d] him as he [fell] from the saddle."[17]) However, it was not necessarily only cowardice, or even a too-obliging bartender, that explains why he remained in town; there had been bloody skirmishes around the city, and government restrictions on foreigners made leaving Havana somewhat dangerous.[18] Luks returned to the United States in early March 1896, having been fired by the *Bulletin* for drunkenness and for missing deadlines. He continued to portray events in Cuba, however, and found an eager market for his most sensational images in Joseph Pulitzer's *World*.

Not to be outdone, Hearst (who had bought the *Journal* just a year earlier) hired celebrity reporter Richard Harding Davis and acclaimed cowboy artist and illustrator Frederic Remington to be *his* men on the scene (see Fig. 33). The *Journal* and the *World* were the leaders of the activist press, involved with making news as much as reporting it. Hearst's slogan was "While Others Talk, the *Journal* Acts!"[19] His action took the form of provocation, stirring up feelings among American citizens, who began pressuring the US government to consider some kind of intervention in Cuba.

By 1896, Cuban rebels—the insurgents—were pressing hard for independence. An illustration by Frederic Remington for the March 7, 1896, issue of *Harper's Weekly* (Fig. 41)[20] showed local forces rallying behind the Cuban flag. The rebels mounted a guerilla campaign against railroads and sugar plantations—the colonizing population's economic lifelines—and they sniped at Spanish soldiers. To try to quell the insurrection, Spain increased its military presence on the island and set up a naval blockade to keep out guns and other supplies. These actions caused hardship among the local citizenry, who not surprisingly increasingly supported the rebels. Money and arms were also coming

Fig. 41
Frederic Remington
The Flag of Cuba—Insurgent Cavalry Formed for a Charge, 1896
Published in *Harper's Weekly* 40, no. 2046 (March 7, 1896): 217

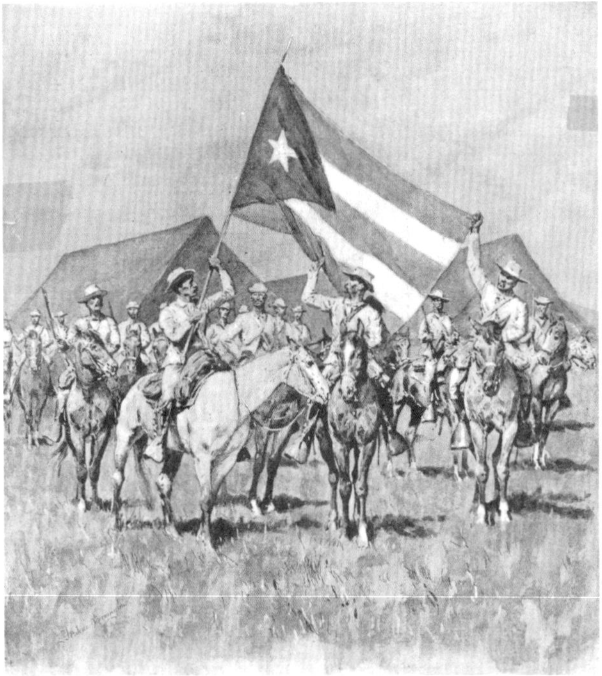

from Cubans living in the United States, who had fled their country after the last war of independence and who were now lobbying for help from the US government. The American press was divided at first. Editorials like the one accompanying Remington's image expressed sympathy for the struggle of the Cuban people but argued that the United States should not intervene: "The recognition of belligerency [that is, of the insurgency as legitimate] would be extremely expensive to our business interests."[21] Other voices opposed intervention in Cuba as a violation of Spain's national sovereignty.[22] But more and more, those favoring involvement in Cuba had begun to dominate the debate in the press and in the government.

In November 1896, William McKinley was elected president of the United States. To satisfy the mounting demands for an American response to events in the Caribbean, McKinley sent his recently appointed commissioner for Cuba, Illinois attorney William J. Calhoun, on a fact-finding mission. Based on Calhoun's report, McKinley announced to Congress that destabilized conditions so close to American shores posed a threat to both national security and the United States' commercial interests. He noted that lucrative trade with Cuba was endangered, as were the many US-owned businesses there. He then requested $50,000 for the relief of the eight hundred Americans in Cuba, who were "in a state of destitution, suffering for want of food and medicines."[23]

American concerns about events in Cuba were also affected, if indirectly, by the findings of the 1890 census, which reported that the United States no longer had a frontier—there was no more land for white settlers to claim on the continent. Testosterone-fueled expansionists,

Fig. 42
George Luks
Torture by the Garrote in Morro Castle, 1896
Published in *New York World*, April 1, 1896, 4 (from Robert L. Gambone, *Life on the Press: The Popular Art and Illustrations of George Benjamin Luks* [Jackson, MI: University Press of Mississippi, 2009], 99)

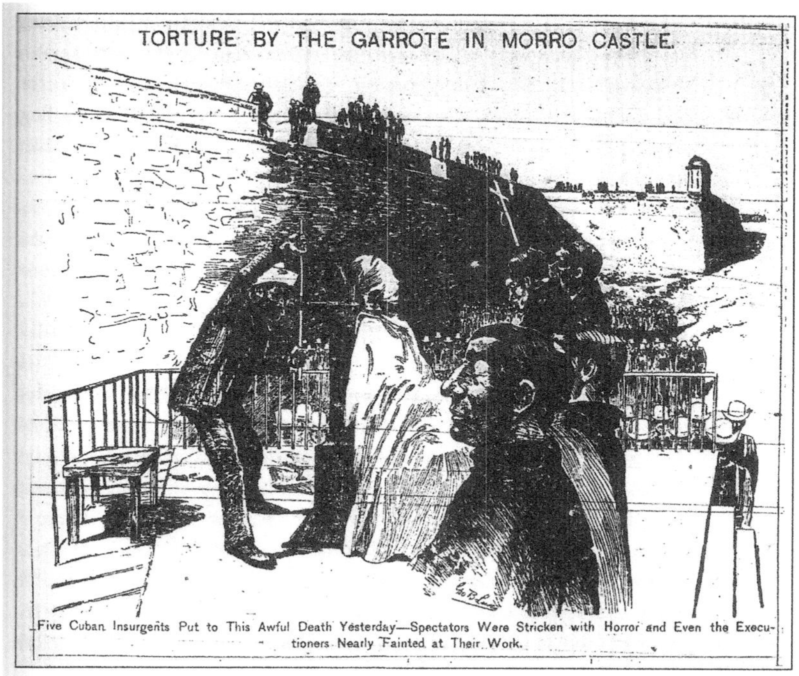

among them Assistant Secretary of the Navy Theodore Roosevelt, began looking elsewhere to extend America's reach. Cuba, being so close and in increasing disarray, was an obvious target for their territorial ambitions. Already in 1895, Roosevelt had proclaimed, "I should welcome almost any war, for I think this country needs one . . . [and] the most righteous of all wars is a war with savages."[24] Artists assisted in this campaign by stepping up their portrayals of the Spanish in Cuba as barbarians. Luks, in one of his first pictures for Pulitzer (Fig. 42), depicted a particularly cruel and primitive kind of execution (to underscore the point, the accompanying caption reads, "Five Cuban Insurgents Put to This Awful Death Yesterday—Spectators Were Stricken with Horror and Even the Executioners Nearly Fainted at Their Work"). Remington's illustration, "Murdering the Cuban Wounded," accompanying one of Richard Davis's articles, showed Spanish soldiers killing local fighters in an outdoor field hospital.[25] While not as gruesome as Luks's image, it records a clear violation of provisions of the Geneva Convention, which covered treatment of the sick and wounded on the battlefield.

Another vital issue was the Spanish treatment of civilians. In October 1896, General Valeriano Weyler, the recently appointed commander of the Spanish forces in Cuba, introduced his "reconcentrados" policy. For their own safety (the Spanish argued, but in fact to keep them from providing support to the rebels), Cuban civilians living in contested areas were to be herded into internment camps, where food was minimal and living conditions deteriorated rapidly. In an illustration for the *Journal* published in 1897, Remington depicted Cuban civilians being marched into the resettlement camps.[26] The

Fig. 43
Frederic Remington
Moonlight Execution of Young Rodriguez, 1897
Published in *New York Journal and Advertiser*, February 2, 1897, 1
Library of Congress, Washington, DC

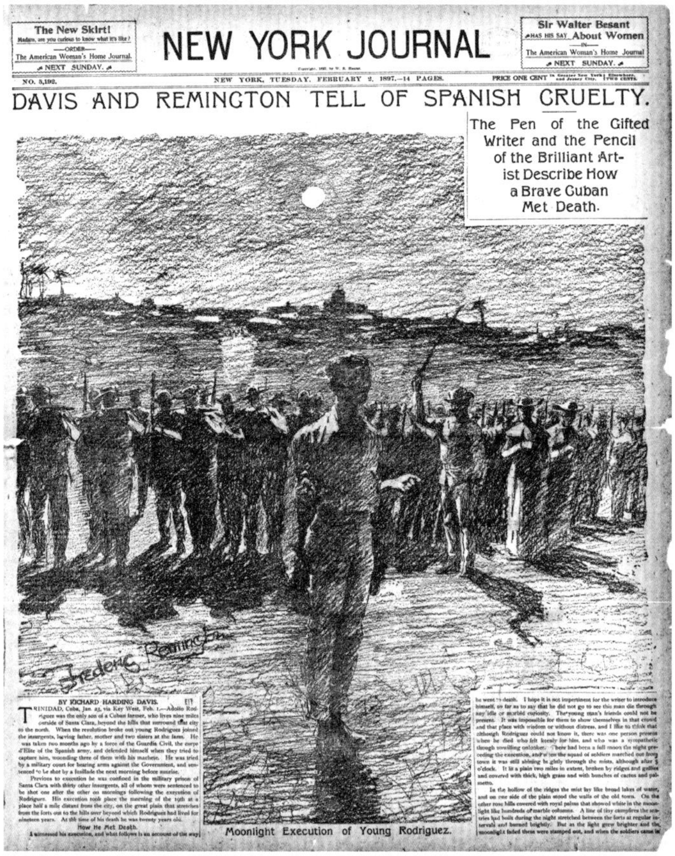

The New Skirt!
Madam, are you curious to know what it's like?
—ORDER—
The American Woman's Home Journal.
NEXT SUNDAY.

NEW YORK JOURNAL

Sir Walter Besant
HAS HIS SAY About Women
—IN—
The American Woman's Home Journal
NEXT SUNDAY.

NO. 5,192. NEW YORK, TUESDAY, FEBRUARY 2, 1897.—14 PAGES. PRICE ONE CENT

DAVIS AND REMINGTON TELL OF SPANISH CRUELTY.

The Pen of the Gifted Writer and the Pencil of the Brilliant Artist Describe How a Brave Cuban Met Death.

BY RICHARD HARDING DAVIS.

TRINIDAD, Cuba, Jan. 23, via Key West, Feb. 1.—Adolfo Rodriguez was the only son of a Cuban farmer, who lives nine miles outside of Santa Clara, beyond the hills that surround that city to the north. When the revolution broke out young Rodriguez joined the insurgents, leaving father, mother and two sisters at the farm. He was taken two months ago by a force of the Guardia Civil, the corps d'Elite of the Spanish army, and defended himself when they tried to capture him, wounding three of them with his machete. He was tried by a military court for bearing arms against the Government, and sentenced to be shot by a fusillade the next morning before sunrise.

Previous to execution he was confined in the military prison of Santa Clara with thirty other insurgents, all of whom were sentenced to be shot one after the other on mornings following the execution of Rodriguez. His execution took place the morning of the 19th at a place half a mile distant from the city, on the great plain that stretches from the forts out to the hills over beyond which Rodriguez had lived for nineteen years. At the time of his death he was twenty years old.

How He Met Death.

I witnessed his execution, and what follows is an account of the way

Moonlight Execution of Young Rodriguez.

he went to death. I hope it is not impertinent for the writer to introduce himself, so far as to say that he did not go to see this man die through any idle or morbid curiosity. The young man's friends could not be present. It was impossible for them to show themselves in that crowd and that place with wisdom or without distress, and I like to think that although Rodriguez could not know it, there was one person present when he died who felt keenly for him, and who was a sympathetic though unwilling onlooker. There had been a full moon the night preceding the execution, and when the squad of soldiers marched out from town it was still shining brightly through the mists, although after 5 o'clock. It lit a plain two miles in extent, broken by ridges and gullies and covered with thick, high grass and with bunches of cactus and palmetto.

In the hollow of the ridges the mist lay like broad lakes of water, and on one side of the plain stood the walls of the old town. On the other rose hills covered with royal palms that showed white in the moonlight like hundreds of marble columns. A line of tiny campfires the sentries had built during the night stretched between the forts at regular intervals and burned brightly. But as the light grew brighter and the moonlight faded these were stamped out, and when the soldiers came in

horrors of Weyler's resettlement policy were subsequently described by the expansionist Senator Redfield Proctor of Vermont, who visited Cuba in early 1898: "Torn from their homes, with foul earth, foul air, foul water, and foul food or none, what wonder that one half [of the reconcentrados] have died and that one quarter of the living are so diseased that they cannot be saved."[27]

In early 1897, Davis and Remington informed Hearst's readership of two of the most incendiary incidents in the run-up to US intervention. "The Death of Rodriguez" was Davis's most famous dispatch of the war, relating the execution of Adolfo Rodriguez, an insurgent captured in a fight with Spanish soldiers. While most reporters characterized Cubans as helpless victims, Davis stressed their heroism. He compared Rodriguez to Nathan Hale, the young patriot and martyr in America's own revolution: "The Cuban's arms were bound, as are those of the statue, and he stood firmly, with his weight resting on his heels like a soldier on parade, and with his face held up fearlessly, as is that of the statue."[28]

By the time Davis filed his dispatch, Remington was back in New York, and so he used Davis's account to shape his picture (Fig. 43). He showed the executioners, rifles at the ready, lined up in the middle distance. The condemned man is between them and the viewer, who sees what Rodriguez could not. Rodriguez's pose roughly echoes Nathan Hale's (as dramatized in a famous statue by Frederick MacMonnies; Fig. 44), underscoring Davis's association between Cuban and American revolutionaries. Remington emphasized Rodriguez's isolation, reflecting the most poignant passage of the account: none of his friends dared be there to support him, Davis noted, but "I like to think that, although Rodriguez could not know it, there was one person present when he died who felt keenly for him, and who was a sympathetic though unwilling spectator."[29]

Ten days later, the *Journal* published another dispatch from Davis. It was given the title "Does Our Flag Shield Women?" and again Remington furnished the picture.[30]

Davis's article related the story of three well-bred, well-educated Cuban women who were suspected of carrying letters to rebel supporters in Florida. They were seized and strip-searched on an American boat. Davis's article focused on the issue of unlawful search and

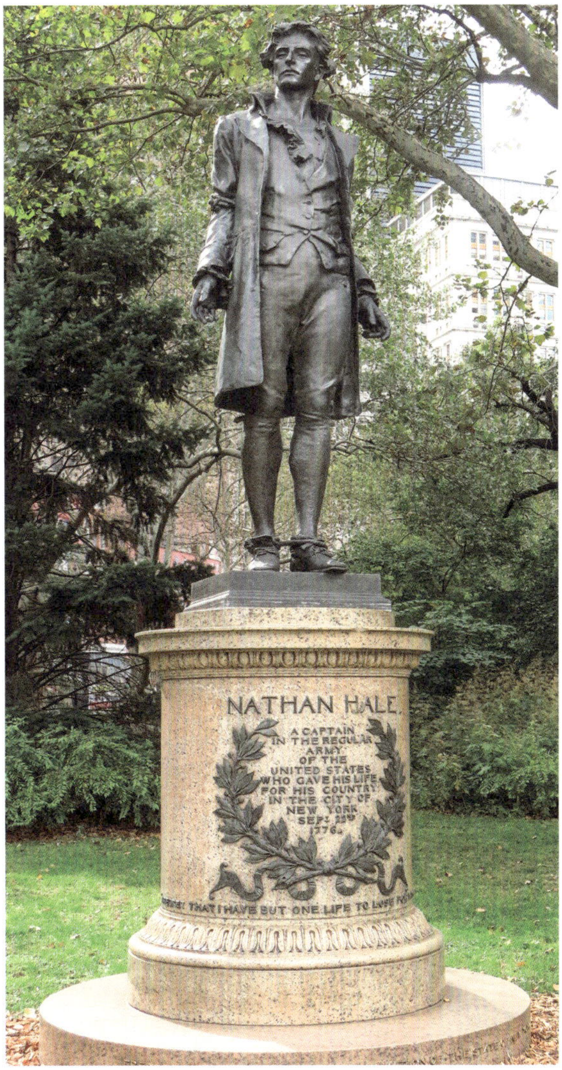

Fig. 44
Frederick MacMonnies
Nathan Hale, cast 1890
Bronze
9 × 3 × 2 ft. (274.3 × 91.4 × 61 cm)
New York City Parks Commission, City Hall, New York

Fig. 45
Frederic Remington
Spaniards Search Women on American Steamers, 1897
Published in *New York Journal and Advertiser*, February 12, 1897, 2
Library of Congress, Washington, DC

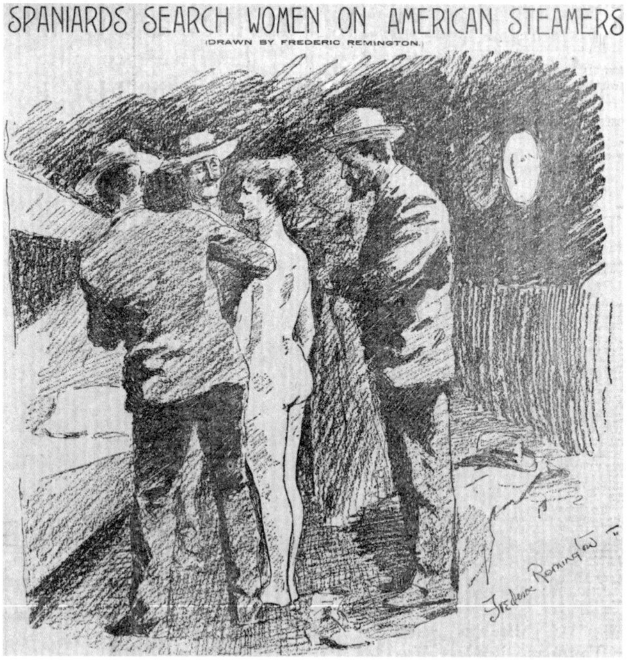

seizure, but in Hearst's and Remington's conception of the story, the issue became Spanish violation of women's honor, and the search, actually performed by women detectives, became the work of "brutal" Spanish men (Fig. 45).

Though not particularly erotic, Remington's illustration of an attractive nude young woman pawed at by dark, mustachioed Spaniards brings to mind representations of Susanna and the Elders, or Jean-Léon Gérôme's slick views of Roman slave markets. It was designed to provoke American outrage at the treatment of innocent (white) womanhood and to reinforce the view of the Spanish as predators. Davis was furious about the repurposing of his message and the falsification of facts. He resigned from the *Journal*, and the rival *World* forced Hearst to publish a retraction. But as a call to Americans to protect the defenseless against the villainy of the Spaniards, the image had done its work.

A growing number of reporters—both those who were respected for their objectivity and those more willing to bend the truth for a good story—were urging American intervention on grounds of compassion for the Cubans. Already by 1897, Davis had joined their ranks:

> Before I went to Cuba I was ... opposed to our interfering there ... but since I have seen [things] for myself I feel ashamed that we have stood so long idle.... We have been patient with men who have put back the hand of time for centuries, who lie to our representatives daily, who butcher innocent people ... who send American property to the air in flames and murder American prisoners.... But why should

we not go a step farther... and interfere in the name of humanity? Not because we are Americans, but because we are human beings, and because, within [a few] miles of our coast, Spanish officials are killing men and woman as wantonly as though they were field mice.[31]

A cartoon by noted illustrator Grant E. Hamilton, published as a two-page spread in *Judge* magazine at the same time that Davis's dispatches were appearing in the *Journal*, similarly plays on popular sympathy for an oppressed people (Fig. 46). A portent of imperialist and racist attitudes, Cuba is personified as a helpless baby, bloodied, bandaged, and brown. He is shown chained to a sign enumerating Spain's atrocities and reaches out to America. Uncle Sam—the US government—is blindfolded and so cannot see what is right in front of his eyes, while Columbia, representing the American people, extends her arms in welcome.

The debate would continue in this vein for another year. The press called for empathy, while the government debated how best to protect American economic interests in Cuba. At the core of the debate was whether the crisis in Cuba should be regarded as an internal Spanish matter—in which the United States therefore had no legitimate role to play—or as a call to show compassion for a people oppressed as Americans once had been, while perhaps also scratching the nation's expansionist itch.

Matters were brought to a head with the explosion that destroyed the battleship *USS Maine* on February 15, 1898. The *Maine* had been sent to Cuba as a warning to the Spanish. It was anchored in Havana Harbor just beneath Morro Castle, a symbol of Spanish power. The explosion, which killed 258 Americans, was believed to have been engineered by the Spanish, and the *Journal*, among other papers, made clear what the US should do about it. One of its headlines, set in type several inches high, proclaimed: "WAR! SURE! *Maine* Destroyed by Spanish; This Proved Absolutely by Discovery of the TORPEDO HOLE."[32] The story appeared before there was a chance to determine whether the Spanish really were responsible (they were not; the cause

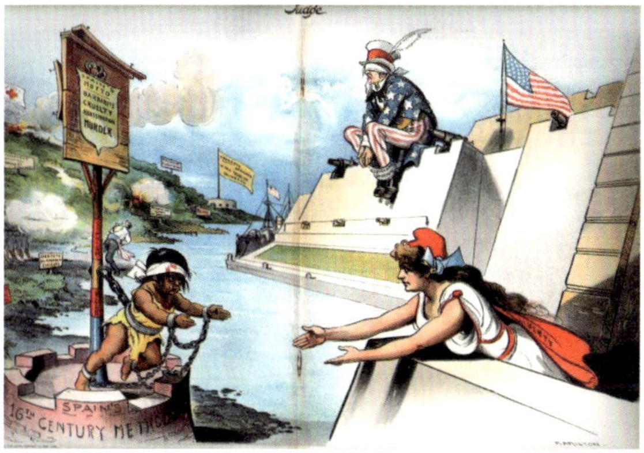

Fig. 46
Grant E. Hamilton
Columbia Reaches Out to Oppressed Cuba, c. 1897
Lithograph
Published in *Judge*, February 6, 1897, centerfold

was most likely an internal explosion)—but the facts had become irrelevant; the explosion provided the pretext for intervention that many had been waiting for.

Early the next month—March 1898—the United States demanded that Spain end the war against the Cubans. Spain refused. In April, Congress passed a resolution demanding that Spain withdraw from Cuba (essentially an acknowledgment of Cuba's independence) and authorized McKinley to intervene, militarily if necessary. Within a week, the United States and Spain had declared war on one another. McKinley called for 125,000 volunteers, while huge numbers of journalists prepared to go to Cuba to cover the war.

Coverage took several forms. First, there was the continuing demonization of the enemy. Luks was a key figure in this campaign. He had been providing anti-Spanish drawings to the bellicose *World* for several years by this time, with such images of Spanish atrocities as *Torture by the Garrote in Morro Castle* (see Fig. 42). Even in his *Hogan's Alley* cartoons he kept interest in the Cuban situation simmering. He tucked "Cuba Libre" signs into the background of cartoons on unrelated subjects, for example, *Hogan's Alley Attacked by the Hoboken Pretzel Club* (*New York World*, May 31, 1896, Comic Weekly Section, 8). He also made drawings that focused directly on the situation in Cuba. In *A Cuban Filibustering Expedition in Hogan's Alley* (*New York World*, January 17, 1897, Comic Weekly Section, 4), the gang organizes a filibustering—gunrunning—expedition to Cuba.[33] More

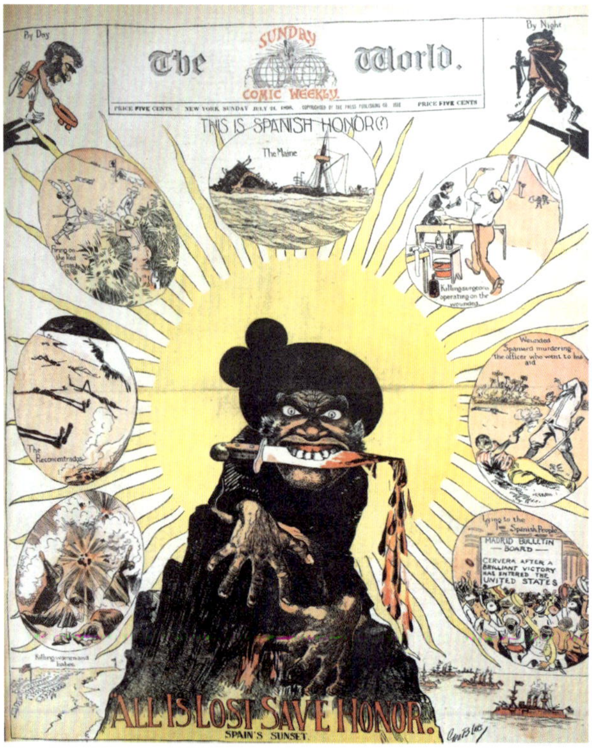

Fig. 47
George Luks
All Is Lost Save Honor. Spain's Sunset, 1898
Published in *The World, Sunday Comics Weekly*, July 24, 1898, 1

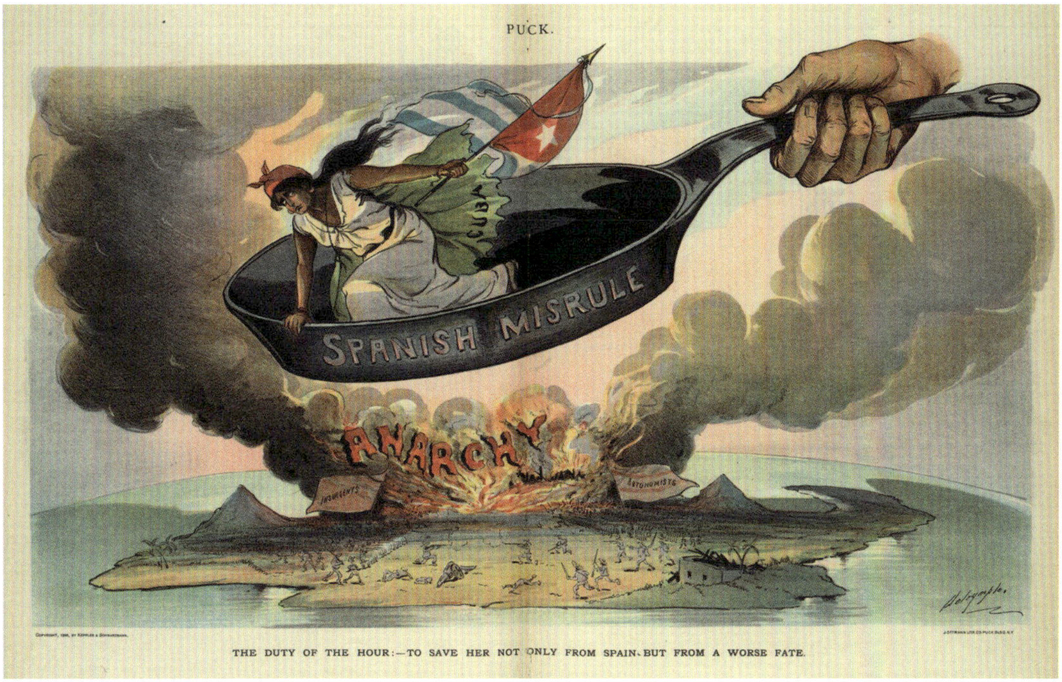

Fig. 48
Louis Dalrymple
The Duty of the Hour:—to Save Her Not Only from Spain, but from a Worse Fate, 1898
Chromolithograph
Published in *Puck*, May 11, 1898, centerfold
Library of Congress Prints and Photographs Division, Washington, DC

inflammatory were images like *All Is Lost Save Honor. Spain's Sunset* (Fig. 47), featuring a vicious figure (Spain), surrounded by vignettes illustrating attacks on Red Cross volunteers, the murder of women and babies, the explosion on the *Maine*, and other atrocities supposedly perpetrated by the Spanish. The purpose of such images was to remind Americans that the enemy was barbaric, and American intervention was therefore justified.

The second kind of coverage provided commentary on the situation as it evolved, supplied for the most part by artists and writers who had not been to Cuba. Initially, the press urged support for Cuba's liberation movement as an echo of America's own—that is, as an expression of solidarity with an oppressed people. But soon, editorials began to voice concern that Cubans were perhaps not ready to govern themselves—that the insurgents might represent "a worse fate" whose government would likely deteriorate into anarchy (Fig. 48). In other words, the United States was urged to assist in the fight for independence, but also to exercise jurisdiction over the people it was supposedly liberating.

This argument had a strong racist undercurrent. American soldiers and correspondents arriving in Cuba were shocked to discover that many of the rebels—the fighters and future leaders of Cuba—were people of color. This was the era of the "white man's burden,"[34] and newspapers that had initially portrayed the insurgents as valiant patriots began describing them as a "primitive, thieving rabble." Or, as General William Shafter, commander of US forces in Cuba declared, Cubans were "no more fit for self-government than gunpowder is for hell."[35]

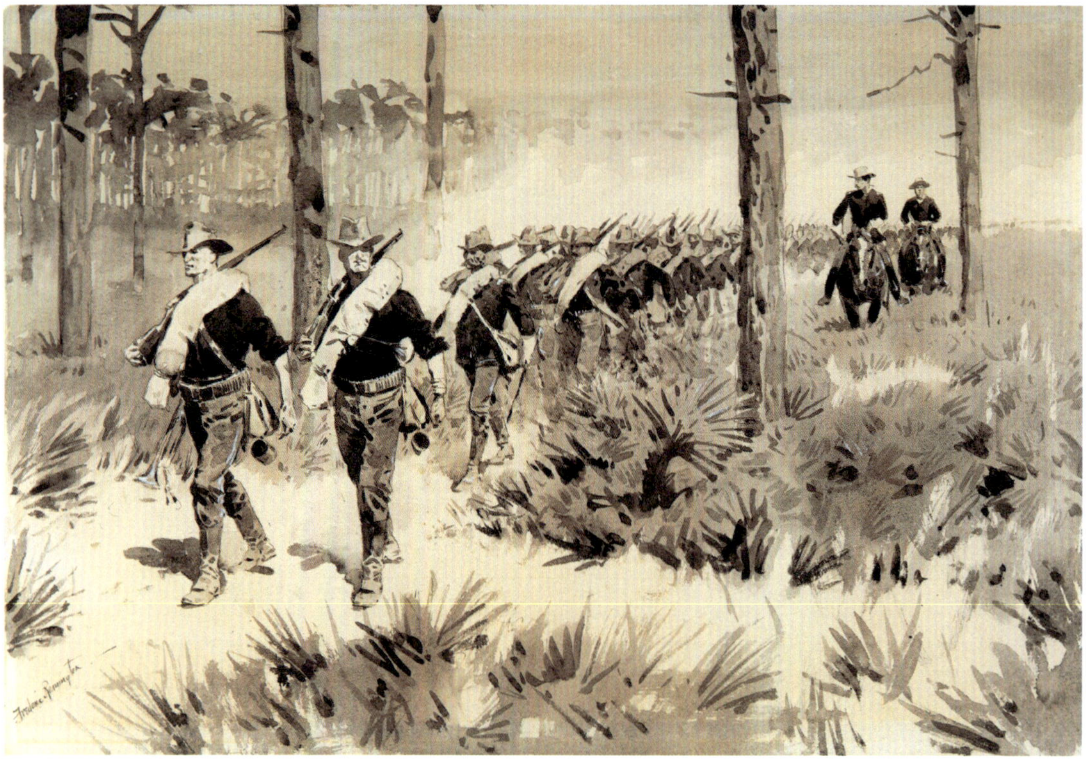

Fig. 49
Frederic Remington
United States Troops Practicing Marching in the Palmetto, 1898
Ink wash on paper
19½ × 29½ in. (49.5 × 74.9 cm)
Frederic Remington Art Museum, Ogdensburg, NY; Museum Purchase 1947 (1966.069)

The third kind of reporting came from the many journalists actually *in* Cuba. For the first time, because of enhanced communications technology, Americans could follow the progress of a war as it was being fought. Improvements in the photogravure process meant that images, whether maps, photographs, or drawings, could also be reproduced clearly.[36] There was rich visual coverage, as artist-journalists poured into Cuba. Of the many who were there in the summer of 1898, Glackens, Remington, and Christy were among the most productive and the most widely followed.

Of those three, Remington was the first to be hired. Immediately upon hearing of the explosion of the *Maine*, he signed on with several publications to provide illustrations.[37] He also sent in his own dispatches. Glackens was probably the first to arrive on the scene, reaching Tampa, where the troops were assembling, in late May. He accompanied the respected journalist Stephen Bonsal and would be identified as a "special artist for *McClure's Magazine*" in Bonsal's report, published in *McClure's* that fall.[38] Christy was the youngest: he was only twenty-five years old when he went to Cuba as a freelance artist, and at the beginning of his career. His drawings were published by several magazines, including *Harper's* and *Scribner's*. Though none of these artists had previously expressed significant interest in politics, they were all swept up in the debate, and their points of view did differ. For all three, their work in Cuba came at critical junctures in their careers.

Both Remington and Glackens documented the American preparations in Florida; all three artists followed the war through the main battles in Santiago. Remington left in July, while Glackens and most likely Christy were still in Cuba when the Spanish surrendered in mid-August. Remington subscribed to Teddy Roosevelt's view that war was a big adventure, "the greatest thing which men are called on to do."[39] Even Remington's scenes of preparation reflect this idea: his soldiers are athletic; they train hard; they are disciplined, fit, and handsome (Fig. 49). Christy's images of soldiers are equally idealized (see Fig. 56). Glackens described the soldiers and their routines quite differently. His men are not glamorous or athletic or good-looking. Soldiering is portrayed as hard, physical work. In a drawing documenting horses being loaded onto a transport ship (Fig. 50), he shows soldiers struggling to keep the animals under control. The men are awkward and not at all attractive.[40] In other drawings Glackens made on the boat going to Cuba (e.g., *Berth Deck of Transport* [1898; Library of Congress, Washington, DC]), he depicts military life as mundane and decidedly unromantic.

Not all of Glackens's Cuba pictures were gritty. An image of transports leaving Tampa Bay (Fig. 51) is elegantly rendered in soft, pale washes that evoke the drifting clouds, swirls of smoke from the ships, and the striated pattern of wake in the bay. The transports, massed along the horizon, are precisely detailed but are subsumed in the quiet

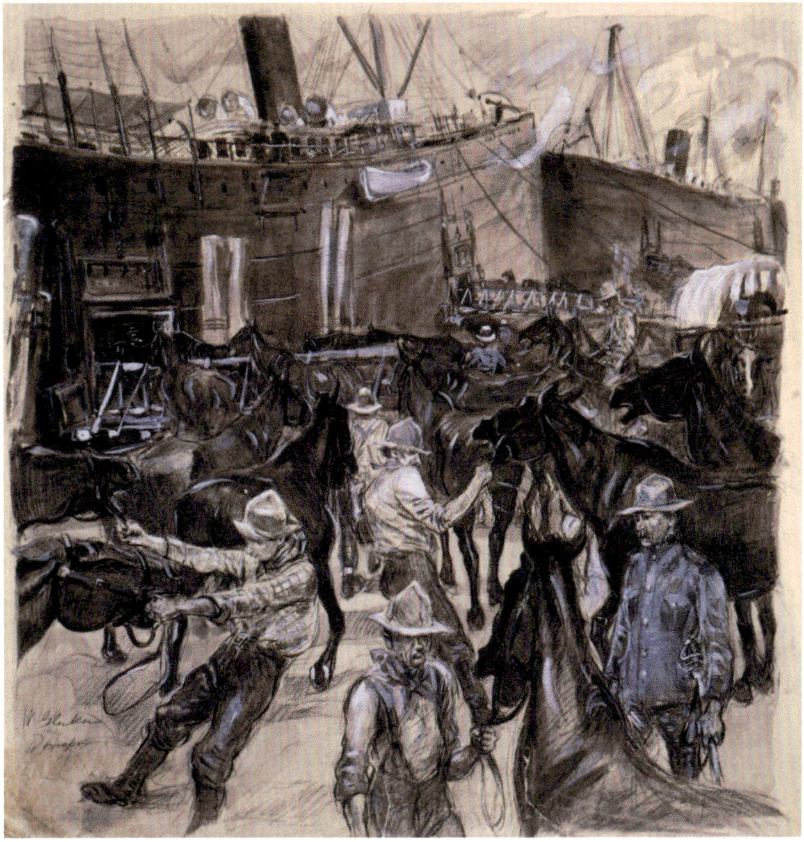

Fig. 50
William Glackens
Loading Horses onto the Transports at Port Tampa, 1898
Pen and ink, wash, Chinese white, charcoal on paper
17 × 18¼ in. (43.2 × 46.4 cm)
Library of Congress Prints and Photographs Division, Washington, DC

Fig. 51
William Glackens
Fleet of Transports Just Before the Start, Tampa Bay, 1898
Wash and graphite on paper
12½ × 18 in. (31.8 × 45.7 cm)
Library of Congress Prints and Photographs Division, Washington, DC

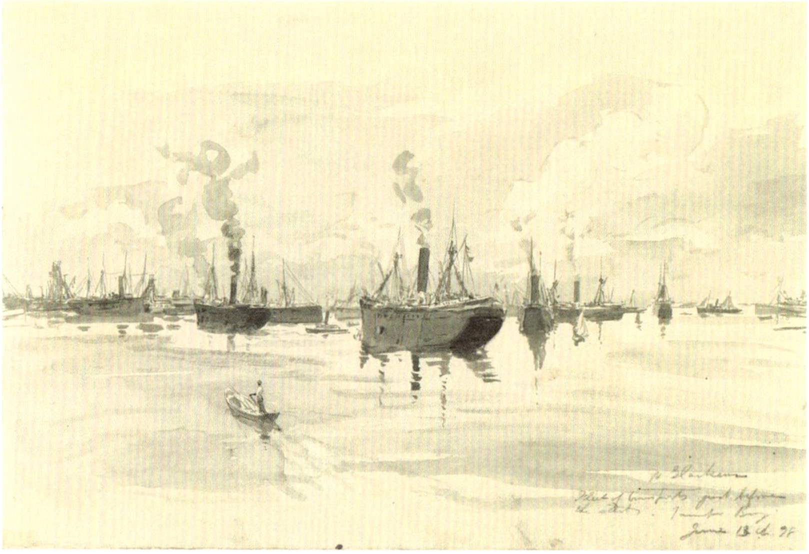

atmosphere of the whole. It is the most aestheticized of Glackens's Cuba illustrations and owes a greater debt to Whistler's images of Venice than to conventional wartime imagery.[41] Other pictures of troops and transports assembling along the shore are far more detailed, constructed with an eye to conveying information, and include storytelling vignettes that added interest. (In *The Beginning of Debarkation of Troops at Daiquiri* [1898; Library of Congress], for example, soldiers on a ship in the immediate foreground wave excitedly to other troops across the bay.) Compiled from graphite or pen-and-ink sketches made on the spot, these drawings were worked up later and were clearly intended for publication.

By and large, while Remington focused on American heroism, Glackens emphasized human interest in his Cuba pictures and made clear the grim toll of the war. The difference between their approaches is especially apparent in their battle scenes. Glackens's *A ford in River Guama* (Fig. 52) and Remington's *At the Bloody Ford of the San Juan* (Fig. 53) describe the same event. At the outset of the attack on Santiago on July 1, 1898, soldiers had to ford the junction of Las Guamas Creek and the San Juan River, where they were especially vulnerable to enemy fire. They were marching toward San Juan Hill, outside of Santiago; the famous battle was imminent.

Remington's scene is highly choreographed. The composition is divided into three horizontal bands of dark to light tones, from the dense woods to the shallow stream traversed by soldiers to the bright, debris-strewn riverbank in the foreground. The men pour out of the woods in columns perpendicular to the creek; highlights on their hats move the eye along. The soldiers in the foreground advance in frieze-like procession across the picture plane, in rhyming poses and "stoop[ing] as low as they anatomically could," as the artist wrote.

As dictated by romantic formula, the central figure, the commanding officer, is tall and handsome and directs his men with a broad rhetorical gesture. Despite the enemy fire, Remington noted, he "stood up straight as if on parade."[42] For scenes like this one, Remington relied on sketches and photographs. A photograph he had of the "bloody ford" shows the soldiers moving in a far less organized fashion and without a presiding officer to guide them.[43]

Glackens's design, on the other hand, communicates the chaos rather than the pageantry of war. His soldiers, scattered along the shallow diagonal formed by the creek bed, are not idealized, and their poses do not rhyme. The men's faces are schematically rendered, but they nonetheless convey pain and fear. The soldiers crawl along the ground on their bellies and shield their heads with their arms. Some have been hit; others struggle to aid the fallen. Glackens's seemingly haphazard distribution of his figures and the awkwardness of their poses and gestures cause the viewer's eye to dart nervously around the page. The scribbly lines, rapid washes, and scattered white highlights convey the muckiness of the terrain, the heat and humidity, and the terrifying randomness of the attack. Glackens's caption is terse: "Many men were hit at this spot . . . called . . . The Bloody Creek. Not a mile from San Juan."

Another group of pictures shows groups of soldiers at the battle of El Pozo, a hill just east of Santiago.[44] Glackens was probably an eyewitness; Remington was not. Obesity and the fever Remington contracted after arriving in Cuba meant that he experienced the key events of the war from far behind the battle lines.[45] His images reflect this: of the six major paintings he made to accompany his own

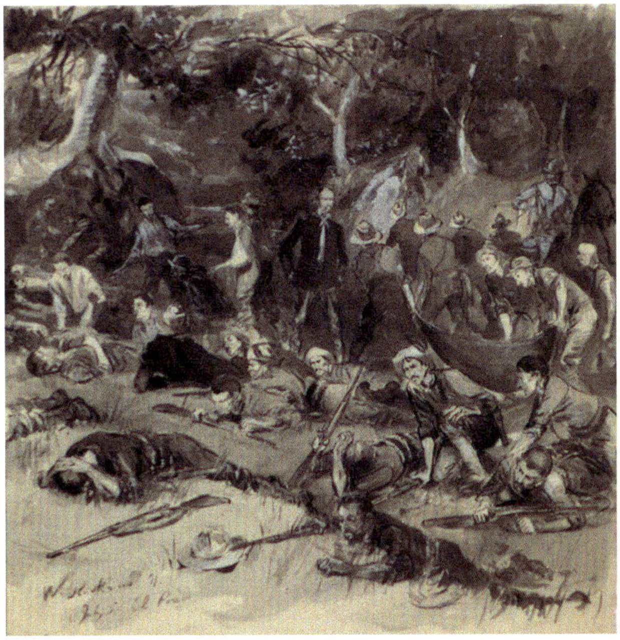

Fig. 52
William Glackens
A ford in the River Guama markes [i.e., marks] the commencement of the [?] on the center, July 1st, 1898
Wash, Chinese white, pencil on paper
16¾ × 17½ in. (42.6 × 44.5 cm)
Library of Congress Prints and Photographs Division, Washington, DC
Reproduced as *The Ford of the San Juan—"The Bloody Bend"* in *McClure's Magazine* 11, no. 6 (October 1898): 505

compelling dispatch, "With the Fifth Corps," published in *Harper's New Monthly Magazine* in November 1898, few are battle scenes.[46] Most depict the movement of wounded soldiers to the rear. The bitter realism of his written account contrasts markedly with the idealism of his illustrations, which do not dramatize the sobering cost of war but rather focus on the heroism of soldiers aiding their comrades or the nobility of the wounded who salute the troops returning to the front. The drama of the battle for Santiago is conveyed in only one picture, *Capt. Grimes's Battery Going Up El Poso Hill* (Fig. 54). In it, Remington showed a long line of soldiers from an artillery unit charging across a field to aim their howitzers toward Santiago. Each of the soldiers in the foreground is shown driving a pair of horses, cracking their whips above their wild-eyed animals' heads and leaning forward, muscles straining, to amplify the sense of urgency. They seem to pass close by the viewer; the noise, the energy, the smell of battle is palpable. Remington was already known for his stirring depictions of cowboys on horseback (e.g., *A Dash for the Timber* [1889; Amon Carter Museum of American Art, Fort Worth, TX]), images meant to inspire admiration for the intrepid men helping to conquer the frontier. Here, the image of heroic soldiers and their mounts, charging headlong into battle, was designed to drum up enthusiasm for the American struggle against the Spanish.

In *Capt. Grimes's Battery Going Up El Poso Hill,* the athleticism of the soldiers and their ability to maintain control, despite their breakneck speed, also suggest a well-coordinated battle plan: a romanticization of the facts. On the other hand, *Just Before the Opening Engagement, El Pozo* (1898; Library of Congress), one of Glackens's images of the same battle, is a more accurate portrayal of the disarray of the American army. Glackens presents a panoramic

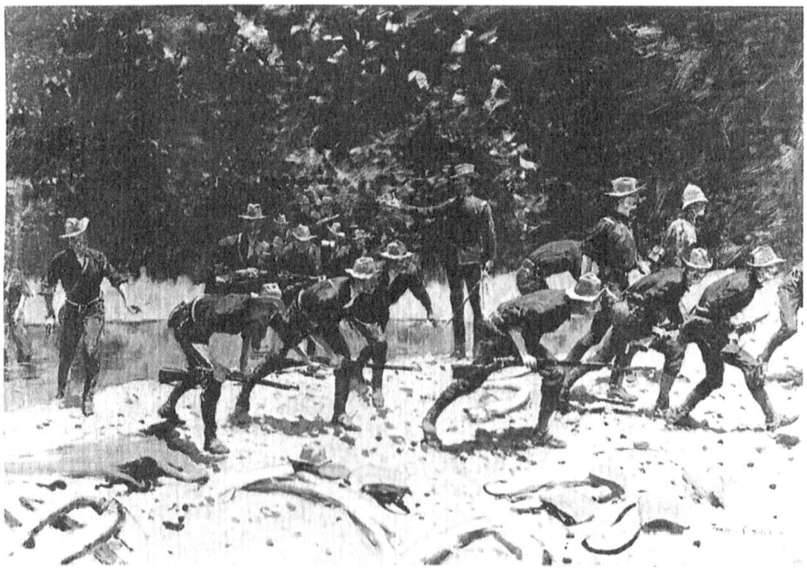

Fig. 53
Frederic Remington
At the Bloody Ford of the San Juan, 1898
Black and white oil on canvas
27 × 39 in. (68.6 × 99.1 cm)
Reproduced in *Harper's New Monthly Magazine* 97, no. 582 (November 1898): 967

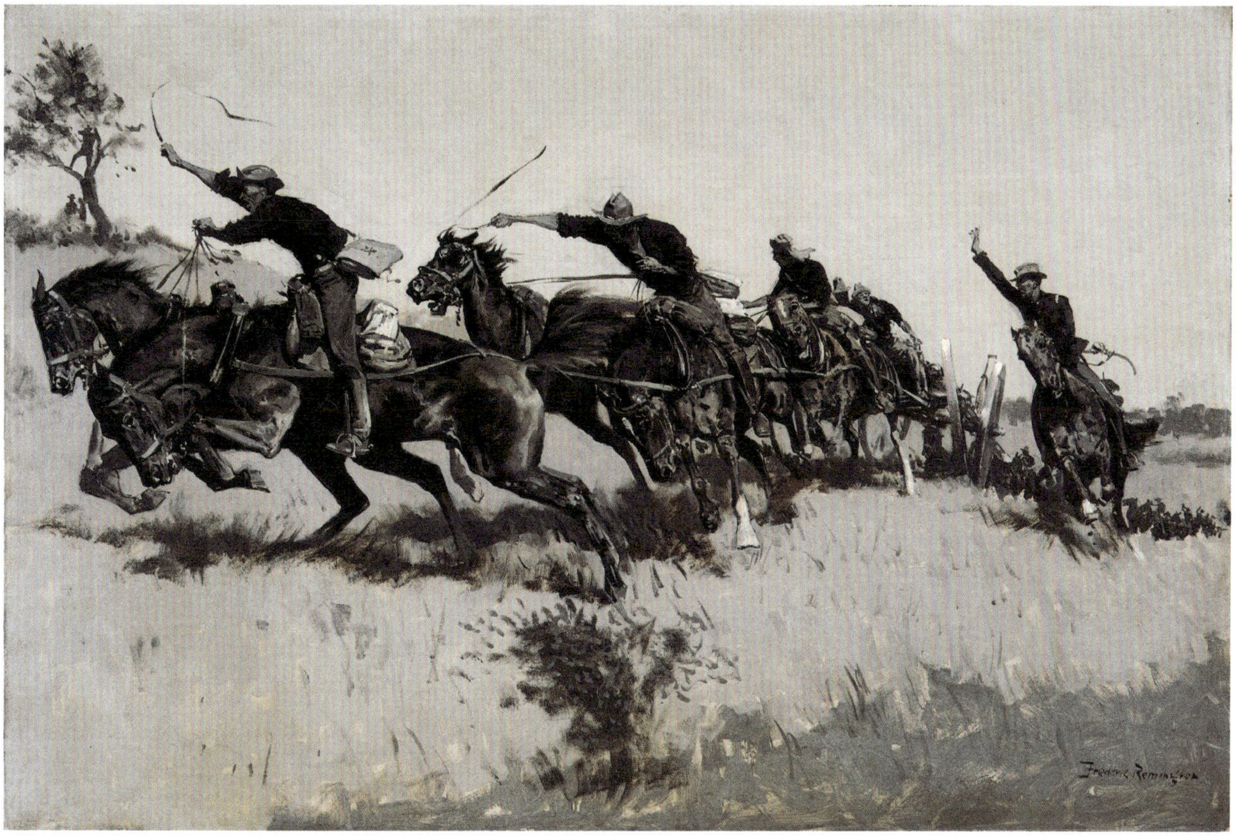

Fig. 54
Frederic Remington
Capt. Grimes's Battery Going Up El Poso Hill, 1898
Black and white oil on canvas
26½ × 39¾ in. (67.3 × 101 cm)
Frederic Remington Art Museum, Ogdensburg, NY; Bequest of Mr. Robert Purcell (1992.002)

view of the American camp, with cavalry and artillery and a few foot soldiers milling around with no clear direction or purpose. He includes vignettes—such as a mounted soldier trying to seize the harness of a panicked riderless horse—that express the anxious uncertainty and disorganization in the moments before the battle. In another image, *El Pozo Centra, Santiago* (Fig. 55), he focused on infantrymen. They are carefully described and fully modeled, and Glackens's academic training is apparent in his accomplished rendering of the stretch and creases of the soldiers' uniforms over well-constructed musculature. At the same time, the skillful balance between open space and the concentration of figures serves his storytelling: he arranged the soldiers in a dense swirl that leads around the hill toward their goal, the Spanish blockhouse.

Images like this one are almost painterly in execution and seem to have little in common with the witty, schematic, rapid-fire drawings of New York streets that Glackens would make in the next decades (for example, *Far From the Fresh Air Farm* [1911; NSU Art Museum, Fort Lauderdale, FL]). Nonetheless, the way the figures are individuated in *El Pozo Centra* foreshadows his mature, lively drawing style. One soldier holds his hat as he charges up the hill; one turns to look at the viewer; one, just shot, grimaces in pain; one falls as he is hit. The men

Fig. 55
William Glackens
El Pozo Centra, Santiago, [1898?]
Pen and ink, wash, Chinese white, crayon on paper
21 × 16⅛ in. (53.3 × 41 cm)
Library of Congress Prints and Photographs Division, Washington, DC
Reproduced as *The "Rough Riders" Charging Up the San Juan Hill* in *McClure's Magazine* 11, no. 6 (October 1898): 506

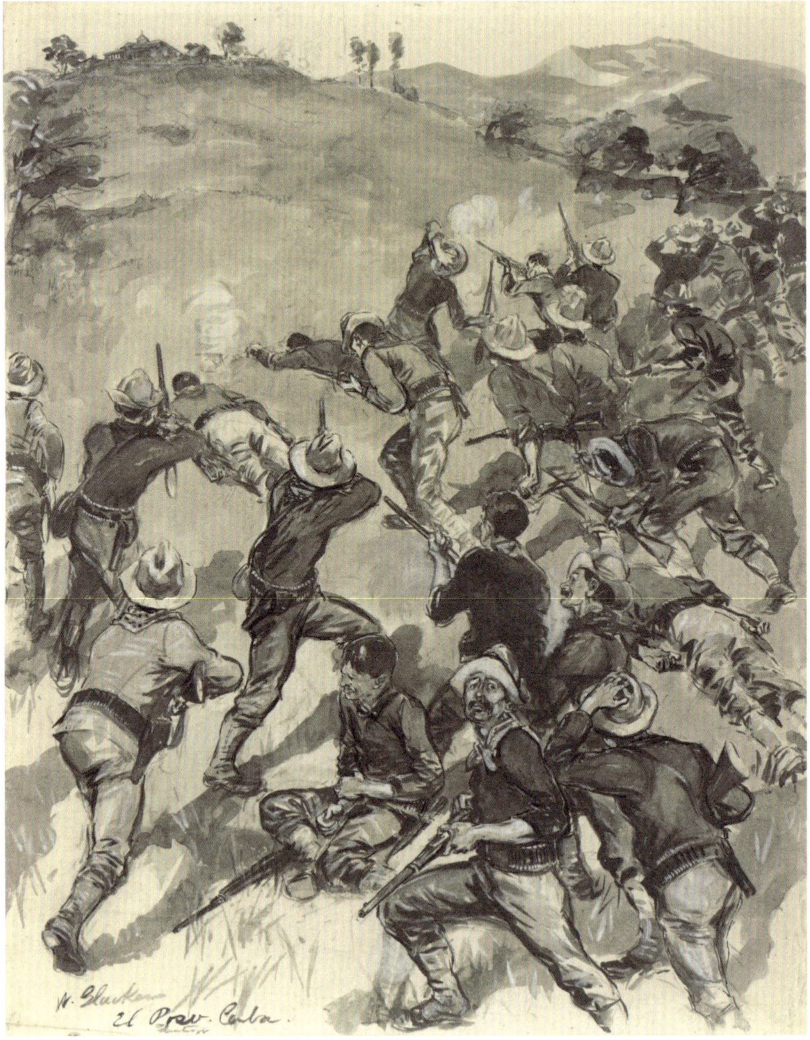

are given individual personalities that grab the viewer's attention and contribute to the vividness of the whole.

Howard Chandler Christy's images were among the most exciting and engaging of the war. He was in Cuba by mid-June and seems to have been fearless, creating tense battle scenes that put the viewer in the middle of the action, as he himself might have been.[47] He did not eschew graphic depictions of violence: in his *Capture of San Juan Blockhouse, July 2* (1898; Pritzker Military Museum and Library, Chicago), he showed a rather gruesome bayoneting in the foreground. His figures are large-scale and immediate. For the most part, he followed Roosevelt's Rough Riders and portrayed them as uniformly valiant. Full of energy and motion, Christy's images were designed to pull the viewer directly into the scene. While Glackens often used an elevated viewpoint, likely reflecting his actual position on a hill above the event, and Remington tended to imagine the spectator a safe distance away, as though he were attending a theatrical performance, in such images as *The Fight at the*

San Juan Block-house, July 1st (Fig. 56), Christy's vantage point is boots-on-the-ground. He positions the viewer as though he were just behind the soldiers, determinedly charging ahead with dead and wounded all around.

Remington's *Capt. Grimes's Battery*, Glackens's *El Pozo Centra*, and Christy's *Fight at the San Juan Block-house* all represent the campaign for Santiago, which took place over a few days in early July 1898. At the same time, the United States Navy was conducting a vicious bombardment of Santiago's harbor, eventually destroying the Spanish fleet. The navy blockaded the harbor and laid siege to the city until Spanish forces signed a "protocol of peace" on July 16.

It was Glackens who most compellingly depicted the aftermath of the big battle and the human cost of the war. He drew a highly sympathetic image of refugees from Santiago clamoring for food in a nearby town—a result of the blockade but also of years of Spanish repression (*Starving Refugees from Santiago Congregating at El Caney* [1898; Library of Congress]). He also drew compassionate pictures of the terrible carnage—the casualties were extremely high at San Juan Hill.[48] *The Night After San Juan* (Fig. 57) shows dead and wounded strewn across the fore- and middle ground and soldiers fanning out around the blockhouse to be sure no enemy remained. It conveys with terrifying eloquence the agony and fear described by a number of journalists on the scene. As Frank Norris wrote for *Century* magazine,

> The blockhouse was a horror, the trenches beyond description. The first Spaniard I saw was lying at the bottom of a trench. He was a young fellow—they were all young fellows—his face the color of wax; one poor, dirty hand hooked like a buzzard's claw. . . . The dead were everywhere . . . in corners of the blockhouse, and in grisly postures halfway down the slope of the hill. The air was full of smells—the

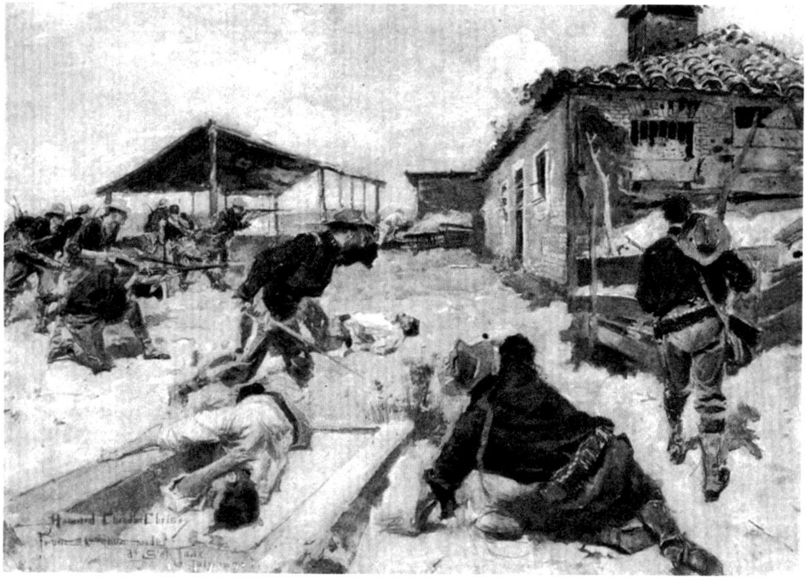

Fig. 56
Howard Chandler Christy
The Fight at the San Juan Block-house, July 1st, 1898
Published in *Scribner's Magazine* 24, no. 3 (September 1898): 280

smell of stale powder, of smoke, of a horse's carcass two days unburied, of shattered lime and plaster in the blockhouse, and the strange, acrid, salty smell of blood.[49]

Glackens's last images of the war commemorated the Spanish surrender. *Raising the Flag over the Governor's Palace, Santiago* (1898; Library of Congress) shows top military brass watching as the American flag goes up over a government building. The drawing, documenting American triumph with no indication of the horrific cost, was published in *McClure's Magazine* in October 1898. Not surprisingly, few of his more compassionate drawings, such as those of the starving refugees or the corpse-strewn roads after the battle for San Juan Hill, made it into print.

Glackens left Cuba on August 14. He contracted malaria on the trip home, from which he never fully recovered. His Cuba pictures would appear in various magazines during the following year, keeping

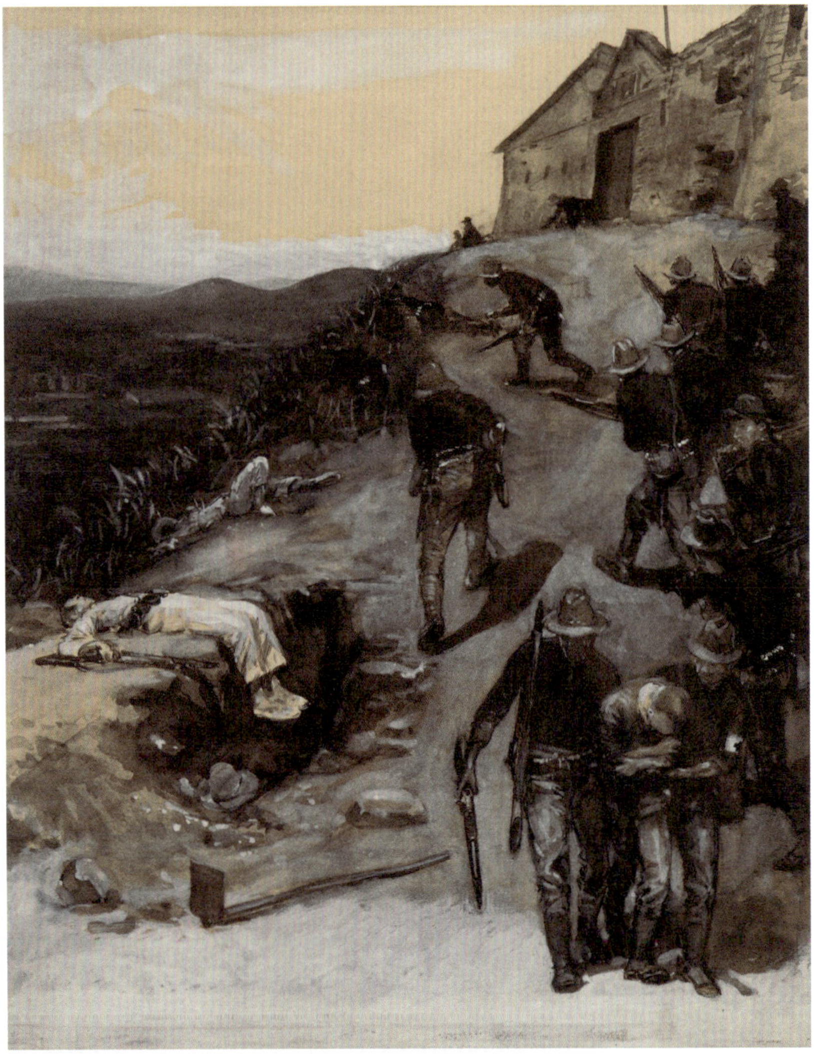

Fig. 57
William Glackens
The Night After San Juan, 1898
Conté crayon, charcoal, gouache on paper
16⅜ × 12⅝ in. (41.6 × 32.1 cm)
NSU Art Museum, Fort Lauderdale, FL; Bequest of Ira D. Glackens 91.40.67

Fig. 58
Howard Chandler Christy
Col. Roosevelt Tells the Story of the Rough Riders in Scribner's Magazine, c. 1898
Advertising poster
15½ × 23 in. (39.4 × 58.4 cm)
Library of Congress Prints and Photographs Division, Washington, DC

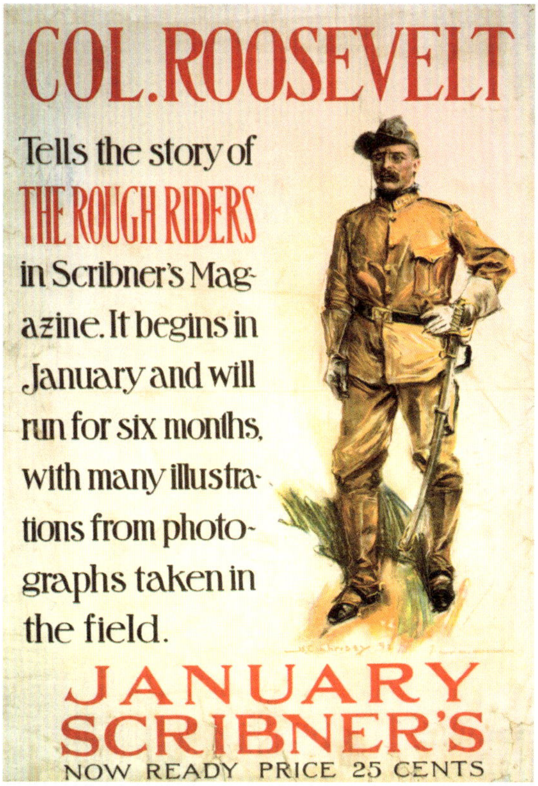

his work in the public eye.[50] Nonetheless, he did not work as an artist-reporter again. He concentrated instead on magazine illustration—his main source of income for more than a decade—while also devoting his energies to painting.[51]

The war had a more transformative effect on Christy's career. During his time in Cuba, he traveled with the Rough Riders and was befriended by Roosevelt. While with their regiment, he made sketches of the soldiers and also of his fellow reporters, several of which were used in advertisements for *Scribner's* magazine. One featured a dashing portrait of correspondent Richard Harding Davis. Another, of Roosevelt, became one of the signature images of the future president (Fig. 58). These portraits and others were then reproduced in a book, *Men of the Army and the Navy*, which made Christy's reputation. And although he would later create a celebrated series of posters encouraging support of the American effort in World War I, when he came back from Cuba he proclaimed he had gotten tired of the "soldier stuff" and developed the character known as the Christy Girl.[52]

Remington left Cuba in mid-July. He too had been close to Roosevelt, and at Roosevelt's urging he created two monumental war pictures, *Charge of the Rough Riders* (Fig. 59) and *The Scream of Shrapnel at San Juan Hill* (1898; Yale University Art Gallery, New Haven, CT).[53] The paintings are frequently described as focusing on the "great game" of warfare, more closely resembling a play on the football field than a battle. (Remington had played on his college football team; *Charge of the Rough Riders* is often compared with his illustration *A Run Behind Interference*, published in *Harper's Weekly* in 1893.)[54] Like Remington's other depictions of the war, the paintings are highly choreographed and idealized, full of handsome figures who advance manfully and die beautifully. His subjects were the Rough Riders, but the San Juan assault was an infantry operation, and as such lent itself to a much less dignified pictorial presentation than did soldiers on horseback. Remington nonetheless made them heroic; the single mounted figure in the vanguard of *Charge of the Rough Riders*, Roosevelt, was made to seem the most noble of all. Due in part to images like these, the charge up San Juan Hill came to be celebrated as the iconic battle of the war and served as a boost to Roosevelt's political ambitions.

Although immediately afterwards Remington declared that "I would in the future paint [only] 'set pieces for dining-rooms,'"[55] by February 1899 he was back in Cuba as a correspondent for *Collier's Weekly*, covering the US Army (Fig. 60). A number of his illustrations from this third tour indicate the tension between native Cubans and the Americans stationed there (see, for example, *Under Which King* [1899; Frederic Remington Art Museum, Ogdensburg, NY], reproduced in *Collier's Weekly*, April 8, 1899). Americans had become convinced that the Cubans were capable neither of governing their own country nor of protecting American interests, and Cubans no longer regarded American soldiers as co-combatants but rather as occupying forces. The evolution—from partners in a noble struggle for freedom to mutually suspicious rivals for domination of Cuba—took place within a very brief period. Although there were dissenting voices, many of the editorials and cartoons in American papers celebrated the United States' new identity as an increasingly powerful player on the international stage.[56]

In 1900, McKinley was elected to a second term. Roosevelt had been chosen as his vice president, an indication that the expansionist argument had prevailed. Cuba had been declared a republic—but one under an American military governor and subject to other forms of regulation. Cuba saw some benefit from US occupation—infrastructure was improved, yellow fever was brought under control[57]—but American domination made the country into a kind of colony, with deleterious effects for the Cuban people.

For American tourists, however, Cuba seemed to have returned to the kind of place it had been before all the fighting. American investments were thriving; tourism was up. Cuba was once again a "garden of delight,"[58] and after the turn of the century, several American artists painted it that way, in images that mirrored those made before the war. Childe Hassam, who had painted some of the loveliest of those pictures, never went back to the Caribbean—in fact, he became so alarmed by the war that in the summer of 1898 he declined to visit his beloved Isles of Shoals, fearing Spanish bombardment of the east

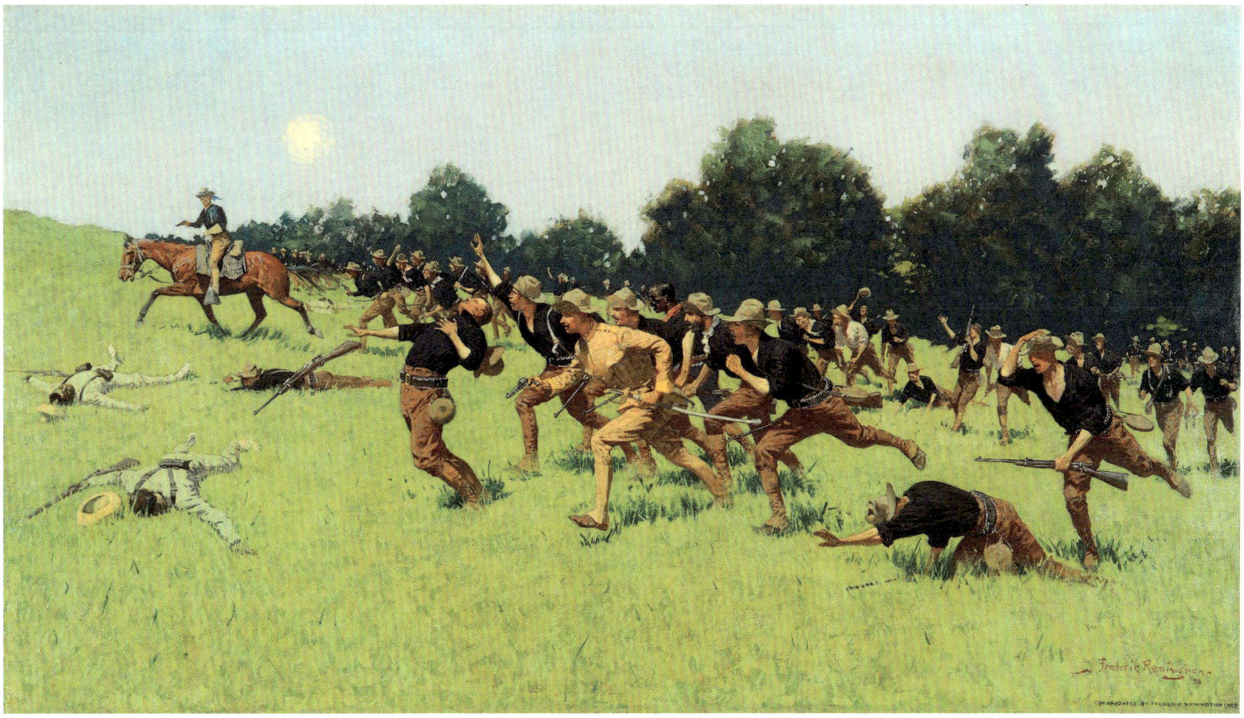

Fig. 59
Frederic Remington
Charge of the Rough Riders, 1898
Oil on canvas
35 × 60 in. (88.9 × 152.4 cm)
Frederic Remington Art Museum, Ogdensburg, NY; Gift of the Remington Estate (66.52)

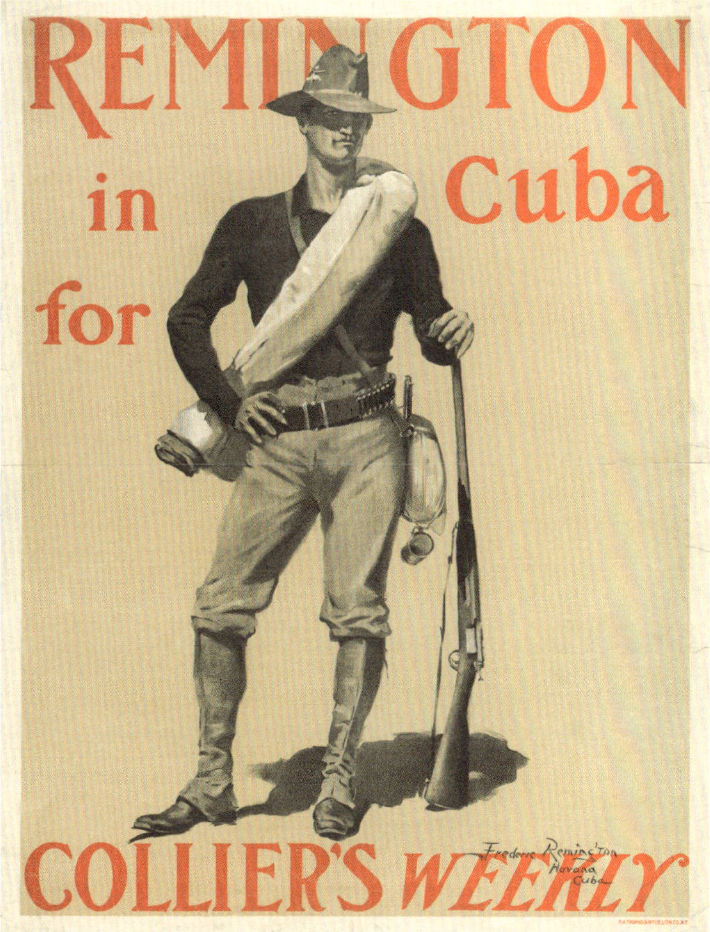

Fig. 60
Frederic Remington
Collier's Weekly: Remington in Cuba, March, 1899
Color lithograph
Sheet: 24$\frac{3}{16}$ × 18 in. (61.4 × 45.7 cm).
Image: 22$\frac{7}{8}$ × 16$\frac{3}{4}$ in. (58.1 × 42.6 cm)
The Metropolitan Museum of Art, New York; Gift of Helen L. Card, 1944 (44.36.1)

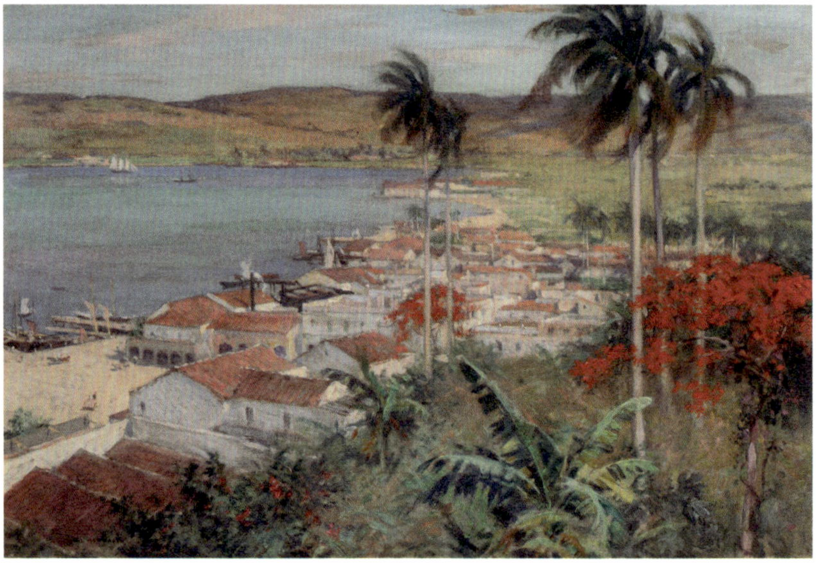

Fig. 61
Willard Metcalf
Havana Harbor, 1902
Oil on canvas
18$\frac{5}{16}$ × 26$\frac{1}{8}$ in. (46.5 × 66.4 cm)
Terra Foundation for American Art, Chicago; Daniel J. Terra Collection, 1992.49

coast of the United States.[59] However, one of his colleagues in the Ten American Painters group, Willard Metcalf, did visit Cuba in 1902, on commission from the American-owned Havana Tobacco Company. The company was building a new store in New York, and Metcalf was hired to decorate it. His paintings for that project show Cuba with clean, wide streets, beautiful old architecture, hard-working peasants, palm trees swaying in the breeze, and brilliantly colored foliage (Fig. 61).

There was at least one artist of this era who seems to have had a more nuanced understanding of recent Cuban history. In late 1901, more than fifteen years after his original visit to Cuba, Winslow Homer sent his just-completed *Searchlight on Harbor Entrance, Santiago de Cuba* (Fig. 62) to his dealer, Knoedler in New York. At the time, Cuba was very much in the news, and Homer urged Knoedler to show the picture right away, "as the subject is now before the people."[60] The immediate issue was a court of inquiry, convened in September 1901, to determine which of two commanding officers should be credited for the American naval victory in Santiago Harbor and whether there had been any improper conduct on the part of one of the officers.[61]

Far more momentous was the debate over legislation proposed early in 1901 by Senator Orville Platt, Republican of Connecticut, which would make Cuba an American colony in all but name—not officially annexed, but firmly under US control. It gave the United States the right to intervene in Cuban affairs and to establish a naval base there and prohibited Cuba from entering into treaties with any other foreign power. McKinley signed the legislation in the spring and then, under intense pressure from the United States, in December Cuba revised its constitution, acceding to these demands.

Completed just at this time, Homer's painting of Morro Castle is chillingly beautiful and full of foreboding. The castle is a massive stone fortress built in the seventeenth century to guard the entrance to Santiago Bay. It had a grim history: it was where political prisoners were held before they were executed. It also was the principal point of defense against naval attack for the city of Santiago and a key stronghold during the bombardment of Santiago Harbor in July 1898. In that battle, the Spanish were outmanned and hampered by obsolescent weaponry. But it was the new American technology—electric searchlights that effectively blinded the defenders of the fortress—that was the decisive factor in the US victory.[62]

Homer shows Morro Castle from the interior. The viewer is positioned near one of the parapets, as though standing behind the Spanish guns and sought by the searchlight's beams—in other words, looking out onto the harbor not as a detached observer but as the Spanish soldiers had in July 1898.[63] Now, however, the heat and noise and terror of the bombardment are stripped away; the fortress is eerily empty. Homer tells his story with starkly reduced means: a limited palette of slate blue, silver, black, and searing white. The cannon and watchtower are silhouetted and simplified into geometric shapes. His composition is taut.

In 1898, one reporter described Morro Castle as "the last stronghold of medievalism" in the Americas.[64] Another attributed a "certain massiveness"[65] to the searchlight beams. Homer opposes the old-fashioned solidity of the military architecture with the modernity of the searchlight beams, evanescent yet deadly.[66] A late twentieth-century scholar has described the painting as a "stark image of ominous soli-

Fig. 62
Winslow Homer
Searchlight on Harbor Entrance, Santiago de Cuba, 1902
Oil on canvas
30½ × 50½ in. (77.5 × 128.3 cm)
The Metropolitan Museum of Art, New York; Gift of George A. Hearn, 1906 (06.1282)

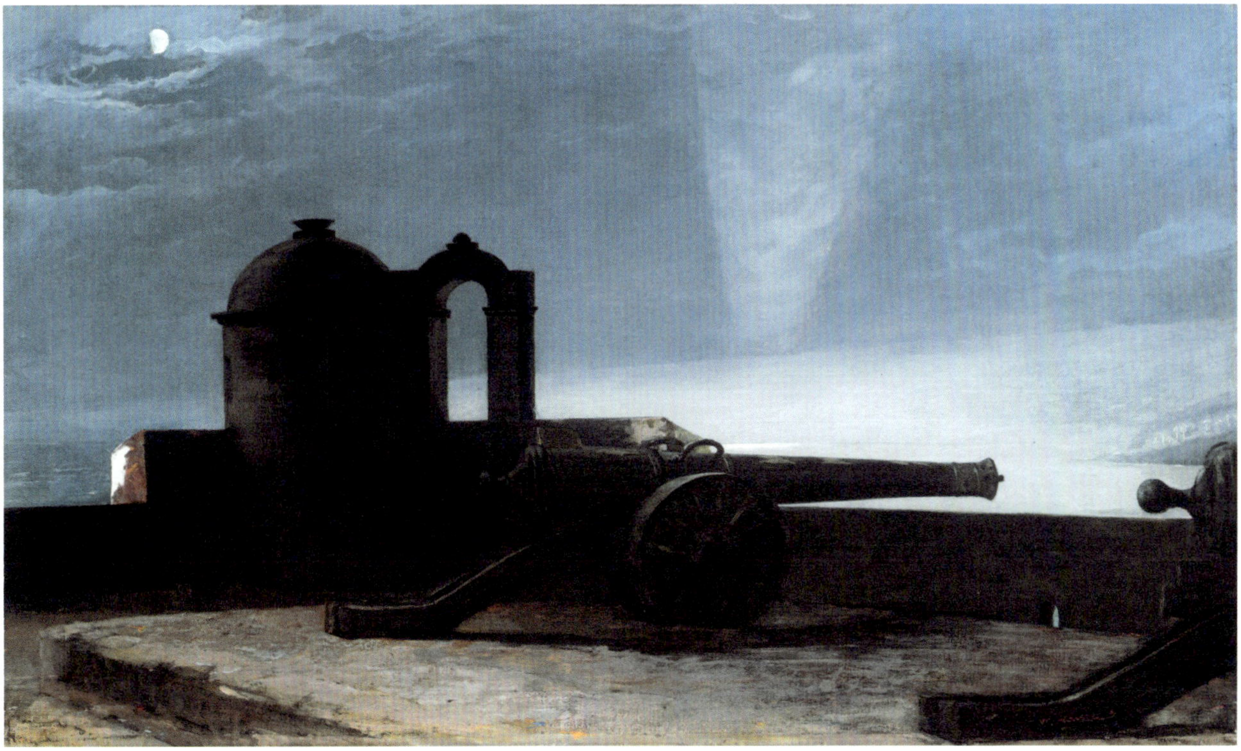

tude in the romantic tradition" and as "one of Homer's most abstract compositions"—in other words, as both retrospective and forward-looking.[67] It was painted one year into what came to be called "the American Century"—the beginning of the United States extending its reach into the Western Hemisphere. The contrast between antiquated Spanish and innovative American military technology can be seen as a metaphor for Spain's old-style subjugating dominance and the US's promise of "enlightened" oversight of Cuba.

Searchlight on Harbor Entrance, Santiago de Cuba is a work of cold beauty and tremendous unease. It speaks to the present day like no other American work from the period. Homer probably had no special insight into the cascading effects of American intervention in Cuba. Nonetheless, for the contemporary viewer looking back, the sinister mood of this picture calls those consequences to mind.

NOTES

1. This famous anecdote was first recorded by journalist James Creelman in his memoir *On the Great Highway: The Wanderings and Adventures of a Special Correspondent* (Boston: Lothrop, 1901), 178. Despite the fact that the story has often been repeated, it is likely fictional. See W. Joseph Campbell, *Getting It Wrong: Ten of the Greatest Misreported Stories in American Journalism* (Berkeley, CA: University of California Press, 2010), 9–25.
2. Linda H. Davis, *Badge of Courage: The Life of Stephen Crane* (Boston: Houghton Mifflin, 1998), 246–47.
3. Commonly known—in the United States—as the Spanish-American War, the War of 1898 culminated in the United States seizing control of several territories (Cuba, Puerto Rico, Guam, and the Philippines) that had long been dominated by Spain. The United States then identified the conflict as the "Spanish-American War," disregarding Cuba's agency in its decades-long struggle for independence, even though Cuba's Third War of Independence (1895–98) was a major factor in Spain's defeat. (The name also ignores local efforts to achieve independence from Spain in the Philippines and elsewhere.) As described by Cuba scholar Ada Ferrer, "In the struggle between Cuba and Spain, then, it was the United States that emerged victorious." Ada Ferrer, *Cuba: An American History* (New York: Scribner, 2021), 166. Ferrer also points out that when in December 1898 "representatives of Spain and the United States met in Paris to sign the treaty that sealed the end of Spanish rule in Cuba," no delegates from Cuba, the Philippines, Guam, or Puerto Rico were present. And when the Spanish flag came down over Morro Castle, it was replaced not by the Cuban flag, but by the American one; Ferrer, *Cuba: An American History*, 165. See also the website and catalogue accompanying the National Portrait Gallery's 2023 exhibition *1898: US Imperial Visions and Revisions*, which makes the case for using "the War of 1898" to describe the conflict.
4. Of the several fronts on which the war was waged, the Philippine theater saw the longest-lasting and most horrific fighting. After the peace treaty with Spain was signed, Filipinos battled American forces for their independence for several years,

finally surrendering, after much brutality and destruction, in 1902. The visual history of that war was recorded in photographs for the most part; the Cuban theater, on the other hand, saw the greatest number of artist-reporters on the scene.

5. See, for example, Richard Henry Dana Jr.'s account of an idyllic evening in Havana: "There is a clear moon above, and a blue field of glittering stars; the air is pure and balmy; the band of fifty or sixty instruments discourses most eloquent music under the shade of palm-trees and mangoes; the walks are filled with promenaders, and the streets around the square lined with carriages." Richard Henry Dana Jr., *To Cuba and Back: A Vacation Voyage* (Boston: Ticknor & Fields, 1859), 48–49.
6. Thomas Moran, letter to Mary Moran, January 31[?], 1883, quoted in Nancy Anderson, *Thomas Moran* (Washington, DC: National Gallery of Art, 1997), 236.
7. Winslow Homer, quoted in Helen Cooper, *Winslow Homer Watercolors* (New Haven, CT, and London: Yale University Press, 1986), 143.
8. Cooper sees this as a liability in the Cuba watercolors, noting that Homer had difficulty "join[ing] in one work the needs of architectural description with those of atmosphere and color." Cooper, *Winslow Homer Watercolors*, 146. See also Martha Tedeschi, *Watercolors by Winslow Homer: The Color of Light* (Chicago: Art Institute, 2008), 176. Tedeschi suggests that Homer's physical discomfort explains why he did not make excursions into the countryside while he was in Cuba as he had in the Bahamas, and also finds the Cuba watercolors "finicky in handling and more neutral in color" than those made in the Bahamas.
9. Homer made three images of cockfights. One was destroyed in the hurricane that struck Galveston, Texas, in 1900; a second is privately owned. The latter shows the birds still tethered to posts and represents the preamble to combat. See Lloyd Goodrich, *Record of Works by Winslow Homer*, vol. 4.2, ed. Abigail Booth Gerdts (New York: Spanierman Gallery, 2005–13), 381–83, nos. 1319, 1320, and 1321.
10. H. Barbara Weinberg, "Hassam's Travels, 1892–1914," in Weinberg, *Childe Hassam: American Impressionist* (New York: Metropolitan Museum of Art, 2004), 182.
11. This image is half of a stereograph and was made of the cathedral square at about the same time as Hassam's painting. It shows a much poorer, Blacker Cuba than the one Hassam describes.
12. Hassam misremembered the date—he actually docked in New York on February 5, 1895, and the insurrection began on February 24. Weinberg, *Childe Hassam: American Impressionist*, 198 n17. Hassam's statement, quoted on 183, comes from DeWitt McClellan Lockman, "Interview with Childe Hassam," February 2, 1927, DeWitt McClellan Lockman Papers, New-York Historical Society, Archives of American Art, Smithsonian Institution, reel 503.
13. Charles N. Sheldon, "Just Before Santiago's Surrender," *Leslie's*, August 4, 1898, quoted in Charles H. Brown, *The Correspondents' War: Journalists in the Spanish-American War* (New York: Charles Scribner's Sons, 1967), 336.
14. "The Insurrection in Cuba," *Harper's Weekly* 39, no. 2004 (May 18, 1895): 471–72.
15. Robert L. Gambone, *Life on the Press: The Popular Art and Illustrations of George Benjamin Luks* (Jackson: University Press of Mississippi, 2009), 97. "Morning Review of Volunteers" appeared on page 1 of the *Bulletin* on January 18, 1896; "Sacking of the Town of Jaruco, Cuba," appeared on page 1 on March 2, 1896.
16. James Creelman, "Famine and Flames: Spain May Destroy, but She Cannot Keep Cuba Even with an Army of 180,000," *New York World*, May 17, 1896, 1.
17. Bennard B. Perlman, *The Immortal Eight: American Paintings from Eakins to the Armory Show, 1870–1913* (Westport, CT: North Light Publishers, 1979), 63.
18. *Harper's* reporter Thomas Dawley said, "The American consul tells me that [American newspaper correspondents] are not allowed to go outside the city, under penalty of being shot, while by others we are informed that we may travel

through the country at our own risk, and that our only danger is from the numerous bands of robbers." Thomas Dawley, "Our Correspondent in Cuba," *Harper's Weekly* 40, no. 2046 (March 7, 1896): 222.

19. Brown, *Correspondents' War*, 16.
20. According to the caption, the illustration was "Drawn by Frederic Remington After a Photograph by an Insurgent Officer." *Harper's Weekly* 40, no. 2046 (March 7, 1896): 217. Remington would not go to Cuba for another ten months.
21. [Unsigned], "The Cuban Question," *Harper's Weekly* 40, no. 2046 (March 7, 1896): 219.
22. The issue of national sovereignty was later summarized by Republican Representative David Henderson of Iowa in the *Indianapolis News*, who noted that "no international law makes the United States the regulator of the wrongs of the earth. . . . We all sympathize with the liberty-loving and fighting Cubans, but they are citizens of another government." Quoted in Stephen Kinzer, *The True Flag: Theodore Roosevelt, Mark Twain, and the Birth of American Empire* (New York: Henry Holt, 2017), 35–36.
23. William McKinley, "Message to Congress on the Condition of American Citizens in Cuba," May 17, 1897, quoted in Robert W. Merry, *President McKinley: Architect of the American Century* (New York: Simon & Schuster, 2017), 218ff.
24. Theodore Roosevelt, quoted in Kinzer, *The True Flag*, 22.
25. Richard Harding Davis, "The Fate of the Pacificos," *Cuba in War Time* (New York: R. H. Russell, 1897), 41–55.
26. Remington commented, "The acts of the terrible savages . . . pass all understanding by civilized man. . . . Their treatment of women is unspeakable, and as for the men captured by them alive, the blood curdles in my veins, as I think of the atrocity, of the cruelty, practiced on these helpless victims. My picture illustrates one case where they saw fit to bring their captives into the lines, trussed up at the elbows." "Cuban War Sketches Gathered in the Field by Frederic Remington. Spanish Guerillas Bringing 'Pacificos' into Camp," *New York Journal and Advertiser*, January 24, 1897, quoted in Douglas Allen, *Frederic Remington and the Spanish-American War* (New York: Crown Publishers, 1971), 12.
27. "What He Saw in Cuba," *Washington Post*, March 18, 1898, quoted in Merry, *President McKinley*, 265.
28. Davis's account first appeared in the *New York Journal and Advertiser* on February 2, 1897, and was reprinted in *Cuba in War Time*, 59–73. The quotation appears on p. 67.
29. *Cuba in War Time*, 60.
30. *New York Journal and Advertiser*, February 12, 1897, 2.
31. Davis, "The Right of Search of American Vessels," *Cuba in War Time*, 129–33.
32. The headline appeared on the first page of the evening edition of the *New York Journal and Advertiser*, February 17, 1898. See Brown, *Correspondents' War*, 123.
33. For a discussion of Luks's images referring to Cuba made after he returned to New York, see Gambone, *Life on the Press*, 169–71.
34. Rudyard Kipling's poem, first published in the *New York Sun* on February 10, 1899, was specifically about the Philippines (its original title was "The White Man's Burden: The United States and the Philippine Islands") and it urged American colonization of that country. The phrase "white man's burden" soon came to be used more generally as an expression of the belief that the white race had a moral obligation to civilize the world's nonwhite peoples.
35. Kinzer, *The True Flag*, 137. General William Shafter, quoted in Kinzer, *The True Flag*, 188.
36. Whereas these improvements, which allowed photographs to be reproduced in newspapers, may have cut into opportunities for artist-reporters, the ability of

these draftsmen to amplify the drama and select the most sensational details from any particular scene made them valuable to their editors.

37. Augustus Thomas, a friend of Remington's, reported that when he called the artist to tell him that the *Maine* had been blown up in Havana harbor, "his only thanks or comment was to shout 'Ring off!' In process of doing so I could hear him calling the private telephone number of his publishers in New York. In his mind the campaign was already actively under way." Augustus Thomas, "Recollections of Frederic Remington," *Century* 86, no. 3 (July 1913): 357, as quoted in Allen, *Frederic Remington and the Spanish-American War*, 24.
38. The byline reads in full, "Illustrated with drawings by W.J. Glackens, special artist for *McClure's Magazine* with the Army of Invasion," in Stephen Bonsal, "The Fight for Santiago: The Account of an Eye-Witness," *McClure's Magazine* 11, no. 6 (October 1898): 499.
39. Remington, "With the Fifth Corps," *Harper's New Monthly Magazine* 97, no. 582 (November 1898): 962.
40. In a drawing by Remington of the same subject, the horses move onto the transport in orderly fashion while the attending soldiers stand by quietly. See *Loading Battery and Cavalry Horses on the Transports*, 1898 (private collection; reproduced in the *New York Journal and Advertiser*, May 20, 1898, 3).
41. Compare, for example, Glackens, *Fleet of Transports Just Before the Start, Tampa Bay* (1898; Library of Congress, Washington, DC) and Whistler, *Nocturne* (1879; Metropolitan Museum of Art, New York), as discussed by Avis Berman in her essay, "Glackens and Whistler: A Young Man's Attraction," *The Magazine Antiques* 181, no. 1 (January–February 2014): 211, 214.
42. Frederic Remington, "With the Fifth Corps," in *The Collected Writings of Frederic Remington*, ed. Peggy and Harold Samuels (Garden City, N.Y.: Doubleday & Co., 1979), 345.
43. Remington's photographic aide-memoire is reproduced in Peter H. Hassrick and Melissa J. Webster, *Frederic Remington: A Catalogue Raisonné of Paintings, Watercolors, and Drawings* (Cody, WY: Buffalo Bill Historical Center, 1996), vol. 2, no. 2379a.
44. The battle site is usually spelled El Pozo. However, "Poso" appears in the captions of some of the illustrations and is used here in those instances.
45. Remington did not try to mask his distance from the front lines, or his fear: "A ball struck in front of me, and filled my hair and face with sand, some of which I did not get out for days. It jolted my glass and my nerves, and I beat a masterly retreat, crawling rapidly backwards, for a reason which I will let you guess." Remington, "With the Fifth Corps," 974. Historian David McCullough describes the war as "the most wrenching, disillusioning experience of Remington's life . . . It bore no resemblance whatever to the high drama and heroics he had been painting and writing about for so long. There were no horses this time, no grand, silent country for background. There was smothering heat instead, mud, rain, yellow fever." David McCullough, "Remington, The Man," in Michael Edward Shapiro and Peter H. Hassrick, *Frederic Remington: The Masterworks* (St. Louis, MO: St. Louis Art Museum, 1988), 30.
46. For the pictures accompanying "With the Fifth Corps," Remington worked in grisaille, on canvases approximately 26 by 40 inches; the images were then reproduced in halftone. He also made smaller, highly finished illustrations in pen and ink and wash on paper or board, sometimes animated with touches of gouache; see, for example, *The Artful Dodgers: Shrapnel Coming Down the Road* (1898; The Art Institute of Chicago), reproduced in the *New York Journal and Advertiser* on August 14, 1898. In addition to these elaborate images, which were presumably intended for sale, he made simplified versions of some

of the same compositions in pen and ink, to be reproduced as line engravings. Remington's illustrations were based on memory and on quick sketches made in the field, although he bemoaned the loss of his sketchbook on the road to San Juan Hill (see "With the Fifth Corps," 972).

47. Christy's observations from the battlefield were recorded in his dispatch "An Artist at El Poso," *Scribner's Magazine* 24, no. 3 (September 1898): 283–84.
48. American casualties were 144 killed, 1,024 wounded, 72 missing. Spanish casualties were 58 killed, 170 wounded, 39 captured. The American forces numbered about 8,412; the Spanish forces, 800. Micheal Clodfelter, *Warfare and Armed Conflicts: A Statistical Encyclopedia of Casualty and Other Figures, 1492–2015*, 4th ed. (Jefferson, NC: McFarland, 2017), 255.
49. Frank Norris, "With Lawton at El Caney," *Century*, June 1899, quoted in Brown, *Correspondents' War*, 349–50.
50. Glackens published fourteen illustrations in *McClure's Magazine* (vols. 11, 12): six (plus an uncredited headpiece) to accompany Stephen Bonsal's article "The Fight for Santiago" (October 1898), two to accompany Bonsal's "The Night after San Juan" (December 1898), and five to illustrate Stephen Crane's "Marines Signaling Under Fire at Guantanamo" (February 1899). Four more drawings, presumably made after his return to New York, illustrated Crane's short story "The Lone Charge of William B. Perkins," published in *McClure's* in July 1899. Seven of Glackens's drawings were published to illustrate Richard H. Titherington's multipart article "Our War with Spain" in *Munsey's Magazine* (vol. 20): three in March 1899, three in April 1899, and two in May 1899. He also produced an illustration titled "An Attack of Marines" that appeared in the article "Dewey's Invincible Squadron" in *Munsey's Magazine* (vol. 19), June 1898—the last clearly based either on a photograph or from a reporter's dispatch. See Nancy E. Allyn and Elizabeth H. Hawkes, *William Glackens: A Catalogue of His Book and Magazine Illustrations* (Wilmington: Delaware Art Museum, 1987). In addition, at least one of his sketches, "U.S. Troops Embarking at Tampa for the Cuban Coast," appeared in the May 15, 1898, issue of the *New York World*; it may have been worked up for publication by another artist. See Edgar John Bullard III, "John Sloan and the Philadelphia Realists as Illustrators, 1890–1940" (master's thesis, University of California, Los Angeles, 1968), ch. 3, p. 8; ill. on 153. While Glackens made many more drawings than were ultimately published, this small percentage reflects both the publishers' preference for action scenes over his human-interest drawings and the fact that by the time many of the images reached New York, the war was over and the appetite for war stories was diminishing.
51. Emily C. Wood, "Chronology," and Heather Campbell Coyle, "The Character and Rhythm of Modern Life: Glackens as an Illustrator," in Avis Berman, ed., *William Glackens* (Philadelphia: Barnes Foundation, 2014), 272, 46–47.
52. Susan E. Meyer, *America's Great Illustrators* (New York: Harry N. Abrams, 1978), 239. An illustration titled *The Soldier's Dream* (location unknown), in which a vision of a beautiful woman appears in the pipe smoke of a young soldier, is often cited as the origin of the type known as "the Christy Girl." See *Howard Chandler Christy* (Allentown, PA: Allentown Art Museum, 1977), n.p.
53. Roosevelt requested that Remington paint *The Charge of the Rough Riders* to illustrate his article "The Cavalry at Santiago," which appeared in the April 1899 issue of *Scribner's Magazine* (421). See Shapiro and Hassrick, *Frederic Remington: The Masterworks*, 122 and 263n32. Roosevelt's six-part series of articles for *Scribner's* was shortly thereafter published as a book, *The Rough Riders* (New York: Charles Scribner's Sons, 1899), and also included Remington's image.
54. See John Seelye, "Remington: The Writer" in Shapiro and Hassrick, *Frederic Remington: The Masterworks*, 239–41, and Alexander Nemerov, *Frederic Remington*

and Turn-of-the-Century America (New Haven, CT, and London: Yale University Press, 1995), 54–62.

55. Remington, "With the Fifth Corps," 975.
56. The most notable dissenter was Mark Twain, whose dark satire of American imperialism, "To the Person Sitting in Darkness," was published in the *North American Review* in February 1901. Among the cartoons, "Declined with Thanks" by John S. Pughe (*Puck* [US edition], September 5, 1900), is typical. It shows a fat, self-satisfied Uncle Sam being fitted by tailor McKinley for a suit of clothes emblazoned with "Hawaii, Porto Rico," and other territorial acquisitions, while declining "anti-expansionist medicine" offered by a group of anti-imperialists.
57. According to an American guidebook to Havana, "before they relinquished Havana to the Cubans, on May 21, 1902, [the Americans] had made it one of the cleanest of cities. The Government of Intervention paved the streets, remodeled the parks and boulevards . . . introduced an American school system of public education, put in operation modern and efficient systems of sanitation; and above all and beyond all, eradicated the yellow fever, and converted Havana from the foul pest hole it had been for a century and a half into one of the healthiest cities of the world." Charles B. Reynolds, *Standard Guide to Havana: A Complete Handbook for Visitors* (New York: Foster & Reynolds, 1905), 127.
58. As expressed in a testimonial from that guidebook: "Cuba to me was a garden of delight, where my heart was dilated and my anxiety ceased." Reynolds, *Standard Guide to Havana*, 8.
59. Hassam was not alone in fearing a Spanish attack on American shores. Winslow Homer's father and some of their Maine neighbors also worried. Around the time the war began, Homer drew a cartoon (Bowdoin College Museum of Art, Brunswick, ME) that pokes gentle fun at their fears that remote Prout's Neck could be in danger of attack by the enemy fleet.
60. Winslow Homer, letter to M. Knoedler & Co., Scarborough, ME, December 30, 1901, M. Knoedler & Co. Archives, quoted in Natalie Spassky et al., *American Paintings in the Metropolitan Museum of Art*, vol. 2 (New York: Metropolitan Museum of Art, 1985), 491.
61. See Spassky, *American Paintings in the Metropolitan Museum of Art*, 490.
62. The devastating effect of the searchlights was described in a contemporary account by the Associated Press's representative stationed on the flagship, commanded by Admiral William Sampson: "The steady glare of the search-light, that never moved from Morro for many nights . . . tried the souls of the Spanish sailors and soldiers, who were so blinded that neither from the castle top nor from the harbor below could they see even the huge shadows of the ships." W. A. M. Goode, "The Inner History of Admiral Sampson's Campaign," *McClure's Magazine* 12, no. 1 (November 1898): 95. For an excellent discussion of Homer's painting in light of this new technology, see Nicolai Cikovsky Jr., "Homer Around 1900," in *Winslow Homer: A Symposium*, Studies in the History of Art 26, ed. Cikovsky (Washington, DC: National Gallery of Art, 1990), 132–54.
63. Scientific examination of the painting revealed a form—which may well have been a figure, a Spanish soldier, standing to the left of the guard tower—which Homer painted out, making the image even more unnervingly austere. See Stephanie L. Herdrich, "Crosscurrents: Conflict, Nature, and Mortality in Winslow Homer's Art," in Stephanie L. Herdrich and Sylvia Yount, *Winslow Homer: Crosscurrents* (New York: Metropolitan Museum of Art, 2022), 190n81.
64. Stephen Bonsal, "How the War Began. With the Blockading Fleet off Cuba," *McClure's Magazine* 11, no. 2 (June 1898): 124.
65. Rear Admiral William T. Sampson, U. S. N., "The Atlantic Fleet in the Spanish War," *Century* 57, no. 6 (April 1899): 901.
66. Cikovsky, "Homer Around 1900," 148.
67. Spassky, *American Paintings in the Metropolitan Museum of Art*, 491.

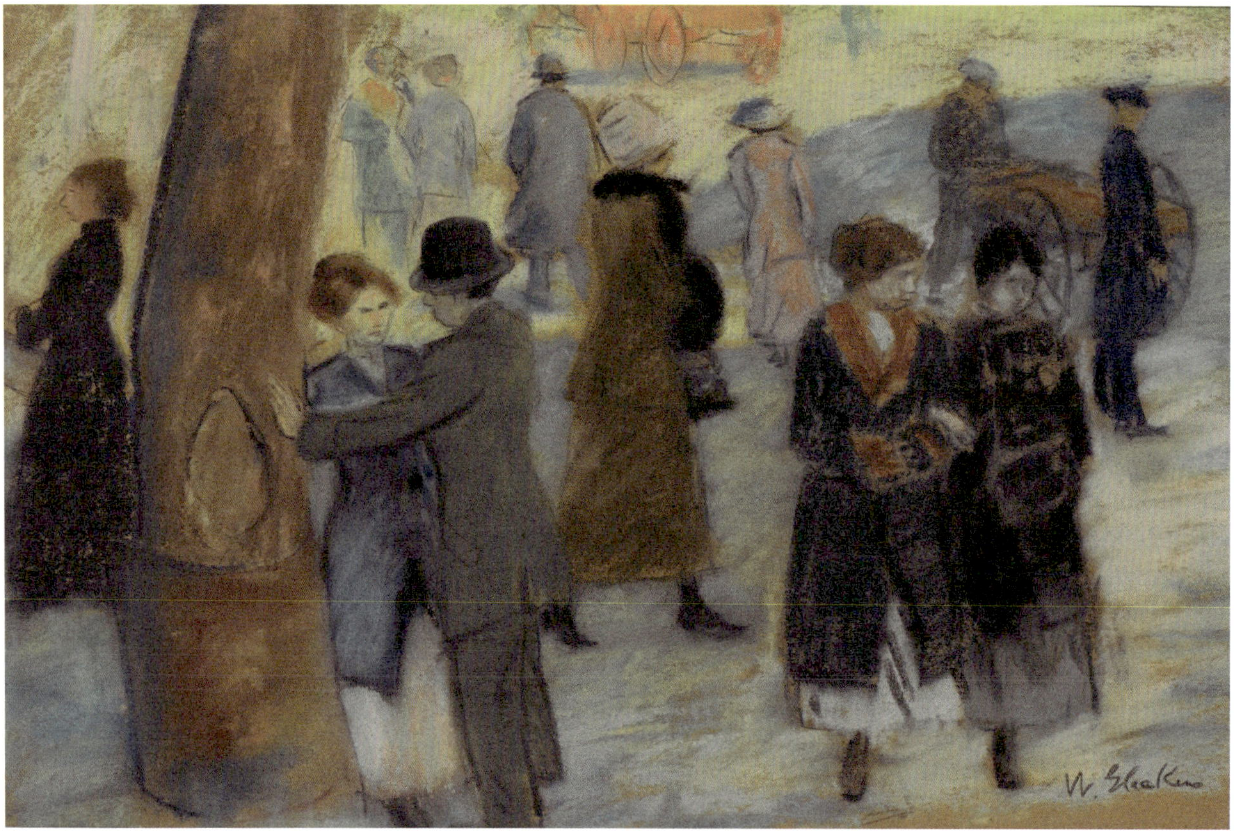
W. Glackens

Lecture given on
May 2, 2019

New-York
Historical Society

New York City

Was the Medium the Message? American Artists Rediscover Pastel at the Turn of the Twentieth Century

KATHLEEN A. FOSTER

"It is rumored that another society of painters, to be known as the Pastellists, is soon to be formed," reported *American Art News* in December of 1910.[1] A few weeks later, on January 10, 1911, the group opened its first exhibition in New York, perhaps including *City Scene* (Fig. 63) by William Glackens, under the title *Washington Square.* A motley network of friends, including several of Glackens's cronies from The Eight (Ernest Lawson, Everett Shinn, and later Arthur B. Davies, George Luks, and Maurice Prendergast); some younger progressive realists from the wider circle of Robert Henri, such as George Bellows, plus a number of older, well-known Post-Impressionist painters (Mary Cassatt, Thomas Wilmer Dewing, and Julian Alden Weir); and several obscure newcomers, the group presented an eclectic survey of current practice in pastel. "Pastelling makes strange bedfellows!" commented the critic in the *New York Sun*, who nonetheless enjoyed the mix: "It is one of the most delightful exhibitions thus far of the season."[2] For the most part warmly received by the press, the Pastellists were not long-lived, however, and presented just four exhibitions: three in rapid succession in January and December 1911 and February 1912, followed by a final showing two years later in February 1914. Never officially disbanded or broken by discord, the club simply disappeared thereafter.

The story of the Pastellists was outlined by Doreen Bolger in the Metropolitan Museum of Art's 1989 catalogue of American pastels, revisited by Susan G. Larkin in 2013 in the context of the Armory Show, and briefly touched on in 2014 by Carol Troyen in her study of the Independents exhibition of 1910, which involved many of the same artists.[3] These recent mentions inspired the present essay, sparking an examination of the makeup and motives of this short-lived club and launching a deeper consideration of its place within the march of groundbreaking new artists' organizations and provocative special exhibitions during this period, from The Eight, formed in 1908, to the famous Armory Show in 1913, when modern art took root in the United States.[4]

Fig. 63
William Glackens
City Scene, c. 1910
Pastel on rust-colored reverse side of wallpaper fragment
12¼ × 18 in. (31.1 × 45.7 cm)
Brooklyn Museum; Bequest of Laura L. Barnes, 67.24.28

From a longer, wider perspective on modernism, the Pastellists also joined the remarkable proliferation of American artists' clubs and exhibition projects dating back to the 1860s, and the simultaneous, related expansion of interest in "minor" media, including all the graphic arts. The American watercolor movement, the first widespread turn by American artists to work on paper for exhibition and sale, began with the foundation of the American Watercolor Society (AWS) in 1866.[5] By the early 1880s, all corners of the American art community had been drawn into this energetic society and its popular annual exhibitions, which generated a second wave of more focused clubs and displays promoting other graphic media. First came etching, wood engraving, and black-and-white studies in ink and charcoal, and then a pastel society—the Society of Painters in Pastel—which presented its first exhibition in 1884 and also flourished for exactly four exhibitions before disappearing after 1890. The larger stories of the club explosion and the movement into new media might be viewed as an interconnected, modern social and economic phenomenon, fueled by the struggle of American artists to create a market for their work and find professional solidarity in a moment of tremendous change and insecurity. New talent, with few opportunities to show their work, took the situation in hand by forming groups, creating venues, and generating buzz. "Nobody can blame the artists for associating themselves in little coteries of their own. If they did not organize themselves into flying wedges of this kind they would never make any impression on the mob," noted the New York *Evening Mail* upon the debut of the Pastellists in 1911.[6] But alongside the challenge of earning a living and the appeal of camaraderie, there is also an artistic story, driven by restless curiosity and creativity; together practical, social, and aesthetic impulses propelled the choice to pursue new effects and materials.

This story of American artists' exploration of media low in the academic hierarchy of Western art has been noted before—by Theodore E. Stebbins Jr. in 1976[7] and by Dianne Pilgrim in her study of the first pastel society in 1978[8]—but this essay was focused by discovering the connection between watercolor and pastel, seen in the migration of key members of the AWS into the first pastel club in 1884, and the crossover in visual effects between the two media (or their outright mixing) in the next decades. This prompted the questions: Why pastel in 1884 and again in 1910? Who were the players, and what did they seek or gain from it? Perhaps pastel is a particularly modern choice, well adapted to modern concerns, carrying a message about the values and intentions of artists drawn in 1911 to this "brilliant, pleasing, graphic, subtle and alluring medium."[9]

To begin to answer these questions, one must consider the nature of pastel and its history, because the attributes of the medium have attracted artists over time for the same fundamental reasons. Based on the Italian term *pasta,* or paste, pastels are made from pure pigment, often modified with a white mineral filler and moistened with just enough binder—some form of sugar, glue, or gum—to make a dough that can be shaped into sticks and dried. Although they can vary in hardness according to the amount of binder, the sticks are inherently soft and crumbly, producing a powdery line that clings to the support largely by pressure.[10] The principal appeal of pastel resides in its bright, pure color, as the pigment particles are unsullied by a darkening or discoloring vehicle, like oil. More dense and saturated than watercolor, which shares a similar purity, a pastel "crayon" can deliver unsurpassed intensity of hue. Additionally, because the pigment particles are not coated in a vehicle that shines and reflects light sharply, the surface of the pastel drawing is matte. Each pigment particle absorbs and disperses light in all directions, creating a glow that produces rich color and a characteristic velvety texture.

Pastel is also quickly applied, offering line and color in one stroke. A rainbow of prepared colors saves the artist time in mixing tints, and there is no need to wait for work to dry, as with oil or watercolor. Speedy to use, it is also simple to correct, as false marks are quickly erased. All these qualities make pastel easy to learn—much easier than watercolor—for artists already adept at drawing as well as for amateurs with no experience. To this accessibility would be added the portability of the materials, which are lightweight; not messy, smelly, or oily; and ideal for fieldwork. In addition, pastels are inexpensive; they can be made at home or cheaply purchased. Although the finest, most costly French pastels, made with the most permanent pigments, would be preferred by discriminating artists, even an impoverished painter could acquire adequate materials, including proper paper, that allowed the production of images that were likewise less expensive to patrons. Finally, and most ineffably, its reputation as a secondary, less important, and less prestigious medium, by comparison to higher-status oil, tempera, or fresco painting, makes pastel an underdog that allows a certain freedom to the artist. Working in cheap materials frequently seen as second-rate, the artist is granted leeway to experiment and test expectations.[11]

These same qualities have a downside, beginning with the likelihood that artists working in a disparaged medium may find themselves struggling to be taken seriously or to claim just remuneration for their work. Materially, the most important drawback to pastel is its fragile surface, which can be easily disturbed by the artist in reworking, or by careless handling. Attempting to protect this delicate surface, most artists place their pastel work under glass, which reduces the tactile impact of the velvety texture, and many have sprayed their pastels with a fixative, which may alter the color and add shine, likewise diminishing the unique qualities of the work. The thrilling purity of the color and its tenuous adherence to the support produces the paradox of pastel, reiterated by writers since the eighteenth century: it is at

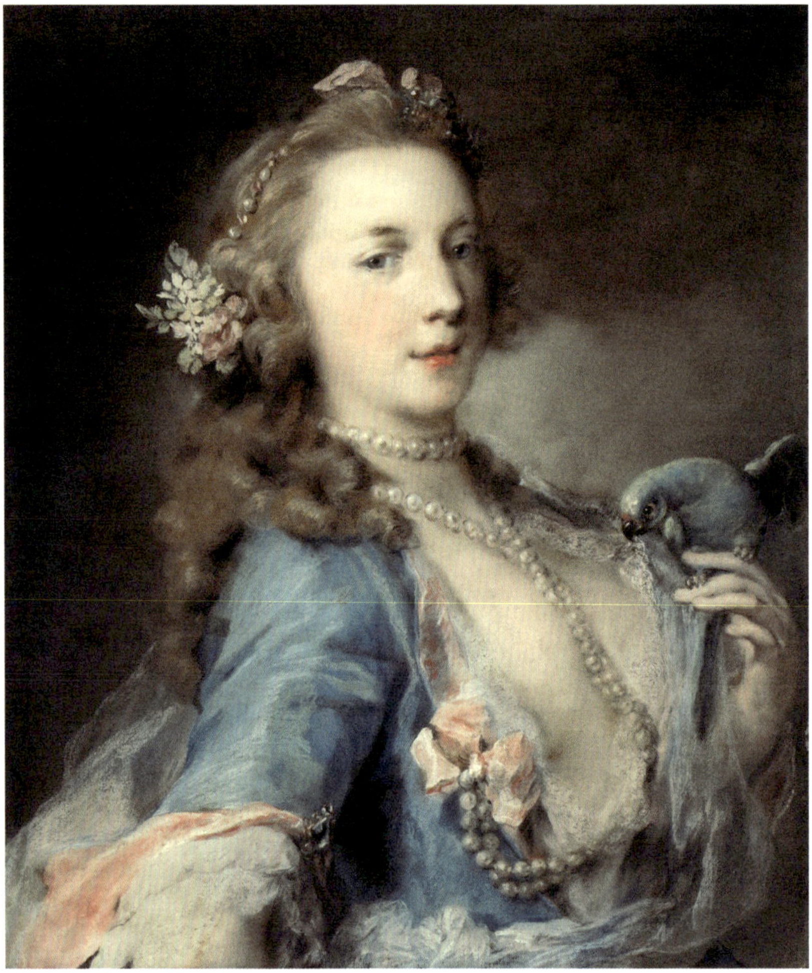

Fig. 64
Rosalba Carriera
A Young Lady with a Parrot, c. 1730
Pastel on blue laid paper mounted to laminated paperboard
23⅝ × 19¹¹⁄₁₆ in. (60 × 50 cm)
The Art Institute of Chicago; The Regenstein Collection, 1985.40

once the most permanent and the most fragile of media. Simplicity and accessibility also have had a negative effect: pastel is easy to learn, but it is also easy to be mediocre in pastel. The prevalence of weak or superficial work undermined respect for the medium at the height of its first popularity in the eighteenth century, when it came to be associated with amateurs, imitators, and women artists. In fact, pastel requires great drawing skill, along with confidence, decisiveness, and a light touch; done badly, however, the effect can be glib, flabby, or overly labored and woolly.

These qualities shaped the reputation of both the medium and its message, beginning in the eighteenth century, when pastel was first cultivated. From the outset, it embodied ideas of class status, stylishness, sensuousness, and affordability—a veritable package of modern concerns. Like watercolor, pastel as we know it is a recent invention, materially and artistically developed in the eighteenth century from older techniques, for new effects and purposes. Descended from Renaissance tricolor drawing, which combined black, white, and red or yellow chalk designs on tinted paper, the full-color, highly finished pastel portrait emerged in the early 1700s. Brought to Paris from Italy by the talented Rosalba Carriera (Fig. 64), pastel became all the rage by the midcentury in the hands of masters such as Maurice-Quentin de La Tour, who established the prestige of the medium among courtly patrons. These pastels prized realism and finish; their pink and blue "pastel" colors signaled Rococo gaiety. A light, fresh touch conveyed a sense of spontaneity that, along with the affluence and stylishness of the sitter, delivered a message of immediacy: the joy of the moment and of life "a la mode." The sensuality of pastel enhanced the mood of pleasure, adding to the sexy, intimate, visually delicious spirit of the image.[12]

The success of the early pastel masters bred contempt, however, as imitators flooded the market with mediocre, inexpensive portraits, while haughty academicians did their best to maintain a hierarchy of media based on the priority of oil painting. Watercolor would find a place of prestige in Britain, but pastel fell out of favor everywhere after 1800, when it became associated with lady amateurs and the frivolity of the ancien régime. Its reemergence in the 1830s accompanied the restoration of the monarchy in France, which inspired waves of Rococo nostalgia that would continue for decades, enduring in the United States as the "Colonial Revival" well into the 1920s.

A new kind of modernity in pastel came first from Jean-François Millet, who broke from the aristocratic portrait mold to produce a torrent of large, defiantly underclass, outdoor figure subjects in the late 1860s. Remarkable for their broad, hatched color, with little detail and no careful modeling, Millet's pastels let the medium (and the artist) find blunt expressiveness. His innovation was taken up by the Impressionists—including Édouard Manet, Berthe Morisot, Camille Pissarro, Pierre-Auguste Renoir, and, most enthusiastically, Edgar Degas and Mary Cassatt—who revived the spirit of Rococo spontaneity and consistently included pastels in their exhibitions beginning in 1874. Bringing pastels to the modern venues favored by the Impressionists, Degas in particular sought out subjects in cabarets, ballet theaters, and intimate boudoir settings, employing his idiosyncratic viewpoints and awkward, cropped figures. His first interest in the medium in the 1870s grew more serious in the 1880s, when he needed income and deliberately sought the attention of collectors, who admired the strong color, suggestive handling, and affordability of pastels. Long practice, as well as the weakening of his eyesight, made pastel his preferred medium after 1890, when he produced many of his largest and most adventuresome pastels. An experimental technician, Degas pushed the medium with novel techniques, adding pastel over his monotypes and wetting and steaming the pigments so they could be worked with a brush. Like the artists of the past, he used tinted paper to create a middle tone, but frequently buried the surface completely with dense hatchings of color, fixing interim layers in order to pile on new pigment.[13] An example of such work, *The Ballet*, probably the mixed-media pastel now known as *Rehearsal of the Ballet* (Fig. 65), was seen in New York in 1878 at the AWS annual, where work on paper appeared in all media, including prints and pastels.

Work by Degas also would have been known to American artists and patrons in Paris, including Mary Cassatt, who eagerly studied his pastels before ever meeting him in person. Ultimately, their friendship would propel her development in the medium. Taking on a classic Impressionist subject of seeing and being seen in a concert hall, Cassatt employed Degas's arsenal of dense layering techniques in *At the Theater* (Fig. 66), shown at her debut with the Impressionists in 1879. Although the themes of modernity, stylishness, and display carry over from eighteenth-century pastel, Cassatt's glowing color, augmented with metallic pigment in the fan, demonstrates how the modern palette moved beyond the stereotypical "pastel" tints of the Rococo. Likewise, although the skin and facial features of the woman are delicately modeled in the best eighteenth-century fashion, Cassatt ranged to a new extreme of gesture and suggestiveness in the costume

Fig. 65
Edgar Degas
Rehearsal of the Ballet, c. 1876
Gouache and pastel over monotype on laid paper
23¹³⁄₁₆ × 29³⁄₁₆ in. (60.5 × 74.2 cm)
The Nelson-Atkins Museum of Art, Kansas City, MO; Purchase: The Kenneth A. and Helen F. Spencer Foundation Acquisition Fund, F73-30

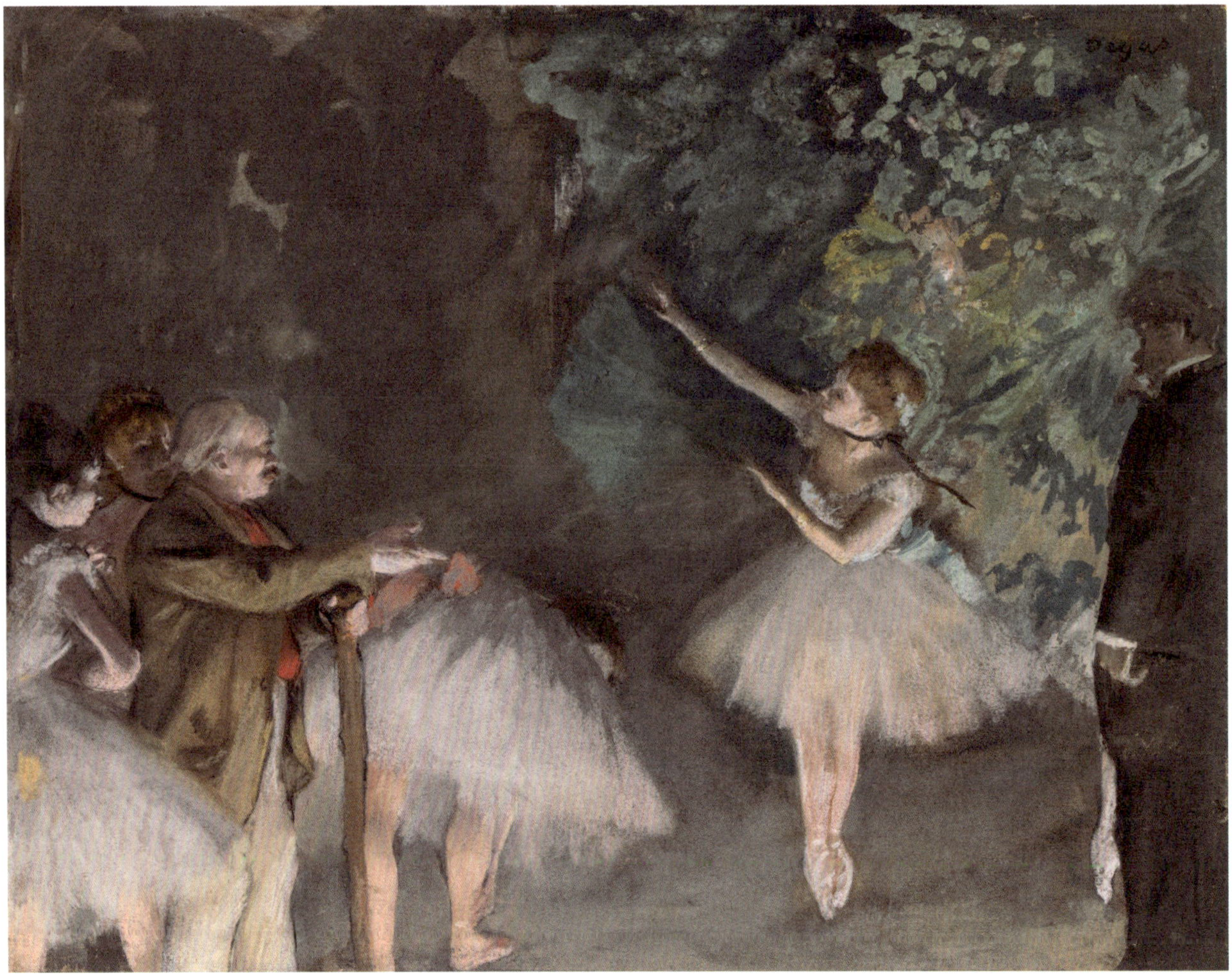

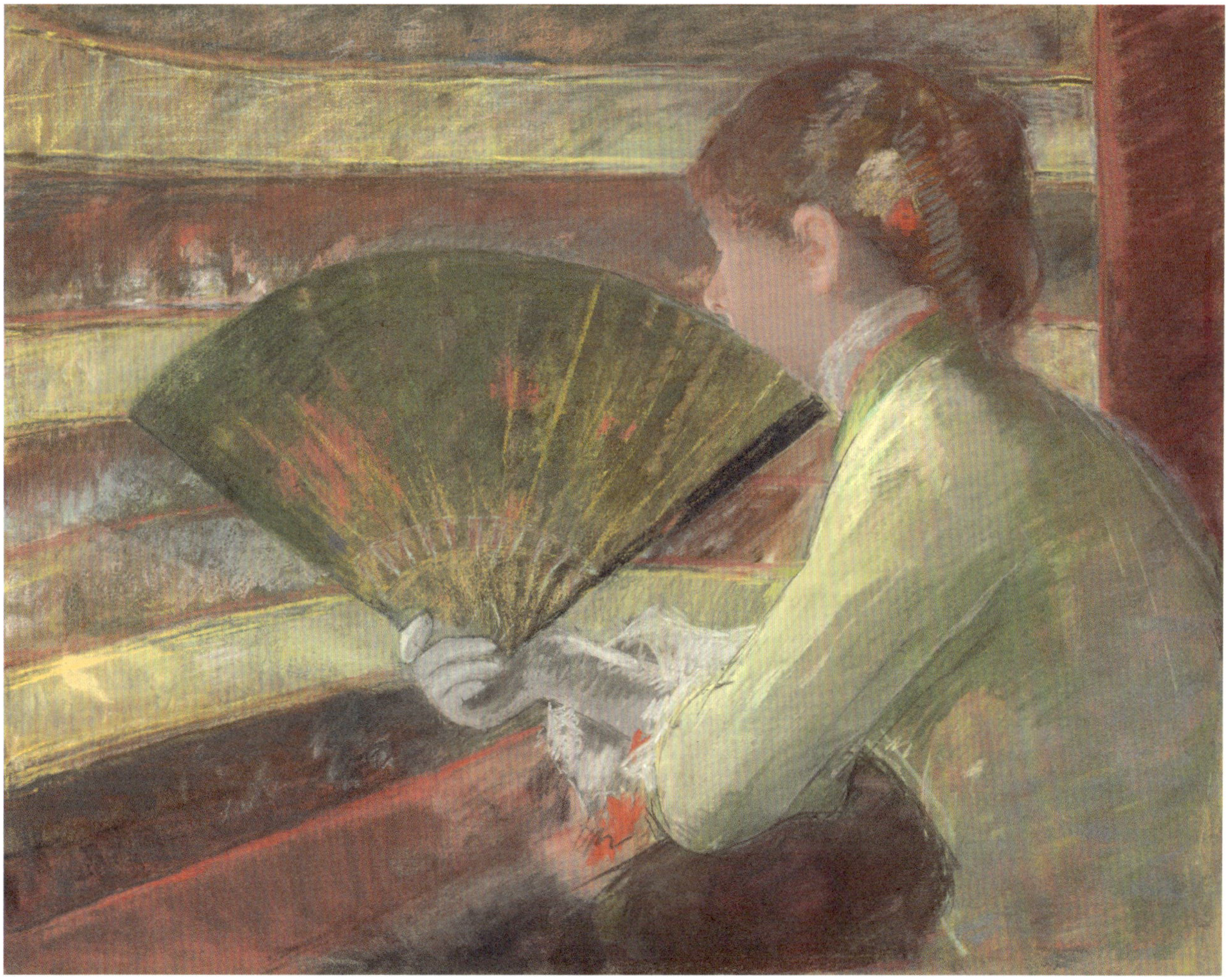

Fig. 66
Mary Cassatt
At the Theater (*Au théâtre*) or
In the Loge, c. 1879
Pastel with gold metallic paint
on canvas
Sheet: 25⁹⁄₁₆ × 31¾ in. (64.9 × 80.6 cm)
Philadelphia Museum of Art; Gift of
Mrs. Sargent McKean, 1950, 1950-52-1

and background.[14] Such large, heavily worked pieces by Degas and Cassatt joined a wider enthusiasm for exhibition pieces in pastel by other European artists, particularly Degas's friend, the Italian Giuseppe De Nittis, whose noteworthy exhibition of big, bravura figure compositions in pastels in Paris in 1881 sparked widespread commentary and enthusiasm among American artists.[15]

However, the most important catalyst for many American artists was James McNeill Whistler, who would pioneer a diametrically opposed style in pastel in this decade. Following his victorious but financially disastrous lawsuit against John Ruskin, Whistler spent fourteen months in Venice, beginning in the fall of 1879, hoping to recover from bankruptcy with a suite of etchings. Taking up pastels at the same time, he returned to London late in 1880 to mount successive exhibitions of prints and pastels in 1881 that redeemed both his critical reputation and his bank account. Noting that his fellow artists were "quite startled" by the brilliancy of his drawings, he predicted correctly that "the pastel business will become quite the fashion."[16]

Whistler applied pastel to landscape with an Impressionist mission, working quickly on small sheets to capture elusive effects of light and color. Choosing tinted paper, including unusual tan and brown pages, he sketched in charcoal or black chalk a drawing that echoes the liveliness of his etching line, and then added small flecks or rubbed veils of bright pastel (Fig. 67). Intending an effect of spontaneity and immediacy, these works were in fact carefully studied and restrained, exquisitely economical and without the flash or elaboration of Salon pastels. The small scale, delicate handling, atmospheric power, and simplicity of these pastels offered something startlingly new: framed and exhibited, they were (as many critics complained) remarkably unfinished by conventional standards, but complete statements of Whistler's aesthetic, first seen in the famous minimalist Nocturnes a decade earlier.[17]

Whistler's revolutionary approach shaped a band of American artists, mostly students in Munich of the Cincinnati artist Frank Duveneck. The "Duveneck Boys" shared lodgings with Whistler in Venice in 1879–80 and witnessed the creation of his new work in etching and pastel. Among them, the illustrator, printmaker, and painter Robert Blum would become the driving force of the American Society of Painters in Pastel, the first group to promote the medium and the only one in this decade entirely inaugurated by artists.[18] Blum returned to New York from Venice late in 1880, just as Whistler headed back to London. Within weeks, he submitted blurred, atmospheric watercolors to the AWS exhibition of 1881, such as *To the Lido* (private collection), inspired by both Whistler's etchings and his pastels.[19] Within a year, his enthusiasm for pastel sparked the creation of thc ncw group, and his entries in its first exhibition in 1884, including *A Chat* (now titled *Girls Sewing*; Fig. 68), echoed the fashionable contemporary figures and avant-garde composition of De Nittis's work. Blum's other entries

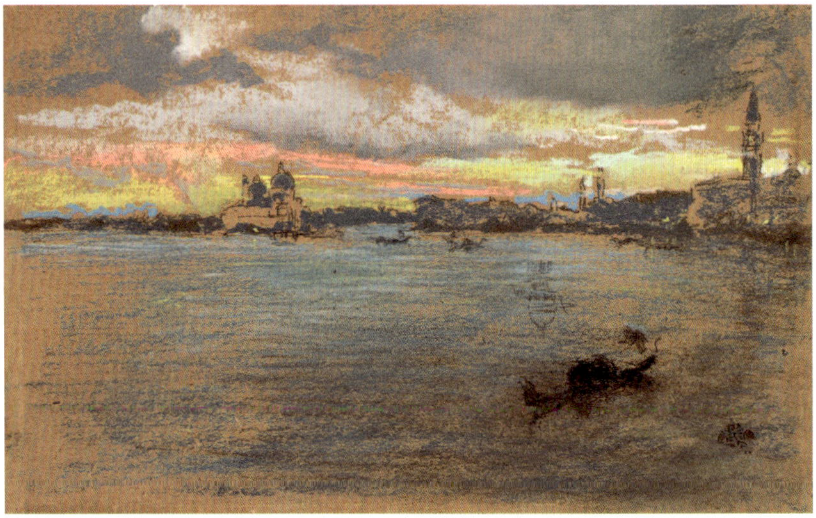

Fig. 67
James McNeill Whistler
The Storm—Sunset, 1880
Pastel on brown wove paper
7⁵⁄₁₆ × 11⁷⁄₁₆ in. (18.6 × 29 cm)
Harvard Art Museums, Fogg Museum, Cambridge, MA; Bequest of Grenville L. Winthrop, 1943.624

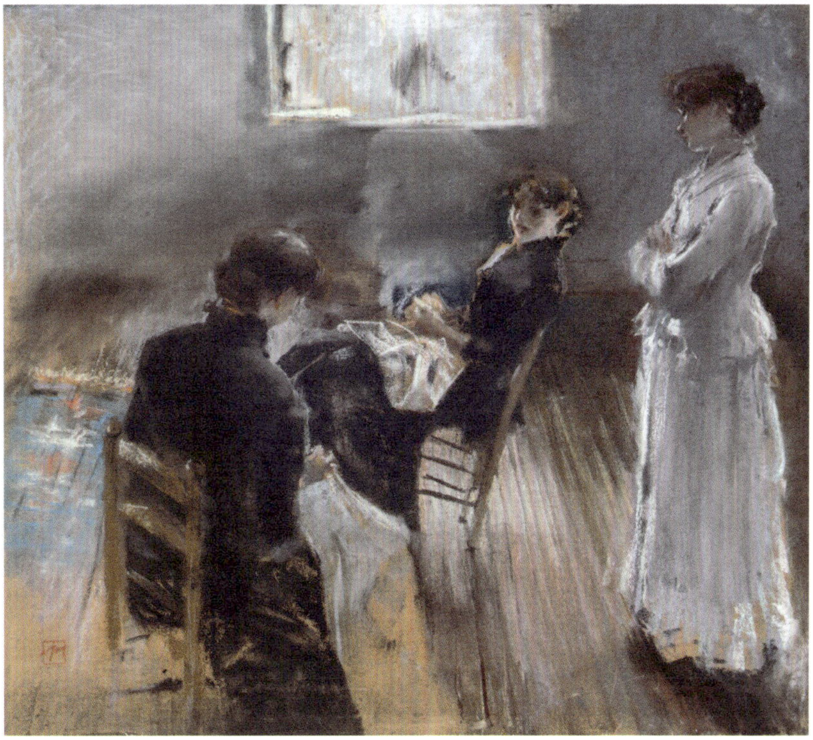

Fig. 68
Robert Blum
Girls Sewing, c. 1884
Pastel on fine sandpaper mounted on heavy board
17½ × 19⅝ in. (44.5 × 49.8 cm)
Cincinnati Art Museum; Museum Purchase 1925.51

evoked the atmospheric urban views of Whistler, reflected in *58th Street Station at Sixth Avenue, New York City*, shown in 1884 as *The L Road—Impression* (Pennsylvania Academy of the Fine Arts, Philadelphia).

Blum, the first president of the Painters in Pastel, cofounded the group with William Merritt Chase, another friend from the Duveneck circle in Munich. Older, better established, and unfailingly tuned into the newest thing, Chase also followed the mode of De Nittis, contributing work to the group's first exhibition that shared the dense, brilliant style of the mainstream in Paris and the masters of the eighteenth century. With lush, saturated color and a polished finish, Chase's figure subjects, such as *Study of Flesh Color and Gold* (Fig. 69), sought the sensuous, velvet surface effects typical of Carriera (see Fig. 64). Landscapes by Chase, such as *Terrace, Prospect Park* (c. 1887, Smithsonian American Art Museum, Smithsonian Institution, Washington, DC) with its bright flecks of color, strike an Impressionist note, although larger and more formal in composition and finish than Whistler's intimate pastels.[20] These two poles would bracket the American pastel world of the 1880s: an intense, developed figure style, and the impressionistic landscape mode of Whistler, gently represented in the work of another of the Duveneck Boys, John Henry Twachtman (Fig. 70), and more expressionistically seen in the work of the American lodestar in Munich, J. Frank Currier.[21]

The excitement of Blum, Chase, and their friends in Painters in Pastel (including German-trained Twachtman and the French-trained

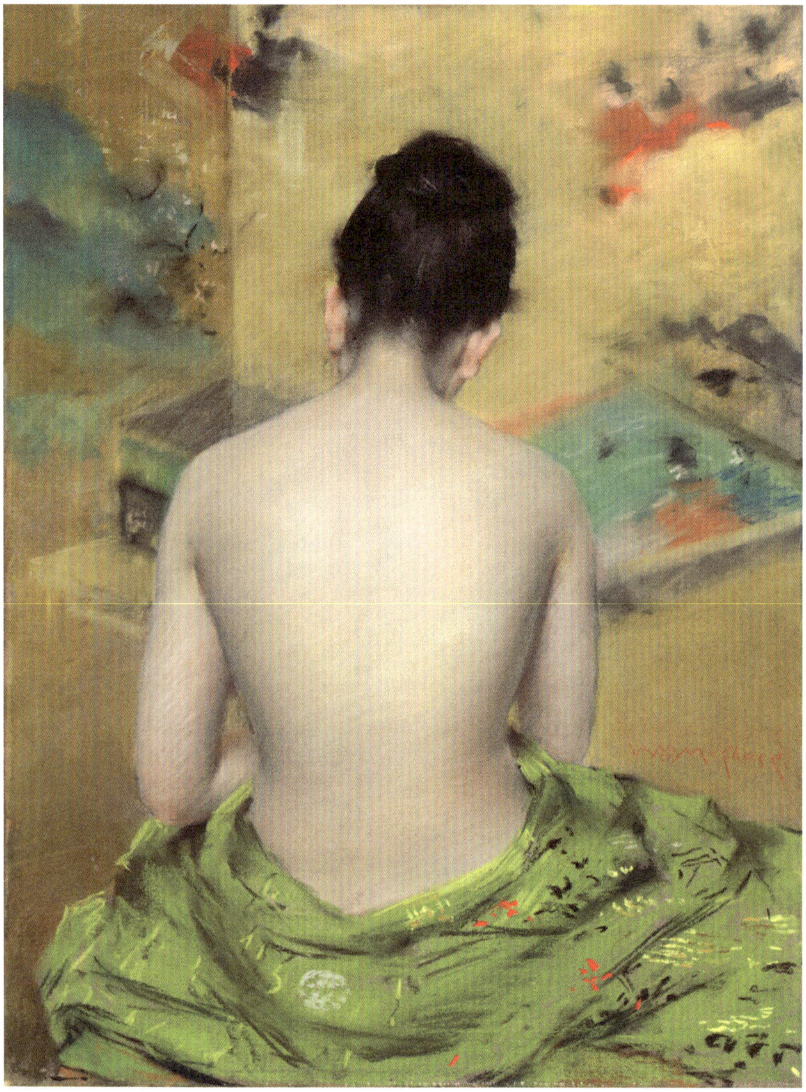

Fig. 69
William Merritt Chase
Study of Flesh Color and Gold, 1888
Pastel on paper coated with mauve-gray grit (on strainer)
18 × 13 in. (45.7 × 33 cm)
National Gallery of Art, Washington, DC; Gift of Raymond J. and Margaret Horowitz 2007.94.2

J. Carroll Beckwith, Childe Hassam, and Weir), all echoing the rising interest in the medium in Europe, prompts the question, why pastel, at this moment? As noted, this was a time of expansion into all the graphic arts, when restless artists were seeking new expressive frontiers and new sources of inspiration. Adventurousness and experimentation characterized the transatlantic art community. Ambitious and cosmopolitan Americans like Chase and Blum sampled different fields, including illustration and decoration, and various media, such as charcoal, pen and ink, watercolor, pastel, and etching. Disdaining specialization—in one subject or medium—these artists exemplified the notion that to be modern is to experiment and to work across media.

Visually, this generation was enticed by effects of bright, saturated, pure color—which could be delivered instantly in pastel. They were also compelled by the search for personal style or "signature" handling—that is, individuality expressed in spontaneous, calligraphic gesture—likewise accomplished with flair in pastel. Both artists and connoisseurs began to value the sketch for its revelation of process and artistic personality. The appearance of the sketch as a legitimate exhibition piece, first debated in the United States in the exhibitions of the AWS in the mid-1870s and then asserted in the annuals of the rebellious Society of American Artists after 1877, signaled the arrival of Impressionist aesthetics.[22] Avant-gardists, in both Europe and the United States, were also cultivating a flat, dry, matte surface, soft and blurred, as seen across all the graphic media of the 1880s, especially as artists begin to mix materials in unorthodox ways, layering watercolor and gouache over pastel or charcoal or monotypes (see Fig. 65), adding pastel to watercolor, or glazing with metallic pigment (see Fig. 66) for an iridescent glow. Seeking visual unity and a stronger sense of two-dimensional design, oil painters valued the flattening effect of a matte surface and ceased varnishing their pictures.[23]

Accompanying all this artistic exploration was also a search for patronage, hoping to tempt collectors with small, affordable works on paper. Trading on the novelty of the medium and the popularity of the sketch, and pricing their works on paper lower than oils, the Painters in Pastel were very disappointed by lack of sales in 1884. Although the group's exhibition was a critical success, the failure to recoup the costs of mounting the show may have been one major reason members did not muster another display for four years.[24]

For the Painters in Pastel, the message in the medium was familiar from the previous century: modern, intimate subjects conveyed a sense of contemporary life, stylishness, and the momentary. The small scale of

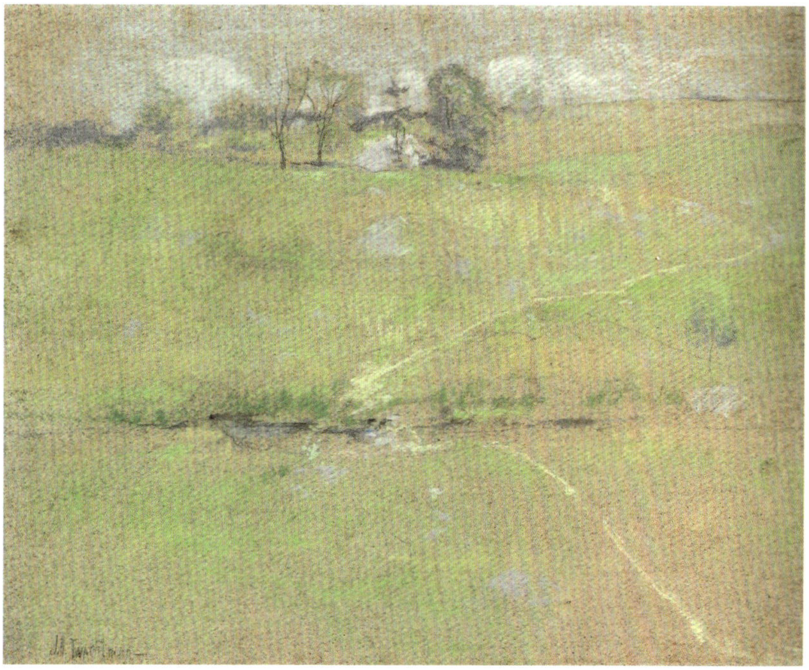

Fig. 70
John Henry Twachtman
Path in the Hills, Branchville, Connecticut, c. 1888–91
Pastel on paper
10 × 12 in. (25.4 × 30.5 cm)
Location unknown (Spanierman Gallery, New York)
In Lisa N. Peters, *John Twachtman (1853–1902): A "Painter's Painter"* (New York: Spanierman Gallery, 2006), 129

most of the works anticipated domestic placement; affordable for both artists and patrons, the pastel beckoned (or aspired) to a wider market of collectors. What was new was the focus on the informal side of the artist and the display of spontaneous, experimental, personal expression. As the critics recognized, the launch into a new medium brought risk and invited edgier as well as more playful work. Also new was an interest in the inherent qualities of pastel and the condemnation of those working against the "natural" virtues of the medium. While this call for truth to materials had a modern ring, the flip side of this argument reinforced old stereotypes, as some voices insisted that pastel was only appropriate to lighthearted subjects and impressionistic handling.[25]

The disappearance of the Society of Painters in Pastel after 1890 has been credited to the distraction of the founders: Blum took off on an illustration assignment to Japan for three years in the spring of 1890, and Chase launched his school in New York's Shinnecock Hills the following summer. But the project was ephemeral from the outset, with no constitution or bylaws, no clubhouse, and no dues, entirely driven by the enthusiasm of the participants, who changed over time at the invitation of the core members. Inherently bohemian, the group prized the qualities of spontaneity and fun that they also enjoyed in the medium itself. If the wish to bring work before the public for sale was a motive, new exhibition opportunities opened in December 1890 with the formation of the New York Water Color Club. Led by Childe Hassam, a veteran of the Painters in Pastel, this new venue—and others in Boston, Chicago, and Philadelphia—offered a forum for pastels, which were by this time disallowed at the AWS annual.[26] In fact, the death of the Painters in Pastel did nothing to slow the rising popularity of the medium, which received a jolt of support from a major exhibition of Whistler's pastels in New York in 1889. Societies in France (1885) and England (1888–90; 1898) manifested the new surge of interest in pastel, Cassatt and Degas produced some of their finest work, and startling new talent, such as Odilon Redon, arose among a crowd of European pastellists. Even as Whistler's evanescent style rose in influence, large and complex work remained popular. Among Americans, new converts such as Edwin Austin Abbey (Fig. 71) shaped the popularity of the medium with major shows of pastels in New York and London in 1895 and again in New York the following year.[27]

The taste for pastel was especially strong in Philadelphia, where Cassatt's family and most of the faculty at the Pennsylvania Academy of the Fine Arts (PAFA) were boosters. Thomas Anshutz, Cecilia Beaux, Hugh Breckenridge, John McClure Hamilton, Henry McCarter, and Chase—all teaching at PAFA at the turn of the century—used the medium and encouraged their students, who would include a new generation of realists and illustrators, including most of The Eight. With the exception of John Sloan, all of the members of the Ashcan School would often work in pastel, and some from this group—especially

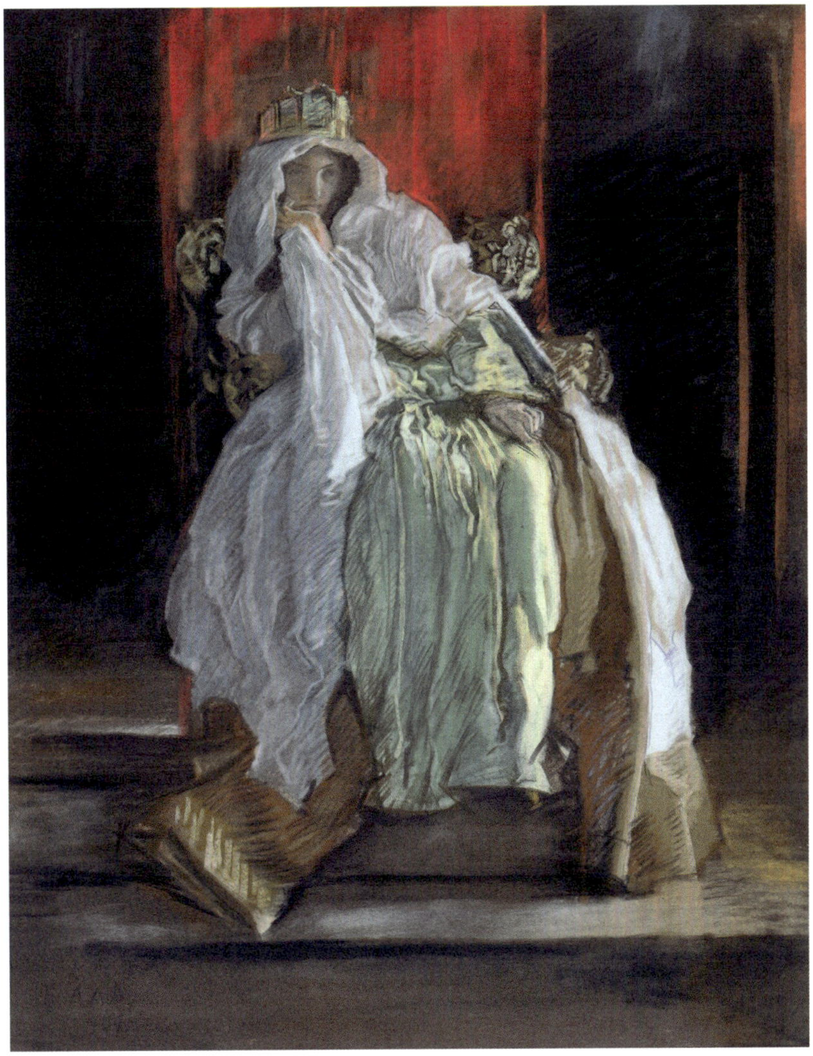

Fig. 71
Edwin Austin Abbey
The Queen in "Hamlet," 1895
Pastel on paperboard
Sheet: 27⅞ × 21⅞ in. (70.8 × 55.6 cm)
Smithsonian American Art Museum, Smithsonian Institution, Washington, DC; Gift of Sen. Stuart Symington and Rep. James W. Symington, 1973.28.1

William Glackens and Everett Shinn—would be at the center of the next pastel society, while many young moderns, such as Morton Schamberg, Joseph Stella, and Georgia O'Keeffe, would learn from the example of these same teachers during the 1890s.

For this new generation, pastel was not a discovery, as it had been in the 1880s, so much as a rising tide of interest, best demonstrated by the belated attention of the increasingly old-fashioned American Watercolor Society. As its fortunes sagged around 1905, the AWS reconsidered its exclusive policies and expanded its show in 1906 to include etchings and black-and-white illustrations; in 1907, the society invited pastellists, who showed up "by the square yard" in 1908.[28] A vogue seems to have taken hold of many of the society's old guard, who took a stab at pastel in the years between 1908 and 1912, while many younger artists—such as Elmer Livingston MacRae, Jerome Myers, and Shinn—would send pastels to the AWS before leaping to form a new club, the Pastellists, in 1910.[29]

The general wish to appreciate the increasingly popular medium of pastel on its own, in a more intimate space apart from large, mixed exhibitions, may have been an impetus for the formation of the new society. However, as with the case of Robert Blum in the 1880s, it was one enterprising pastel specialist, MacRae, who made things happen. Less well known today as an artist than as an organizer, MacRae was one of those gregarious, indefatigable, indispensable persons capable of running a guesthouse at an artist colony (Holley House, in Cos Cob, Connecticut) while being willing to serve as secretary or treasurer of three different artists' groups, including the Pastellists, the Greenwich Society of Artists, and, most notably, the American Association of Painters and Sculptors (AAPS), the society propelling the Armory Show in 1913. A pupil of Twachtman and a disciple of Weir, who both taught him at the Art Students League in New York and then at the summer colony of Cos Cob, MacRae produced Impressionist winter landscapes, Japanese-inspired still lifes, portraits, and figure studies of his family in both pastel and oil.[30] It was in pastel, however, that the critic Henry Tyrell found "real distinction and individuality" in MacRae's work, which took advantage of the atmospheric qualities of the medium.[31] The examples MacRae produced in pastel showed him working in both of the medium's recent traditions: the Whistlerian path of suggestive landscape (also seen in Weir's and Twachtman's pastels), and the market-savvy Rococo tradition of portraiture, particularly of children, in a delicate, animated style (Figs. 72, 73).

MacRae's pastels won more attention than his oils in his first major showing in New York, in a 1909 group exhibition at the home and shop of the decorator Clara Davidge, a few doors away from Glackens's studio on Washington Square. He featured pastels in his two solo shows at Davidge's new Madison Gallery (which Davidge opened late in 1909),

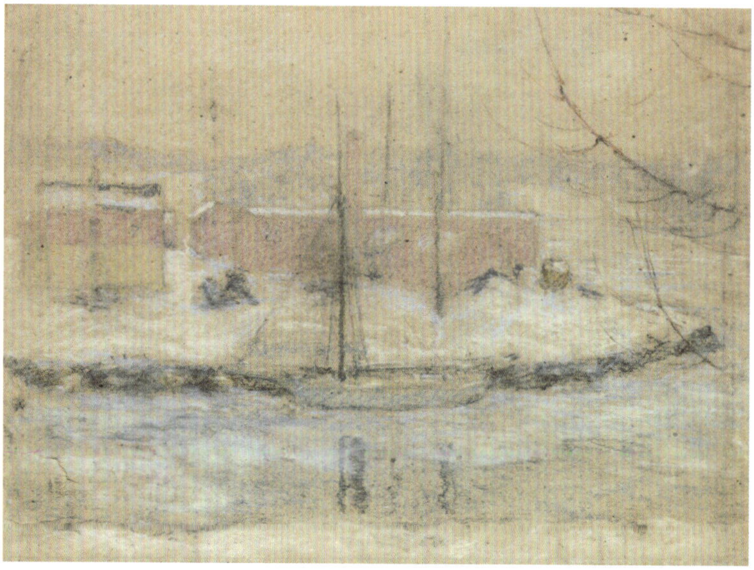

Fig. 72
Elmer Livingston MacRae
Harbor Scene in Winter, n.d.
Pastel on paperboard
18½ × 24⅜ in. (47 × 61.9 cm)
Location unknown
In Swann Auction Galleries, New York, *American Art*, June 4, 2015, no. 2386, lot 24

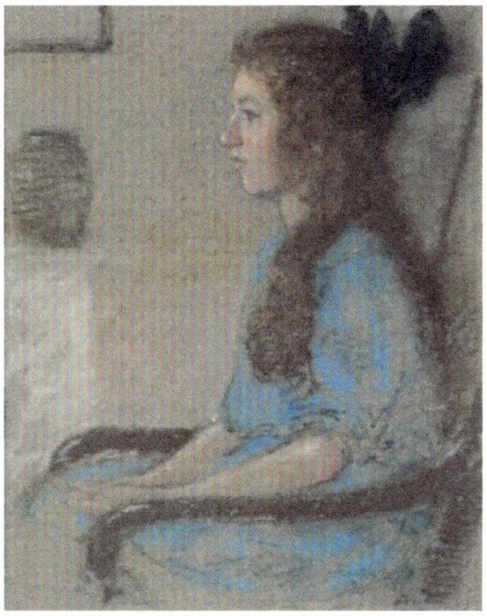

Fig. 73
Elmer Livingston MacRae
Portrait of a Seated Girl in Blue, 1911
Pastel on tan paper
13¾ × 11 in. (34.9 × 27.9 cm)
Location unknown
In Northeast Auctions, Portsmouth, NH, *28th Annual Summer Americana Auction*, August 2, 2014, lot 212

presented them in group shows at the Powell and Macbeth galleries, and tirelessly sent them to all the watercolor annuals.[32] From the look of his campaign, it might appear that the hungry, thirty-five-year-old MacRae's search for exposure and for portrait clients instigated the meeting the artist called to organize the Pastellists in August 1910. Perhaps he hoped to follow the example of the attention-grabbing group exhibition of the Independents that April, although no critique of the establishment seems to have been intended, apart from a wish for a new, more sympathetic, more inclusive forum; in fact, members of the National Academy of Design and the American Watercolor Society supported the new group. It sufficed that energy and ambition were rising; a time for new venues and art associations had dawned.[33]

The Pastellists mobilized quickly to open an inaugural show on Tuesday, January 10, 1911, at the new Folsom Galleries,[34] packed with sixty-seven works by twenty-one artists, including a stated limit of twenty members and one guest exhibitor (Cassatt). The following Sunday, according to MacRae's diary, an afternoon reception was thronged with visitors. Some must have been enticed by a press release quoted in several papers, promoting the new group and its avowedly noncommercial mission "to exhibit intimate studies or pictures which the artists have enjoyed in the performance; also to get away as far as possible from the commercial aspect."[35] Echoing the sentiments of the earlier Painters in Pastel, who likewise were praised for work done "out of genuine love of the doing," with "no mercenary or commercial serpent lurking under the flowers," the Pastellists were nonetheless—like their forebearers—keen to put work before the public, courting critical attention and hoping for patronage.[36] MacRae, for one, tracked every visiting critic and every sale in his diary. Taking a cue from Whistler's famous 1883 "Yellow and White" exhibition in its tiny, color-coordinated room, the group would seek out the cozy scale and red walls of the Folsom "parlor" to create an invitingly intimate installation, suited to the scale of most pastels and apt for collectors sizing up work that might fit in their own homes.[37] The publicity and the staging paid off: unlike the Painters in Pastel in the 1880s, the Pastellists' first show was a financial success, doubtlessly encouraging the second show ten months later, in time for Christmas, and a third one just a few months later, in February 1912.[38] From their announced intentions as well as their actions, it was clear that the medium had a message: pastel signaled personal, experimental work, not major, labored, "serious" effort. And it was an affordable and accessible commodity, suited to the domestic spaces of modest collectors.

Progressive in its art-for-art's-sake posture, the exhibition also conjured eighteenth-century taste, encapsulating this moment when both the Rococo (Colonial) revival and the advent of modernism surged simultaneously on both sides of the Atlantic. MacRae's profile portraits stand with the stylish charcoal and pastel society portraits by John

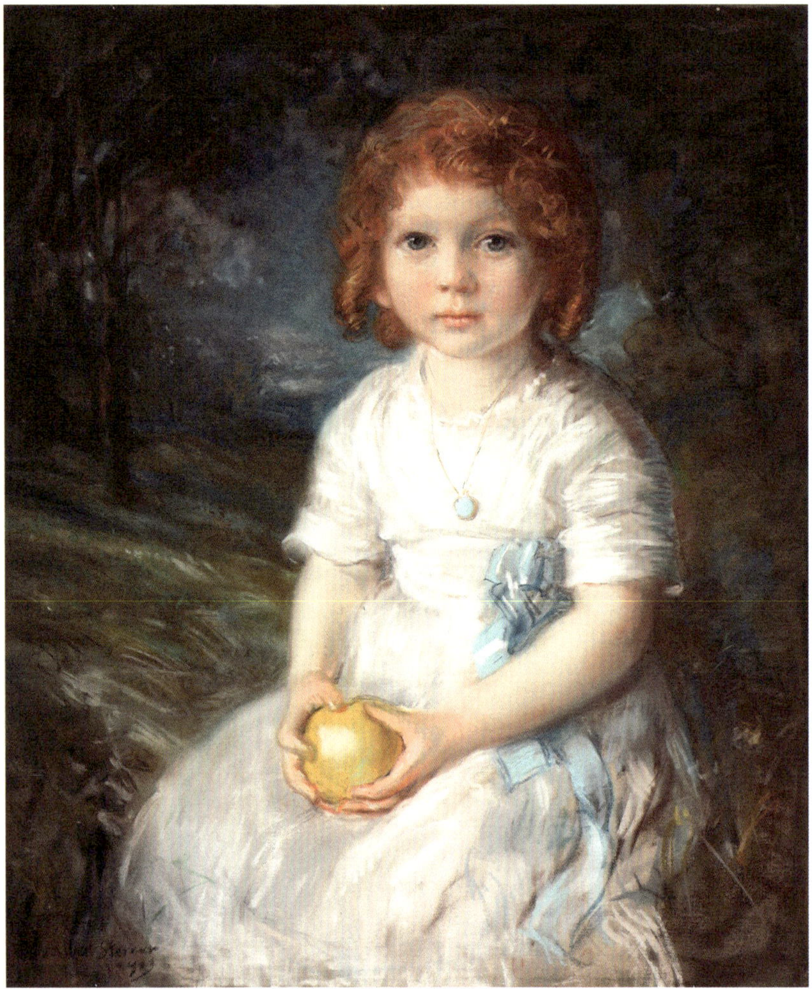

Fig. 74
Albert Sterner
Olivia, 1903
Pastel on canvas
27 × 22 in. (68.6 × 55.9 cm)
Location unknown
In Heritage Auction Galleries, Dallas, *American and European Fine Art*, November 11–12, 2009, no. 5030, lot 65069

Singer Sargent and another club member, Albert Sterner, whose work added a note of Gainsborough to the first two shows of the Pastellists (Fig. 74). Sterner, an English-born, French-trained illustrator, cultivated an elegant class of crayon and pastel portraiture that echoed both Holbein and the Rococo masters.[39] The figure subjects of Sterner and MacRae also make us look again at the pastels of Mary Cassatt, such as the work probably shown late in 1911 at the second exhibition of the Pastellists as *L'Enfant à l'Orange* (*Portrait of Margaret Milligan Sloane [no. 2]*, Fig. 75), to consider the legacy of eighteenth-century portraiture in Europe and the United States. Cassatt was well known in New York at this time, when her work was promoted by her dealer, Durand-Ruel, and seen in the watercolor annuals. She had also been represented in the first of the Pastellists shows in January, probably thanks again to the Durand-Ruel Gallery, where a solo exhibition of her work appeared simultaneously.[40] Her work was given a place of honor in each of these first two displays, adding a note of seniority, costliness, and accomplishment in the more intense pastel mode popular in the 1880s. "Cassatt is, of course a past master in the art of using

Fig. 75
Mary Cassatt
Portrait of Margaret Milligan Sloane (no. 2), 1893
Pastel on gray paper
32 × 26 in. (81.3 × 66 cm)
Private collection

pastel," noted the *New York Times*, "but her method is not that used by most of her companions. Crisp and fresh as her colors are she uses a fuller palette and covers her ground more completely than they and achieves a result more nearly akin to oil painting."[41]

Seeking similarly prestigious names, MacRae recruited others of this older generation from his own circles at the Art Students League and the Cos Cob artists' colony. Predictably, he first turned for support from his teacher, Weir (a member of the earlier Painters in Pastel), and the well-established pastellist Thomas Wilmer Dewing.[42] From Weir, or their network of friends, probably came two examples by Twachtman (another alum of the earlier group, who had died in 1902) that

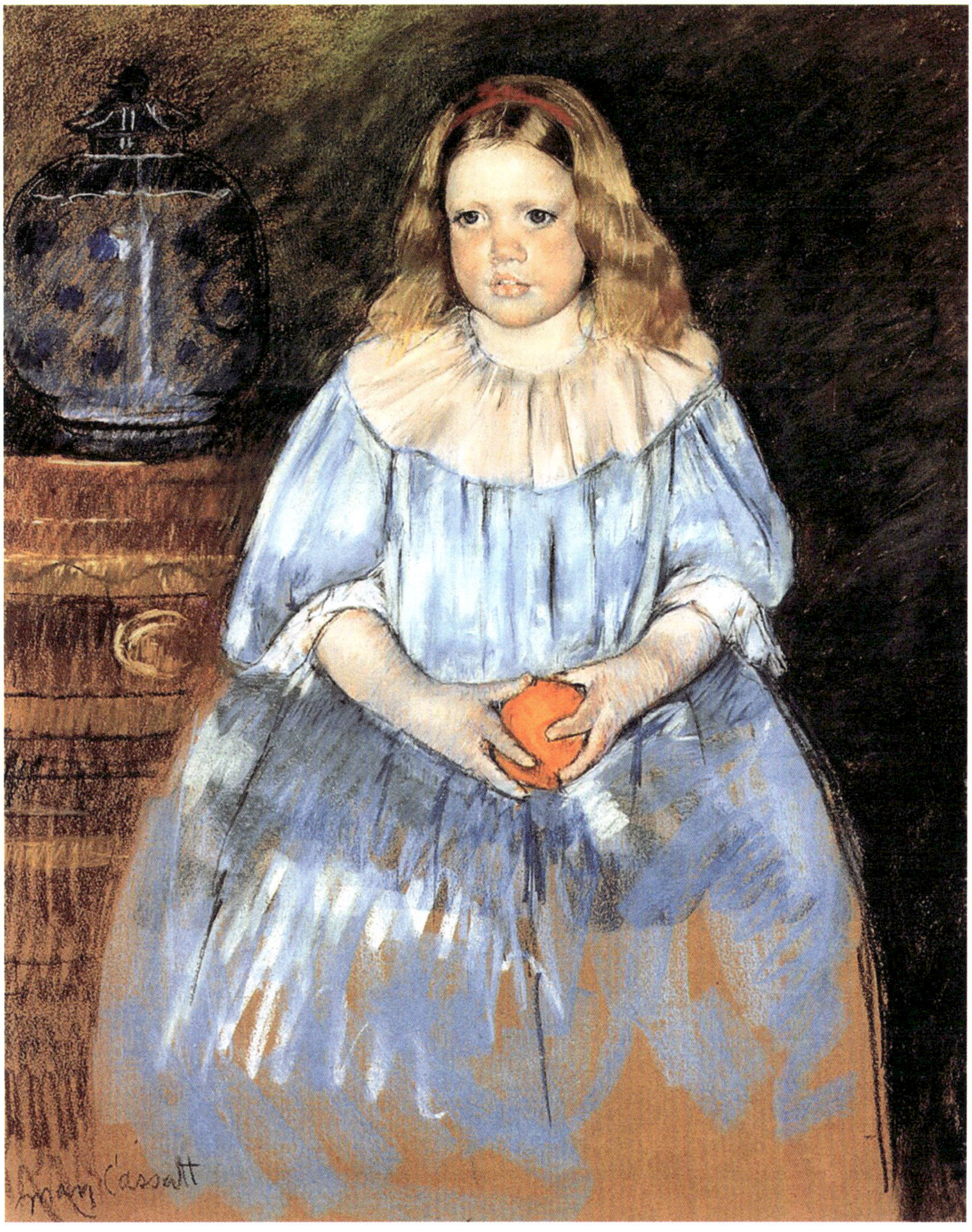

Fig. 76
Jerome Myers
Park Bench at Night, 1909
Pastel on paperboard
15 × 18 1/16 in. (38.1 × 45.9 cm)
Hirshhorn Museum and Sculpture Garden, Smithsonian Institution, Washington, DC, Gift of Joseph H. Hirshhorn, 1966, 66.3759

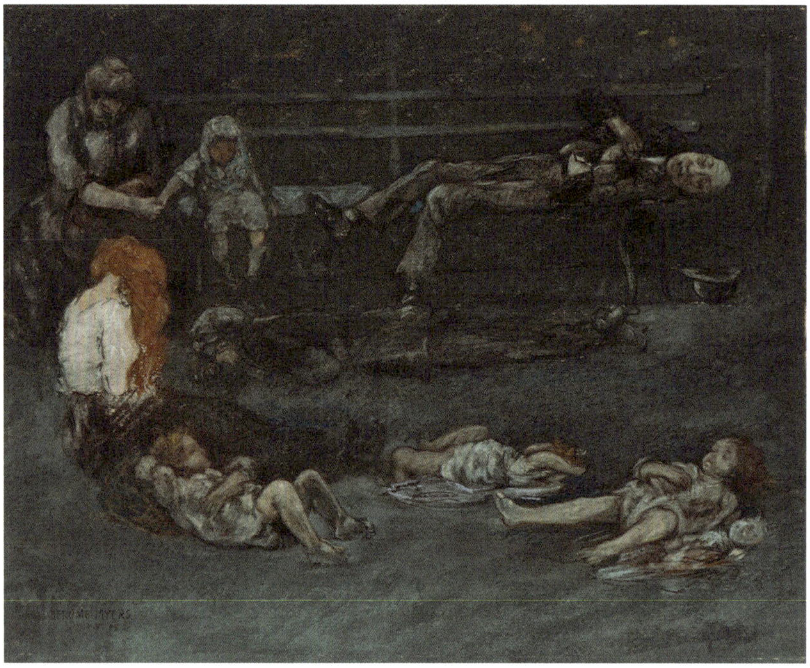

appeared in the club's second show, late in 1911. From this same Cos Cob circle came Childe Hassam—also an experienced pastellist and an exhibitor with the earlier society—although he did not submit work until sending five in 1914. A younger landscapist in the Twachtman-Weir community, Ernest Lawson, was recruited right at the outset: with no previous experience in the medium, he submitted two pastels to the group's first two shows.

MacRae then reached out to Jerome Myers to help build a list of additional recruits.[43] One of the few in the group who might have been described as a pastel specialist, Myers did not take up oils until about 1907. He worked in the urban realist circle of Henri and Sloan, producing generally upbeat New York street scenes, usually with children, only occasionally showing poverty and squalor. His *Park Bench at Night* (Fig. 76), perhaps a work shown in the third pastel exhibition of 1912, uses dark paper to create the predawn atmosphere of the Lower East Side, where whole families might sleep along the shore of the East River on a hot summer night. "Here were no derelicts," wrote Myers, "only industrious people enjoying their night of cool river breezes."[44] With Myers, MacRae would invite the progressive artists that showed with him at the Madison Gallery or were part of the Independents, such as Bellows, Glackens, Lawson, Samuel Halpert, Walt Kuhn, Jonas Lie, and Allen Tucker.

Neither MacRae nor Myers was elected to the society's most public-facing post, however; that honor (chairman of the Board of Control) went to the French-born and trained Léon Dabo, who represented the Whistler lineage of delicate, poetic pastel. Four to six "low-keyed, blue tonal river scenes . . . by that modern Whistler, Léon Dabo," appeared in each of the society's four exhibitions.[45] Probably resembling the banded, misty marine *Seascape* (Fig. 77), such work was praised as a "soothing caress," akin—like Whistler's Nocturnes—to music.[46] Such work was old-guard by 1911, although Dabo consistently identified with the progressives, showed with the Independents in 1908 and 1910, and would be among the organizers of the Armory Show; his genteel, liberal position made him an acceptable leader to most parties in the new group.[47]

The other veteran pastellist in the first two exhibitions was Everett Shinn, who sent *Fifth Avenue Bus in Snowstorm* (similar to his *Winter on 21st Street, New York*, Fig. 78), recognized by the critics as dating from his earliest days in the city.[48] The precocious Shinn had been holding large exhibitions of pastels since 1899, first in Philadelphia, at PAFA, and then in a series of New York galleries almost annually from 1900 to 1905. Like many illustrators, he was happy to mix media, building on top of a charcoal drawing or a monotype with watercolor, gouache, and pastel; like fellow Ashcan artists, who were trained as visual journalists, he was awake to the pictorial possibilities of modern life. His sojourn in Paris in 1900 inspired a brilliant series of café and boulevard subjects that would play out in his work for years, showing the inspiration of Degas and Toulouse-Lautrec.[49] His predilection for wind and snow, as seen in *Winter on 21st Street*, was perfectly suited to pastel, which cleverly suggested the blur of a blizzard; likewise, pastel captured the hot colors of the gaudy costumes and glaring spotlights of the theatrical world so dear to Shinn, a sometime playwright and thespian.[50]

Although modern subjects dominated Shinn's early work, an eighteenth-century playfulness also rose up in chalk figure drawings

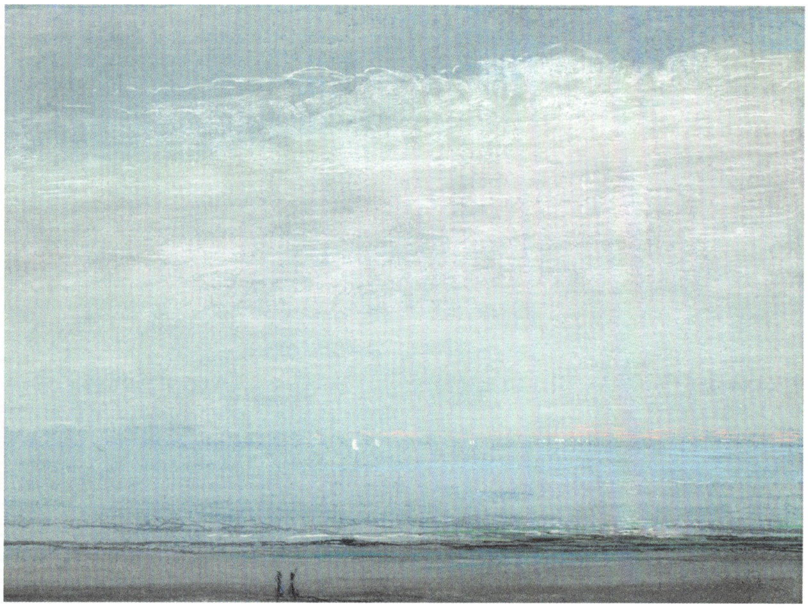

Fig. 77
Léon Dabo
Seascape, c. 1900–10
Pastel on paper
17⅛ × 21½ in. (43.5 × 54.6 cm)
Courtesy of Sullivan Goss Gallery

for the mural decorations that occupied Shinn's imagination at the time of the Pastellists. Painted for homes designed by Stanford White and for David Belasco's Stuyvesant Theatre on West 44th Street, Shinn's murals embraced a lively Rococo revival manner, with cavorting nudes and amorous couples. Three red-chalk figure studies in this spirit appeared in the first Pastellists exhibition of 1911; according to the artist and critic A. E. Gallatin, these "gay little decorations in red chalk," evoking Fragonard or Watteau, "are most charming souvenirs of the joyous days when Louis XVI sat upon the throne of France."[51]

Shinn was also, like Lawson, one of The Eight, and was a link to this older circle as well as to the more adventuresome younger talents, such as George Bellows, who all made a splash in 1910 as the Independents. Bellows, generally regarded as "a revolutionary pure and simple"[52] in the moment before the Stieglitz group set a new standard for extremism, added avant-garde spice to the mix in the first Pastellist exhibition. His rugged sporting subjects, including *Football Game* (Fig. 79), played against the traditional expectations of pastel content seen in Shinn's boudoir nudes or portraits by Cassatt, Sterner, and MacRae. Pushing the Impressionist bravura seen in Cassatt and Shinn into new territory, Bellows's dark, expressionistically worked tangle of monstrous modern athletes willfully—and wittily—flouted the dainty Rococo tradition of the medium. The contrariness worked: one critic smiled at the attempt to convey in "soft, feminine pastel the

Fig. 78
Everett Shinn
Winter on 21st Street, New York, 1899
Pastel on gray paper mounted overall to pulpboard
20⅜ × 24⅜ (51.8 × 61.9 cm)
Brooklyn Museum; Gift of Solton Engel, 56.3

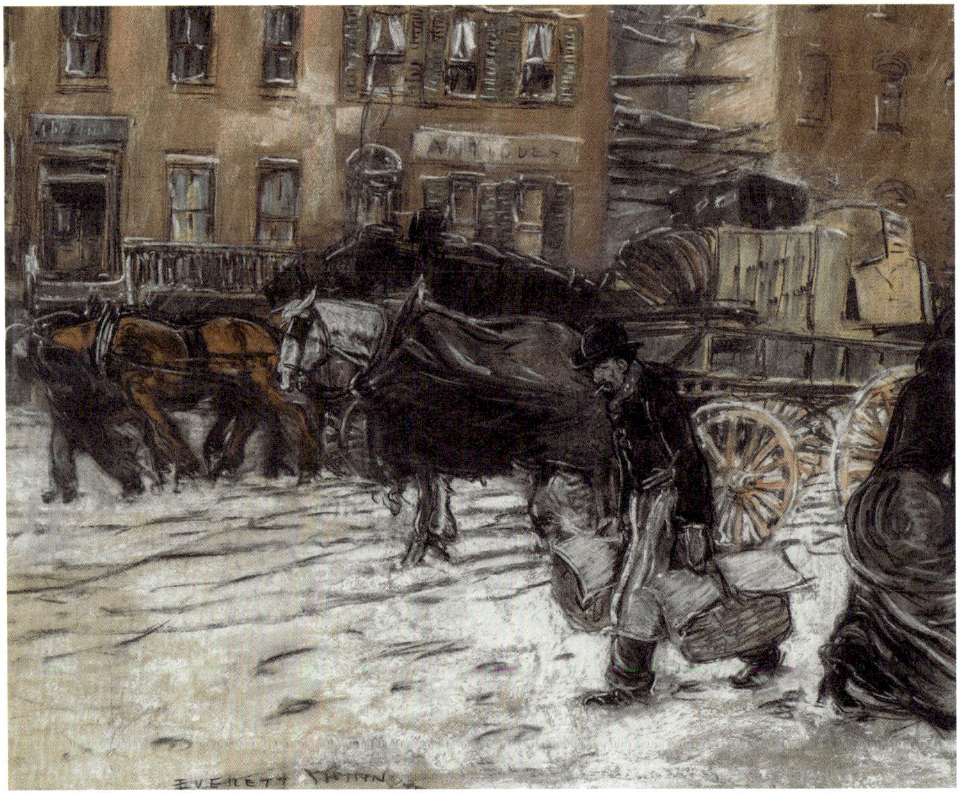

Fig. 79
George Bellows
Football Game, 1910
Pastel on paper
14⅝ × 24 in. (37.2 × 61 cm)
Private collection

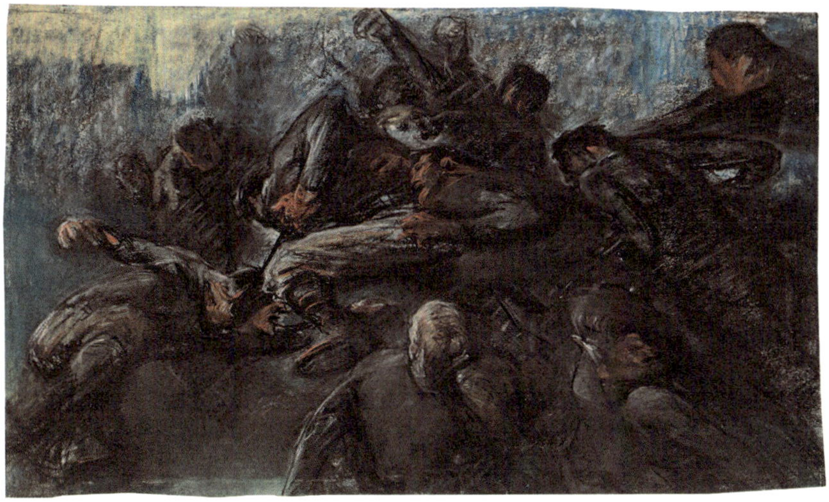

furious exhilaration of dashing polo players or the riot of action of a football game," and others liked these pastels even better than Bellows's big oils of the same subjects, shown a few months earlier with the Independents. As one viewer put it, his polo subject in pastel was "a dashing, slashing melee that makes his treatment of the same subject in oils at the recent academy look like a Saint Patrick's Day parade."[53]

More moderate than Bellows, but experimental and forward-looking, William Glackens also used pastel to further the effects made in his oils. From the same circle of The Eight, he was an accomplished draftsman, like his friends Shinn, Sloan, and Luks; comfortable with many graphic media; and willing, like most commercial artists, to mix materials in unorthodox ways.[54] All were trained as newspaper illustrators, but Glackens was the consummate observer and sketcher, whose speedy notations of urban figures in motion captured the essence of modern city life. Glackens had used pastel sporadically, but his interest in the medium was kindled around 1910, probably as a result of his involvement in the Pastellists, and he began to use the medium for studies and for autonomous exhibition pieces. Coinciding with his search for stronger color and a more powerful sense of design, his new work in pastel included *City Scene* (see Fig. 63), probably one of the two items titled *Washington Square*, listed among the ten works he sent to the first two Pastellist exhibitions.[55]

City Scene, with its bundled figures, was probably made in cold weather shortly before the first Pastellist exhibition in January 1911, or perhaps in advance of the second show that December. In Impressionist fashion, Glackens chose a modern site—a park, an intersection of paths and a bustling crowd—to give a sense of the chaotic congestion and movement of the city. Like Shinn, he learned from Degas (see Fig. 65), abruptly cropping his figures to give a sense of motion and a casual, fleeting, snapshot composition. The speed of his stroke suggests

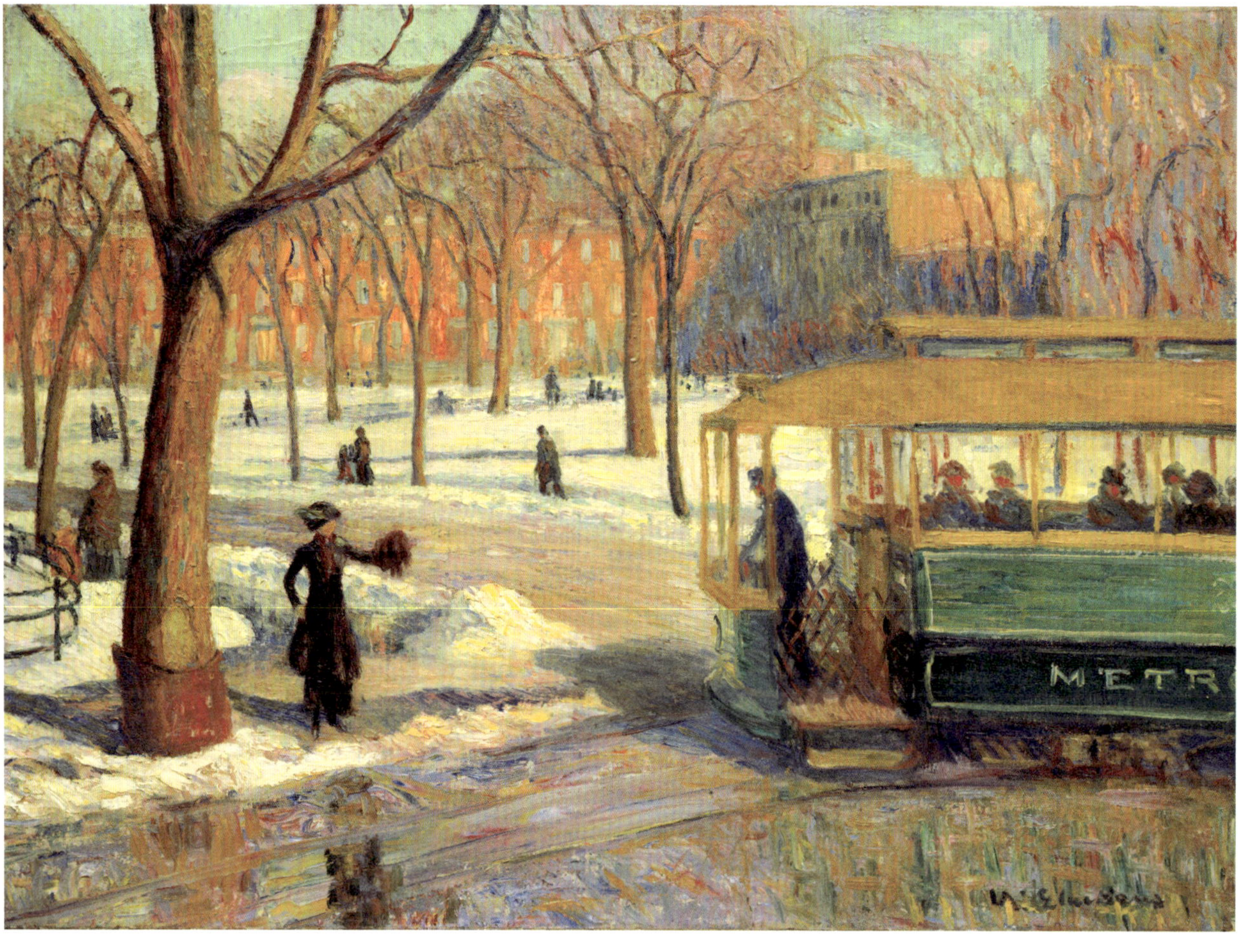

Fig. 80
William Glackens
The Green Car, 1910
Oil on canvas
24 × 32 in. (61 × 81.3 cm)
The Metropolitan Museum of Art, New York; Arthur Hoppock Hearn Fund, 1937 (37.73)

the movement of the figures, who appear as blurred vignettes of life interrupted, seen at a glance.

Glackens undertook this subject many times around 1910, perhaps because its appealing contemporary scene lay beneath the window of his studio at 50 Washington Square South. Larger, more delicately finished oils of this moment, such as *The Green Car* (Fig. 80 and cover), show the same pattern of sidewalks, the same scarred tree, and the same stylish women.[56] Typically, although his work in oil performs the Impressionist ideal of spontaneity, Glackens studied and redrew his subjects repeatedly, rehearsing figures until he could command them with seeming effortlessness.[57] The distinction between his relatively more studied oils and the bolder, rougher pastels illustrates the different spirits of these media in his method at this time.

This pattern is clearest in a related pastel of this same corner, *Woman with Umbrella, Washington Square* (Fig. 81), also a composite of figures and perhaps also one of the works shown in 1911. It seems to have been a study for a small oil that repeats the identical composition, but less incisively.[58] Showing all the vivacity of Glackens's drawn line, the pastel makes for a lively, anecdotal image that uses the bare paper (now discolored by exposure to light) for a sweeping curvilinear pattern into space and on the page, more complex than the impressionistic oil. More extreme is *City Scene*, with its greater size, larger figures, cropped and crowded composition, broad and restless handling, and ominous interactions—particularly the man accosting the woman by the tree. No oil of this composition exists, and indeed by comparison his oils of Washington Square are much daintier, more conventional in their suggestion of space, and less unsettling; this seems to have been an experimental composition inspired by the pastel medium—and perhaps a random piece of scrap wallpaper—that creates a bolder, harsher image. Its force may explain why one critic described Glackens's pastels in 1911 as "charged with life and humor," while another dismissed them as "brutalities."[59]

Glackens's freewheeling approach to pastel, like Bellows's, was in keeping with the principles the Pastellists announced in their press release, demonstrating a wish for freedom and experimentation, for the pleasure in making rather than the strategic production of marketable commodities or "important" artistic statements. Such a deliberately art-for-art's-sake stance was, of course, a strategy in its own right, and judging from the response in the press, the results were rewarding. So why then, with this promising start, did the Pastellists fade away? As with the earlier society, the leadership of the group and the commitment of the membership played the largest part. Although the prime movers—such as MacRae and Myers—were dedicated to pastel, many of those invited to exhibit were new to the medium and not very successful, not deeply engaged, or just tapped out by three exhibitions in very short order. As with the earlier club, the turnover

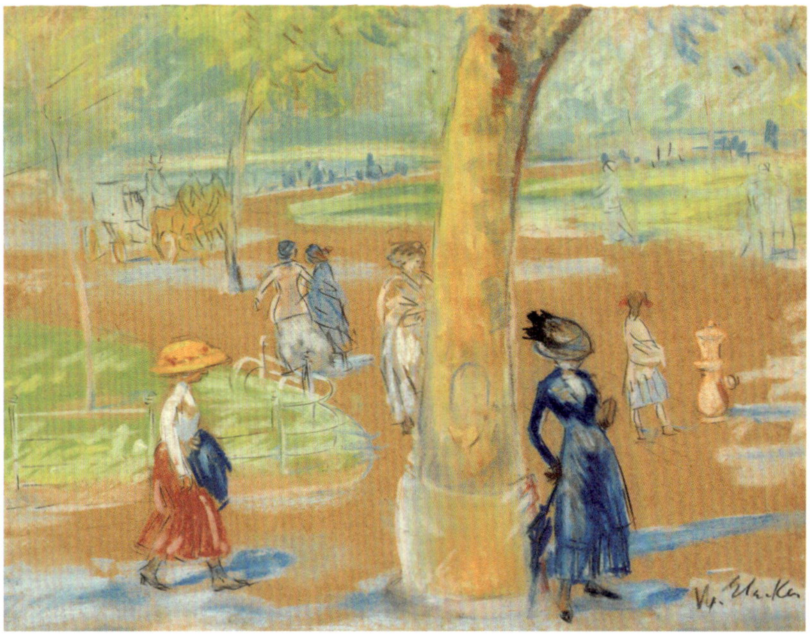

Fig. 81
William Glackens
Woman with Umbrella, Washington Square, c. 1910
Oil pastel and black crayon on brown wove paper
10 15/16 × 13 7/8 in. (27.8 × 35.2 cm)
The Barnes Foundation, Philadelphia; BF694

in the membership as well as in the venue probably contributed to instability. Many strong participants, including Glackens and Bellows, fell away in the gap that opened up between the third exhibition, in February 1912, and the fourth one, two years later.[60] Their distraction into other projects was shared by the core members, who were drawn away into the formation of the AAPS and the planning for the Armory Show, which was literally born in the Pastellists' exhibition at the Madison Gallery in December 1911.[61] Led by MacRae, Kuhn, Glackens, and Davies, all Pastellists, this new adventure would also draw many artists from their circle, and its staging in February and March of 1913 probably goes a long way toward explaining why there was no pastel exhibition that year and why the final Pastellist display in 1914 came off as a weak sidebar to a larger, more radical group show.[62]

Davies, one of the most provocative exhibitors in the last three pastel shows, represented a link to the antiacademic wing of the Pastellists, enticed by the excitement of the new European art that would be the centerpiece of the Armory Show. Like many others in the circle of The Eight, such as Anshutz and Shinn, he was introduced to pastel in the 1890s in France, where he was equally inspired by Rococo and Symbolist examples. Davies's eclectic sources and wide-ranging intellectual interests made him hard to categorize stylistically but infallibly interesting to critics; his presence in the pastel exhibitions indisputably lent prestige and sanction to those with experimental leanings, including the "old" progressives from The Eight, such as Glackens and Maurice Prendergast, and the more radical modernists of Alfred Stieglitz's gallery, named "291" after its address on Fifth Avenue. As the president of the AAPS, Davies was the driving—and sometimes annoying—force of the Armory Show, where he showed three

Fig. 82
Arthur B. Davies
Birth of Tragedy, c. 1912–13
Pastel on paper
18 × 34½ in. (45.7 × 87.6 cm)
Colby College Museum of Art, Waterville, ME; Gift of Mrs. Jacob Kaplan, 1965.004

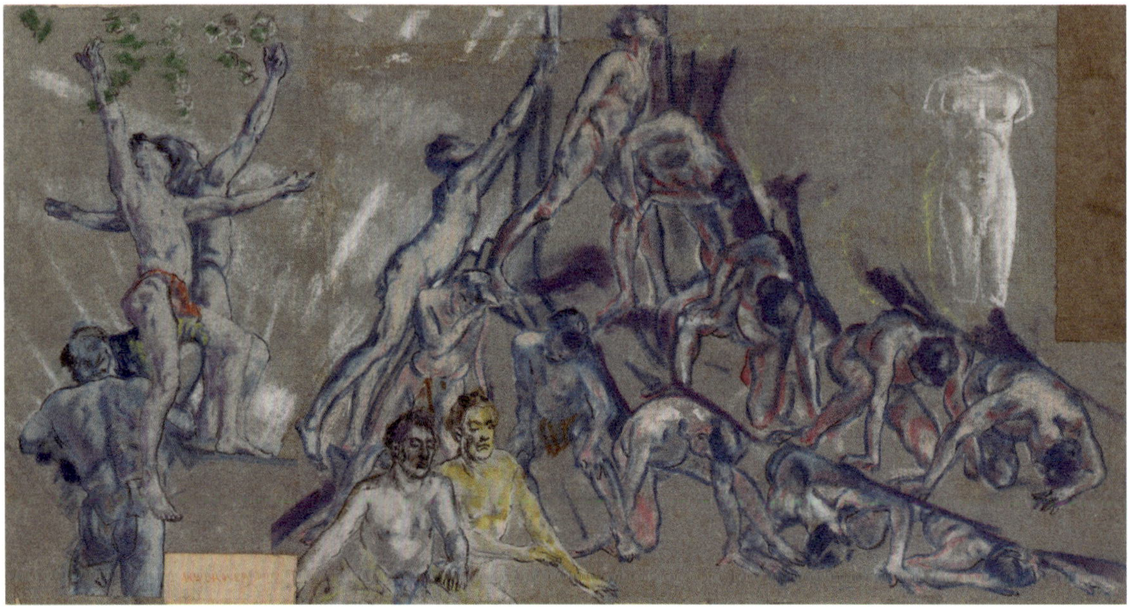

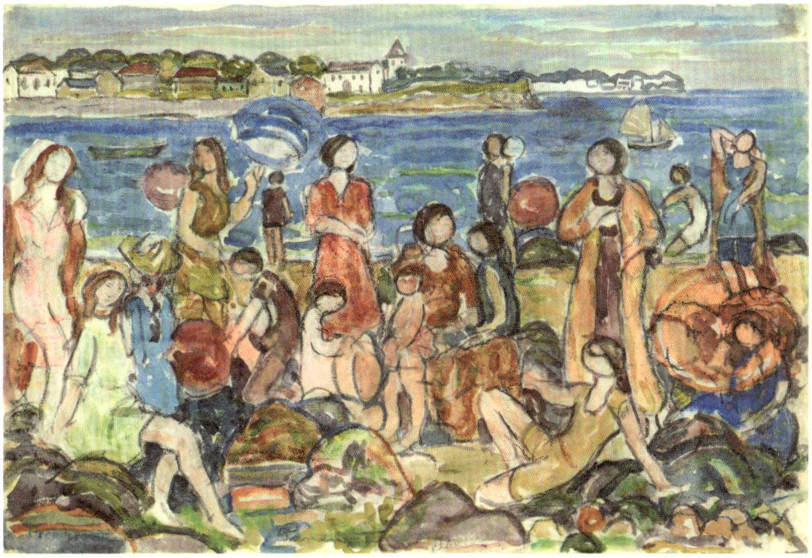

Fig. 83
Maurice Prendergast
Bathers, New England, c. 1916–19
Watercolor and pastel with graphite on wove paper
Sheet: 15¾ × 22⁷⁄₁₆ in. (40 × 57 cm)
Philadelphia Museum of Art; 125th Anniversary Acquisition, Gift of C.K. Williams II, 2003, 2003-63-2

oils and three pastels, including the characteristically emotional and enigmatic *Birth of Tragedy* (Fig. 82), in which figures in a rhythmic, dancelike sequence are successively brought low.[63] Suggesting mural studies, Davies's complex figure compositions inspired one critic to speculate that one day such pastels would be more esteemed than his finished paintings.[64]

Like Davies, Prendergast bridged the gaps opening in New York's art community. Respected in old-guard circles such as the American Watercolor Society, he was also consistently present in the most progressive exhibitions, including those of the Independents and the Pastellists, offering some of the most advanced painting in the country. Powerfully shaped by many trips to Paris, Prendergast brought Post-Impressionist decorative design and color to his work, as well as an experimental sensibility that freely mixed media for new formal effects. Around 1907, he began to layer pastel over his charcoal, crayon, and watercolor compositions, which repeatedly explored friezelike figure subjects such as *Bathers, New England* (Fig. 83), seeking a dense, visually integrated two-dimensional pattern, equally animated across the surface.[65] Seen in the fourth, largest (with twenty-nine artists and eighty-three entries), and last Pastellist exhibition of 1914 at the National Arts Club, *Bathers, New England* appeared adjacent to a larger group of works by Prendergast within a new, larger exhibition of Independents at the same venue.[66] About twice as many works by provocative so-called Cubists from the Stieglitz circle, such as Arthur B. Carles, Andrew Dasburg, Arthur Dove, Marsden Hartley, Alfred Maurer, Abraham Walkowitz, and Marguerite and William Zorach, took over most of the space. The eclipse of the Pastellists, whose showing in one gallery received almost no critical attention thanks to the shadow cast by the partner display and two equally controversial exhibitions across town, probably made little difference to the five artists (Marion Beckett, Fanny Willcox Brown, Samuel Halpert, Edward Kramer, and Prendergast) who showed on both sides.[67] The most faithful Pastellists—Dabo, Davies, MacRae, and Myers—were on hand to support their group, but the context nonetheless showed the society drifting away from their original center—demonstrated by the absence of Bellows, Glackens, Henri, Lawson, Lie, Luks, Shinn, Sterner, and others—toward a company of more radical artists whose work pointed to the future of pastel as a modernist medium.

A few of these new voices had appeared with the Pastellists, including artists typically seen as associated with Stieglitz. In fact, most of the artists affiliated with 291 worked in pastel, demonstrating the appeal of the medium that had spread beyond the club and continued to flourish after its disappearance.[68] Max Weber, one of the most surprising new names in the third, somewhat smaller exhibition of the Pastellists in 1912, was the harbinger, demonstrating by his presence the liberality of the group and its crossover terrain.[69] Weber emigrated as a boy from what is now Poland and probably learned both charcoal and pastel from his progressive teacher in New York, Arthur Wesley Dow, who set him up for four galvanizing years in Paris in the circle of Matisse and Picasso, from 1905 to 1909. He returned to camp out at 291 and teach Stieglitz and his friends about the newest trends in France, including—as Weber's *Composition with Four Figures* (Fig. 84) demonstrates—lessons from Cubism and non-Western art. Weber shocked New Yorkers with what was described as savage work in Stieglitz's "Younger Painters" show in 1910, and his solo shows in 1911 and 1912, coincident with the Pastellists, confirmed his reputation as a wild man. Weber's entries with the Pastellists were praised as "milder" and "rather more comprehensible" than the work in his solo shows, but if his *Composition with Four Figures* resembles the *Interior with Figures* shown in 1912, his work added an edginess to the exhibition that stimulated visitors and demonstrated the versatility of the medium.[70]

Joseph Stella, another modernist maverick, sent two items—*Emigrant* and *Old Peasant*—to the fourth and final exhibition of the Pastellists in 1914, evidently drawing on a side of his work very unlike his Futurist *Coney Island, Battle of Lights* (Yale University Art Gallery, New Haven, CT), which was attracting attention at the Montross Gallery exhibition of "extremists" at the same time. He probably learned charcoal and pastel at the Art Students League with William Merritt Chase from 1902 to 1904, building skills seen in a masterful series of charcoals made in about 1908 that depicted the steelworkers and smoky skies of Pittsburgh. By 1909, he produced a large, finished pastel, *The Bagpipers* (private collection), very much in the tradition of the Italian Baroque.[71] As with Prendergast and Weber, Paris opened Stella's eyes to new ways of painting, and he fell under the spell of Matisse and

Fig. 84
Max Weber
Composition with Four Figures, 1910
Charcoal and pastel on moderately thick, moderately textured laid paper
Sheet: 24¼ × 18¼ in. (61.6 × 46.4 cm)
Brooklyn Museum; Dick S. Ramsay Fund, 57.17

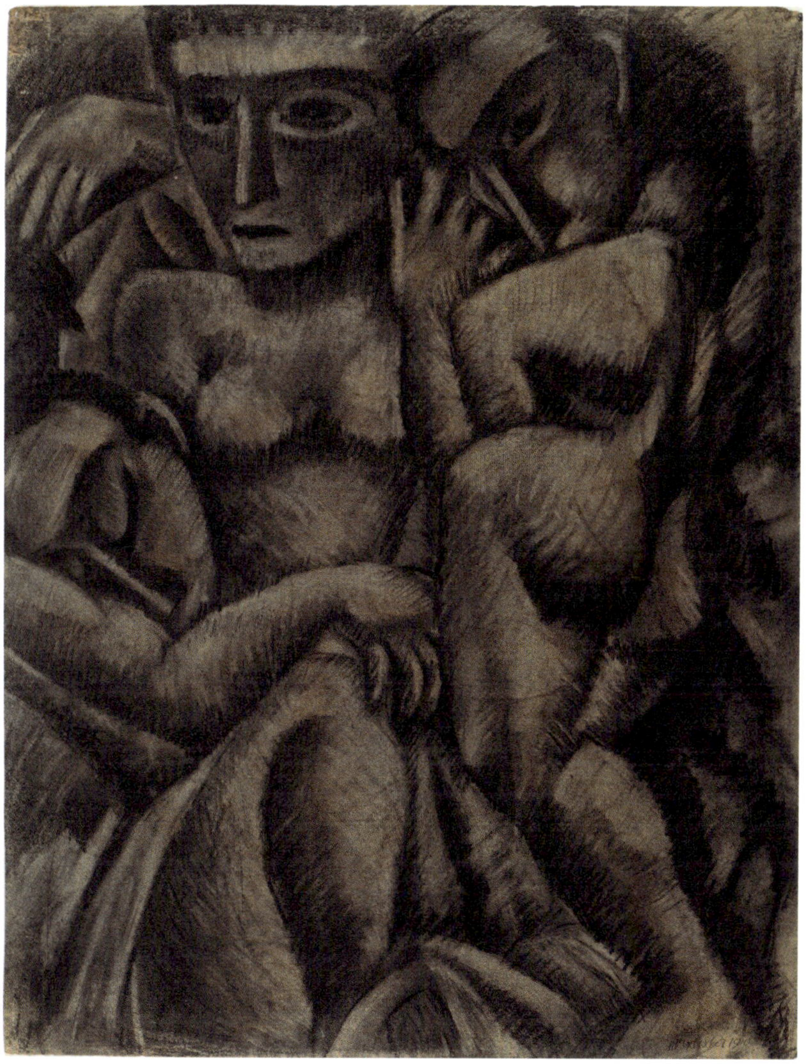

the glorious color of the Fauves during four years in Europe, from 1909 to late 1912. Returning in time to exhibit in the Armory Show, Stella launched an astonishing series of pastels following his debut with the Pastellists—some very abstract, others Symbolist in feeling—such as *Abstraction* (Fig. 85), that suggest Odilon Redon's work, seen frequently in Paris and in New York in this period.[72] Like Redon, Stella loved the intense color of pastel—the gemlike saturation of blue and red—that has a purity not found in oil paint. The softness of the medium and Stella's ethereal handling make the forms float in a dreamlike space, conjuring the sense of an underwater hallucination.[73]

Stella would remain devoted to pastel for the rest of his career, but he also embraced many other media, showing an experimental curiosity as well as phenomenal energy and imagination, working at small and large scale, from dainty silverpoint to epic oil canvases. The variety of his work and the monumental scale of his pastels demonstrate two of the cardinal directives of modernism that we have seen growing

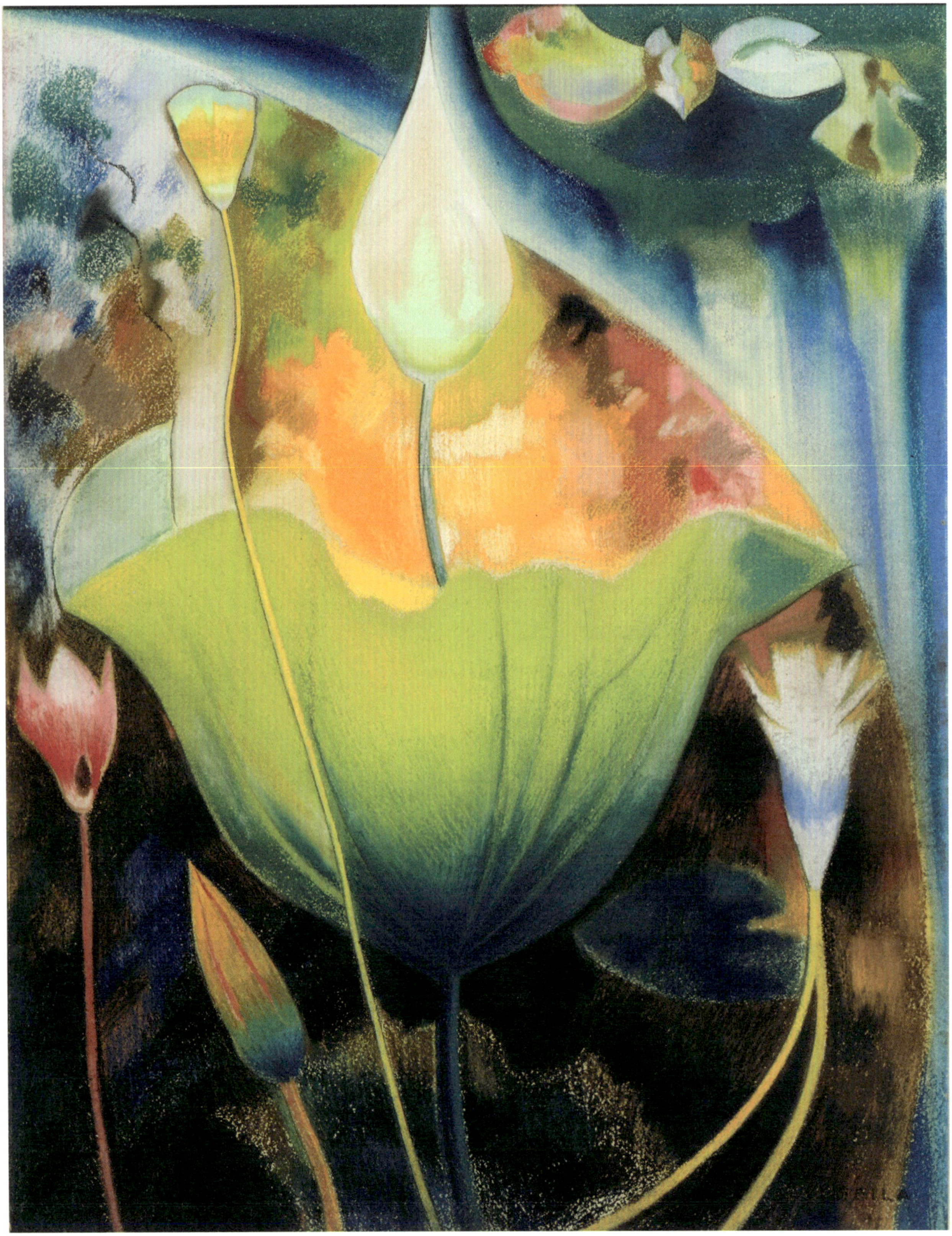

Fig. 85 (*opposite*)
Joseph Stella
Abstraction, c. 1913–14
Pastel on paper
39¼ × 29¼ in. (99.7 × 74.3 cm)
Newark Museum of Art, NJ; Gift of Mrs. Rhoda Weintraub Ziff, 1983.83.264

from the era of the watercolor movement in the 1870s: explore many genres and materials, and overthrow media hierarchies. Stieglitz would insist on the expressive potential of all media, and Stella—like many artists of his generation—would demonstrate that to be modern is to work seriously in many materials.

Taking a step back to witness the wide appeal of pastel that radiated from the exhibitions of the Pastellists as well as the shifting art politics of this moment, we discover Arthur Dove, who presented a sensational series of ten pastels, including *Nature Symbolized No. 2* (Fig. 86), in his debut at Stieglitz's gallery in February and March 1912, just two months after the second Pastellists show.[74] Selections from this group, all titled *Nature Symbolized*, may have comprised the three entries Dove sent to the so-called "Cubist" exhibition at the National Arts Club early in 1914 that included the Pastellists' final show. His work did not appear in the Pastellists' gallery, however, but in the rooms containing the works of his friends Carles and Maurer and others from the Stieglitz circle. Like Weber, Dove was excoriated for his work, which was characterized as incomprehensibly Futurist. Based on nature, his work pushed—in advance of all his American colleagues—into total abstraction, and most contemporary viewers were amazed.

Tellingly, Dove chose pastel for his most radical statements. At this moment of breakthrough, reaching for nonobjective art, he began with small, rough oil studies, but concluded with carefully finished work, four times larger, in pastel. Why did Dove prioritize the medium, and how did it suit his purposes at this moment? Perpetually impoverished

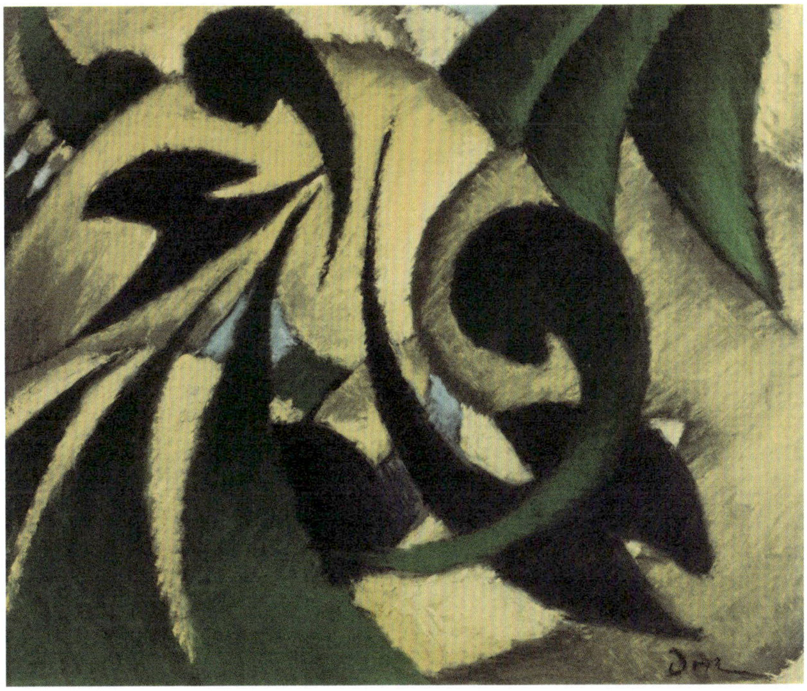

Fig. 86
Arthur Dove
Nature Symbolized No. 2, c. 1911
Pastel on paper on Masonite
18$\frac{1}{16}$ × 21$\frac{11}{16}$ in. (45.8 × 55 cm)
The Art Institute of Chicago; Alfred Stieglitz Collection, 1949.533

and distracted by the need to complete illustration work and run a farm to support his family, he probably appreciated fast, inexpensive materials. Certainly, he must have been drawn to the intimate scale, always characteristic of his work (and required by Stieglitz's tiny gallery), and he valued the ability to pack a wallop in a small package. But most of all, it was the color and texture of pastel that suited Dove's search for an intense, integrated image. Grinding the pigments and preparing the sticks himself in carefully graduated tints, he sought saturation of color and density, covering the ground with heavy, felt strokes. And such softness! As Stella understood, this velvety texture creates visual depth, while the matte surface gives flatness and overall unity to the surface. Space is generated optically, by the layering of planes and the movement of value and color. As in the work of Mark Rothko and the abstract color field painting of the 1960s, the surface cannot be rough or shiny if it is to open up this kind of pictorial space.

Dove, like Prendergast, Weber, and Stella, also represents the modernist willingness (perhaps enhanced by the illustrator's pragmatism) to try new materials and mix media in unorthodox combinations. Conservators still have not identified some of Dove's inventive kitchen-sink components: oil, wax, watercolor, tempera, charcoal, pastel, sand, moss, metallic paint, collaged fabric, wood, and objects. In the tradition of Degas, Dove experimented and used whatever worked. His unconventional technique hints at dissatisfaction with available solutions and a deliberate search for a particular visual effect. He chose pastel because he needed its special qualities.[75]

Georgia O'Keeffe, by contrast, was a media purist. She was another student of Chase and probably learned charcoal and pastel from him, like Stella. But O'Keeffe was away from New York during the era of the Pastellists, and did not return until the fall of 1914, after their fourth and last exhibition. In 1915, while studying at Columbia (like Weber) with Dow, she began her deliberate and systematic exploration of different media—examining and rebuilding her skills.[76] This was in itself a modernist undertaking of a different order: the challenge to understand, master, and exploit the inherent qualities of each medium. If media mixing is one story, then media purification—first heard in the "truth to materials" commentary of the late nineteenth century; embraced by early twentieth-century sculptors such as John Flannagan, Robert Laurent, and William Zorach; and made canonical in the midcentury by critics such as Clement Greenberg—is another trope of modernism.

O'Keeffe began with the groundbreaking series of abstract charcoals in 1915 that would draw the attention of Stieglitz, winning an invitation to exhibit them at his 291 gallery the next year. After mastering all the effects of light, shade, and texture in velvety black and white, she allowed herself color—launching a series of pastels that likewise explored the brilliance of pure hue and abstract form, seeking maximum visual expressiveness in the medium. Although she did not know him yet, her master in pastel was Dove, whose works she sought out and studied carefully; her earliest pastels, like *Special No. 32* of 1915 (Fig. 87) were inspired—like Dove's—by observation of nature (in this case, a muddy river) later remembered and conveyed abstractly.[77]

O'Keeffe's methodical exploration of the inherent qualities in each medium paid off in the 1920s, when she began to synthesize the lessons of the previous decade. Instead of mixing, like Dove and Stella, she cross-pollinated, bringing themes and techniques explored in oil or charcoal to her work in pastel. She would continue to work in pastel for decades (after oil, it was second in frequency in her work), regularly showing a group of pastels in all her exhibitions with Stieglitz. Perhaps it was marketing savvy, bringing smaller, less expensive work into the mix, and perhaps it was logistical, as Stieglitz continued to have small spaces (such as "the Intimate Gallery"), but clearly O'Keeffe took a great deal of pleasure in the medium, judging from immaculate, hypnotic works such as *Slightly Open Clam Shell* (Fig. 88). Bringing her experience in oil to her work in pastel, she took on similar magnified natural subjects, but with a keen, delicate sense of the particular. The opposite of Dove and Stella, this is now the Precisionism of the '20s, a throwback to the intense pastel manner of Chase and Maurice-Quentin de La Tour. Suppressing gesture and seeking refinement of surface,

Fig. 87
Georgia O'Keeffe
Special No. 32, 1915
Pastel on paper
Sight: 14 × 19½ in. (35.6 × 49.5 cm)
Smithsonian American Art Museum, Smithsonian Institution, Washington, DC; Gift of Georgia O'Keeffe Foundation, 1995.3.2

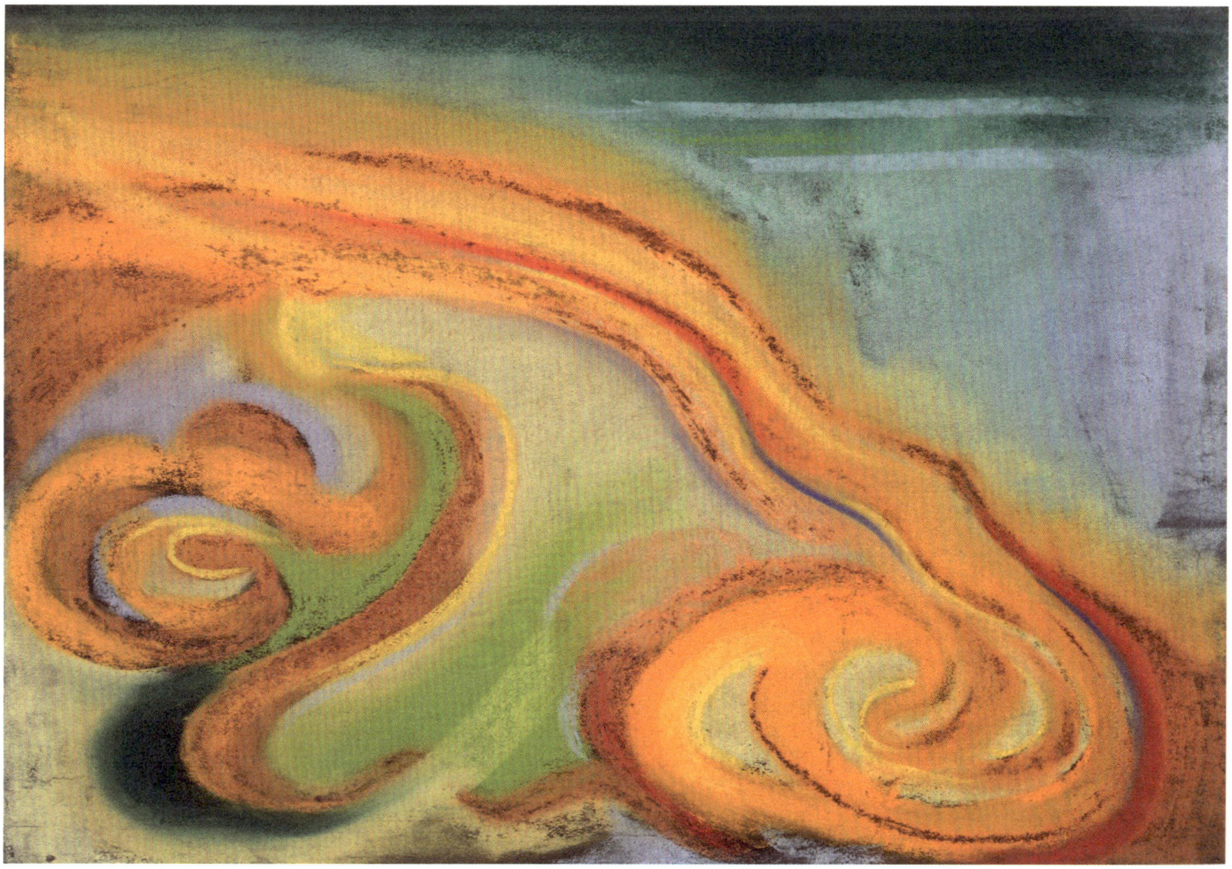

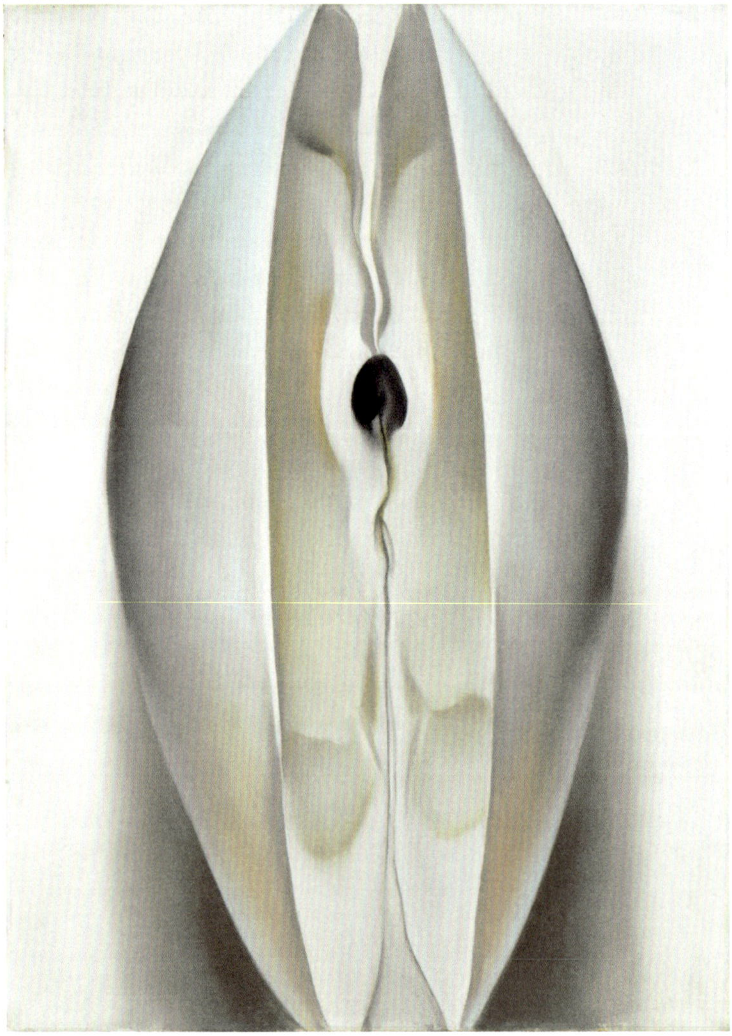

Fig. 88
Georgia O'Keeffe
Slightly Open Clam Shell, 1926
Pastel on white ground on artist board
18½ × 13 in. (47 × 33 cm)
Wadsworth Atheneum Museum of Art, Hartford, CT; The Douglas Tracy Smith and Dorothy Potter Smith Fund: Purchased in honor of Elizabeth Mankin Kornhauser, Krieble Curator of American Painting and Sculpture, in gratitude for her many years of extraordinary service to the Wadsworth Atheneum Museum of Art (1983–2010), 2009.1.1

O'Keeffe creates surprise in the contrast of soft pastel versus hard shell and in the discovery of subtle color, inspiring the impulse to hold your breath as you explore the secret interior of the shell.

Regardless of subject, in choosing pastel, Stella, Dove, and O'Keeffe capitalized on a sense of the unexpected: that pastel is a secondary, slightly offbeat choice. And for all three it is an intimate and enthralling encounter, offering a deep dive into the pleasure of making and looking. Their choice signals a message: to be surprising, exploratory, and personally expressive by exploiting—each of them—different inherent qualities in the medium. For these artists, and for others introduced above, the intimacy of pastel, its visual sensuality, made it the perfect vehicle to advance the emotional and visual goals of modernism.

NOTES

I wish to thank Elizabeth Hawley and Kelsey Gustin, successive Barra Fellows at the Philadelphia Museum of Art, for their research assistance with this project, and Avis Berman for her helpful reading of the text.

1. [James B. Townsend], "New Artist's Society," *American Art News*, December 17, 1910, 2. This and many clippings cited below can be found in the Holley/MacRae Family Papers, Historical Society of the Town of Greenwich, Connecticut (hereafter MacRae Family Papers).
2. [Untitled], *New York Sun*, January 15, 1911. The first exhibition included Marion Beckett, Bellows, Mary Helen Carlisle, Colin Campbell Cooper, Paul Cornoyer, Léon Dabo, Dewing, Glackens, Edward Adam Kramer, Lawson, Jonas Lie, Elmer Livingston MacRae, Jerome Myers, Henry Reuterdahl, Shinn, Albert Sterner, Juliet Thompson, Weir, and Henry C. White. Other reviews were warm and noted the novelty of the show: "The display is a new departure, for we do not recall where there has been a show of pastel work in this city" ("Art and Artists," *New York Globe*, January 12, 1911). The installation was described as "harmonious, intimate and delightful" by Henry Tyrell ("Up and Down Picture Lane," *Evening World*, January 14, 1911, 15). J. B. Townsend commented on the "most delightful and refreshing display" ("Exhibitions at the Galleries," *Arts and Decoration* 1, no. 4 [February 1911]: 172). Checklist and clippings, MacRae Family Papers.
3. Doreen Bolger, "The Pastellists 1910–15," in *American Pastels in the Metropolitan Museum of Art* (New York: Metropolitan Museum of Art, 1989), 20–21; Susan G. Larkin, "So Many Thrills, So Much Excitement: Elmer MacRae's Role in the Armory Show," in *The Armory Show at 100: Modernism and Revolution* (New York: New-York Historical Society, 2013), 75–77; Carol Troyen, "'Wonderful Color Palpitating About Us': William Glackens and the Independents Exhibition of 1910," in *The World of William Glackens*, Vol. II, *The C. Richard Hilker Art Lectures & New Perspectives on William Glackens* (New York: Sansom Foundation Inc., 2017), 223–24.
4. See Troyen, "'Wonderful Color Palpitating About Us,'" 223–49, and Charles Brock, "The Exhibition Game: Rockwell Kent and The Twelve," in *The World of William Glackens*, Vol. II, 123–63.
5. The story of the watercolor movement and its relationship to the club movement and the interest in new media is told in Kathleen A. Foster, *American Watercolor in the Age of Homer and Sargent* (Philadelphia: Philadelphia Museum of Art, with Yale University Press, 2017); see also the website with related research materials: https://philamuseum.libguides.com/AmericanWatercolors.
6. "A New Artist Society," (New York) *Evening Mail*, January 14, 1911, MacRae Family Papers.
7. Theodore E. Stebbins Jr., with John Caldwell and Carol Troyen, *American Master Drawings and Watercolors: A History of Works on Paper from Colonial Times to the Present* (New York: Harper & Row, 1976), 233. Astute critics contemporary to the artists also noted this trend: see Mary Gertrude Van Rensselaer, "American Painters in Pastel," *Century* n.s. 7 (December 1884): 204–10.
8. Dianne H. Pilgrim, "The Revival of Pastels in Nineteenth-Century America: The Society of Painters in Pastel," *The American Art Journal* 10, no. 2 (November 1978): 43–62. See also Dianne H. Pilgrim, "Introduction," in *Painters in Pastel: A Survey of American Works* (New York: Hirschl & Adler Galleries, 1987), 7–12; and Mary L. Sullivan, "American Pastels 1880–1930: Revival and Revitalization" and "The Society of Painters in Pastel and the International Revival of the Medium," both in *American Pastels in the Metropolitan Museum of Art*, 1, 6–17.
9. "A New Artist Society."

10. On the materials of pastel, see Marjorie Shelley, "American Pastels of the Late Nineteenth and Early Twentieth Centuries: Materials and Techniques," in *American Pastels in the Metropolitan Museum of Art,* 33–45; and Thea Burns and Philippe Saunier, "Technical Appendix," in *The Art of the Pastel* (New York and Paris: Abbeville Press, 2014), 369–73. A hands-on approach to pastel, with a brief sketch of its history, comes from a contemporary master of the medium, Ellen Eagle, in *Pastel Painting Atelier: Essential Lessons in Techniques, Practices and Materials* (New York: Watson-Guptill, 2013).
11. Pilgrim, "The Revival of Pastels in Nineteenth-Century America," 44.
12. On the origins and development of the medium, see Geneviève Monnier, *Le Pastel* (Paris: Skira, 1983), translated as *Pastels: From the Sixteenth to the Twentieth Century* (Geneva: Skira, 1995); and Burns and Saunier, *Art of the Pastel*, which surveys work through 1900.
13. Monnier, *Pastels*, 48–64, 120–21.
14. On Cassatt's pastels and *At the Theater*, see Kathleen A. Foster, "Cassatt and Pastel: Working Old and New," in *Mary Cassatt at Work* (Philadelphia: Philadelphia Museum of Art, with Yale University Press, 2024), 201–14; and Kathleen A. Foster and Thomas Primeau, "Cassatt's Pastels: Materials and Techniques," in *Mary Cassatt at Work*, 241–50.
15. Pilgrim noted the impact of De Nittis, who showed with the Impressionists in 1874 but moved on to conquer the Salon; "The Revival of Pastels in Nineteenth-Century America," 47–48. On De Nittis and the other stylish pastellists of the 1880s, see Burns and Saunier, *Art of the Pastel*, 283–99. The *New York Times* reported De Nittis's untimely death in 1884, describing him as "the avowed head of the impressionists," whose recent work in pastel had given "new life and interest" to the medium ("De Nittis," *New York Times*, December 24, 1884, 6).
16. James McNeill Whistler, letters to Anna Matilda Whistler, n.d. [1880], and to Matthew R. Elden, n.d. [1880], quoted in Margaret Macdonald, *Palaces in the Night: Whistler in Venice* (Berkeley, CA: University of California Press, 2001), 146, 149. Whistler's impact in the United States is surveyed by Linda Merrill, ed., *After Whistler: The Artist and His Influence on American Painting* (New Haven, CT: Yale University Press, 2003).
17. For a compendium of reviews of Whistler's pastels and commentary on his technique, see Robert H. Getscher, *James Abbott McNeill Whistler Pastels* (New York: Braziller, 1991); Fig. 67 in the present essay, *The Storm—Sunset*, is discussed on p. 100.
18. The French Société was founded in 1885 by Degas and other artists recruited by the dealer Georges Petit; the London Society, organized in 1888 by the head of the Grosvenor Gallery, Sir Coutts Lindsay, folded when his gallery failed. See Burns and Saunier, *Art of the Pastel,* 304–8, 315–17. On Blum's career, see Bruce Weber, "Robert Frederick Blum (1857–1903) and his Milieu" (PhD diss., City University of New York, 1985).
19. Critics complimented them as "tinted Whistler etchings," though many had a blurred, foggy surface that also emulated pastel; see Foster, *American Watercolor in the Age of Homer and Sargent*, 190, Fig. 157.
20. Shown as *Sunlight and Shadow* in the second exhibition of the Painters in Pastel in 1888. All of Chase's pastels are included in Ronald G. Pisano, *William Merritt Chase: The Paintings in Pastel, Monotypes, Painted Tiles and Ceramic Plates, Watercolors, and Prints*, vol. 1, *The Complete Catalogue of Known and Documented Work by William Merritt Chase (1849–1916)* (New Haven, CT: Yale University Press, 2006), 1–47.
21. On Twachtman, see Lisa Peters, *John Henry Twachtman: An American Impres*

sionist (Manchester, VT: Hudson Hills, 1999). On Currier, see Foster, *American Watercolor in the Age of Homer and Sargent,* 197–200.

22. Pilgrim, "The Revival of Pastels in Nineteenth-Century America," 43; Mary L. Sullivan, "The Society of Painters in Pastel," in *American Pastels in the Metropolitan Museum of Art,* 13. William H. Gerdts argued that pastel forwarded the aesthetic of Impressionism in the United States; *American Impressionism* (Seattle: Henry Art Gallery, 1980), 29. On the arrival of Impressionism and the exhibition sketch in the United States in the 1870s, see Foster, *American Watercolor in the Age of Homer and Sargent,* 185–89.
23. Anthea Callen, "The Unvarnished Truth: Mattness, 'Primitivism' and Modernity in French Painting, c. 1870–1907," *The Burlington Magazine* 136, no. 1100 (1994): 738–46. For this effect on paper, see Stebbins, *American Master Drawings and Watercolors,* 236; for examples of this intermedia effect, see Foster, *American Watercolor in the Age of Homer and Sargent,* 185, 210, 221–22, 234, 243, 247, 295.
24. See Sullivan, "The Society of Painters in Pastel," in *American Pastels in the Metropolitan Museum of Art*, 9.
25. J. L. Sprink, in *A Guide to Pastel Painting* (London: Rowney, 1886), characterized the medium as "charming, soft, and sweet," suited to "flowers, children, and feminine beauty;" vii, ix. A wish to characterize the essential quality of pastel appears in all of the critical commentary from the 1880s forward, with a focus on lightness and spontaneity, and a corollary critique of artists who over-finish and attempt to rival the effect of oils or adopt subject matter outside the "proper scope and limits" of the medium, such as Bellows's sporting subjects, discussed in this essay. As one critic noted, it is unwise to seek in pastel the "serious treatment of form" and "nobility of motive" appropriate to oils; "The Pastel Exhibition," (New York) *Evening Post,* April 22, 1889, 7. This theme of truth to materials and suitable subject matter recurs in the discussion of watercolor in this period.
26. On the reasons the club folded, see Pilgrim, "The Revival of Pastels in Nineteenth-Century America," 60–62. The AWS exhibitions before about 1880 were eclectic, but they gradually purified as special-interest groups in etching and "black and white" work formed their own shows. Many catch-all work on paper exhibitions after 1890 welcomed pastels, although the medium is often not listed in the exhibition catalogue entries. See Sullivan, "The Society of Painters in Pastel," in *American Pastels in the Metropolitan Museum of Art*, 15–16.
27. See note 17. Abbey is credited with stirring up interest in pastel in England; he was among the founders of a new Pastel Society in London in 1898; Mary L. Sullivan, "Edwin Austin Abbey," in *American Pastels in the Metropolitan Museum of Art*, 61. He used pastel for his mural studies after 1894 but soon developed a series of stand-alone costumed figures such as shown in Fig. 71 that were a popular exhibition item. His pastels are notably broader than his exhibition oils or watercolors.
28. "The Water Color Society," *Brooklyn Daily Eagle*, May 5, 1908, 4. "The Water Color Society has liberated itself by opening its exhibitions to etchings and drawings, pastels, and pen-and-ink illustrations," noted the *New York Times*, "Etchings, Pastels, and Charcoals Lend Variety to the New Art Exhibition," May 2, 1907, 7. The 1905 AWS annual was restricted to members' work and unusually small; the expansion in 1906 must have been an attempt to recapture the inclusiveness of the early exhibitions of the Society in the 1870s and compete with the more liberal New York and Philadelphia watercolor clubs, which included pastels and prints in their annuals. The stratagem did not pay off, as the 1907 exhibition hit a record low in sales. From an excited peak of about sixty pastels in 1908 (within a show of 610), the presence of pastels diminished to between twenty-five and fifty each year through 1912. Perhaps the invention of the Pastellists in 1911

made the AWS less welcoming to the medium after 1912; Bolger notes that they were excluded in 1913 and then allowed again in 1915; "The Pastellists 1910–15," in *American Pastels in the Metropolitan Museum of Art*, 21. Tracking this pattern is difficult, as the catalogues between 1908 and 1912 indicate medium, but those after 1912 seldom do. The New York Water Color Club and the Philadelphia club's catalogues likewise rarely describe media other than prints, making it hard to tally the pastels. The catalogues of these three exhibitions through 1922 can be searched at https://philamuseum.libguides.com/AmericanWatercolors.

29. Veteran members of the AWS such as Jennie Brownscombe, James W. Champney, Charles C. Curran, Charles W. Eaton, Childe Hassam, Frank Jones, George Maynard, Hermann D. Murphy, and Rosina Emmett Sherwood all submitted a few pastels in this period.
30. On MacRae and the Cos Cob artists, see Susan G. Larkin, *On Home Ground: Elmer Livingston MacRae at the Holley House* (Greenwich, CT: Bruce Museum, 1990), 35–37, where his role in the Pastellists and the critical response to his work are discussed; and Susan G. Larkin, *The Cos Cob Art Colony: Impressionists on the Connecticut Shore* (New Haven, CT: Yale University Press, 2001), both based on Larkin's doctoral dissertation, "'A Regular Rendezvous for Impressionists': The Cos Cob Art Colony 1882–1920" (City University of New York, 1996). The pertinence of the Pastellists to MacRae's role in the Armory Show is discussed by Larkin in "So Many Thrills, So Much Excitement: Elmer MacRae's Role in the Armory Show," in *The Armory Show at 100*, 75–77.
31. Tyrell, "Up and Down Picture Lane."
32. See Larkin, *On Home Ground*, 35, 50–51, and MacRae's diary at the Archives of American Art, Smithsonian Institution, for his activities in all these endeavors. Apparently his Madison Gallery show of March 1911 also was seen later that spring at the Copley Gallery in Boston. A final solo show in 1912, shortly before the Madison Gallery closed, was also dominated by pastels. See Christine I. Oaklander, "Clara Davidge's Madison Art Gallery: Sowing the Seed for the Armory Show," *Archives of American Art Journal* 36, no. 3/4 (1996): 20–37; MacRae's gallery brochure from 1911 is reproduced on page 23. MacRae would show six pastels and three oils at the Armory Show in 1913.
33. See Troyen, "'Wonderful Color Palpitating About Us,'" 223–49. The exhibition was presented as the work of the members and invited guests, so it did not advertise the "no jury, no prizes" ethos promoted by Henri and the Independents. On the flowering of exhibitions in this period, see Judith Zilczer, "'The World's New Art Center': Modern Exhibitions in New York City, 1913–1918," *Archives of American Art Journal* 14, no. 3 (1974): 2–7.
34. First opened in 1906 at 11 East 33rd Street, the gallery moved nearby to 396 Fifth Avenue above 36th Street in 1907 as the Bauer-Folsom Galleries, under the partnership of Otto H. Bauer and Arthur H. Folsom. In 1909, Folsom took over sole ownership, renamed the gallery, and commenced a program of contemporary, mostly Impressionist American art. See https://research.frick.org/directory/detail/4873.
35. These remarks and the limits to the membership appear in an untitled clipping from the *New York Sun*, January 8, 1911. The same text appears in "The Pastellists: A New Art Society," *The Craftsman* (March 1911), 639. The distinction between members and guests is not made in the one-page exhibition brochure, which gives the exhibitors listed in note 2 above. Another printing of the checklist deletes no. 62, Gladys "Thaer" [Thayer], who evidently did not join. John White Alexander is listed among the paid members in MacRae's papers, although he never exhibited with the group. All sources in this note are in the MacRae Family Papers.
36. "The Pastel Club," *New York Tribune*, April 21, 1889, 7. Clarence Cook, "The Painters in Pastel: The Fourth Exhibition," *The Studio*, May 17, 1890, 237–38.

37. On Whistler's innovation, see Sylvia Yount, "Whistler and Philadelphia: A Question of Character," in Merrill, ed., *After Whistler*, 52. Henry Tyrell commented on the "crimson-walled parlor" of the Folsom Galleries and its "intimate, and delightful" ambiance in "Up and Down Picture Lane."

38. The second exhibition, also at the Folsom Galleries, December 9–30, 1911, was similar in size and makeup to the first, with sixty-six works by twenty-one artists. Seventeen members appeared again, with new exhibitors Bryson Burroughs, Davies, and Henri, plus a work by Twachtman, who had died in 1902. First-year exhibitors absent from the second exhibition were Bellows, Carlisle, and Dewing. Checklist brochure, MacRae Family Papers.

39. See Ralph Flint, *Albert Sterner: His Life and Art* (New York: Payson & Clarke, 1927), 26–28. A founder of the Painter-Gravers of America in 1915 (which included many of the Pastellists, such as Bellows, Hassam, Myers, and Weir), Sterner was a pioneering lithographer, but not an exhibitor at the Armory Show.

40. Two similar pastels from 1893 of the same sitter with an orange are listed in Adelyn Breeskin, *Mary Cassatt: A Catalogue Raisonné of the Oils, Pastels, Watercolors, and Drawings* (Washington, DC: Smithsonian Institution Press, 1970), cat. 219 and cat. 220. The second one, *Portrait of Margaret Milligan Sloane (No. 2)* (Fig. 75), is the likely exhibition piece in 1911, as the first version descended in the Sloane family, while *No. 2* was deposited with Durand-Ruel in New York. An annotated catalogue of the second Pastellist show (MacRae Family Papers) lists this pastel for sale at $1,100, by far the most expensive work in an exhibition where most pieces were less than $150. Created and shown in Paris in 1893, it also appeared among nine pastels seen in Cassatt's large exhibition at Durand-Ruel's New York gallery in 1895. One of these two pastels of Margaret was probably shown as *Girl with Orange* at the Philadelphia Art Club in their fifteenth annual exhibition of watercolors and pastels in 1906; see the review of this exhibition in the *Philadelphia Inquirer*, March 18, 1906, 2. Cassatt's agency in all these displays seems unlikely, given her poor health and unhappiness following her brother Gardner's death in Paris that spring. The work in the first Pastellist exhibition of 1911, *Mère et enfant*, has not been identified.

41. "The excellent drawing of her round-faced little model strikes a note of authority in the exhibition, and the science of her execution is admirable," "The Pastellists," *New York Times*, December 17, 1911, 15.

42. Weir would show one pastel in the first, third, and fourth exhibitions of the Pastellists; Dewing exhibited only one item in the first show.

43. Larkin, *On Home Ground*, 35–36. MacRae's initiative, "backed by the energy of Jerome Myers," was credited by several journalists as the origin of the group; see "Drawings by Pastellists," *New York Post*, January 13, 1911; MacRae Family Papers.

44. Jerome Myers, *Artist in Manhattan* (New York: American Artist Group, 1940), 217. This text faces a related image, *Summer Night*, 1919, oil on canvas, Whitney Museum of American Art, New York. The *Brooklyn Daily Eagle* commended the work *Night*, shown in 1912, of sleepers stretched on benches in hot weather; "Pastels at Powell Gallery," February 23, 1912, 9.

45. "Pastellists at Folsom's," *American Art News*, January 14, 1911, 6. The other officers were MacRae (secretary and treasurer), and Board of Control members Jerome Myers, Everett Shinn, and Juliet Thompson. "The Pastellists: A New Art Society," *The Craftsman*, March 1911, 639.

46. Andre Tridon, "An Exhibition of Pastels," *New York Call*, January 24, 1911, 6; "First Exhibition of 'The Pastellists' Suggests the Revival of a Charming Form of 18th Century Art," *New York Times*, January 15, 1911, 51.

47. See Merrill, ed., *After Whistler*, 168. Dabo's position in the art world might be measured by Walt Kuhn's plans for the new AAPS in 1911, which he felt should

include "the opposite type" from the Henri circle: "Even Dabo (the limit) should be in it"; Milton W. Brown, "Walt Kuhn's Armory Show," *Archives of American Art Journal* 27, no. 2 (January 1987): 5. On Dabo's work, see William H. Gerdts, Cody Hartley, Frank Goss, and Nathan Vonk, *The Pastels of Leon Dabo* (Santa Barbara, CA: Sullivan Goss, Ltd., 2012).

48. *Fifth Avenue Bus in a Snow Storm* (unlocated) is reproduced in A. E. Gallatin, "The Pastellists," *Art and Progress*, March 1911, 142.
49. Shinn worked almost exclusively in pastel until 1901. In *Everett Shinn: The Spectacle of Life* (New York: Berry-Hill Galleries, 2000), 19, Janay Wong focuses on his modern subject matter, noting his mixing of media. Facsimiles of Shinn's early exhibition checklist brochures are reproduced in Edith De Shazo, *Everett Shinn 1876–1953: A Figure in His Time* (New York: Clarkson N. Potter, 1974), including for the shows at PAFA (1898), 36–37; Boussod Valadon [Goupil] (1900, 1901), 38, 44; and Durand-Ruel (1904), 55. Shinn also showed pastels at the AWS, including several pastel monotypes in 1910, following the example of Degas; see his exhibition record at https://philamuseum.libguides.com/AmericanWatercolors.
50. On this series of Fifth Avenue snow scenes and Shinn's interest in New York's old-fashioned horse-drawn buses, see Wong, *Everett Shinn: The Spectacle of Life*, 19, 27–30.
51. Gallatin, "The Pastellists." The checklist titled two of the chalk drawings "Period Louis XIV," perhaps intending "Louis XVI," the era of Shinn's typical frame of reference. Other reviews compared Shinn's work to that of François Boucher. For a reproduction of one of these drawings, see "Art News from New York," *New York Tribune*, January 22, 1911; MacRae Family Papers. On these drawings and mural decorations, see De Shazo, *Everett Shinn 1876–1953*, 89–95, 101–3. Shinn exhibited two Paris street scenes and *Scene from a Music Hall* at the second Pastellist exhibition in December 1911; like the entries in the first show, these may have been older drawings.
52. "Art and Artists," *New York Globe*.
53. Tridon, "An Exhibition of Pastels"; Tyrell, "Up and Down Picture Lane." The three entries from Bellows in the first exhibition were *Polo Game*; *Mardi Gras, Coney Island*; and *Foot Ball Game*. In the third exhibition in 1912, he showed *Knock Out* and *Polo Game*.
54. On Glackens's media preferences and mixtures, see Everett Shinn, "William Glackens as an Illustrator," *American Artist*, November 1945, 36–37; on his inspiration from contemporary French drawing in the 1890s, particularly Théophile Alexandre Steinlen, Jean Louis Forain, and Toulouse-Lautrec, see Elizabeth Wylie, "William Glackens," in *American Pastels in the Metropolitan Museum of Art*, 90.
55. I thank Avis Berman for pointing me to what could be Glackens's earliest surviving pastel, *Interior* from 1899 (New Britain Museum of American Art). A subject from the demimonde reprising Édouard Manet's notorious *Nana*, it is too skilled to be a first attempt and suggests prior work in Philadelphia, in the circle of his teacher Anshutz and working alongside his friend Shinn. Sketchbooks from this period, still not systematically studied, may show more of his early work in the medium. On Glackens's transitional period after 1910 and its relationship to his pastels, see William H. Gerdts and Jorge H. Santis, *William Glackens* (New York: Abbeville Press and the Fort Lauderdale Museum of Art, 1996), 89–101; and Troyen, "'Wonderful Color Palpitating About Us,'" 223–24. Glackens's entries in the first Pastellist exhibition included no. 26, *Washington Square*, and no. 27, *Washington Arch*; in the second exhibition was no. 25, *Washington Square*.
56. Glackens lived on the tonier side, Washington Square North, from 1904 to 1908, before moving a few blocks north on Fifth Avenue, but he retained his studio at 50 Washington Square South. This was the street with the trolleys, bordering

the ethnic neighborhoods below the square. On the history and character of the park as seen in the work of Shinn, who lived nearby on Waverly Place, see Janay Wong, "Washington Square Park," in *Everett Shinn: The Spectacle of Life*, 52–57. Other paintings showing this same perspective include Glackens's *Washington Square* (1910; New Britain Museum of American Art); *Mother and Baby, Washington Square*, 1914 (NSU Art Museum, Fort Lauderdale, FL); *Parade, Washington Square*, 1912 (Whitney Museum of American Art); and *Winter, Washington Square* (1912; Sotheby's New York, May 22, 1996, lot 17). Also from the same vantage point is the mixed-media cover design for the April 16, 1910, edition of *Collier's Weekly*: *A Spring Morning in Washington Square, New York*, which is an amusing, action-packed crowd scene showing the popular, commercial side of Glackens's work; see https://www.illustrationhistory.org/illustrations/a-spring-morning-in-washington-square.

57. John Sloan commented on Glackens's draftsmanship and his astonishing memory, as well as his repeated studies, in *Artists of the Philadelphia Press: William Glackens, George Luks, Everett Shinn, John Sloan* (Philadelphia: Philadelphia Museum of Art, 1945), 7–8. Glackens's methods are also discussed in Ira Glackens, *William Glackens and the Ashcan Group* (New York: Crown, 1957); Gerdts and Santis, *William Glackens*; and Avis Berman, ed., *William Glackens* (New York: Skira Rizzoli, in association with the Barnes Foundation, 2014).
58. The oil version of the pastel shown in Fig. 81, formerly in the Evans collection, was sold on May 19, 2011. The pastels shown in Figs. 63 and 81 were purchased by Albert Barnes about 1913; Mrs. Barnes (Laura) later gave *City Scene* to the Brooklyn Museum. Fig. 81 is marked on the verso "Washington Square, $75"; see Richard Wattenmaker, *American Paintings and Works on Paper at the Barnes Foundation* (New Haven, CT: Yale University Press, 2010), 112.
59. Tridon, "An Exhibition of Pastels." "Blundering use of the wrong medium" wrote the *New York Sun*, December 1911; MacRae Family Papers. Occasionally, Glackens's oils from this period adopt the unblended, hatched stroke of pastels, suggesting some cross-fertilization of ideas; see for example *Breezy Day, Tugboats, New York Harbor* (c. 1910; Milwaukee Art Museum).
60. On the participants in the 1912 Pastellists exhibition, see note 69.
61. MacRae records in his diary the meeting on December 14 with Kuhn, Myers, and Henry Fitch Taylor that launched the new society. MacRae diary, AAA.
62. Davies was in Europe for the first exhibition; he showed at the following three. Kuhn exhibited in the third and fourth shows. On the Pastellists at the Armory Show, see Roberta J. M. Olson, "Drawings at the Armory Show: The Currency of Change and Modernism," in *The Armory Show at 100*, 302–3. MacRae showed pastels, but few others did; see the exhibition checklist at http://armory.nyhistory.org/category/artworks. For a survey of bibliography and recent archival discoveries, see Laurette E. McCarthy, "Armory Show: New Perspectives and Recent Discoveries," *Archives of American Art Journal* 51, no. 3/4 (Fall 2012): 22–35.
63. On Davies as a pastellist, see Elizabeth Wylie, "Arthur B. Davies," in *American Pastels in the Metropolitan Museum of Art*, 74–76, 83–84. His role in the Armory Show is studied in Kimberly Orcutt, "Arthur B. Davies—Hero or Villain," in *The Armory Show at 100*, 29–39. Bernard B. Perlman discusses this pastel, its symbolic meaning, and its relationship to motion photography in *The Lives, Loves, and Art of Arthur B. Davies,* (New York: SUNY Press, 1998), 223–26. Exhibited at the Armory Show as *Design, Birth of Tragedy*, this pastel may relate to a group of four works similarly subtitled "Design" at the Pastellists second exhibition in 1911. Davies also showed three items titled *Design* at the AWS earlier that year.
64. "The Pastellists Show," (New York) *Evening Mail,* February 24, 1912; MacRae Family Papers.

65. The gradual incursion of pastel in Prendergast's work to a peak of intensity in 1916–18 can be tracked in Carol Clark, Nancy Mowll Mathews, and Gwendolyn Owens, *Maurice Brazil Prendergast, Charles Prendergast: A Catalogue Raisonné* (Williamstown, MA: Williams College Museum of Art; Munich: Prestel-Verlag, 1990). After a few instances in 1907, pastel appears more often from about 1910–11, in tandem with the pastel exhibitions, although the preponderance of undated work and the possibility that he added pastel to earlier work makes a precise pattern elusive. Warren Adelson argues for a coherent body of pastel work by Prendergast from about 1910 to 1920 that "sought to synthesize the fluidity and clarity of watercolor with the density and impasto of oil," achieving a new effect of saturated color and textural complexity; see *The Unknown Pastels: Maurice Brazil Prendergast* (New York: Universe Books, with Coe Kerr Gallery, 1987), 5. In Boston or in Europe during most of the period of the Pastellists, Prendergast may have been encouraged by the example of Glackens or other friends in New York; his participation in the fourth exhibition at the National Arts Club followed shortly after a visit to New York in December 1913.

66. Prendergast showed *State House Grounds*, no. 176 in *Exhibition [of] Contemporary Art*, with a preface by J. N. L. [J. Nilsen Laurvik] (New York: National Arts Club, 1914). A work by the same title was shown at PAFA in 1913 and at the Boston Art Club in 1914; see Clark, Mathews, and Davis, *Maurice Brazil Prendergast, Charles Prendergast: A Catalogue Raisonné*, no. 2165, currently unlocated. This larger exhibition at the National Arts Club ran from February 15 to March 7, 1914; the gallery of pastels may have appeared for a shorter period. The Pastellists' display included numbers 140–223, by twenty-nine artists; from the checklist and reviews, it appears that prints and watercolors were included. New to the Pastellists this year were Childe Hassam, George Hart, Ernest Haskell, Eugene Higgins, Nathaniel Dolinsky, Vernon Ellis, Leo Mielziner, Walter Pach, Telford Paullin, Maurice Prendergast, Joseph Stella, and ten new women exhibitors: Fanny Brown, Aileen King Dresser, Sarah Freedman, Anne Goldthwaite, Edith Haworth, Herminie Kleinert, Ella Condie Lamb, Charlotte Meltzer, Ethel Myers, and Mary C. Rogers.

67. Simultaneous "extremist" exhibitions at the National Arts Club, the Montross Gallery, and at the Macdowell Club created a vortex of controversy. Many journalists reviewed all three shows together, with simply a mention of the Pastellists; for example, see "'Progressive' Art Exhibited at National Club," *New York Times*, February 7, 1914, 10; "What Is Happening in the World of Art," *New York Sun*, February 8, 1914, 70; and William B. McCormick, "Cubists and Other Obscurants Have Their Innings this Month," *New York Press*, February 1, 1914, 8. See also Carol Lowrey, "The National Arts Club, Its Founding, Early History, and the Artist Life Membership Program" (PhD diss., City University of New York, 2003), 58–60.

68. For an overview, see Mary Wayne Fritzsche and Gail Stavitsky, "Pastel and the American Modernists," in *American Pastels in the Metropolitan Museum of Art*, 21–28.

69. No checklist has been located for the third exhibition, held at the Powell Gallery from February 19 to March 9, 1912, although press accounts suggest a group of about forty-eight objects by fourteen artists. The majority of the artists were new: Gutzon Borglum, John Breyfogle, Samuel Halpert, Walt Kuhn, George Luks, Ivan Olinsky, Allen Tucker, and Max Weber. Returning artists were Bellows, Dabo, Davies, Kramer, MacRae, and Myers. The smaller group and high turnover imply a loss of interest, and Susan Larkin suggests that both the third and fourth exhibitions were driven more by MacRae than by the group; see *On Home Ground*, 36n25. Attention to this smaller exhibition was less than seen

in 1911, but accounts were warm: "A more stimulating pastel show has seldom been seen in this bailiwick. . . . This exhibition is the talk of the studios," said *The Sun* (New York) in "Things Seen in the World of Art," February 25, 1912, 10.

70. According to accounts in the press, Weber also showed an "extremely unpleasant" figure study and a still life of "strange uncouth beauty" in the third Pastellist show; "The Pastellists' Show," (New York) *Evening Mail*, February 24, 1912; "Matters of Art," *New York Daily Tribune*, February 25, 1912, 7; "Pastels in Variety," *New York Times*, February 25, 1912, SM15. More cordially, the critic of the (New York) *Sun* described Weber's work as "mild, as if this unquestionably able young man had said: 'Let them have something they can understand'"; "Things Seen in the World of Art," *The Sun* (New York), February 25, 1912, 24. All articles can be found in MacRae Family Papers. Weber's career was first surveyed in Alfred H. Barr, *Max Weber Retrospective Exhibition* (New York: Museum of Modern Art, 1930); see Percy North, *Max Weber* (New York: Jewish Museum, 1982).
71. The work shown in 1914 has not been identified. On the development of Stella's technique and style in works on paper, see Joann Moser, *Visual Poetry: The Drawings of Joseph Stella* (Washington, DC: Smithsonian Institution Press, for the National Museum of American Art, 1990); *The Bagpipers* is reproduced on 11 and examples of his Pittsburgh series appear on pages 41–50. See also Barbara Haskell, *Joseph Stella* (New York: Whitney Museum of American Art, 1994), 44–45, with examples of his old-masterly figure studies in charcoal from 1908–10 on pages 24–26, 32–33, 36. See also Irma B. Jaffe, *Joseph Stella* (New York: Fordham University Press, 1970, 1988), plates 12–23.
72. Odilon Redon had a major show of pastels in Paris in 1908; his work appeared at the Durand-Ruel Gallery in New York in 1906 and 1910 and at the Carroll Gallery in 1915. Other pastels by Stella from the 1914–19 period are reproduced and discussed in Haskell, *Joseph Stella*, 48, 52, 56–68.
73. Moser discusses the symbolic and poetic content of these pastels and notes Stella's search for pure color in these works; see *Visual Poetry: The Drawings of Joseph Stella*, 88–89, and 150n80, which describes his preferred pastel sets and papers.
74. On this series by Dove, see Barbara Haskell, *Arthur Dove* (New York: New York Graphic Society, for the San Francisco Museum of Art, 1974), 15, 20–25. Untitled at first, they were soon dubbed *The Ten Commandments*; Stieglitz later titled some of them *Nature Symbolized.* On this series, its critical response, and Dove's use of pastel, see Melanie Kirschner, *Arthur Dove: Watercolors and Pastels* (New York: Braziller, 1998), 22–35; and Ann Lee Morgan, *Arthur Dove: Life and Work, with a Catalogue Raisonné* (Newark: University of Delaware Press, 1984), 18, 43–44, 104–111.
75. Kirschner argues that Dove's later experimentation with mixed media in the 1920s continued the pursuit of the matte, absorptive surface of his pastels; *Arthur Dove: Watercolors and Pastels*, 30.
76. On the development of O'Keeffe's drawing techniques, see David Turner and Barbara Haskell, *Georgia O'Keeffe: Works on Paper* (Santa Fe: Museum of New Mexico Press, 1985) and Barbara Buhler Lynes, *Georgia O'Keeffe: Catalogue Raisonné*, 2 vols. (New Haven, CT: Yale University Press, in association with the National Gallery of Art and the Georgia O'Keeffe Foundation, 1999).
77. O'Keeffe was enchanted by a reproduction of Dove's pastel *Based on Leaf Forms and Spaces* (now lost) in Arthur Jerome Eddy's influential 1914 book *Cubists and Post-Impressionism*; she later sought out his two pastels shown at the Forum Exhibition of 1916, which were from the group first seen at the 291 gallery in 1912. On their friendship and their mutual interest in pastel, see Debra Bricker Balken, *Dove/O'Keeffe: Circles of Influence* (New Haven, CT: Yale University Press, for the Sterling and Francine Clark Art Institute, 2009).

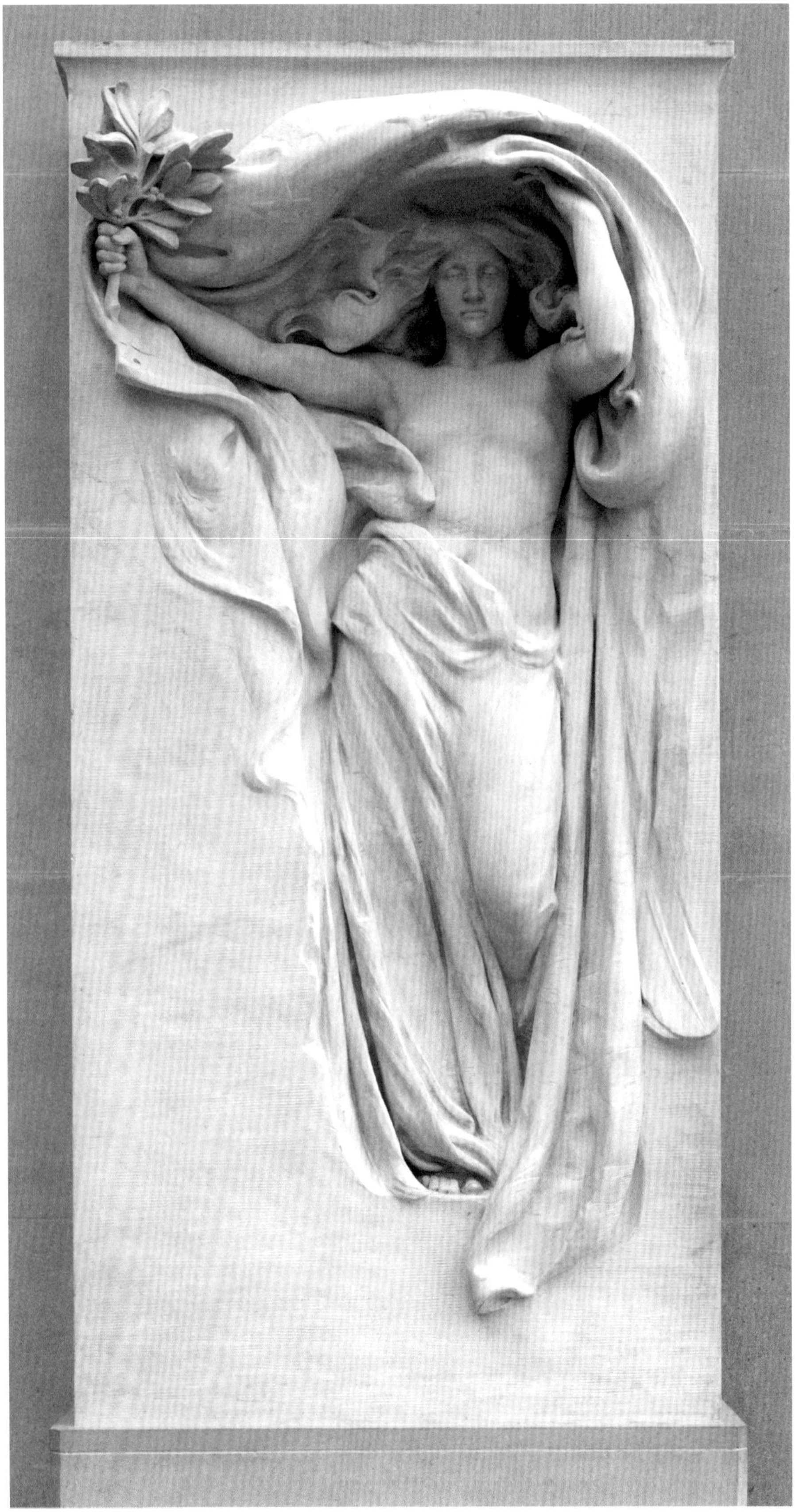

Lecture given on
October 12, 2021

New-York
Historical Society

New York City

What a Relief! Innovations in American Sculpture, 1875–1910

DAVID B. DEARINGER

The aesthetic and technical changes that occurred in American sculpture in the last quarter of the nineteenth century are well documented. They are part of an oft-told tale: after the Civil War, American sculptors went to Europe in record numbers, looking for a more sophisticated educational experience than what was available at home. First-rate art schools, especially in Paris, staffed by successful professional sculptors; an inexpensive and relaxed lifestyle; and a liberal attitude toward gender and race were part of the Continental allure. With their educations completed, most of these Americans eventually returned home, where they set about attracting patrons and sharing their newfound knowledge with other sculptors. "A pronounced and helpful feature of the new order," Lorado Taft, who was one of their number, wrote, "is the fact that as a rule the Parisian-trained sculptors do not remain abroad; they return to live with their own people, and like their French masters, they delight in teaching."[1]

Among the things these artists learned from their French masters was an appreciation for materials other than marble, which had been all the rage in America since the 1820s. Specifically, this meant bronze. Once they witnessed the liberating possibilities of this marvelous material of temporary fluidity and ultimate strength, they began to design their own works with it in mind. Bronze, they realized, would allow them to represent a wider range of movement, render emotions with greater subtlety, and delineate the details of the world as crisply, loosely, or decoratively as they wished. While American painters were redefining the strictures of academic painting by milking the materiality of oil paint, American sculptors were learning how to use their own materials to evoke atmosphere, space, spontaneity, and energy. Therein lurked the origins of modernism.

It is easy enough to see some of the changes that occurred during this period with a simple comparison of objects. Look, for example, at Hiram Powers's quintessentially neoclassical *Eve Tempted* of 1839–42 (Fig. 90) and Frederick MacMonnies's fin-de-siècle *Bacchante and*

Fig. 89
Daniel Chester French
Mourning Victory from the Melvin Memorial, 1906–8, carved 1912–15 by Piccirilli Brothers Carving Studio
Marble
120½ × 57¼ × 28¾ in. (306.1 × 145.4 × 73 cm)
The Metropolitan Museum of Art, New York; Gift of James C. Melvin, 1912 (15.75)

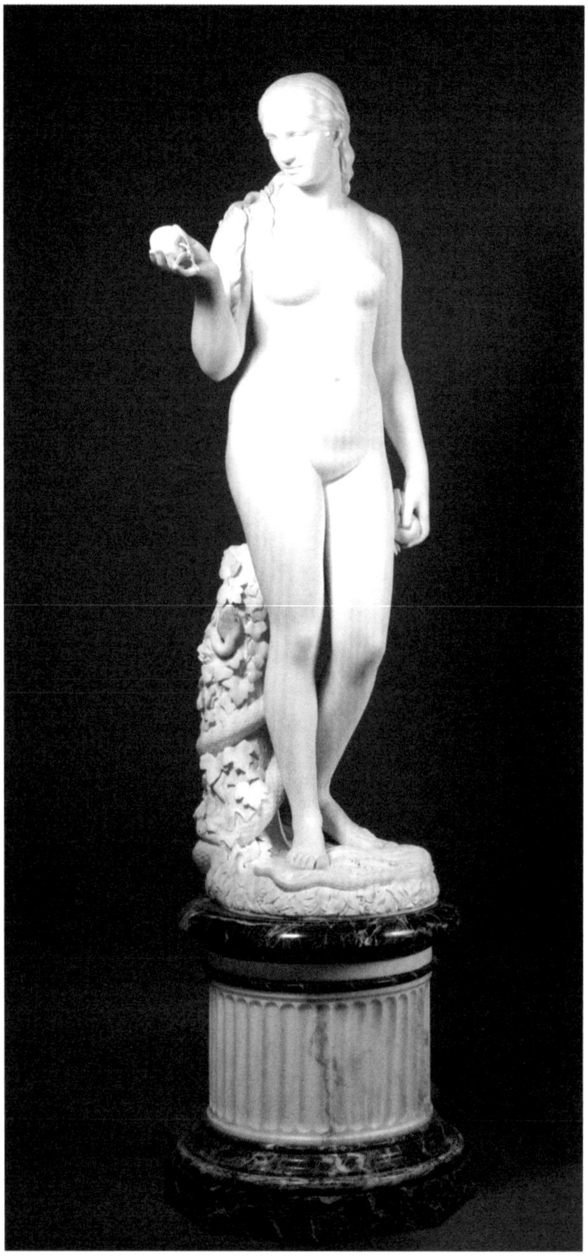

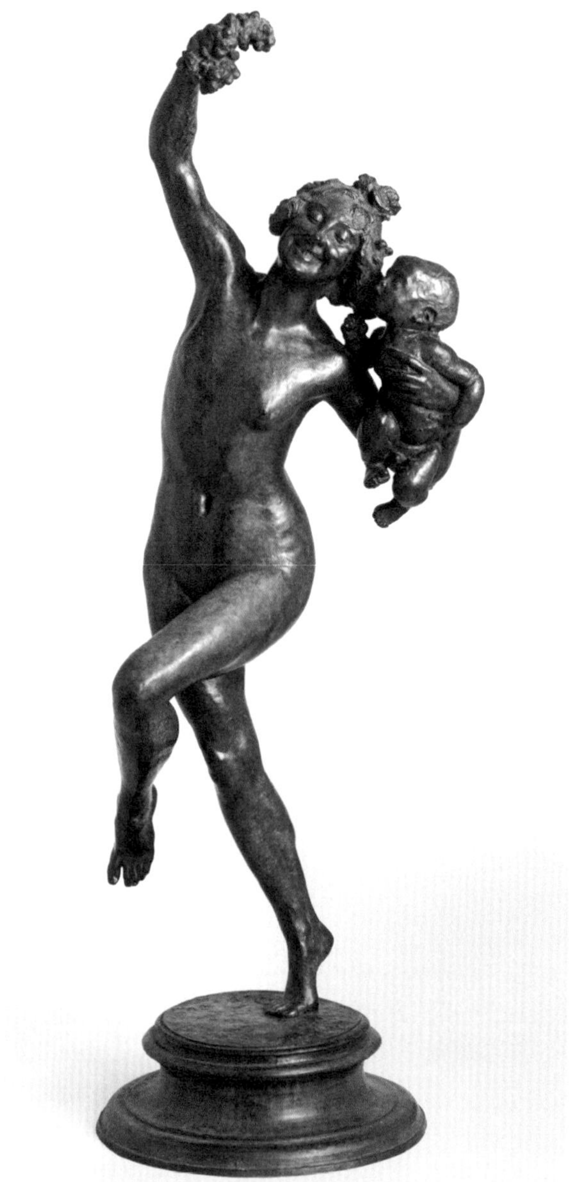

Fig. 90
Hiram Powers
Eve Tempted, modeled 1839–42, carved 1873–77
Marble
68⅞ × 29⅞ × 20½ in. (174.9 × 75.8 × 52 cm)
Smithsonian American Art Museum, Smithsonian Institution, Washington, DC; Museum purchase in memory of Ralph Cross Johnson, 1968.155.126

Fig. 91
Frederick MacMonnies
Bacchante and Infant Faun, 1893–94, cast 1894
Bronze
84 × 29¾ × 31½ in. (213.4 × 75.6 × 80 cm)
The Metropolitan Museum of Art, New York; Gift of Charles F. McKim, 1897 (97.19)

Infant Faun of 1893–94 (Fig. 91).[2] Both sculptures—one marble, the other bronze—depict nude, fetishized women caught in a moment of temptation. But it is their physical and emotional differences that are most striking. Eve is a study in passivity and fecklessness; the Bacchante is a creature of exuberance and abandon. One sculpture, with its scriptural theme, warns of the wages of sin; the other, rooted in myth, celebrates it.

But these three-dimensional, freestanding objects tell us only so much about the formal and functional changes that sculpture underwent during that time. More information emerges when one compares examples of the other major volumetric division of the art: relief sculpture. One can consider, for example, the last-gasp neoclassicist Margaret Foley's *Pascuccia* of about 1865 (Fig. 92) versus the new-wave Augustus Saint-Gaudens's portrait of Samuel Gray Ward from 1881 (Fig. 93). In its seemingly-unfinished sketchiness—a product of quickly applied strokes, gashes, and gouges—Saint-Gaudens's bronze is purposefully at variance with the highly polished, wall-ready neoclassical marble. Stylistically, the changes seen here mirror those that were taking place in American painting at the same time. Indeed, this mention of the two mediums in the same sentence is hardly arbitrary: the symbiosis between painting and relief sculpture has been recognized for centuries and was acknowledged in nineteenth-century America. In 1863, one of this country's earliest art periodicals, the *New Path,* made the point: "The flatter the relief," the journal decreed, "the nearer it [is] to picture-making."[3] A few years later, *Century* magazine told its

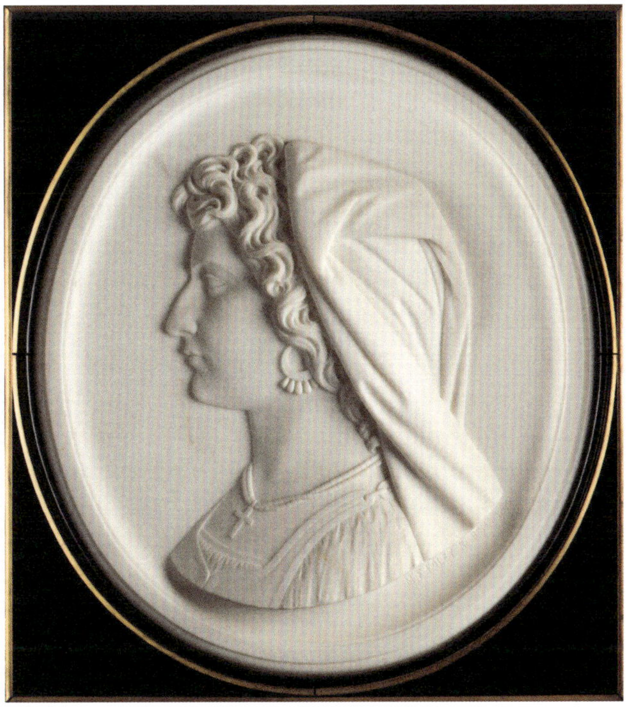

Fig. 92
Margaret Foley
Marble Relief of Pasuccia on Stand (detail), c. 1865
Marble, wood
Overall (framed relief): 28 × 25 × 3½ in. (71.1 × 63.5 × 8.9 cm)
Brooklyn Museum; Bequest of Marie Bernice Bitzer, gift of Mabel Rusch, and bequest of Mrs. John H. Bennett, by exchange, 2003.55b

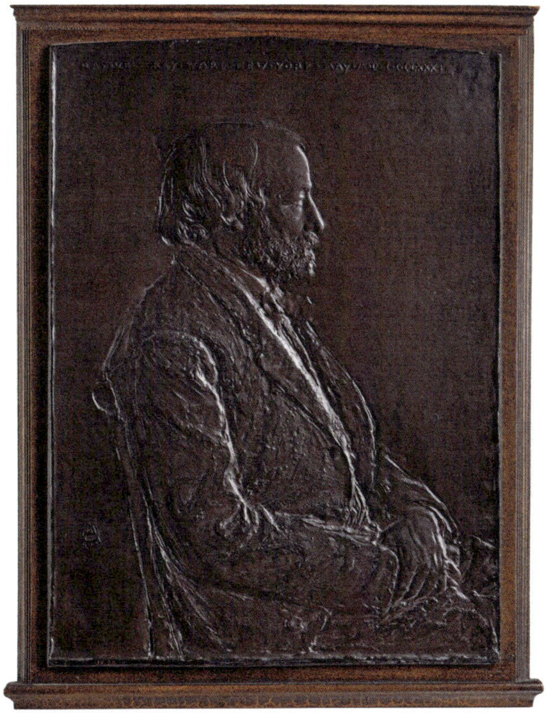

Fig. 93
Augustus Saint-Gaudens
Samuel Gray Ward, 1881, cast c. 1908–9
Bronze
19 × 13⅛ in. (48.3 × 33.3 cm)
The Metropolitan Museum of Art, New York; Gift of Mrs. Augustus Saint-Gaudens, 1912 (12.29)

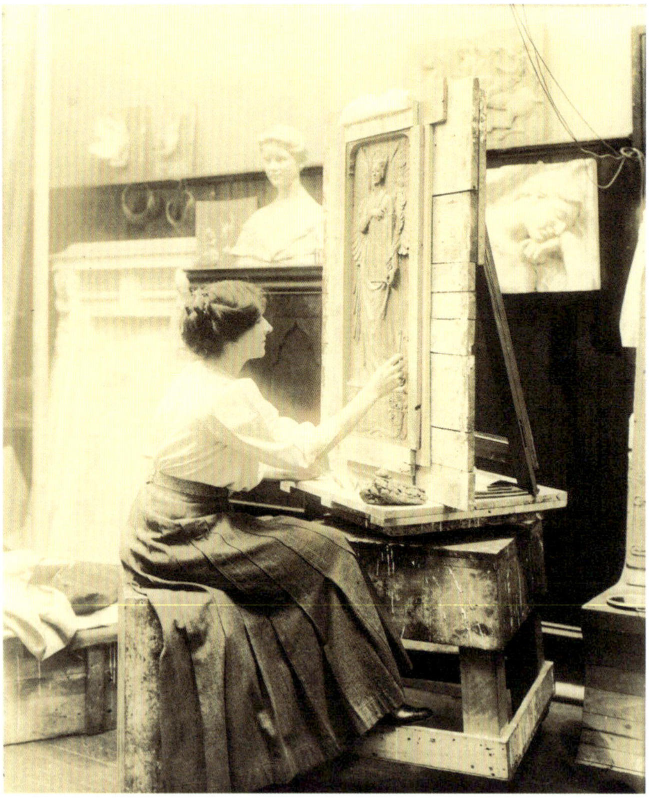

Fig. 94
Jessie Tarbox Beals
Evelyn Beatrice Longman Working on "The Ryle Memorial" in her 14th Street Studio, New York, c. 1905
Photograph
The Loomis Chaffee Archives,
Loomis Chaffee School, Windsor, CT

Fig. 95
Marble grave stele of a little girl, Greek,
c. 450–440 BCE
Parian marble
31¾ × 14⁹⁄₁₆ in. (80.6 × 37 cm).
Base: 15½ × 4 in. (39.4 × 10.2 cm)
The Metropolitan Museum of Art, New York; Fletcher Fund, 1927 (27.45)

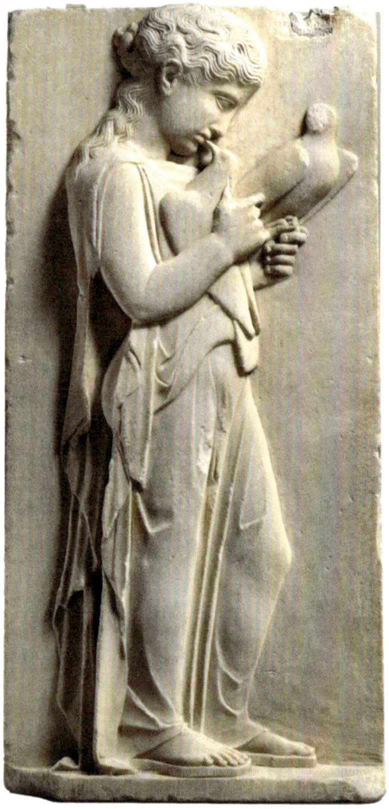

readers that relief sculpture was "a kind of *drawing*... an art nearly allied to painting."[4] Elsewhere, it was described as "pictorial, rather than sculptural" and defined simply as "raised drawing."[5]

Relief sculpture is by nature fully frontal, made so by the thing that distinguishes it from freestanding sculpture. Its structure and stability depend on a planar surface from which its representational bits project or recede. This surface is the relief's "picture plane" and acts as a background for its subject. For both practical and pictorial reasons, it is an integral part of the object from its conception and remains so through the long process of modeling, molding, carving, and casting. Establishing this surface is one of the first things a sculptor does in planning a relief. Clay is pressed into a frame to create a slab, an outline of the intended design is etched into the clay with a blunt instrument, and the area around the outline is scraped down, thereby establishing the plane. From there, projecting or receding shapes that will articulate the thing to be represented are built up and refined until the final form is achieved. At some point, the clay slab might be propped on an easel for ease of access (Fig. 94), thereby establishing a physical relationship between the slab and the sculptor that parallels that between a painter and a canvas. Ultimately, the finished clay model will be cast in plaster and, funds permitting, translated into a more permanent material.

Since it is the projecting or receding parts of the relief that define its subject, it is easy enough for a sculptor to leave the surrounding planar surface—the background—flat and unarticulated, as did most classical (Fig. 95) and neoclassical sculptors (see Fig. 92). A smooth, "perfect" surface, it was thought, ensured that the object would remain purely thematic and didactic. But during the last third of the nineteenth century, in a sort of reverse minimalism that was more baroque than classical, sculptors began to realize that this flat, traditionally blank surface was ripe for artistic innovation. It could be a place to abstract nature's nontactile, ethereal elements—things that would not have a direct narrative or representational function. These ideas were given their first expression in the works of the two sculptors who dominated the period and who will be the focus of this discussion, Augustus Saint-Gaudens (1848–1907) and his near-contemporary Daniel Chester French (1850–1931).

When the American artist and critic Kenyon Cox painted Augustus Saint-Gaudens's portrait in 1887 (Fig. 96), he chose to show his friend at work on a relief sculpture. By placing more of Saint-Gaudens's reliefs in the background of the portrait, Cox made his message clear:

Fig. 96
Kenyon Cox
Augustus Saint-Gaudens, 1887
(replica, 1908)
Oil on canvas
33½ × 47⅛ in. (85.1 × 119.7 cm)
The Metropolitan Museum of Art, New York; Gift of friends of the sculptor, through August F. Jaccaci, 1908 (08.130)

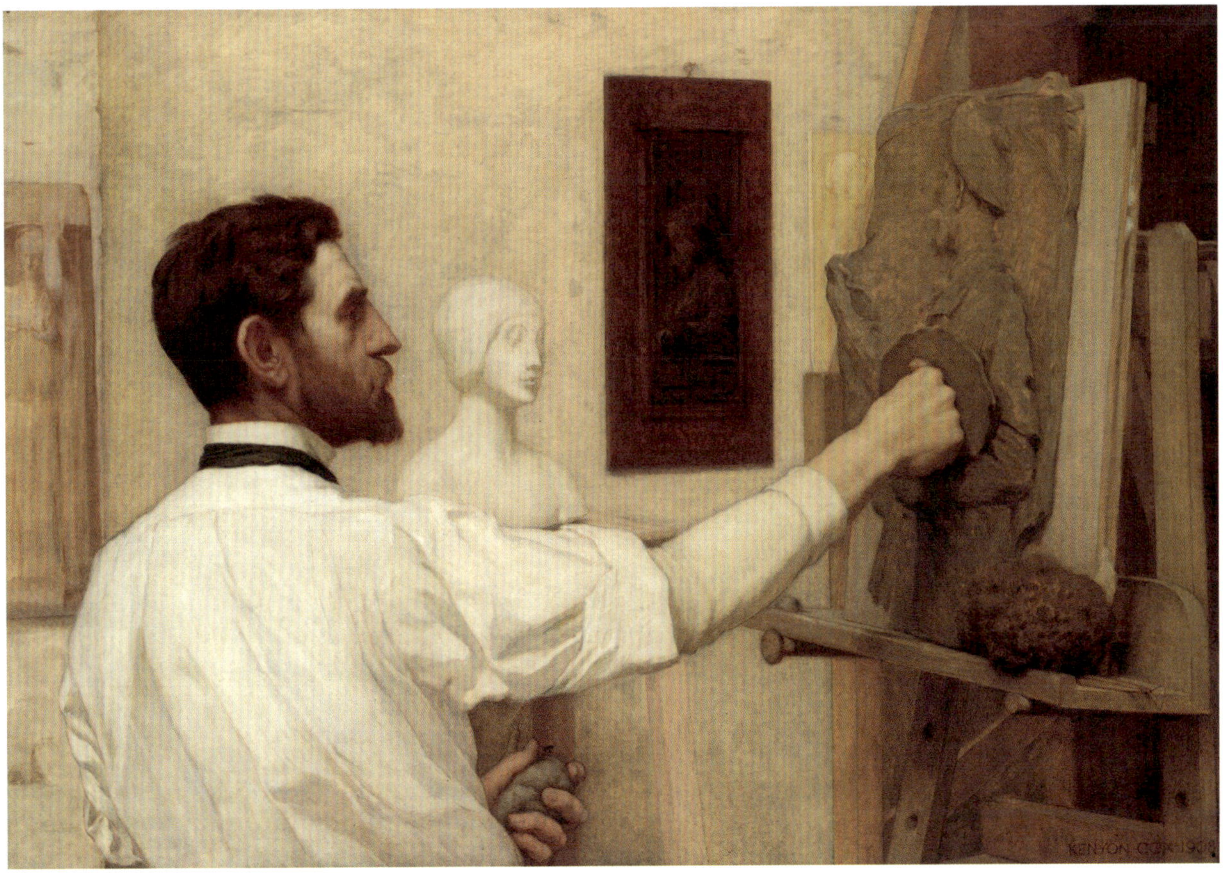

Saint-Gaudens had an apparently natural affinity for modeling in relief and, in fact, did it better than anyone else.[6] In his role as a critic, Cox reiterated this observation every chance he got. From the full-length article he wrote about Saint-Gaudens in 1887 to the eulogy he delivered on the sculptor's death in 1908, Cox praised every aspect of Saint-Gaudens's talents in the highest terms, but especially when it came to the artist's skill at making relief sculptures. Having recognized Saint-Gaudens as "a designer by nature," Cox numbered him among "the supreme masters of relief" and credited him with resuscitating "the dead art of sculpture" by bringing the quintessentially Renaissance form of relief into the modern era.[7]

In fact, Saint-Gaudens's professional life began with relief sculpture, albeit on a tiny scale. Starting in 1861, the sculptor trained with one New York cameo cutter and then worked for another. Cox likened these experiences to the apprenticeships by which Florentine sculptors had learned their trade in the fifteenth century. Living up to this grand tradition, Saint-Gaudens mastered the technique of relief while still in his teens and soon came to appreciate its artistic promise and prefer it above all other forms. In his autobiographical *Reminiscences*, annotated and published after his death by his son Homer Saint-Gaudens, he wrote that this preference, acquired in his youth in New York, was "forcibly renewed" in Paris, where he traveled in 1867 to gain the skills he needed to become a professional sculptor.[8] First at the Petite École and then at the École des Beaux-Arts, he learned about the advantages of bronze, not only for the creation of three-dimensional works but also as a viable medium for relief sculpture on a scale larger than that of the cameos on which he had cut his technical teeth. Kenyon Cox notes that in the Paris studios of some of France's leading sculptors, where reliefs were much in evidence, Saint-Gaudens "became a part of the fresh and vigorous movement of contemporary sculpture."[9]

Saint-Gaudens's next step was to take his newly acquired knowledge of modern sculptural technique and material and see how it fit with traditional ways. In November 1870, he moved to Rome, where he found that tradition in Renaissance portrait medallions by fifteenth-century artists such as Antonio Pisanello and Sperandio Savelli. He was struck by the elegant but simple design that characterized these objects, especially the way they integrated image and typography, an aesthetic that would profoundly inform his own work.[10] He bought casts of several of these medallions and, once back in New York, displayed them in his studio—only to find them intimidating. In 1875, he showed them to the painter John La Farge, with whom he was about to collaborate on several projects, all the while complaining that he would never be able to do anything as good. La Farge's emphatic retort was, "Why not?"[11]

La Farge was not being flippant. He soon put Saint-Gaudens to the test by subcontracting him to create low-relief sculptures for an altarpiece and reredos that he was designing for the high-society St. Thomas Church on Fifth Avenue in New York. Saint-Gaudens's contribution to the project was a series of angels kneeling on either side of a large cross (Fig. 97). They were Saint-Gaudens's first large relief sculptures and constituted his public debut as an artist.[12] When the altar was dedicated in January 1878, critics sat up and took notice. Clarence Cook, one of the most respected of these critics, gave Saint-Gaudens a star-is-born review. "The center of all eyes must be Mr. St. Gaudens' part of this interesting work," Cook wrote for *Scribner's* in February. Like Cox, Cook linked Saint-Gaudens to the artists of the Renaissance, while recognizing his style as something new and innovative. "There is no slavish imitation [here]," Cook wrote, "nor anything out of date nor out of time."[13]

With the support of influencers like La Farge, Cox, and Cook, things began to move quickly for Saint-Gaudens. By the time he had

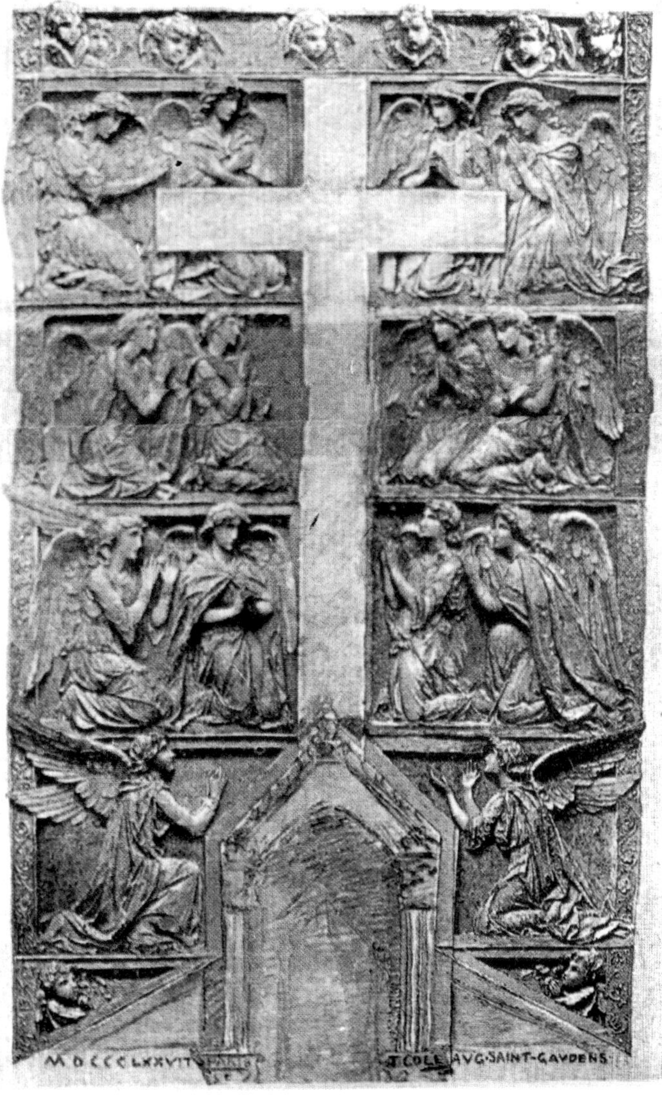

Fig. 97
Timothy Cole
Engraving of Augustus Saint-Gaudens's "Adoration of the Cross by Angels"
Reproduced in *Scribner's Monthly* 15, no. 4 (February 1878): 576

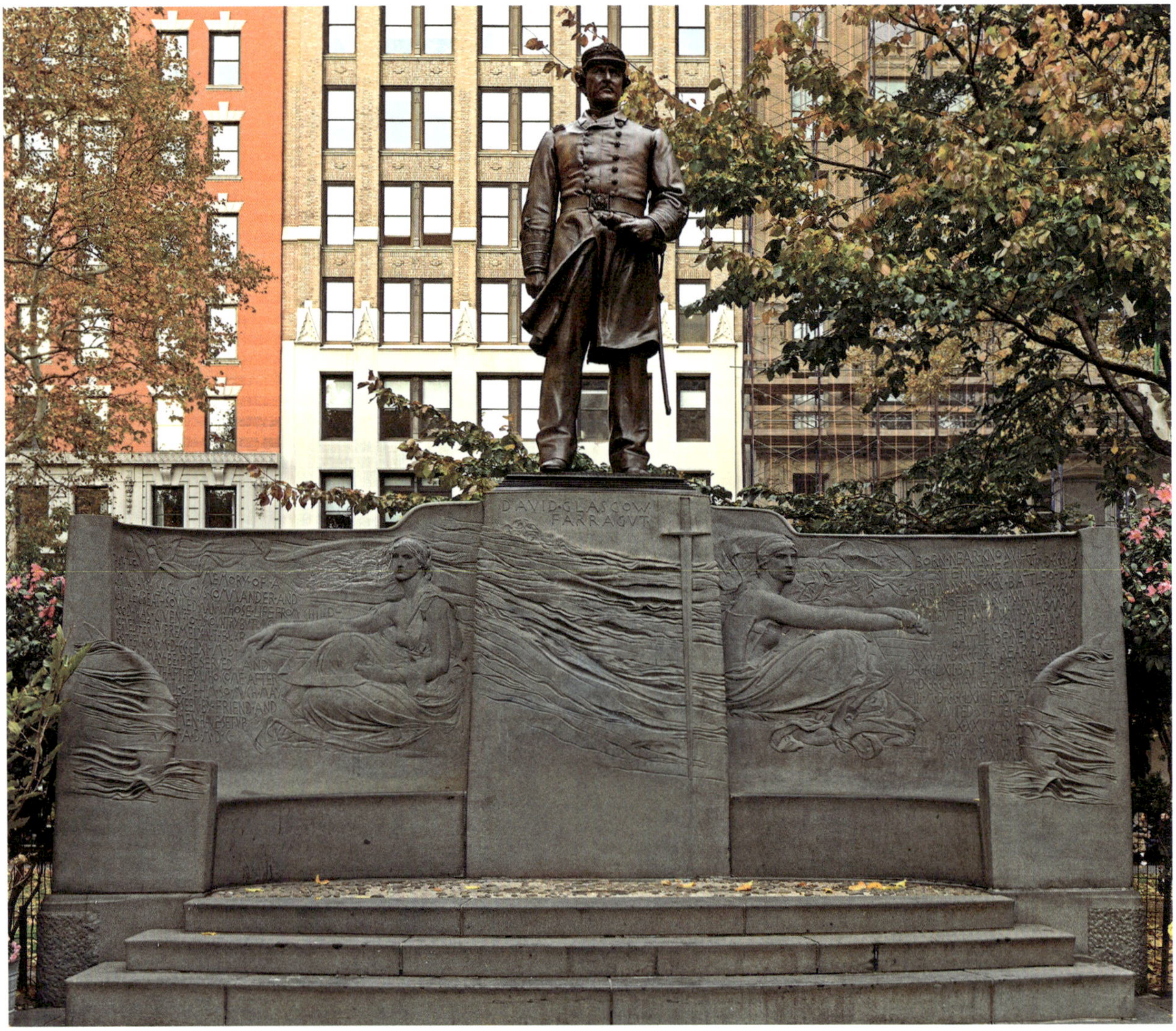

Fig. 98
Augustus Saint-Gaudens
Admiral David Glasgow Farragut Monument, cast 1880
Bronze (figure), black granite (pedestal with exedra wings)
Figure: 9 ft. high. Pedestal with exedra wings: 9 ft. × 17 ft. 6 in. × 9 ft. 6 in. (2.7 × 5.3 × 2.9 m)
Madison Square Park, New York

fulfilled his obligations for the St. Thomas project, he was hard at work on an even more visible commission, the first of over twenty public sculptures that he would design in the coming decades.[14] This was a monument to the Civil War hero Admiral David Farragut, commissioned under the aegis of the New York City Parks Department for Madison Square Park in Manhattan (Fig. 98). The commissioners of this publicly funded project reasonably expected that it would result in a traditional freestanding statue atop a sturdy stone pedestal of standard proportions. They would get their statue, but Saint-Gaudens had his own ideas about its style and that of the environment in which it would stand.[15]

For the latter, he partnered with his friend the architect Stanford White, who was charged with designing the sculpture's pedestal and whatever other architectural bits of business were thought necessary for Farragut's support. Saint-Gaudens gave White carte blanche as to the shape and proportions of the structure, but he reserved its iconographic embellishment for himself.[16] White was an artist of the moment, as was Saint-Gaudens, and his plan called for something more than a mere plinth. Instead, he designed a graceful, classical exedra—"a pedestal with wings," as the *New York Times* called it[17]—with plenty of surface for Saint-Gaudens to cover with reliefs that fittingly would be in a maritime mode. White was confident that whatever Saint-Gaudens came up with would be "bully." His only request was that the sculptor make his imagined sea "stormy."[18] Accordingly, Saint-Gaudens's relief suggests a mid-ocean swell at the moment it passes under Farragut's ship. The admiral stands above, his feet planted on the ship's prow, represented by the centrally placed plinth whose gently curving trapezoidal shape is reminiscent of the entasis of a classical Greek column. The whole affair lifts and thrusts Farragut forward and provides an appropriate stage for his wind-blown performance—and for Saint-Gaudens's dead-on summation of the admiral's personality.[19]

Meanwhile, Saint-Gaudens was planning the relief sculptures that were literally and figuratively to underpin the image of Farragut above. The results suggest that he was already on his way to codifying his own theories about how a relief sculpture, with its limited depth and breadth, could successfully cover as many artistic bases as possible. He would later articulate these theories to his students and followers. Avoid filling the backgrounds of your reliefs with things representational (e.g., flora, fauna, or furniture), he would tell them, and resist the urge to build up multiple planes of perspective. Instead, use the background—the *entire* background—to achieve compositional harmony by concentrating on effects of light, air, and space. "Remember that your background is your atmosphere," he instructed, "and part of the composition, [which] should extend from edge to edge of the frame." Let the "texture, lettering, molding, background, and all" draw the viewer's eyes across the entire surface of the object and unify it as a single and singular work of art.[20]

As he designed the broad oceanic relief for Farragut's "wings," Saint-Gaudens gave his theories tangible form. Pushed to their decorative limits, the watery elements that set the scene flow across the central plinth, extend outward, and spill around the contours and corners of the outer edges of the monument. This sculpted liquid supports self-assured allegories of Courage and Loyalty that, from their positions on either side of the plinth, float comfortably in it. Their inextricable relationship to their environment is expressed by their flowing hair, which melds with the appropriately erratic lines of the water and leads the eye to biographical and hagiographic inscriptions laid out on the face of the exedra. At either end of the structure, leaping dolphins, carved in relief but threatening to become fully three-dimensional, form a parenthetical pair that redirects the viewer's attention back toward the figure of Farragut. In one final gesture of decorative genius,

Saint-Gaudens valorizes the balancing plinth with an image of a large sword, an outsized exclamation point that, with a modernist stroke, he places off-center.

Recent historians have diagnosed Saint-Gaudens's Farragut reliefs as early-onset Art Nouveau.[21] But there is something of the past here too. The "wrapping relief" effect that Saint-Gaudens used to heighten the illusion of three-dimensionality recalls Neo-Assyrian sculptures such as the famous lamassu figures of the ninth century BCE (Fig. 99), which use the same corner-turning device. Saint-Gaudens would have seen examples of these impressive, hard-to-miss objects during his years in Paris, where they had been on display at the Louvre since 1847.[22] Like the creators of those ancient hybrids, Saint-Gaudens pushed his design into a formal territory that falls somewhere between in-the-round and relief and combines attributes of both types. He also understood, as had the Assyrians, how to successfully integrate the textual and figural parts of his sculptures, not hesitating to cover as much surface as necessary to bring the monument's message home. While Saint-Gaudens's narrative and iconographic motives may have differed from those of his ancient predecessors, there can be little doubt that his aesthetic choices echoed theirs.

Whatever their sources, Saint-Gaudens and White's innovative designs for the Farragut pedestal created some unease among the project's commissioners and delayed the monument's completion. But finally, in the spring of 1881, its two great elements—the bronze figure of Farragut, cast in Paris, and the stone base, carved in America—were united and the whole thing dedicated at ceremonies held that May.[23] The figure of Farragut was lauded for capturing the admiral's personality, bravery, and energy. But it was the monument *as a whole* that was immediately recognized as a new kind of American sculpture.[24] The *New York Herald* declared it "the most noble piece of combined architecture and sculpture of its kind in the country."[25] Mariana Griswold Van Rensselaer, a pioneering critic and one of Saint-Gaudens's champions, thought that the monument's relief sculptures deserved special praise. "It is in work similar to this that Mr. St. Gaudens has won a good part of his fame," she wrote, "and it is a fresh proof of his ability that he has been able here to harmonize such delicate work with the strong effect of the crowning statue."[26] Writing for the *Nation,* the critic William C. Brownell stated that this "transmutation of blue-stone into marine significance is an accomplishment which few artists living, probably, could successfully attempt."[27] The ever-faithful Kenyon Cox went so far as to declare that, to his eye, Saint-Gaudens's talents were proven more by the reliefs than by the figure of Farragut, magnificent as it was.[28]

In the end, it is the cohesiveness of the Farragut monument that spells its genius. The hero stands between wind and water in a sea of contrasts that, rather than splintering the monument, unify it. Every

Fig. 99
Neo-Assyrian, Mesopotamia, Nimrud (ancient Kalhu)
Human-headed winged lion (lamassu), c. 883–859 BCE
Gypsum alabaster (relief panels)
122½ × 24½ × 109 in. (311.2 × 62.2 × 276.9 cm)
The Metropolitan Museum of Art, New York; Gift of John D. Rockefeller Jr., 1932 (32.143.2)

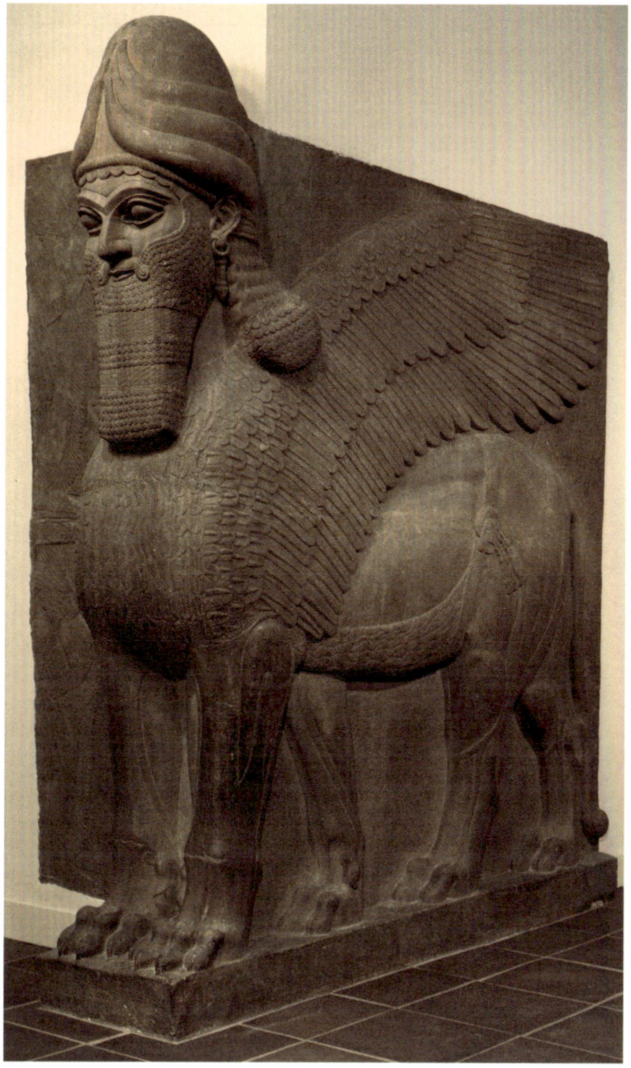

part is in service to the whole: realism balances stylization, decoration tempers representation, determination mitigates uncertainty, bronze converses with stone, and relief supplements statuary. Again, much of this is achieved because Saint-Gaudens insisted that all surfaces of the monument are intrinsic parts of a whole and are fair game for embellishments that extend "from edge to edge," or in this case, from sea to shining sea.

The standard understanding of Saint-Gaudens's chronology is that the Farragut monument made him famous. But the art historian Thayer Tolles has convincingly argued that Saint-Gaudens had already, by 1880, earned the respect of the American art world with a group of relief portraits—or "medallions" as Saint-Gaudens called them—of friends and fellow artists that he made starting in about 1877.[29] Here again is evidence of the influence of John La Farge, who actually gave

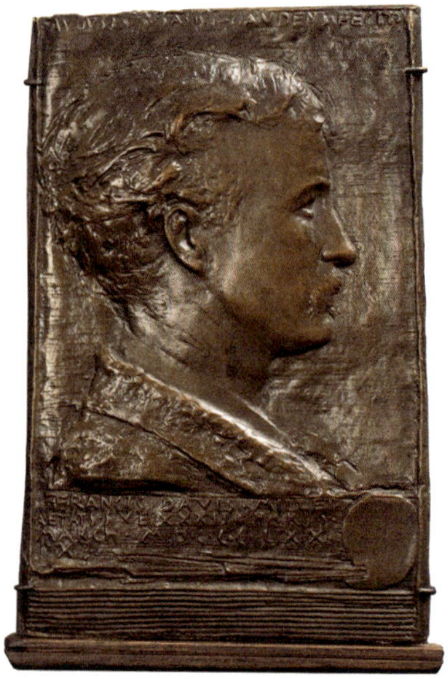

Fig. 100
Augustus Saint-Gaudens
Francis Davis Millet, 1879
Electrotype with bronze patina on wood backing
10½ × 6¾ in. (26.7 × 17.1 cm)
Conner-Rosenkranz, New York

the sculptor the confidence to pursue this tricky art. "There is no doubt that my intimacy with La Farge," Saint-Gaudens wrote, "has been a spur to higher endeavor [and is] no doubt the reason I have modeled so many medallions since."[30] "Paint a bas-relief," La Farge supposedly told him, by which he meant that the sculptor should take full advantage of the fluidity of wet clay by manipulating it the way painters do pigment.[31] Saint-Gaudens took the advice to heart, applying and refining it in over eighty relief portraits that he executed between the late 1870s and his death in 1907.[32] It was in these works that he gave full rein to his own aesthetic theories.

One of the earliest of these was a portrait of the artist and former American consul general in Rome David Maitland Armstrong (1877; Century Club, New York) that Saint-Gaudens made in 1877 for La Farge, who had introduced him to Armstrong.[33] The relief's small scale—about eight by five inches—marks it as a transitional work for Saint-Gaudens, between his cameos and his portrait medallions, and signaled his mastery of the relief form. Over the next five years, he produced more than twenty-five such works, among them several sensitive and highly personal portraits of fellow artists, including the American painter Francis Davis Millet (Fig. 100) and the French painter and sculptor Jules Bastien-Lepage (1880; Conner-Rosenkranz, New York).[34] A number of images of well-to-do patrons, such as Henry Shiff, a doctor (1880; Saint-Gaudens National Historic Site, Cornish, NH), and the financier Samuel Gray Ward, mentioned earlier (see Fig. 93), also belong to this period. In terms of the technique of relief, the portrait of Ward is of special interest, for with it Saint-Gaudens reached a new high in low relief. At only an eighth of an inch deep, it speaks of a spontaneity that, thanks to Saint-Gaudens's extraordinary mind-hand coordination, has nothing of the accidental about it. "My father was taught by hard discipline not to wait upon 'inspiration,'" the sculptor's son Homer later recalled, "but to think best with a modeling tool in his hand."[35]

While the material of Saint-Gaudens's reliefs may be shallow, their notional space is not. With potential distractions eliminated, the relief's background becomes for the sculptor an available and appropriate staging area for the illusions of immediacy, atmosphere, and space that he considered integral to the object's success. And by creating these effects through abstraction, he secured for himself a place in the history of early American modernism. His 1879 portrait of Rodman de Kay Gilder (Fig. 101), the two-year-old child of Saint-Gaudens's friends and supporters, the poet and editor Richard Watson Gilder and his wife, the painter Helena de Kay, is a case in point.[36] With modeling tools as his pencils and brushes and clay as his liquid pigment, Saint-Gaudens modeled as La Farge had urged him to do. Like any good draftsman, he varied the width and depth of the lines that he scratched into the clay to make objects that pointedly illustrate

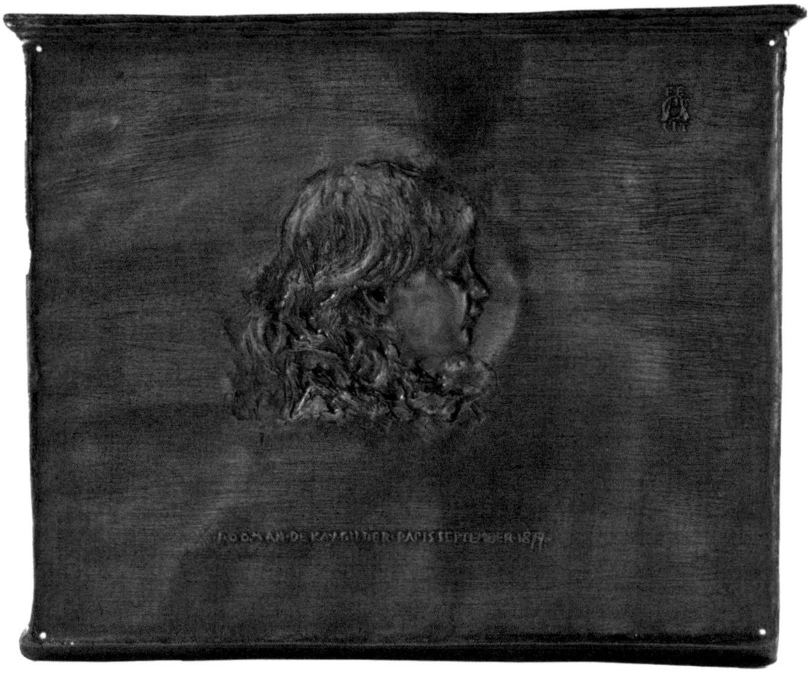

Fig. 101
Augustus Saint-Gaudens
Rodman de Kay Gilder, 1879, cast probably 1880
Bronze
13½ × 16⅞ in. (34.3 × 42.9 cm)
The Metropolitan Museum of Art, New York; Purchase, Morris K. Jesup Fund and Mr. and Mrs. Richard J. Schwartz Gift, 1994 (1994.50)

the kinship of relief sculpture to drawing and painting. As the composition expands to the edges of the object, the bronze subtly shifts and undulates. The child's head becomes a three-dimensional thing by both sinking into and emerging from what passes as malleable space. As though the child's head were pushing into a pillow, the surface seems to give: it is an old sculptural technique used here by Saint-Gaudens, as it had been by the likes of Michelangelo and Bernini, to express both the pliability and the strength of flesh and bone.[37]

Similarly, the painterly effect that Saint-Gaudens achieved as he wielded his tool to model Rodman Gilder's head is reminiscent of the techniques of the great Baroque painters, such as Frans Hals, who loosely limned the edges of forms in much the same way that Saint-Gaudens, two centuries later, made an abstraction out of little Rodman's hair. The sculptor has freely scratched and stabbed the clay, assured that his viewer's eye will successfully translate his marks into space, atmosphere, and solid form. By laying out light-catching striations across the entire surface of the relief, Saint-Gaudens extends and completes the illusion—and then defies it. In the manner of a Japanese printmaker or that of the American painter James McNeill Whistler, Saint-Gaudens floats a monogram at the upper right of the relief to remind us that we are not, after all, looking at real space but at an illusion, a picture plane that he, the artist, is free to define, deny, or embellish as he sees fit.[38]

Fig. 102
Augustus Saint-Gaudens
The Children of Jacob H. Schiff,
1884–85, carved 1906–7
Marble
68⅞ × 51 in. (174.9 × 129.5 cm)
The Metropolitan Museum of Art,
New York; Gift of Jacob H. Schiff, 1905
(05.15.3)

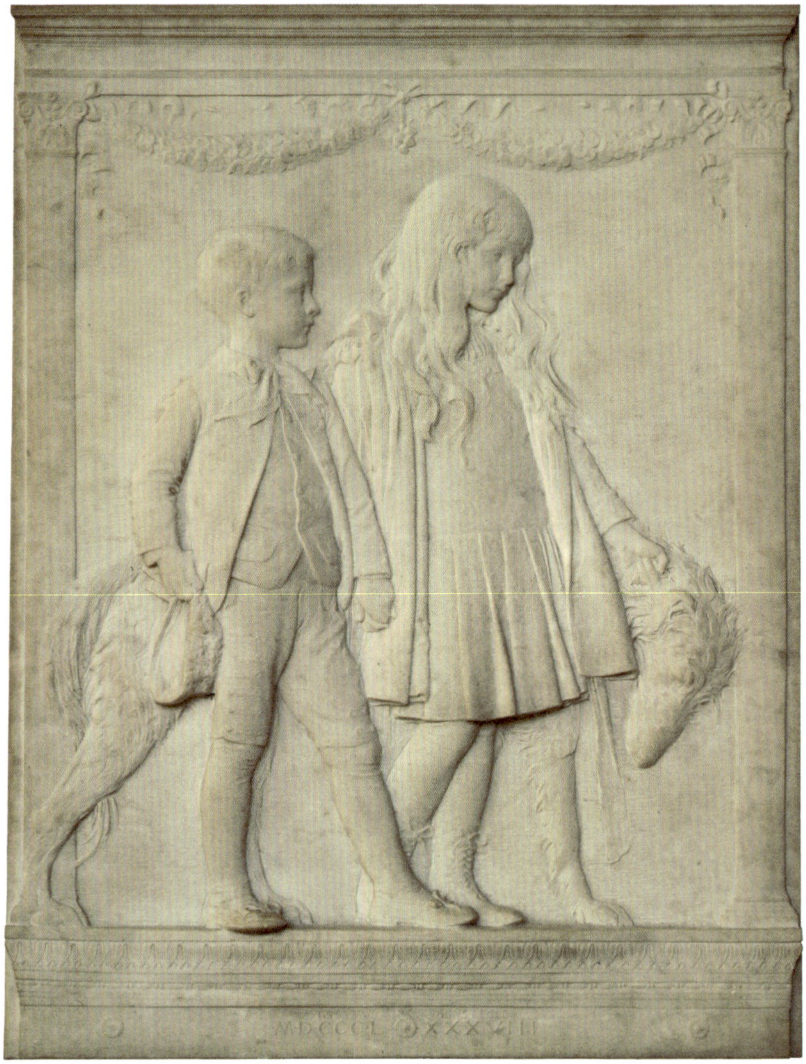

Having successfully applied his skills and theories to smaller reliefs, Saint-Gaudens had no trouble transferring them to larger ones. Among the grandest and most satisfying of these is his 1884 portrait of the children of Jacob Schiff, a wealthy New York banker, which he conceived to be cast in bronze but later replicated in marble (Fig. 102).[39] For such a large work—it is nearly six by four-and-a-half feet—it is modeled in surprisingly low relief. That did not stop Saint-Gaudens from pulling out all the optical stops in order to manipulate the viewer into suspending disbelief and accepting that one is looking at two full-bodied children and a dog strolling through a space that could well be an extension of one's own. He achieves this in various ways, some of which, ironically, are irrational. For one, he places the children in physically impossible poses, with their heads and legs in profile and their torsos turned toward the viewer. This anatomical trick, which is as old as the ancient Egyptians (Fig. 103), allows for a maximum of formal flattening without sacrificing information or spatial illusion. The dog does extra duty as a unifying element: the arc of its body is a furry fulfillment of Saint-Gaudens's case for an all-encompassing composition. Meanwhile, a contrapuntal cadence of limbs makes up the lower quadrant of the relief. One of the dog's legs is first in the sequence, another is last, and a third is tightly bound to one of the little boy's. This further integrates the figures and binds them sculpturally and emotionally. Part of the lower rim of the relief curves outward into the viewer's space to accommodate one of the boy's feet, which twists toward the viewer.[40] At left, the dog's tail and, at right, wisps of its fur overlap the faux pilasters that one might have read as parts of a frame but now realizes are "architecture." As in the portrait of Rodman Gilder, the background gently undulates, and, since the girl is meant to be seen as farther away from the viewer than the boy, her head presses into the background in the same way that Rodman Gilder's does. Parts of a garland at the top of the composition simply disappear into the background as though reacting to the vagaries of light and atmosphere.

The sculpture was a critical success when it debuted at the annual exhibition of the Society of American Artists in New York in 1886, and though it was not originally created as a public work, it was remembered and continued to receive plaudits for decades. When the

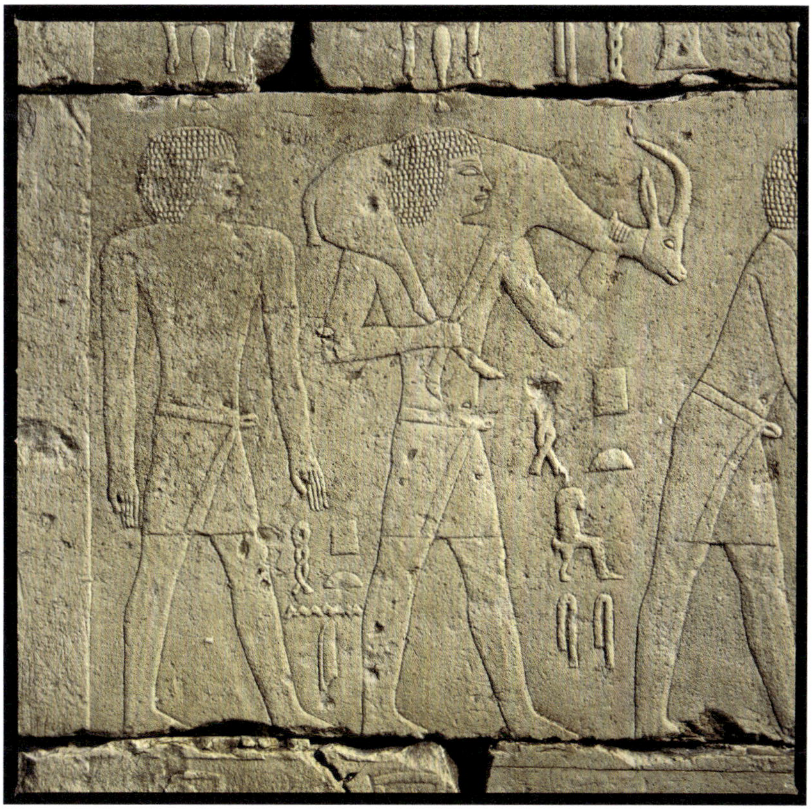

Fig. 103
Tomb Chapel of Raemkai: East Wall,
c. 2446–2389 BCE
From Egypt, Old Kingdom, Memphite Region, Saqqara, North of the Djoser pyramid complex, MarietteD3, Egyptian Antiquities Service/Quibell excavations, 1907–08
Limestone and paint
The Metropolitan Museum of Art, New York; Rogers Fund, 1908 (08.201.1f)

Anglo-American critic Charles Caffin compiled a set of essays on great American sculptors for publication in 1903, Saint-Gaudens was at the top of his list. Like almost everyone else who knew the sculptor's reliefs, Caffin paid them special homage—and he singled out the portrait of the Schiff children as one of the best. "The figures are not merely set against the background," Caffin wrote,

> they grow out of it, forming with it an enclosed parterre of beautiful design, of delicately differing planes of elevation, of subtle tones of gray in between the extremes of light and dark. The effect is not unlike that revealed at early morning when the landscape is flattened in appearance by the mist, and as the latter is loosened and dispersed by the sun, the patterned forms take on infinitesimal degrees of definition and mysteriousness behind the intervening veils of lighted vapour. Through such a simile one may, perhaps, suggest the essential quality of loveliness in these low reliefs.[41]

No discussion of Saint-Gaudens's reliefs would be complete without some mention of the sculptor's Shaw Memorial (Fig. 104), begun in 1884 and finally unveiled on Boston Common in 1897. Its history has been recounted many times, and there is no need to relate more than the basics here.[42] Famously, the memorial is dedicated to the soldiers of the Fifty-Fourth Massachusetts Regiment, the first unit of African Americans to serve in the Union Army, and their commanding officer, Robert Gould Shaw, who died at the Battle of Fort Wagner near Charleston, South Carolina, in 1863. Making the memorial consumed some thirteen years of Saint-Gaudens's career, but it was worth it. Not only is it one of his best-known works, it is arguably the greatest of all American sculptures.

Due to the depth of the modeling and the monumentality of the Shaw memorial as a whole, it is easy enough to overlook the fact that it is a relief sculpture. In fact, when the Commonwealth of Massachusetts awarded Saint-Gaudens the commission for the project in 1884, his immediate inclination was to make a fairly standard freestanding equestrian statue of Shaw.[43] It was a type of sculpture that, he sensed, he was bound to create some day. "[I] felt that . . . I must do an equestrian statue," Saint-Gaudens later wrote,

> and that here I had found my opportunity. . . . I proceeded with this theory until the Shaw family objected on the ground that, although Shaw was of a noble type, . . . he had not been a great commander, and only men of the highest rank should be so honored. In fact, it seemed pretentious. Accordingly, in casting about for some manner of reconciling my desire with their ideas, I fell upon a plan of associating him directly with his troops in a bas-relief, and thereby reducing his importance.[44]

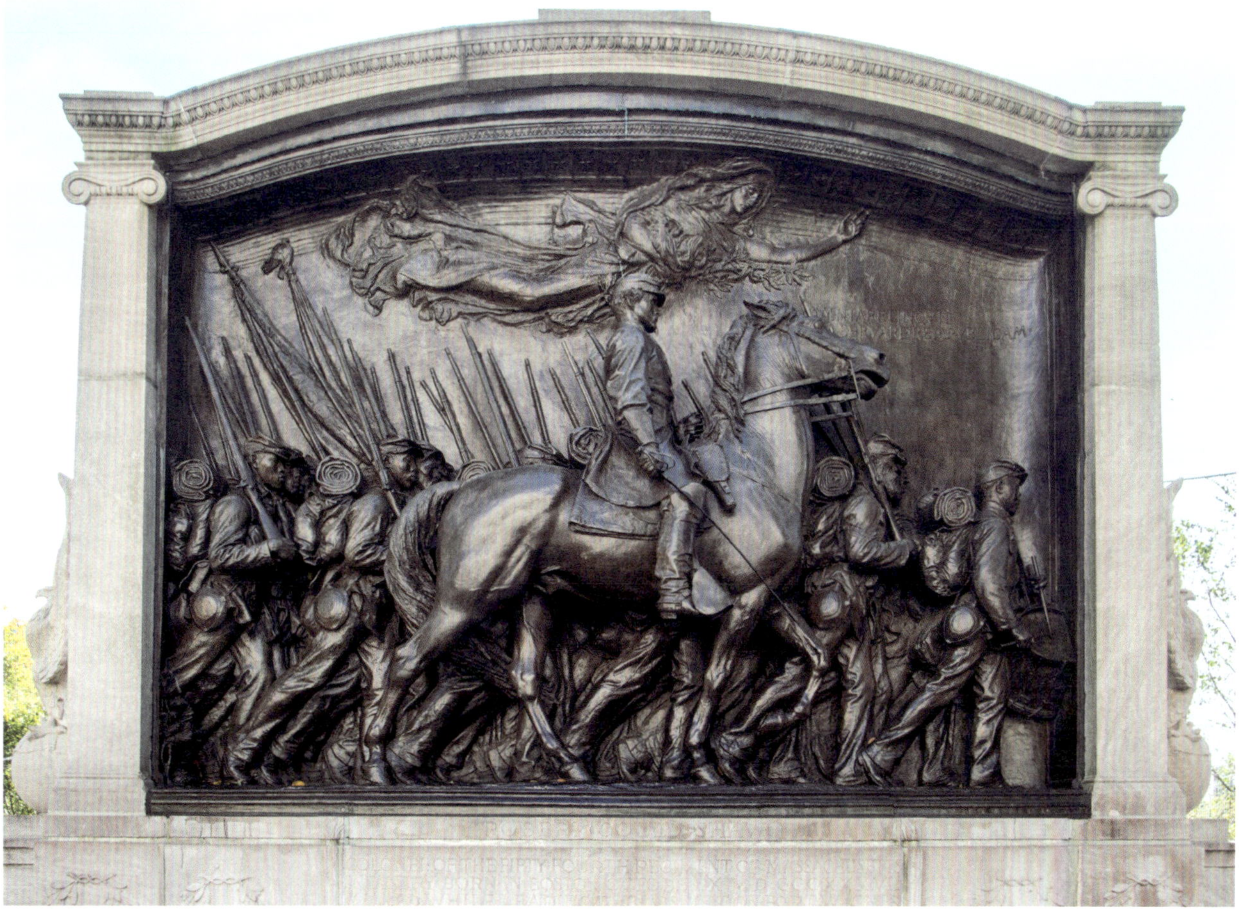

Fig. 104
Augustus Saint-Gaudens
Robert Gould Shaw and the 54th Regiment Memorial, 1884–97
Bronze
11 × 14 ft. (3.4 × 4.3 m)
Boston Common

Subsequently, Saint-Gaudens produced drawings and a rough plaster sketch in relief so low that Shaw, his horse, and the troops were modeled on more or less the same level.[45] This strategy, an echo of Saint-Gaudens's earlier portrait reliefs writ large, had practical as well as aesthetic value. "In justice to myself," he wrote, "I must say here that . . . the low-relief I proposed making when I undertook the Shaw commission . . . reasonably could be finished for the limited sum at the command of the committee."[46] But as he worked on the sculpture in his New York studio, he (again) became engrossed with the contrasts that relief offered and the creative satisfaction that moving between low and high relief in a single project gave him. He wrote, "I, through my extreme interest in it and its opportunity, increased the conception until the rider grew almost to a statue in the round and the negroes assumed far more importance than I had originally intended. Hence the monument, developing in this way infinitely beyond what could be paid for, became a labor of love."[47]

As the image of Shaw rose from the background to near-three-dimensionality, the soldiers, numbering some thirteen men, filled the rest of the composition. By truncating several of them at the left margin and lopping off the drummer boy's instrument at the right, Saint-

Gaudens gave them direction and infused them with energy. With so many players in the drama—Shaw, his horse, the troops, and, eventually, an allegorical figure thrown in for good measure, all conceived at their full length and height—Saint-Gaudens's challenge was not only to fill the background from side to side but also to convincingly compress it from front to back. As several scholars have proposed, Saint-Gaudens took inspiration from a number of sources for the compositional and spatial problems created by his design. His own *Reminiscences* have him looking at Jean Louis Ernest Meissonier's then-famous painting *Campagne de France, 1814* (1864; Musée d'Orsay, Paris), a print of which he had in his studio. This image may have provided tips on how to render convincingly a tightly packed group of marching soldiers, but only in a general sense.[48] For one thing, Meissonier's soldiers come out of the distance, with Napoleon in the lead, and move toward the viewer at a fairly acute angle. It is an arrangement that does not match Saint-Gaudens's strategy, neither in the sculptor's early drawings for the monument nor in its final version. Instead, the composition is more akin to figures in ancient Roman reliefs, such as those on the interior walls of the first-century CE Arch of Titus in the Roman Forum, which Saint-Gaudens almost certainly knew. As in the Shaw Memorial, the figures in the Roman relief energetically enter, move across, and exit the space, as though passing from behind the proscenium arch of a stage on one side and disappearing behind it on the other. Other ancient Roman relief sculptures, such as the long frieze that spirals up the cylinder that is Trajan's Column (107–113 CE; Forum of Trajan, Rome), compress space from foreground to background to accommodate as many figures and objects as possible. Similarly, in order to fit as many soldiers as possible into his composition, Saint-Gaudens squeezes them from front to back into a space that in reality would have been at least six feet deep (the minimum space needed to accommodate three soldiers marching abreast) but here measures less than a foot.[49] The fact that the figures "read" correctly proves Saint-Gaudens's technical virtuosity, just as their individualized faces prove his artistic brilliance. At the same time, the soldiers' steady but relentless movement is accentuated by arms, legs, and weapons placed at various obtuse angles. "The work seems to throb with the sound of drumbeats," one modern scholar has written about the memorial, "their cadence formed of such words as war, valor, patriotism; death, grief, waste."[50] "You have immortalized my native city," Shaw's mother told Saint-Gaudens following the monument's dedication. "You have immortalized my dear son, and you have immortalized yourself."[51]

Saint-Gaudens's closest competitor in the monument-obsessed post-Reconstruction United States was a near-contemporary, Daniel Chester French, best remembered for his commemorative sculptures,

Fig. 105
Peter A. Juley & Son
Daniel Chester French in his studio, c. 1912
Photograph
Smithsonian American Art Museum, Smithsonian Institution, Washington, DC; Peter A. Juley Collection (J00156)

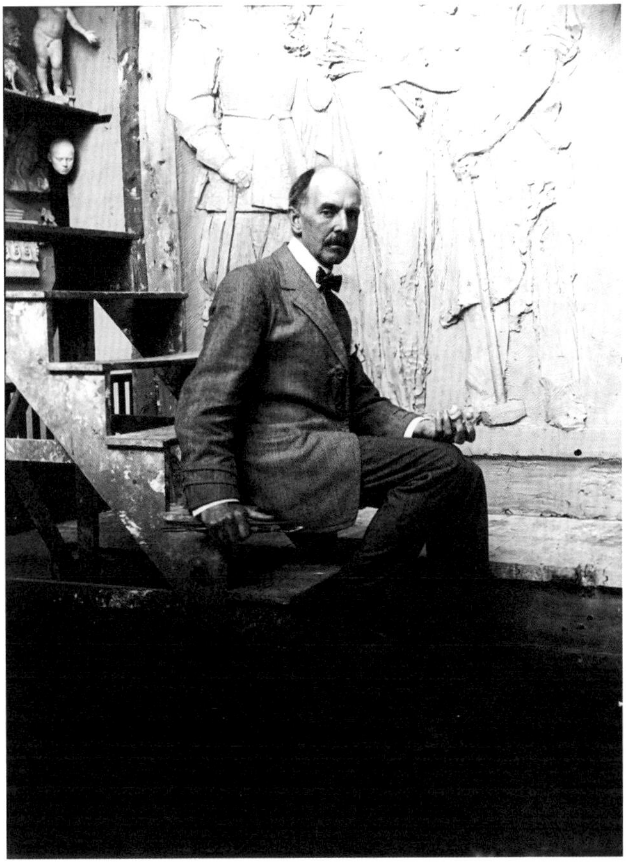

starting with his *Minute Man* (1871–75) in Concord, Massachusetts, and culminating with his colossal statue of Lincoln (1911–22) in the Lincoln Memorial in Washington, DC. Of the more than eighty public works that French created over his long career, most, like these two, are in the round.[52] But French was not a stranger to the relief form and although he may not have had Saint-Gaudens's passion for it, he had no trouble accommodating patrons who wanted it. He was especially adept at combining relief, both high and low, with sculpture in the round in elegant architectural settings. When he posed in his studio for the well-known photographer Peter A. Juley in about 1912 (Fig. 105), he did so in front of the model of one such work, a memorial to Henry Wadsworth Longfellow that he made for Cambridge, Massachusetts. This was appropriate, as by then French was widely known as "the leader in the production of... monumental architectural reliefs," as one critic put it.[53]

Given the reach of the genius and fame of Saint-Gaudens, it was inevitable that French would come under his influence.[54] Something of Saint-Gaudens's angels for St. Thomas Church, for example, can be seen in a pair of similar beings that French designed in 1894 for the Clark family plot at Forest Hills Cemetery near Boston; and Saint-Gaudens's portrait of the Schiff children (see Fig. 102) may have informed French's 1907 memorial to the educator Alice Freeman Palmer at Wellesley College (Fig. 106). French also shared something of Saint-Gaudens's appreciation for the careful integration of text and image, as seen in the bronze doors that he, French, designed for the Boston Public Library in the late 1890s; and his 1917 memorial to the Marquis de Lafayette in Brooklyn's Prospect Park has been interpreted, accurately or not, as a compositional descendant of Saint-Gaudens's Shaw Memorial.[55]

The first masterwork in which French showed his talent at combining various forms of relief with three-dimensional sculpture is the memorial he created for the Milmore family plot at Forest Hills Cemetery in Jamaica Plain near Boston (Fig. 107). A fortuitous commission, it came with few restrictions and a flexible timetable that freed French to show off his technical skills and aesthetic sensibilities.[56] The

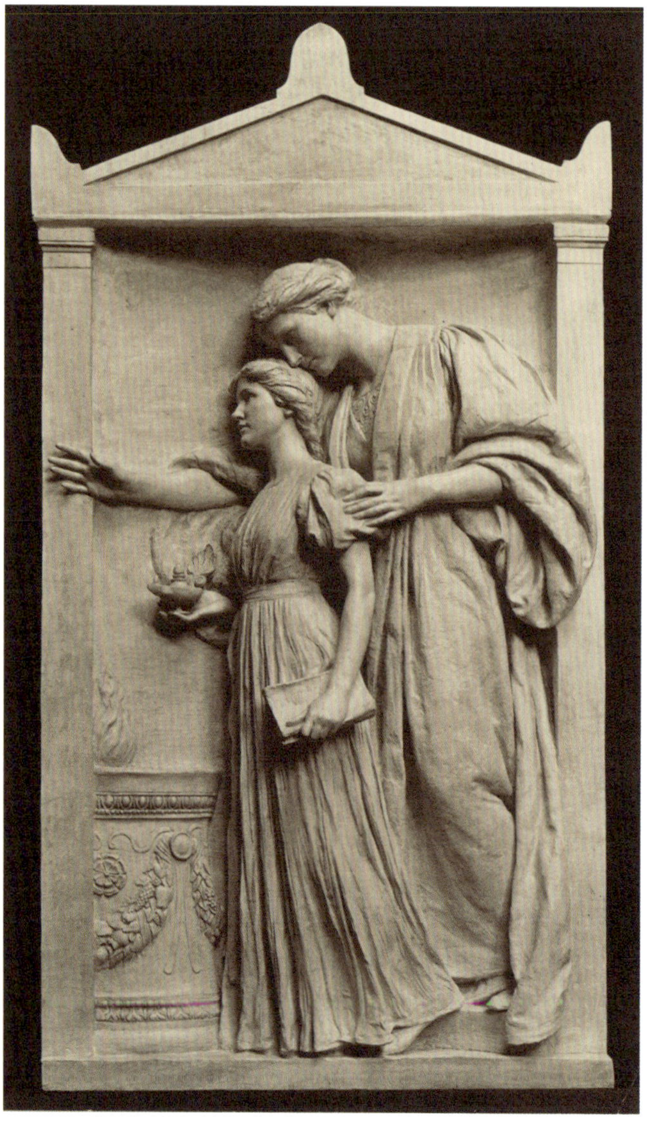

Fig. 106
Daniel Chester French
Alice Freeman Palmer Memorial, 1907
Marble
Houghton Chapel, Wellesley College, Wellesley, MA
Archival photograph
Concord Free Public Library, William Munroe Special Collections, MA
(DCF.001.055)

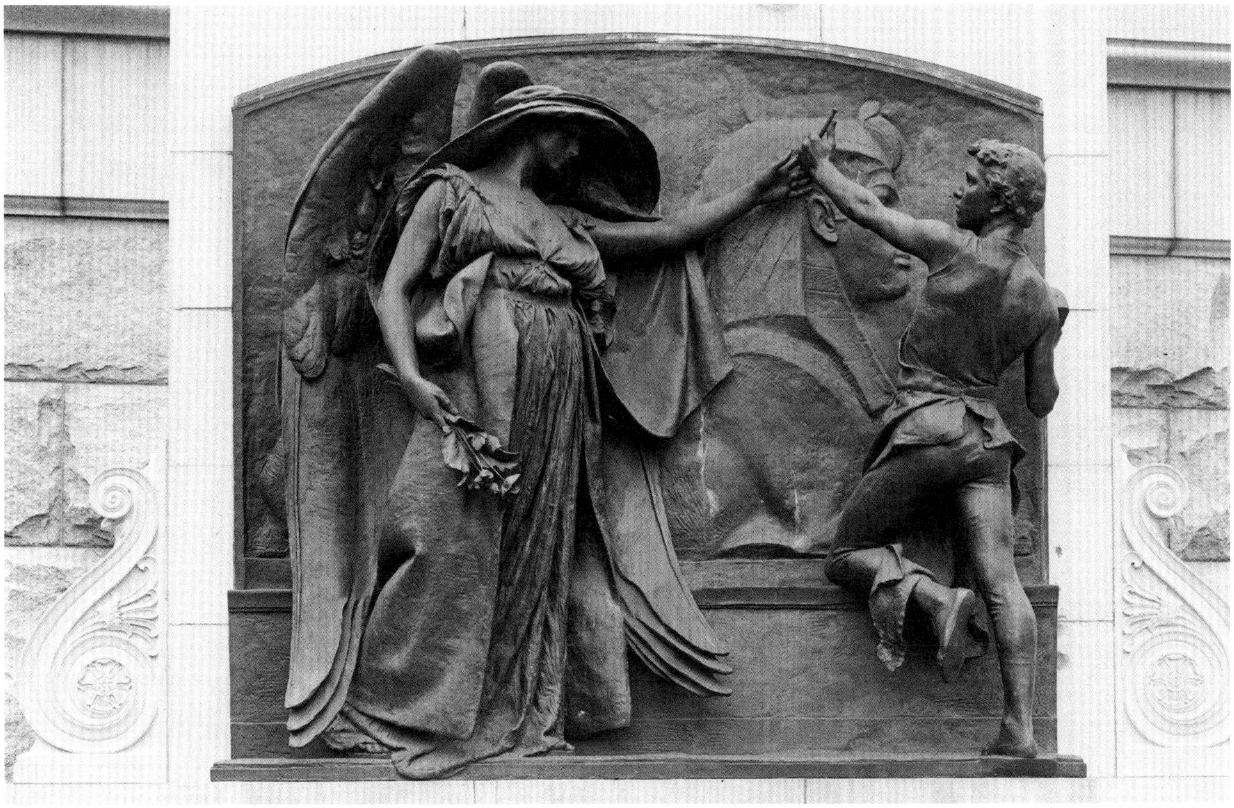

Fig. 107
Daniel Chester French
Milmore Memorial (The Angel of Death and the Young Sculptor), 1889 (photographed c. 1890–1901, with marble pedestal by Henry Bacon)
Bronze
100 × 30 in. (254 × 76.2 cm)
Forest Hills Cemetery, Jamaica Plain, Boston

commission originated with two members of the family, the brothers Martin (1844–83) and Joseph Milmore (1841–86), both of whom were sculptors. Each had specified in his last will and testament that proceeds from his estate should be used to fund a marker for his parents' graves at Forest Hills, with simple inscriptions and modest portraits.[57] Since both brothers died in their thirties, the opportunity to implement their wishes came sooner than expected. Instead of following the brothers' instructions, their heirs adjusted them upward to something more expressive and poetic than either Martin or Joseph had envisioned, a memorial that would reference the brothers rather than the parents. French, who was given the commission in 1889, obliged. He worked on the project for four years, eventually producing a life-size, multifigured bronze that acquired the descriptive titles *The Angel of Death and the Sculptor* and *Death Staying the Hand of the Sculptor.* It was installed at Forest Hills Cemetery in 1893.

Because of the relative youth of the Milmore brothers at their deaths, French chose to commemorate them not with portraits but with an idealized image of a young sculptor diligently executing his craft. Given the tools that the youth holds, a mallet and a chisel, it is obvious that he is carving something in stone, an ironic jab at reality, since the sculpture at Forest Hills—French's sculpture—is bronze. The something that is being "carved" by the young man constitutes the background of French's composition. It is worked in a relief high enough to signal its significance but low enough that it does not interfere with the main action. With iconographic intentionality, French makes the young sculptor's subject a sphinx, an ancient symbol of death. Archival photographs of an early version of the memorial show that French had originally intended the sphinx to face forward.[58] Probably realizing that its direct gaze would be too distracting, even a bit creepy, he shifted it to a profile view. It was a good call, and to French's delight it earned the praise of no less an expert than Saint-Gaudens, who, as has been seen, believed that figures in relief are best shown in profile.[59] In the finished composition, French's young sculptor is putting the finishing touches on his sphinx when he is interrupted by the untimely touch of a benevolent but determined angel of death, identifiable by the poppies, symbols of eternal rest, that she holds. She halts his work, his creativity, and his life in mid-stroke.[60]

Meanwhile, the sculpture within the sculpture serves another purpose, intentional or not. It would have reminded French's contemporaries of one of Martin Milmore's own works: the well-known, thoroughly three-dimensional *American Sphinx* (Fig. 108) that Milmore created for Mount Auburn Cemetery in Cambridge, Massachusetts, in 1872. French made the unlikely claim that the inclusion of a sphinx in his Forest Hills memorial was strictly symbolic and not meant to be a reference to Milmore's sculpture.[61] But if one ignores this and takes French's sphinx to be Milmore's *American Sphinx*, the former must morph in one's imagination from flat to three-dimensional, thereby requiring the transformation of French's background into a space deep enough to accommodate it. This visual vibration of spaces, real and illusionary, creates a frisson of spatial confusion, as art usually does. Such artistry of material and thematic execution, coupled with the memorial's narrative pathos, almost guaranteed that it would be a critical and popular success.

French took the full-scale plaster version of the *Milmore Memorial* to Paris in 1891 to have it cast in bronze at Gruet's, a renowned foundry often used by American sculptors. Once the casting was complete, he exhibited the plaster in his Paris studio and sent the bronze to the 1892 Salon, where it received a medal, the first American sculpture to be so honored.[62] That same year, he showed the plaster in New York and then, in 1893, at the Chicago World's Fair, where it created a sensation.[63] The sculptor-historian Lorado Taft wrote that it "rose superb" above the "indecent extravagances" of European sculpture shown nearby. Taft was impressed by the way French had combined various levels of sculptural form, and he summarized the sculpture's theme as "a great thought simply, adequately expressed."[64] Other critics agreed. Helen Emerson wrote that it was exactly this combining of forms—its "variety of altitude and perspective"—that made the sculpture so visually pleasing. Its theme was irresistible. "It has a universal message to the

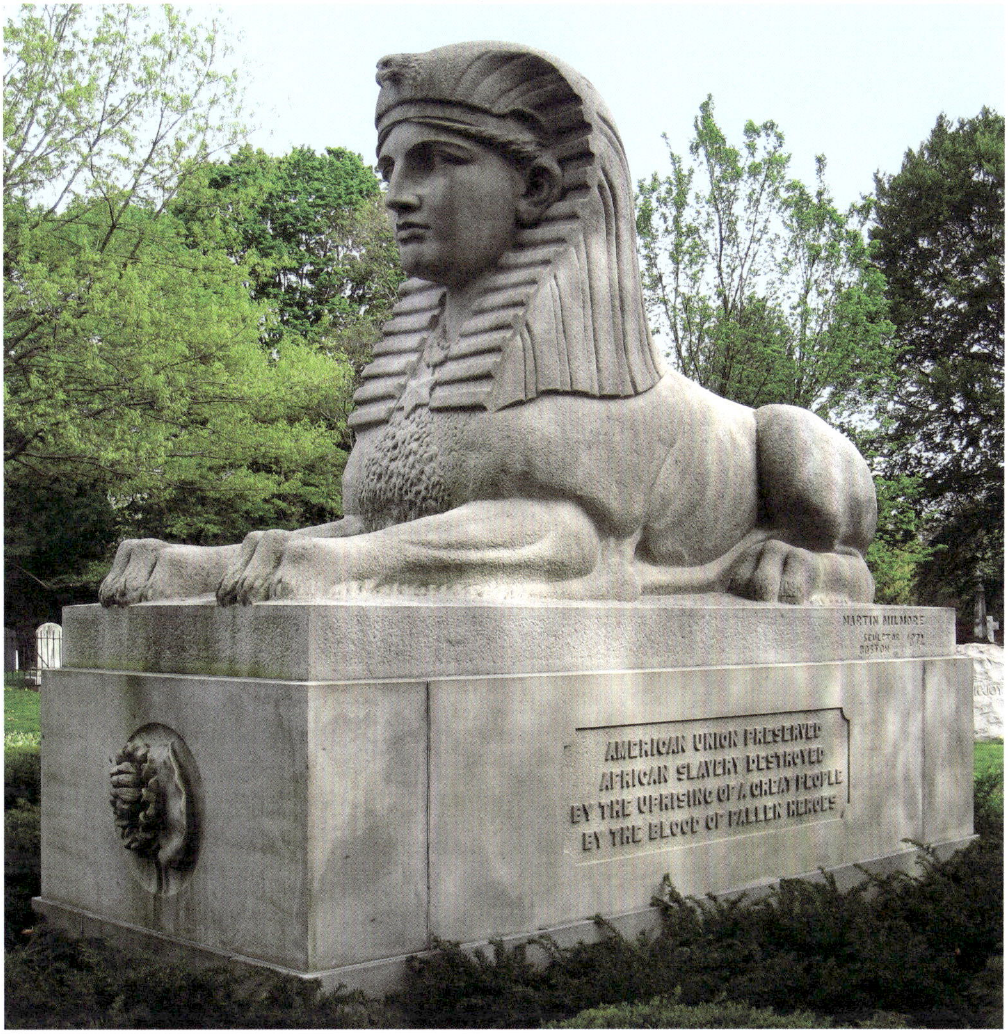

Fig. 108
Martin Milmore
American Sphinx, 1872
Hallowell Maine Granite
Mount Auburn Cemetery, Cambridge, MA

universal heart," she wrote, "a message not of darkness and death, but of life." Its popularity at the fair, she reported, incited "almost daily pilgrimages . . . as to a shrine."[65] Charles Caffin described the sculpture in similarly spiritual terms. "The varied emphasis of these figures in the round, placed against the quiet, smooth levels of low-relief in the background," he wrote, "results in a colour-scheme of striking handsomeness; the gradations from dark to light mingling richness and delicacy of tone, while the passages are distributed with such variety of bold and subtle contrasts as to be exceptionally decorative. And it is by these devices, as well as by the action of the two figures and the expression of their faces, that the sentiment of the subject is conveyed."[66]

The fame of French's *Milmore Memorial* at the turn of the nineteenth century has been forgotten today, but by 1900 it had an international reputation.[67] For a time, photographic reproductions of it graced the walls of hundreds of American classrooms, homes, and offices, where they often joined reproductions of other sentimental and patriotic favorites, such as Gilbert Stuart's *George Washington* (1796; jointly owned by the Museum of Fine Arts, Boston, and National Portrait Gallery, Smithsonian Institution, Washington, DC), Emanuel Leutze's *Washington Crossing the Delaware* (1851; Metropolitan Museum of Art, New York), and Thomas Hovenden's *Breaking Homes Ties* (1890; Philadelphia Museum of Art), the last having been the other big star of American art at the Chicago fair. The *Milmore Memorial*'s popularity in photographic form continued through the 1930s; historian Adeline Adams wrote as late as 1932 that these widely distributed images made it one of the most recognizable of American sculptures, "a household word in American art."[68]

The ultimate tribute to the *Milmore Memorial*, though, came in 1945 when it was moved from the family plot at Forest Hills to a more open, landscaped spot near the cemetery's entrance where it can be more clearly seen and appreciated. Public sculptures have often been moved, usually for negative reasons—the object is found to be blocking

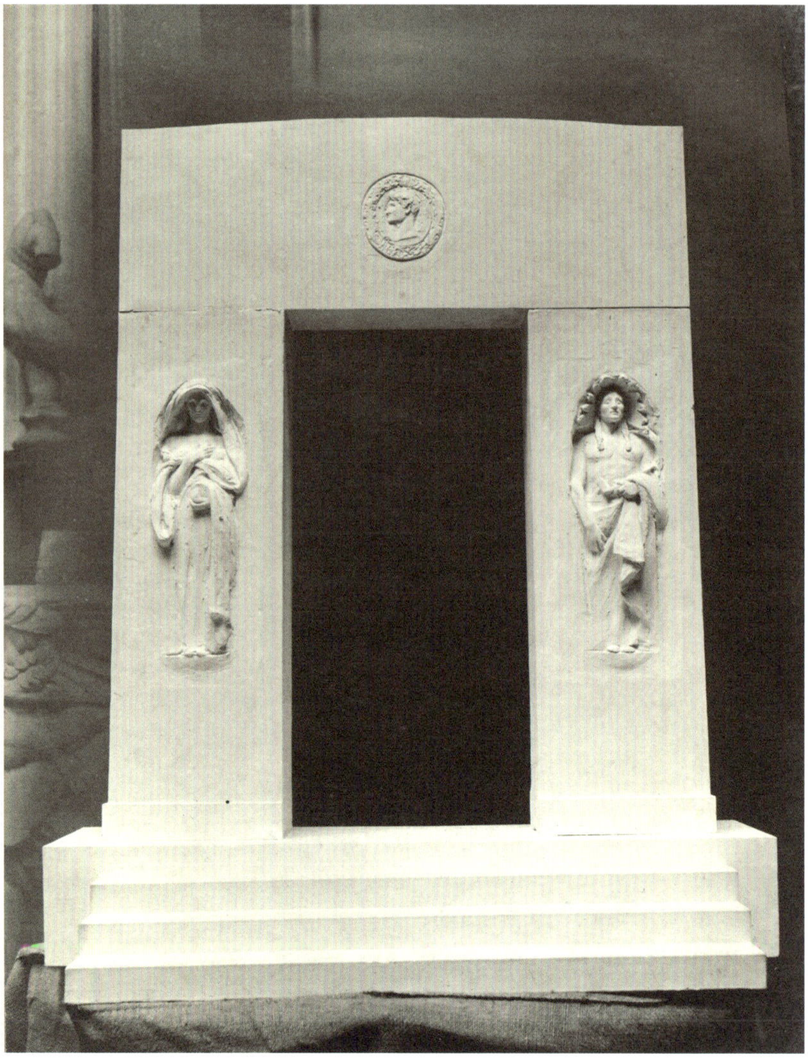

Fig. 109
Daniel Chester French and
Charles Follen McKim
Francis Parkman Memorial, First Model, 1901
Archival photograph
Chapin Library, Williams College, Williamstown, MA; Gift of the National Trust for Historic Preservation/Chesterwood, a National Trust Historic Site, Stockbridge, MA (NT69.38.1289.3)

"progress," has been neglected and become an eyesore, is suddenly deemed to be in bad taste, or has finally been recognized for its racist, treasonous, or misogynistic content.[69] But the relocation of French's *Milmore Memorial* is rare in that it was not undertaken because the sculpture was offensive but because it was admired. In its new location, it also gains in power and purpose, serving now as a dramatic introduction to and a synecdoche for all that stands on and lies in the hallowed burial ground behind it.

As the *Milmore Memorial* suggests, French was aware of and had at least some interest in experimenting with the background of his relief sculptures. True, he was not as consistent as Saint-Gaudens in this and often left alone the flat picture plane in his reliefs. But he did make at least one notable innovation in this area, the fulfillment of which is the monumental relief that he created for the Melvin family for Sleepy Hollow Cemetery in Concord, Massachusetts, between 1906 and 1908 (Fig. 110). A haunting and original work of art, it is one of the most successful odes to death in the history of American sculpture.[70] For French, it was also a synthesis in stone of ideas that he had been contemplating for nearly a decade. It had started with a memorial to the American historian and educator Francis Parkman that French designed for a site near Boston, beginning in 1897. The project originated shortly after Parkman's death in 1894, when a group of Bostonians formed a committee, established a subscription fund, and hired the architect Charles McKim to design something.[71] McKim eventually advised the committee to pursue a sculptural rather than an architectural monument and asked Saint-Gaudens and French, both of whom he knew well, for their advice. Saint-Gaudens immediately recommended that French alone be offered the commission; in April 1897, French accepted the job.[72]

From the start, French's plan called for large, allegorical relief sculptures applied to a simple architectural form of McKim's design. By early 1901, French and McKim had put their initial plan for the memorial into the form of a plaster model (Fig. 109). It consisted of a simple post-and-lintel structure with a portrait of Parkman, carved in negative relief, at the center of its horizontal element. In reference to Parkman's writings about the American West, each of the structure's vertical members was embellished with a full-length figure of a Native American, one female and one male. These were to be modeled in negative relief so that they would appear to be emerging from a picture plane. In reality, that plane is, of course, a solid, flat, and smooth surface; but visually, it becomes a membrane through which the figures break as they advance toward the viewer. The fact that they are not fully formed synchronizes with contemporary stereotypes that viewed Native Americans as somehow unknowable to white people, forever alien, mysterious, and inscrutable.[73] However that might have been, modeling the figures in this way was undoubtedly a technical challenge. The contemporary journalist Omar H. Sample summarized the issue: "The intaglio relief is a very difficult and unusual effect that makes the figures appear as if emerging from the stone ... [an] appearance ... all the more difficult to secure by reason of the fact that the background is a smooth surface instead of being in the rough as in the common form of Rodinesque sculptures."[74]

At some point, McKim amicably withdrew from the Parkman project, and the architect Henry Bacon was brought in as French's collaborator. They revised the design of the memorial several times, simplifying it and eventually eliminating the female figure. The project was finally erected in Jamaica Plain without fanfare in 1906, but the broader interest French had in the theme of a figure in relief, emerging from the background, continued.[75] Happily, two other opportunities to pursue the idea soon came his way.

The first was for a memorial that the state of Connecticut hoped to erect to honor soldiers from that state who had been incarcerated at the Confederate prison near Andersonville, Georgia, during the Civil War. Since the war, Andersonville had become a site for commemoration, and in 1899 several states and patriotic organizations began

Fig. 110
Daniel Chester French
Melvin Memorial, 1906–8
(photographed 1909–12)
Marble
Sleepy Hollow Cemetery, Concord, MA

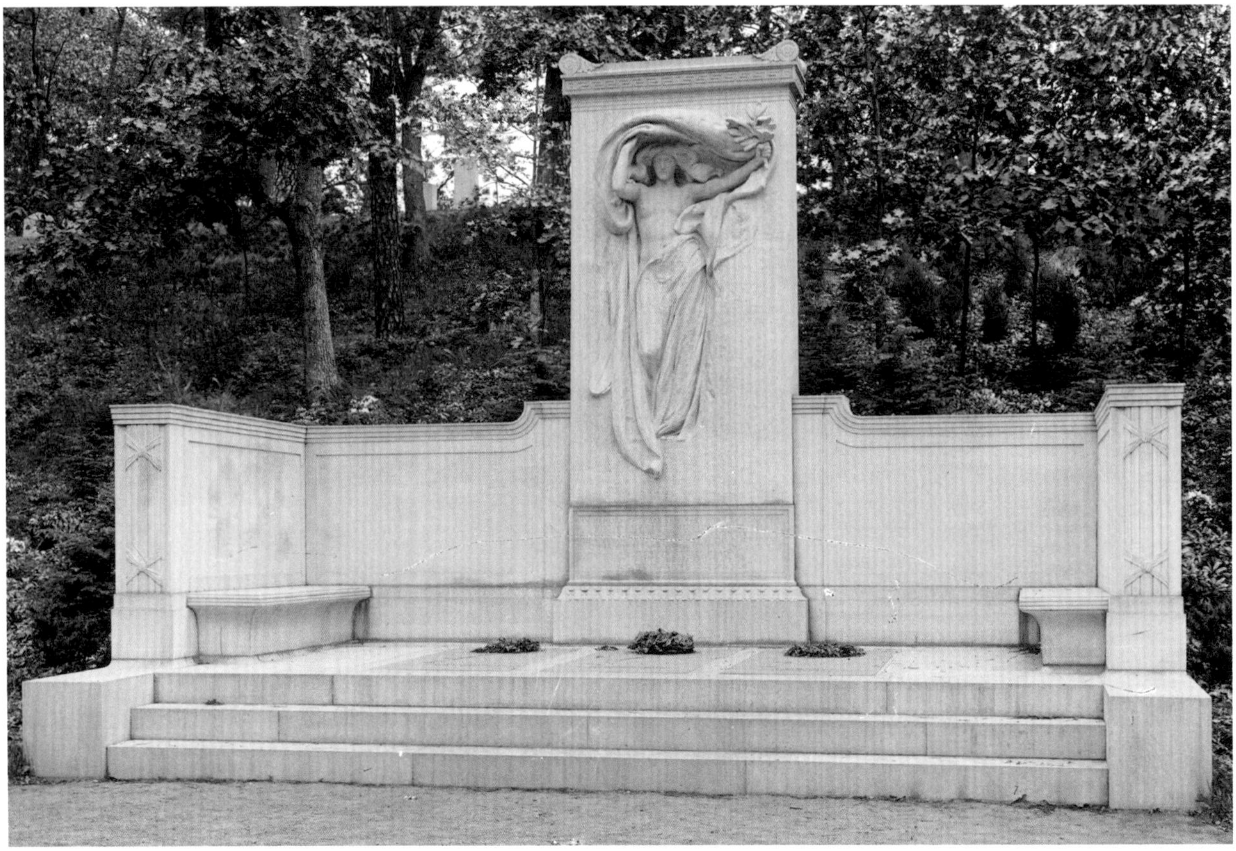

Fig. 111
Daniel Chester French
Melvin Memorial Maquette (relief), 1906
Plaster
14⅞ × 7¾ × 2¾ in. (37.8 × 19.7 × 7 cm)
The National Trust for Historic Preservation, Stockbridge, MA; The Chesterwood Collection NT69.38.1

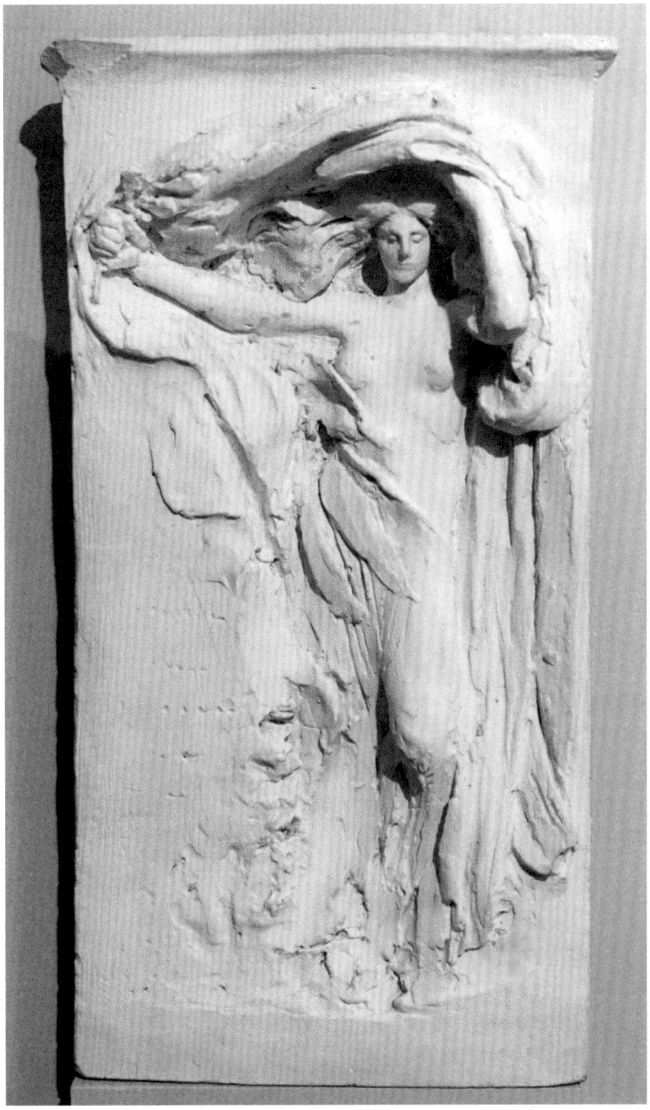

erecting monuments there. The committee overseeing Connecticut's contribution contacted French about taking it on, and by May 1906 he had sent them a proposal in the form of a plaster maquette depicting an allegorical female figure, in relief, that he eventually called *Mourning Victory* (Fig. 111). Thematically, the figure harks back to French's *Milmore Memorial*, but formally it relates to the Parkman monument, proof of French's confidence in the figure-emergent as an effective sculptural relief form. Unable to contain his enthusiasm, French told the chair of the Connecticut committee that it "is one of the best things I have ever done."[76] "The monument must be this design or nothing," he said. "It was . . . only because I was so much interested in this design that I was willing to undertake it."[77] Unfortunately, the committee did not share his excitement in the design, negotiations broke down, and in March 1907 French withdrew from the project.[78]

Despite this failure, French was certain that, given the right project, the ideas he had illustrated with the rejected maquette could serve as the basis of a great work of art. His big break came courtesy of a Boston businessman named James C. Melvin, who proved to be an ideal patron. Three of Melvin's brothers had died as a result of the Civil War, and he and French, who had known each other for most of their lives, had long discussed collaborating on a memorial to them for Sleepy Hollow Cemetery in their hometown of Concord.[79] Now, in 1904, both Melvin and French were economically and professionally secure enough to make it happen. Melvin became especially energized about the project after seeing French's Andersonville maquette, and the two men quickly sealed the deal.[80] As he had done with the *Parkman Memorial*, French asked the architect Henry Bacon to collaborate with him, and by April 1907 they had a small-scale presentation model (Fig. 112) ready to show Melvin, who immediately approved it.[81]

For the *Melvin Memorial*, French took his Andersonville figure and fleshed out both its anatomy and the attributes that define its allegorical function. The fabric the figure holds over her head is now clearly an American flag, and the branch she grasps in her right hand is more obviously laurel, an ancient symbol of posthumous, spiritual victory. An ill-defined shape at the lower left-hand corner of the maquette is now more easily read as the tip of a wing, confirming the figure's celestial origins. Although French left the surrounding surface around it flat

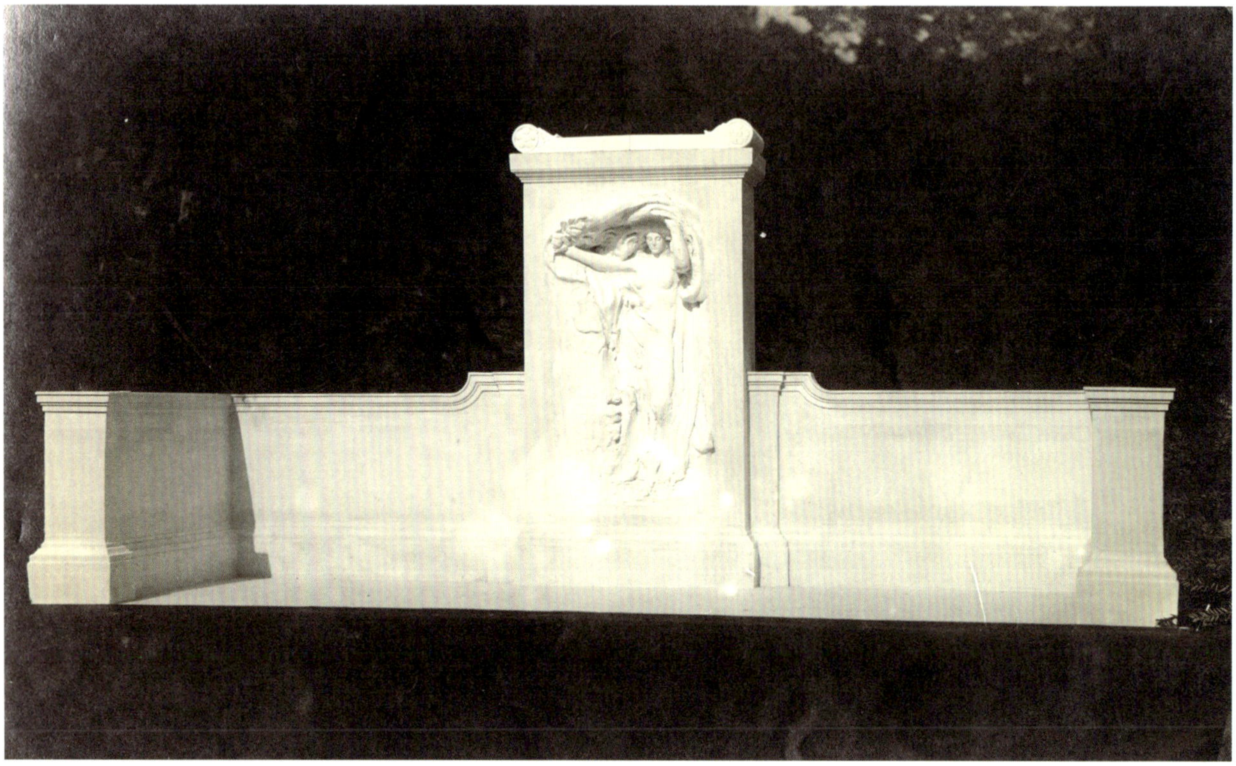

Fig. 112
Daniel Chester French and Henry Bacon
Melvin Memorial, Architectural Model, 1907
Archival photograph
Chapin Library, Williams College, Williamstown, MA; Gift of the National Trust for Historic Preservation/ Chesterwood, a National Trust Historic Site, Stockbridge, MA (NT 69.38.1318.11.1)

and bare, the figure's movements make it clear that this area is meant to be read as an intangible something through which it is passing. Thus transformed, the heretofore sterile background comes to represent the figure's transition from an intangible spirit world to a visible, earthly one. At Sleepy Hollow, the figure, at last able to perform her duties as *Mourning Victory*, hovers as a guardian angel over the site, bowing her head to acknowledge three bronze plaques bearing the departed brothers' names that are embedded in the pavement below.[82]

So certain was French of the perfection of his design that, between the preparatory stage and the enlargement of the figure, first in plaster and then in stone, he made no major alterations to it. But at the end of the summer of 1907, as he was finishing the full-scale model of *Mourning Victory*, he and Bacon realized that if it were installed at Sleepy Hollow in its then-current configuration, it would create a visual complication. As first encountered from the planned approach to the site, the figure's face would be blocked from view by its raised left arm and delay the aesthetic and emotional effect it was meant to have on visitors (see Fig. 89).[83] The solution was to reverse the composition, a process that the Piccirilli Brothers, the professional New York stone carvers whom French had hired to translate his plaster model into marble, could easily do under French's supervision.[84] With this accomplished, the memorial was erected at Sleepy Hollow in the fall of 1907 (see Fig. 110). After delays due to scheduling and weather, it was finally dedicated on June 16, 1909, with family, friends, politicians, and veterans in attendance. But a wider audience had already been reached. Several months before the dedication in Concord, French sent the full-size plaster model of *Mourning Victory* (Chesterwood, National Trust for Historic Preservation, Stockbridge, MA) to the winter exhibition of the National Academy of Design in New York, where it was on view from late December 1908 to early January 1909. It was universally praised, even by New York critics.[85] Its popularity did not wane over the years. In 1931, shortly after French's death, Adeline Adams marveled at this "symbolic figure" that "appears as if summoned from the deeps of the stone which it adorns [and] comes forward to deliver its message." French's relief technique, she continued, "gives a rich deep dark as background for certain significant portions of the figure—perhaps head, arms, and torso—these being sunk beneath the flat surface of the stone, while other parts emerge in the usual manner. I know of no other outstanding American work in which the single figure is thus conceived and executed."[86]

As successful and famous artists, Augustus Saint-Gaudens and Daniel Chester French naturally had a number of followers—assistants, apprentices, students—who were influenced by them. But that influence, which in any event was short-lived, may have been more technical

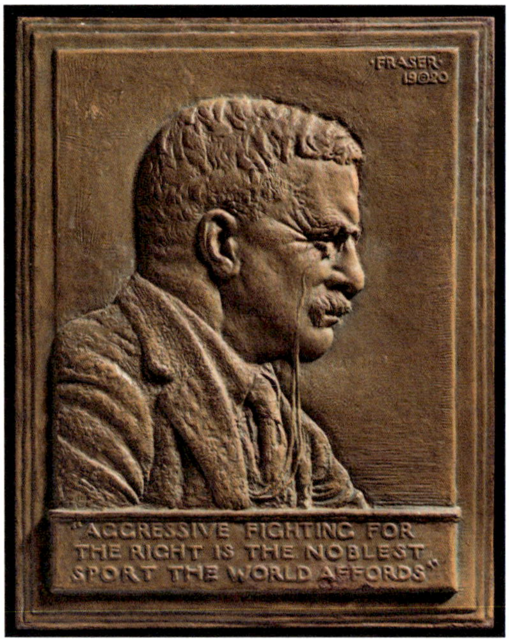
·FRASER·
19©20
"AGGRESSIVE FIGHTING FOR
THE RIGHT IS THE NOBLEST
SPORT THE WORLD AFFORDS"

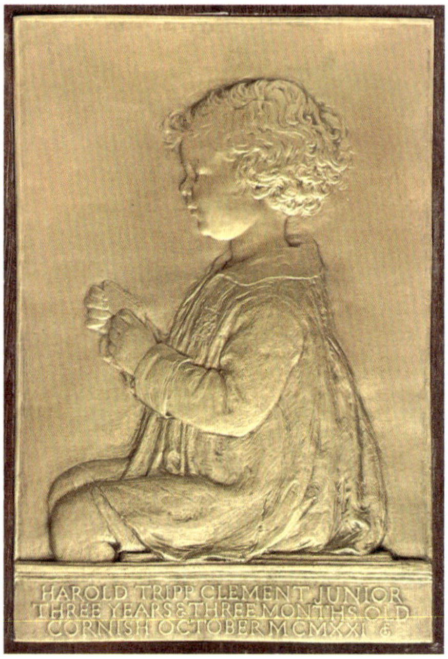
HAROLD TRIPP CLEMENT JUNIOR
THREE YEARS & THREE MONTHS OLD
CORNISH OCTOBER MCMXXI

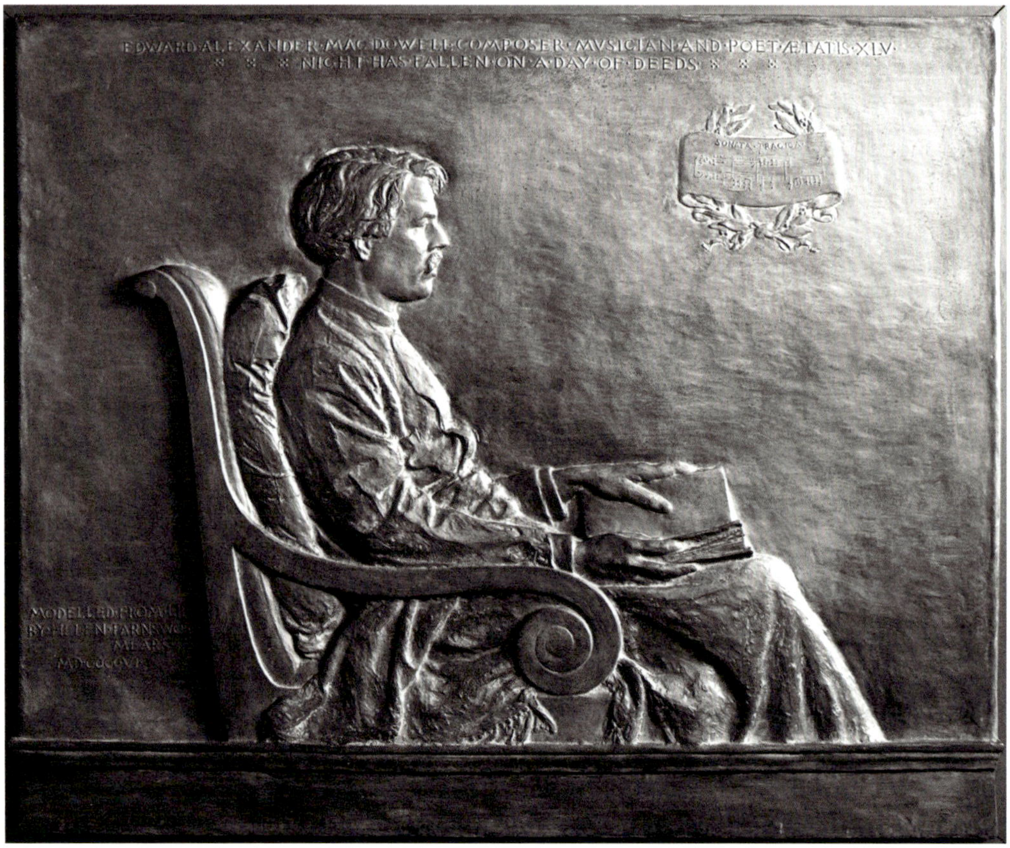
EDWARD·ALEXANDER·MAC·DOWELL·COMPOSER·MVSICIAN·AND·POET·ÆTATIS·XLV·
NIGHT·HAS·FALLEN·ON·A·DAY·OF·DEEDS

Opposite:

Fig. 113
James Earle Fraser
Portrait Plaque of Theodore Roosevelt, 1920
Bronze
12⅝ × 10 × ⅝ in. (32.1 × 25.4 × 1.6 cm)
Crystal Bridges Museum of American Art, Bentonville, AR; Gift of Adam D. Stolpen, 2018.18

Fig. 114
Frances Grimes
Harold Tripp Clement, Jr., 1921
Bronze
10⅜ × 7⅜ × ⅞ in. (26.4 × 18.7 × 2.2 cm)
National Academy of Design, New York; 41-S

Fig. 115
Helen Farnsworth Mears
Edward Alexander MacDowell, 1906
Bronze
33³⁄₁₆ × 39¾ × 1³⁄₁₆ in. (84.3 × 101 × 3 cm)
Brooklyn Museum of Art; Gift of Anne Lupton Prince (16.757)

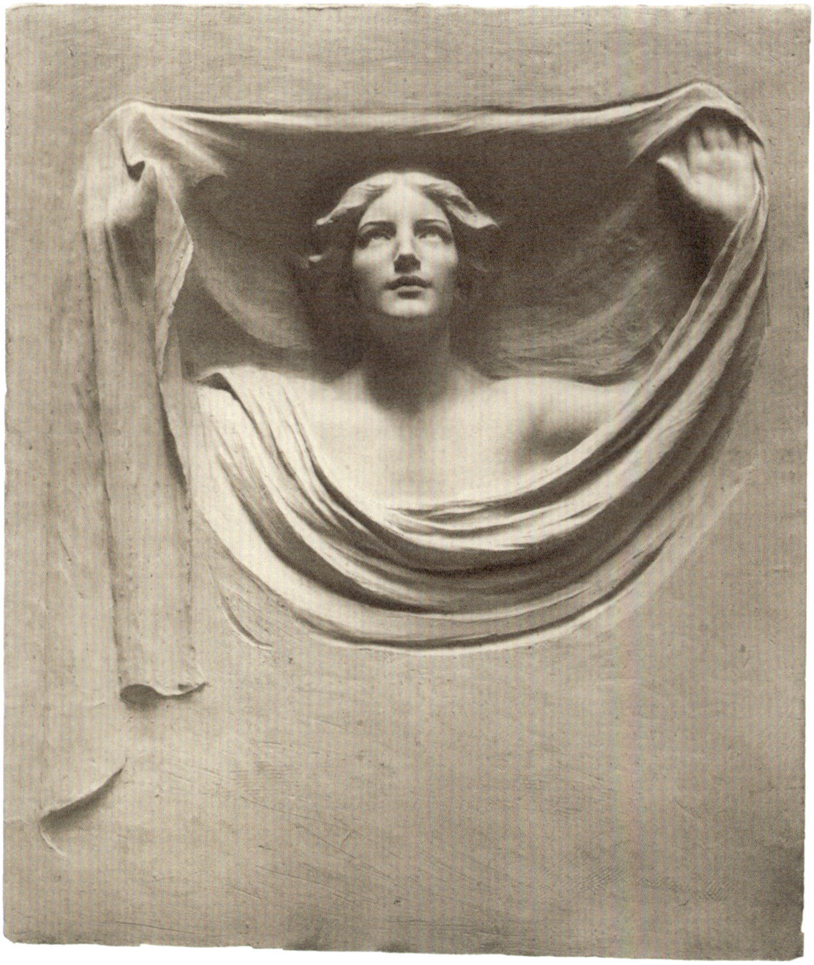

This page:

Fig. 116
A. B. Bogart
Evelyn Beatrice Longman, Hood Memorial, c. 1910
Photograph of original plaster reconceived in marble for the grave of Laura Gamble Thomson, Spring Grove Cemetery, Cincinnati, 1913
Smithsonian American Art Museum, Smithsonian Institution, Washington, DC; Metropolitan Museum of Art Study Collection of American Sculpture Photographs (S0001521)

than stylistic and, especially when it came to relief sculpture, more imitative than innovative.[87]

Having been Saint-Gaudens's supposed favorite assistant, Frederick MacMonnies went on to a successful career as both a sculptor and a painter. He designed several large, public reliefs, none of which have much of Saint-Gaudens in them.[88] Saint-Gaudens's other most successful former assistant, James Earle Fraser, was a sculptor mostly of large freestanding public monuments and small three-dimensional bronzes. But he occasionally made reliefs, some of which are especially reminiscent of Saint-Gaudens's medallions in their use of the profile pose, the variegation of their backgrounds, and the integration of text (Fig. 113).[89] These same attributes appear in the work of two of Saint-Gaudens's other assistants, Frances Grimes and Helen Farnsworth Mears, members of a growing coterie of successful women sculptors who, among other things, excelled in the art of the relief portrait (Figs. 114, 115).[90]

Another member of this group was Evelyn Longman. She worked with French from 1901 to 1904 and, of all his many assistants, was the

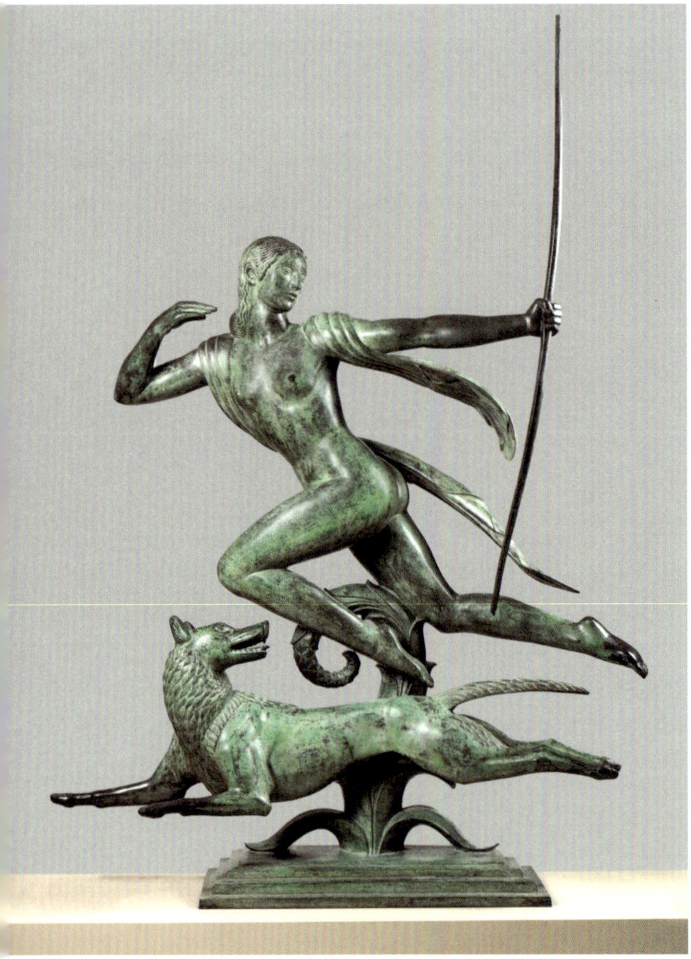

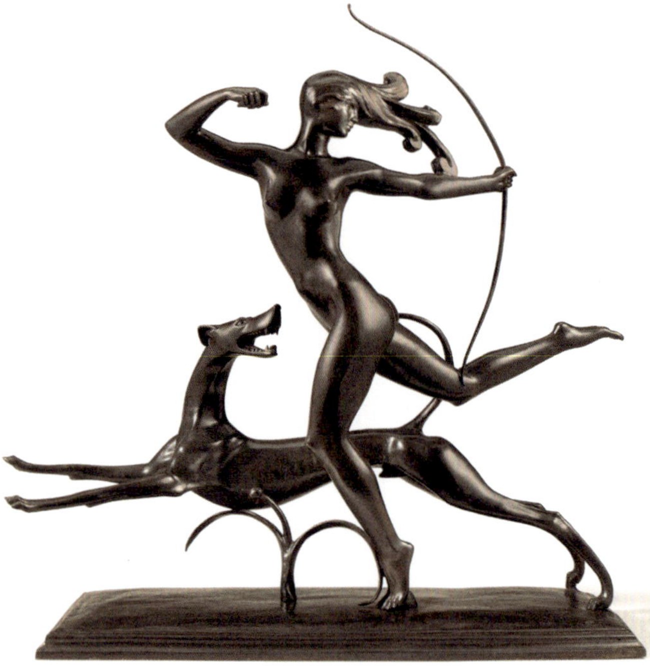

Fig. 117
Paul Manship
Diana, 1925
Bronze
49 × 43 in. (124.4 × 109.3 cm)
Smithsonian American Art Museum, Smithsonian Institution, Washington, DC; Gift of the artist, 1965.16.32A-B

Fig. 118
William (Wilhelm) Hunt Diederich
Diana and Hound, c. 1930
Bronze with dark brown patina
27 in. (68.6 cm) high
Private collection

closest to him, both professionally and personally.[91] French's influence on her work is most obvious in her relief sculptures, especially in her larger commemorative portraits such as the one she made of French himself (1926; National Portrait Gallery, Smithsonian Institution, Washington, DC) or, even more to the point, her marble memorial for the grave of Laura Gamble Thomson, wife of Peter G. Thomson, a wealthy paper manufacturer, in Spring Grove Cemetery in Cincinnati. The latter's emerging figure, which Longman based on one of her slightly earlier conceptions (Fig. 116), makes direct reference, in both its movement and its allegorical purpose, to French's *Mourning Victory*.[92]

As has been seen, Saint-Gaudens and French experimented with the relief form, each in his own way and at his own level of intensity, looking for new ways to use the sculpture's background to create illusions of air and space. A next logical step in this process, had they thought to take it, might have been simply to drop the pretense and dissolve the background altogether, thereby replacing illusion with the real thing. This is more or less what several American sculptors of the next generation—those who came to maturity in the early twentieth century—did. Consider, for example, Paul Manship, many of whose sculptures might as well be reliefs, except for the fact that they are missing that mandatory feature of the type: the background. His 1925 pendants *Diana* (Fig. 117) and *Acteon* (Smithsonian American Art Museum, Washington, DC) are good examples of this. These figures, both individually and together, are typical of the sculptor's style, which has been characterized as retro archaic classicism bumping up against Art Deco. With their insistent frontality, horizontality, and relatively shallow depth, *Diana* and *Acteon* could well be part of a running frieze, minus its architectural surround—relief sculptures stripped of their backgrounds. Similar observations might be made about the work of several of Manship's contemporaries, for example, William (Wilhelm) Hunt Diederich and Carl Paul Jennewein. In both the former's *Diana and Hound* (Fig. 118), which bears an obvious resemblance to Manship's *Diana*, and the latter's *Greek Dance* (Fig. 119), the figures go to some trouble to twist into a position parallel to the plane of their movement. Both beg to be seen from the front and, in fact, are nearly incomprehensible when viewed from the side. In retaining this obvious frontality but letting surrounding space and atmosphere stand for themselves, these objects realize the innovations of Saint-Gaudens and French. They are, in essence, liberated reliefs.

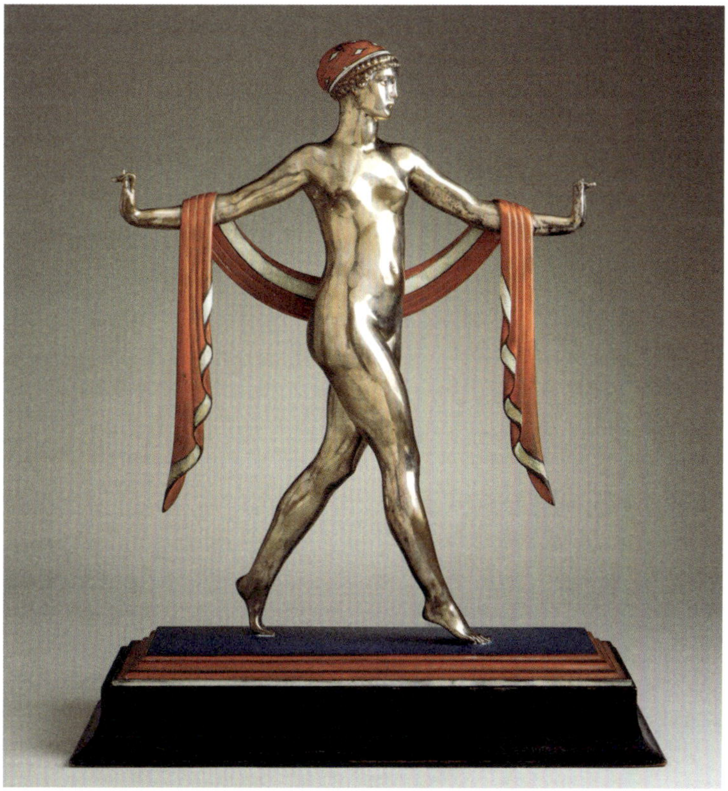

Fig. 119
Carl Paul Jennewein
Greek Dance, 1924
Silver on polychromed wood base
20½ × 16⁷⁄₁₆ × 6½ in. (52 × 41.8 × 16.5 cm)
The San Diego Museum of Art; Gift of Mrs. Henry A. Everett, 1927.84

NOTES

I thank Frank M. Buscaglia, Jorge H. Santis, and Avis Berman of The Sansom Foundation for commissioning this essay and for sponsoring the accompanying lecture that I delivered at the New-York Historical Society in October 2021. I would also like to acknowledge the scholarship of art historians John Dryfhout, Henry Duffy, Donna Hassler, Dana Pilson, Michael Richman, and Thayer Tolles, which provided a firm factual foundation for the interpretations I submit here.

1. Lorado Taft, *The History of American Sculpture* (New York: MacMillan, 1903), 9.
2. For these sculptures, see Richard P. Wunder, *Hiram Powers, Vermont Sculptor, 1805–1873*, vol. 2 of 2 (Newark: University of Delaware Press, 1991), 139–44; and Mary Smart, *A Flight with Fame: The Life and Art of Frederick MacMonnies (1863–1937)* (Madison, CT: Sound View Press, 1996), 292. For a recent assessment of MacMonnies's *Bacchante*, see Thayer Tolles, "*Bacchante and Infant Faun*: Tradition, Controversy, and Legacy," *Metropolitan Museum of Art Bulletin* 77 (Summer 2019): 5–48.
3. "Sculpture," *New Path*, December 1863, 92.
4. Kenyon Cox, "Augustus Saint-Gaudens," *Century* 35, no. 1 (November 1887): 32, 34.
5. Omar H. Sample, "A New Development in Monumental Sculpture," *Art and Progress* 2 (February 1911): 96; Brenda Putnam, *The Sculptor's Way: A Guide to Modelling and Sculpture* (New York: Watson-Guptill, 1948), 49.
6. The subjects of the three reliefs are, respectively, the American painter William Merritt Chase, Saint-Gaudens's infant son Homer, and sixteen-year-old Sarah Redwood Lee. My observations about this painting rely on two sources: Doreen Bolger Burke, *American Paintings in the Metropolitan Museum of Art, Volume III: A Catalogue of Works by Artists Born Between 1846 and 1864* (New York: Metropolitan Museum of Art, 1980), 215–16; and Thayer Tolles in *Augustus Saint-Gaudens 1848–1907: A Master of American Sculpture* (Toulouse: Musée des Augustins, 1999), 100–1, cat. no. 1.
7. Cox, "Augustus Saint-Gaudens," 30; Kenyon Cox, *Old Masters and New: Essays in Art Criticism* (New York: Fox, Duffield, 1905), 266; and Kenyon Cox, "The Saint-Gaudens Memorial Exhibition," *Metropolitan Museum of Art Bulletin*, vol. 3 (February 1908): 20.
8. Augustus Saint-Gaudens, *The Reminiscences of Augustus Saint-Gaudens*, ed. Homer Saint-Gaudens, vol. 1 of 2 (New York: Century Co., 1913), 216. For the facts of Saint-Gaudens's life, I have relied on the chronologies in John H. Dryfhout, *The Work of Augustus Saint-Gaudens* (Hanover, NH: University Press of New England, 1982), 2–21, and the Musée des Augustins' 1999 *Augustus Saint-Gaudens 1848–1907* exhibition catalogue, 209–12.
9. Cox, *Old Masters and New*, 267. Among the contemporary French sculptors whose work Saint-Gaudens saw in Paris were Henri Chapu, Jean Garnier, Jules-Clément Chaplain, and Alexandre Charpentier. See John H. Dryfhout, "Augustus Saint-Gaudens: The Portraits in Bas-Relief," *American Art Journal*, vol. 4 (November 1972): 84.
10. Dryfhout, "Augustus Saint-Gaudens: The Portraits in Bas-Relief," 84; Cox, "Augustus Saint-Gaudens," 32.
11. Saint-Gaudens, *Reminiscences*, vol. 1, 162.
12. Dryfhout, *The Work of Augustus Saint-Gaudens*, 86–87, no. 65. The altarpiece, including Saint-Gaudens's angels, was destroyed when the church burned in 1905. "St. Thomas Destroyed," *New-York Daily Tribune*, August 9, 1905, 4.
13. Clarence Cook, "Recent Church Decoration," *Scribner's Monthly* 15, no. 4 (February 1878): 575, quoted in Thayer Tolles, "Augustus Saint-Gaudens, His Critics, and the New School of American Sculpture, 1875–1893" (PhD diss., City University of New York Graduate Center, 2003), 137.

14. John H. Dryfhout, "The Catalogue," in *Augustus Saint-Gaudens: American Sculptor of the Gilded Age* (Washington, DC: Trust for Museum Exhibitions, 2003), 45. Saint-Gaudens was awarded the Farragut commission in 1876.
15. Tolles, "Augustus Saint-Gaudens, His Critics, and the New School of American Sculpture," 194–95.
16. Saint-Gaudens, *Reminiscences*, vol. 1, 238.
17. "Notes of the Fine Arts," *New York Times*, January 9, 1881, 10.
18. Stanford White, letter to Augustus Saint-Gaudens, December 17, 1899 [*sic*; 1879], quoted in Saint-Gaudens, *Reminiscences*, vol. 1, 240.
19. Cox provides an apt summary: "The feeling for individuality,—the modern idea that a man is not merely one of a species, but is a character,—the caring less for the perfection of a race and more for the man himself as he is, with his defects as well as his merits, is one of the noticeable qualities of Mr. Saint-Gaudens's work." Cox, *Old Masters and New*, 269–70.
20. Augustus Saint-Gaudens, *The Reminiscences of Augustus Saint-Gaudens*, ed. Homer Saint-Gaudens, vol. 2 of 2 (New York: Century Co., 1913), 23–24.
21. Dryfhout, *The Work of Augustus Saint-Gaudens*, 112; Burke Wilkinson, *The Life and Works of Augustus Saint Gaudens* (Fort Washington, PA: Eastern National, 2006; originally published as *Uncommon Clay: The Life and Works of Augustus Saint Gaudens* [San Diego: Harcourt Brace Jovanovich, 1985]), 119.
22. See "The Opening of the Assyrian Museum at the Louvre," https://archeologie.culture.gouv.fr/khorsabad/en/opening-assyrian-museum-louvre. I am grateful to Avis Berman for calling my attention to this information.
23. Tolles, "Augustus Saint-Gaudens, His Critics, and the New School of American Sculpture," 193–94. The original pedestal and exedra were carved in bluestone under Saint-Gaudens's supervision by the firm of Fisher & Bird. By the 1930s, it had seriously deteriorated, and an exact copy of it was made in granite. That is what now stands in Madison Square Park. The original is at the Saint-Gaudens National Historic Site in Cornish, NH.
24. The Saint-Gaudens scholar Henry Duffy has seen this as evidence that Saint-Gaudens was an early proponent of modernism, but he astutely goes on to remind us that Saint-Gaudens was "innovative but not revolutionary." Henry J. Duffy, "American Sculptor of the Gilded Age," in *Augustus Saint-Gaudens: American Sculptor of the Gilded Age* (Washington, DC: Trust for Museum Exhibitions, 2003), 15, 19.
25. *New York Herald*, quoted in Tolles, "Augustus Saint-Gaudens, His Critics, and the New School of American Sculpture," 196.
26. M. G. Van Rensselaer, "Mr. St. Gaudens's Statue of Admiral Farragut in New York," *American Architect and Building News* 10, no. 298 (September 10, 1881): 119. This is not to say that the praise was universal. In this same issue of *American Architect and Building News*, one of Van Rensselaer's colleagues expressed doubts about the pedestal, writing that it "looks like the back of a sofa, and not even a monumental one." "The Farragut Monument," *American Architect and Building News* 10, no. 298 (September 10, 1881), 120.
27. [William C. Brownell], "St. Gaudens' Statue of Farragut," *Nation* 32 (June 2, 1881): 390.
28. Cox, "Augustus Saint-Gaudens," 30–32.
29. Tolles, "Augustus Saint-Gaudens, His Critics, and the New School of American Sculpture," 195.
30. Saint-Gaudens, *Reminiscences*, vol. 1, 161–63.
31. La Farge, as quoted in Dryfhout, *The Work of Augustus Saint-Gaudens*, 32.
32. Dryfhout, "Augustus Saint-Gaudens: The Portraits in Bas-Relief," 84; and Dryfhout, "The Catalogue," in *Augustus-Saint Gaudens: Sculptor of the Gilded Age*, 45.

33. Saint-Gaudens, letter to Armstrong, 1878, quoted in Maitland Armstrong, *Day Before Yesterday: Reminiscences of a Varied Life* (New York: Charles Scribner's Sons, 1920), 264–65; Dryfhout, *The Work of Augustus Saint-Gaudens*, 82, no. 61.
34. For his portrait of Bastien-Lepage, Saint-Gaudens may have been directly inspired by one of the Frenchman's own paintings. In his 1879 portrait of Sarah Bernhardt (private collection), Bastien-Lepage used some of the same devices that Saint-Gaudens did. In both cases, the subject is posed in strict profile against an undefined but highly atmospheric background and holds some career-related objects. A well-integrated inscription "floats" nearby. See Carol Ockman and Kenneth E. Silver, *Sarah Bernhardt: The Art of High Drama* (New Haven, CT: Yale University Press, 2005), 120, fig. 24. I thank Kevin Lane Dearinger for this reference.
35. Homer Saint-Gaudens in Saint-Gaudens, *Reminiscences*, vol. 1, 152.
36. The relief of Rodman is an extraction, with some variations, from a larger portrait that Saint-Gaudens made a few months earlier of the whole Gilder family. See Dryfhout, *The Work of Augustus Saint-Gaudens*, 102, no. 82.
37. See Michelangelo's *David* (1501–4) in the Galleria dell' Accademia, Florence, and Gian Lorenzo Bernini's *Rape of Proserpina* (1621–22) in the Galleria Borghese, Rome, specifically David's right thumb at it presses against his thigh and Pluto's fingers as they push into the unfortunate Proserpina's flesh.
38. See, for example, Hokusai's *Under the Wave Off Kanagawa (The Great Wave)* (c. 1830/33; The Art Institute of Chicago) and James McNeill Whistler's *Harmony in Pink and Grey: Portrait of Lady Meux* (1881–82; Frick Collection, New York).
39. Dryfhout, *The Work of Augustus Saint-Gaudens*, 152–53, no. 119. Bronze was Saint-Gaudens's material of choice. His one-time studio assistant the sculptor Frances Grimes stated that Saint-Gaudens could not abide the feel of marble because, she speculated, it reminded him of his cameo days; see Dryfhout, *The Work of Augustus Saint-Gaudens*, 33. But as the marble replica of *The Children of Jacob H. Schiff* that is in the collection of the Metropolitan Museum of Art clearly indicates, Saint-Gaudens was not averse to having his ideas translated into marble when a patron, public or private, so desired.
40. Saint-Gaudens's relief has been compared to those on the ancient Roman Ara Pacis (c. 13–9 BCE). Thayer Tolles, "The Children of Jacob H. Schiff," in *American Sculpture in the Metropolitan Museum of Art, Volume 1: A Catalogue of Works by Artists Born Before 1865*, ed. Thayer Tolles (New York: Metropolitan Museum of Art, 1999), 283.
41. Charles Caffin, *American Masters of Sculpture* (Garden City, NY: Doubleday, Page, repr. 1913 [1903]), 16–17.
42. Recent scholarship on the memorial includes Katie Mullis Kresser, "Power and Glory: Brahmin Identity and the Shaw Memorial," *American Art*, vol. 20 (Fall 2006): 33–57; Henry J. Duffy, "Consecration and Monument: Robert Gould Shaw, the 54th Massachusetts Regiment, and the Shaw Memorial," in *The Civil War in Memory and Art*, ed. Kirk Savage (Washington, DC: National Gallery of Art, 2016), 191–202; and Charles H. Karelis, "The Problem of Racial Hierarchy in the Shaw Memorial," in *The Civil War in Memory and Art*, 205–12. See also Dryfhout, *The Works of Augustus Saint-Gaudens,* 222–29, no. 166.
43. His early ideas for a Shaw equestrian can be seen in two drawings reproduced in Dryfhout, *The Works of Augustus Saint-Gaudens*, 224.
44. Saint-Gaudens, *Reminiscences*, vol. 1, 332.
45. Some of these sketches, which are in the collection of the Saint-Gaudens National Historic Site in Cornish, NH, are reproduced in Dryfhout, *The Works of Augustus Saint-Gaudens*, 224–25.
46. Saint-Gaudens, *Reminiscences*, vol. 1, 333.
47. Saint-Gaudens, *Reminiscences*, vol. 1, 333.

48. Homer Saint-Gaudens in Saint-Gaudens, *Reminiscences*, vol. 1, 342.
49. I am especially grateful to Josh Craine of Daedalus Inc., Sculpture Conservators, Watertown, MA, for this information.
50. Kathryn Greenthal, *Augustus Saint-Gaudens, Master Sculptor* (New York: Metropolitan Museum of Art, 1985), 145.
51. Sarah (Sturgis) Shaw, quoted in Mark Anthony De Wolfe Howe, *Boston: The Place and the People* (New York: MacMillan, 1903), 295.
52. For a list of French's public sculptures, see Harold Holzer, *Monument Man: The Life and Art of Daniel Chester French* (New York: Princeton Architectural Press, 2019), 320–23.
53. Sample, "A New Development in Monumental Sculpture," 96. Shortly after it was taken, the Juley photograph was translated into a full-size painted portrait of French by the American artist Robert Vonnoh (Chesterwood, National Trust for Historic Preservation, Stockbridge, MA).
54. Homer Saint-Gaudens in Saint-Gaudens, *Reminiscences*, vol. 2, 188.
55. Lois G. Marcus, "The 'Shaw Memorial' by Augustus Saint-Gaudens: A History Painting in Bronze," *Winterthur Portfolio* 14 (Spring 1979): 22.
56. For a contemporary assessment, see, for example, H. C. Howard, "The Art of Daniel Chester French," *Fine Arts Journal* 17 (September 1906): 555. The sculpture historian Michael Richman called the work "the most successful achievement of [French's] early career." Michael Richman, "The Early Public Sculpture of Daniel Chester French," *American Art Journal*, vol. 4 (November 1972): 113.
57. Martin Milmore's will mandated "a monument in my lot in Forest Hills Cemetery to the memory chiefly of my deceased brother James but with such inscriptions and in such way and manner as may be to the taste of [my] executors." Two years later, Joseph Milmore extended the idea by asking for a monument to include "bronze busts or reliefs of my dear mother and my two brothers Martin and James and myself." Will of Martin Milmore, January 5, 1882, probated September 14, 1883; will of Joseph Milmore, October 2, 1885, probated October 11, 1886. Probate Records, Suffolk County, MA, via Ancestry.com; accessed 2023.
58. Michael Richman, *Daniel Chester French: An American Sculptor* (New York: Metropolitan Museum of Art for the National Trust for Historic Preservation, 1976), 73, reproduces a photograph of French working on the early version of the *Milmore Memorial* that shows the sphinx facing the viewer.
59. Daniel Chester French, letter to William M. R. French, February 1, 1891, reprinted in Daniel Preston and Michael Richman, *The Papers of Daniel Chester French*, digital MS, Chesterwood Archives, Chapin Library, Williams College, Williamstown, MA.
60. Contemporary critics noted that Death's action in the *Milmore Memorial* is not aggressive. "Her hand does not snatch the chisel from the youth," one said. "She tempers the sting of fate with gentle sympathy" ("Daniel Chester French: Sculptor," *Munsey's Magazine* 19 [May 1898]: 235). Lorado Taft wrote that "this mysterious angel" is "beautiful and impressive," not "the grisly, threatening *something*" that Death often is in art. She "may be looked upon as a friend, even a benefactress" (Lorado Taft, "Daniel Chester French, Sculptor," *Brush and Pencil* 5 [January 1900]: 152).
61. Thayer Tolles, ed., *American Sculpture in the Metropolitan Museum of Art, Volume 1*, 332, citing Daniel Chester French, letter to Mrs. G. R. Streeter, March 6, 1914, French Family Papers, Library of Congress, Washington, DC, microfilm 19, frame 559.
62. Lois Marie Fink, *American Art at the Nineteenth-Century Paris Salons* (Washington, DC: National Museum of American Art, Smithsonian Institution, 1990), 344; Richman, "The Early Public Sculpture of Daniel Chester French," 114.

63. Society of American Artists, *Catalogue of the Retrospective Exhibition* (New York, 1892), 17, no. 149; Carolyn Kinder Carr, George Gurney, et al., *Revisiting the White City: American Art at the 1893 World's Fair* (Washington, DC: National Museum of American Art and National Portrait Gallery, Smithsonian Institution, 1993), 364.
64. Taft, "Daniel Chester French, Sculptor," 151; Lorado Taft, "Sculpture of the Nineteenth Century," *Fine Arts Journal*, vol. 34 (February 1916): 71. Taft wrote that whenever he visited the sculpture in Chicago, he felt compelled to remove his hat.
65. Helen B. Emerson, "Daniel Chester French," *New England Magazine* 16, no. 3 (May 1897): 261–62.
66. Caffin, *American Masters of Sculpture*, 63.
67. Emerson, "Daniel Chester French," 262; Taft, "Daniel Chester French, Sculptor," 152.
68. Adeline Adams, *Daniel Chester French, Sculptor* (Boston and New York: Houghton Mifflin, 1932), 11.
69. For an excellent case study of one such peripatetic sculpture, Frederick MacMonnies's ill-fated *Civic Virtue*, see Michele H. Bogart, *Public Sculpture and the Civic Ideal in New York City, 1890–1930* (Chicago: University of Chicago Press, 1989), 259–70.
70. The other major contender in this category is Saint-Gaudens's riveting untitled figure on the Clover and Henry Adams lot in Rock Creek Cemetery, Washington, DC.
71. For the history of the *Parkman Memorial*, I have relied on Michael Richman's "Daniel Chester French and Henry Bacon: Public Sculpture in Collaboration, 1897–1908," *American Art Journal*, vol. 12 (Summer 1980): 46–64, and *Daniel Chester French: An American Sculptor*, 97–102. See also David B. Dearinger, *Daniel Chester French: The Female Form Revealed* (Boston: Boston Athenaeum, 2016), 36–40.
72. Charles Follen McKim, letter to Daniel Chester French, April 30, 1897, Charles Follen McKim Papers, Manuscript Division, Library of Congress, Washington, DC, reprinted in Preston and Richman, *The Papers of Daniel Chester French*; and McKim, letter to Charles S. Sargent, June 29, 1897, McKim, Mead & White Collection, New-York Historical Society, quoted in Richman, "Daniel Chester French and Henry Bacon," 54.
73. Historian Richard Heath has suggested that French's source for both the subject and the design of the *Parkman Memorial* was an often-quoted passage in Parkman's *The Conspiracy of Pontiac* (1851): "Some races of men seem moulded in wax, soft and melting, at once plastic and feeble. Some races, like some metals, combine the greatest flexibility with the greatest strength. But the Indian is hewn from rock." Unfortunately, Parkman went on to say that the inflexibility of Native-American character and culture made it inevitable that "he and his forest must perish together." Francis Parkman, *The Conspiracy of Pontiac and the Indian War After the Conquest of Canada*, vol. 1 (New York: Library of America, 1984), 389. See Heath, "Parkman Memorial," Jamaica Plains Historical Society, https://www.jphs.org/people/2005/4/14/parkman-memorial.html.
74. Sample, "A New Development in Monumental Sculpture," 99.
75. Richman, "Daniel Chester French and Henry Bacon," 58.
76. Daniel Chester French, letter to Frank W. Cheney, May 27, 1906, Daniel Chester French Papers, Manuscript Division, Library of Congress, Washington, DC.
77. Daniel Chester French, letter to Frank W. Cheney, May 30, 1906, Daniel Chester French Papers.
78. Daniel Chester French, letter to Frank W. Cheney, March 11, 1907, Daniel Chester French Papers. Following French's withdrawal from the project, the commission went to Boston sculptor Bela Lyon Pratt, who gave the Connecticut

committee exactly what they had wanted all along: a straightforward figure, in the round, of a young soldier. See *Dedication of the Monument at Andersonville Georgia, October 23 1907* (Hartford, CT: Case, Lockwood, & Brainard, 1908).

79. Alfred S. Roe, ed., *The Melvin Memorial: A Brother's Tribute* (Cambridge, MA: Riverside Press, 1910), 1. See also Dearinger, *Daniel Chester French: The Female Form Revealed*, 40–47.
80. Richman, "Daniel Chester French and Henry Bacon," 62; Roe, *The Melvin Memorial*, 27.
81. Daniel Chester French, letters to James C. Melvin, April 1 and April 9, 1907, Daniel Chester French Papers; and Richman, "Daniel Chester French and Henry Bacon," 62–63.
82. It should be noted that the *Melvin Memorial* is not a grave marker. The grave of Asa Heald Melvin (b. 1834), who was killed in 1864 in the Battle of Petersburg, VA, is unlocated; Samuel Melvin (b. 1844), who died at Andersonville Prison in 1864, is buried in the federal cemetery there; and John Heald Melvin (b. 1841), who died of disease at Fort Albany, VA, in 1863, is buried with other relatives in the family plot at Sleepy Hollow, which is some distance from the *Melvin Memorial*. See FindAGrave.com, memorials no. 23323985, 23352783, and 23378019.
83. "Mr. French's Fine Melvin Memorial," *Monumental News*, February 1909, 140, quoted in Richman, *Daniel Chester French*, 119.
84. Daniel Chester French, letter to William Brewster, August 30, 1908, Brewster Papers, reprinted in Preston and Richman, *The Papers of Daniel Chester French*. For the Piccirilli family and firm, see Josef Vincent Lombardo, *Attilio Piccirilli: Life of an American Sculptor* (New York: Pitman Publishing Corp., 1944).
85. See, for example, Charles Henry Meltzer, "Sculptures Rival Paintings at the Academy Display," *New York American*, December 12, 1908; R[oyal] C[ortissoz], "Art Exhibitions: Sculpture and Painting at the Academy of Design," *New York Tribune*, December 16, 1908; and James B. Townsend, "Winter Academy Display (Second Notice)," *American Art News*, December 19, 1908, 4.
86. Adams, *Daniel Chester French, Sculptor*, 54–55.
87. This influence was short-lived because of the advent of a take-no-prisoners modernism that burst on the scene with the famous Armory Show in New York in 1913 and soon made every effort to put paid to the idea that art must be both figurative and didactic.
88. See for example, MacMonnies's over-the-top baroque affair on the *Soldiers' and Sailors' Memorial Arch* in Brooklyn, which, he told Lorado Taft, he had conceived "as an 'explosion'; a mass hurled against a stone wall . . . which, bursting in all directions, has been petrified as it flew." Taft, *History of American Sculpture*, 352.
89. See Barbara A. Baxter, *The Beaux-Arts Medal in America* (New York: American Numismatic Society, 1987), and Alan M. Stahl, ed., *The Medal in America* (New York: American Numismatic Society, 1988).
90. See Lucia Fairchild Fuller, "Frances Grimes," *Arts and Decoration* 14 (November 1920): 34, 74; and "Helen Farnsworth Mears," *Wisconsin History Bulletin* 13 (March 1927): 1–2.
91. Michael Richman, "The French-Longman Connection," in Marilyn and Walter Rabetz, *Evelyn Beatrice Longman Batchelder Exhibition* (Windsor, CT: Richmond Art Center of the Loomis Chaffee School, 1993), 11.
92. Peter Thomson commissioned both the marble memorial to his wife at Spring Grove Cemetery and a bronze replica of it for the College Hill Presbyterian Church, both in Cincinnati. Obituary of Laura Gamble Thomson, *Cincinnati Enquirer*, January 21, 1913, 8; "Laura Gamble Thomson," https://www.findagrave.com/memorial/17957395/laura-thomson; and "Inaugural Recital," *Cincinnati Enquirer*, December 30, 1914, 16.

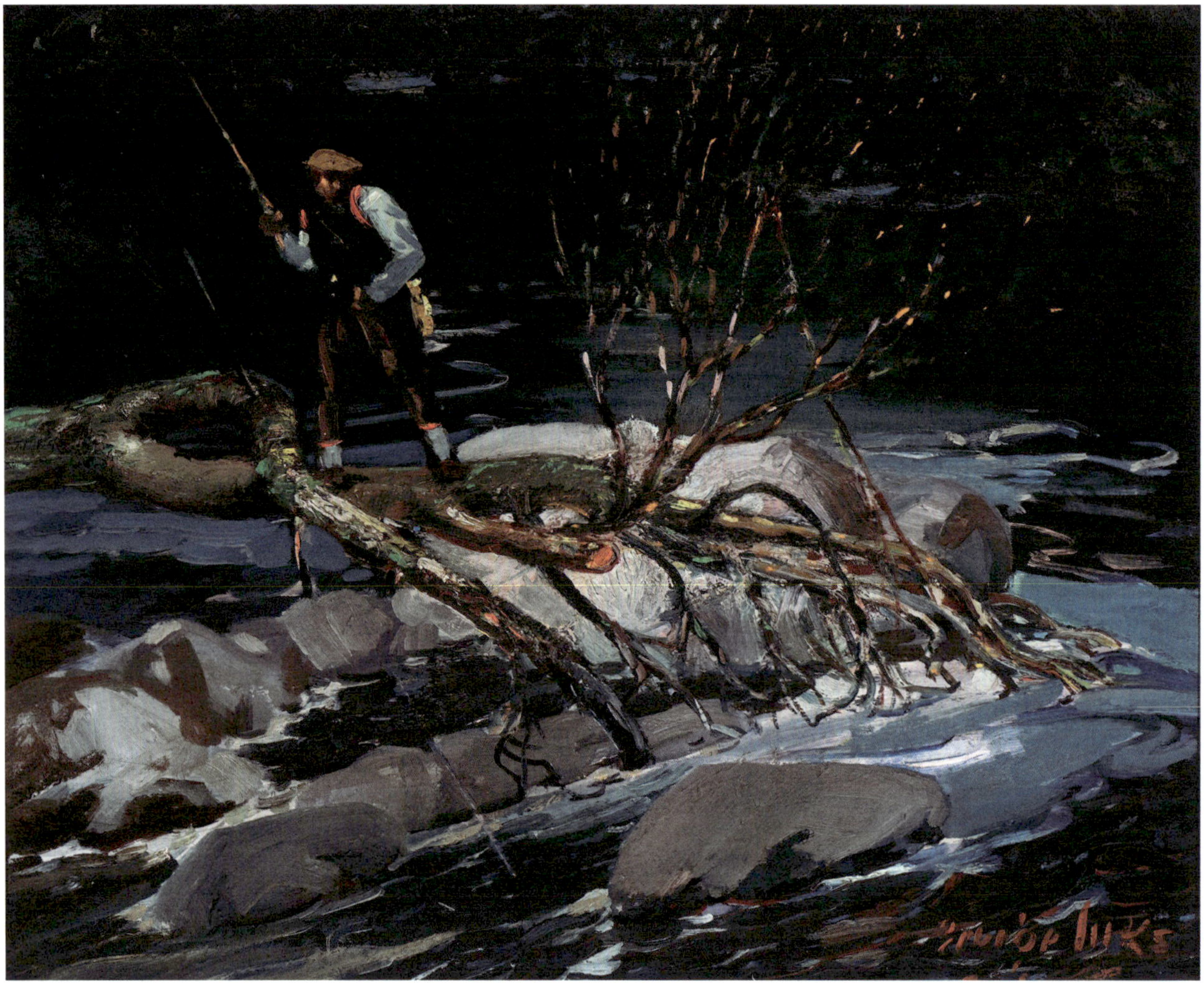

Lecture given on
October 25, 2022

New-York
Historical Society

New York City

Fishing Lure:
George Luks in Nova Scotia

HEATHER CAMPBELL COYLE

Twisted and spotted unevenly with moss, a tree limb arcs over massive rocks, dipping the tips of its branches into the fast-moving water. Atop it, a fisherman stands balanced, with his legs spread more than shoulder-width apart. He needs stability to manage the long bamboo rod and yards of silk line unfurling into a deep eddy. He has something on the line.

This is the solitary sportsman's experience that American realist painter George Luks captured in *Trout Fishing, "The Screecher," Lake Rossignol, Nova Scotia* from 1919 (Fig. 120). The lengthy title—inscribed in large letters on the back of the canvas—anchors the painting in a specific place, claiming authenticity and presence for the artist. It feels natural to imagine the artist as the fisherman poised on a broken branch. He is permanently cut off from the shoreline by the edge of the canvas, and the painted water rushes forward and down, tumbling toward the viewer. Alone in nature, the fisherman becomes heroic. Large and bold, the artist's signature claims equivalent status.

Trout Fishing presents both a moment of leisure and an elemental challenge: man and nature, rocks and water, relaxation and exhilaration. The canvas is brought to life by glittering color and vivid brushstrokes that amplify dramatic tension, effectively conveying the dappled sunlight, rushing water, and textures of moss and bark. Warm tones link things of the earth—the figure, the branch, the artist's signature—and contrast with the blues and grays of rocks and water. The facture—the artist's distinctive handling of the oil paint—expresses energy and motion, and there is a three-dimensional quality to the paint that alternates between fluidity and impasto. Get too close and the scene dissolves into a riot of paint. This is Luks at his finest—laying paint on canvas with vitality and purpose. And while it is certainly a record of a very specific place, *Trout Fishing* is also a painting about painting: a celebration of a mature artist's ability to manipulate his medium.

This canvas is one of twelve oil paintings and about fifteen watercolors that George Luks made based on a trip to Nova Scotia

Fig. 120
George Luks
Trout Fishing, "The Screecher," Lake Rossignol, Nova Scotia, 1919
Oil on canvas
25¼ × 30 in. (64.1 × 76.2 cm)
Delaware Art Museum, Wilmington; Gift of Mrs. Alfred E. Bissell, 1963

in 1919. Critics hailed the oils when Luks exhibited them at Kraushaar Galleries that winter, comparing them to works by John Singer Sargent and Winslow Homer and noting the artist's departure from the manner of his earlier work.[1] A month later, *Century* magazine published eight paintings from the series as a portfolio, bringing Luks's latest work to a national audience. At the time, Luks was fifty-two years old and an established figure in the New York art world. He was best known for his images of New York City and its inhabitants: street scenes of the Lower East Side and hazy portraits of eccentric characters and urban children. Luks's painterly Nova Scotia pictures signaled a new direction and served as his bid to be classed as an American master.

BECOMING GEORGE LUKS

Luks was born in Williamsport, on the Susquehanna River in central Pennsylvania, on August 13, 1867. His well-educated parents had immigrated to the United States from Bavaria and Poland before the American Civil War, and his father worked as a doctor and druggist in various towns in Pennsylvania and New Jersey. Luks was engaged in music and art from a young age, and he developed a theatrical streak. George and his brother Will left their genteel family home and toured the vaudeville circuit, performing in blackface as young men in the 1880s.[2] In the same decade, Luks briefly studied art in Philadelphia at the Pennsylvania Academy of the Fine Arts. He traveled to Düsseldorf in 1889, and, after some formal study at the Academy there, he moved on to Paris and London. In Europe, he developed a particular admiration for Velázquez, Frans Hals, and Édouard Manet. Never

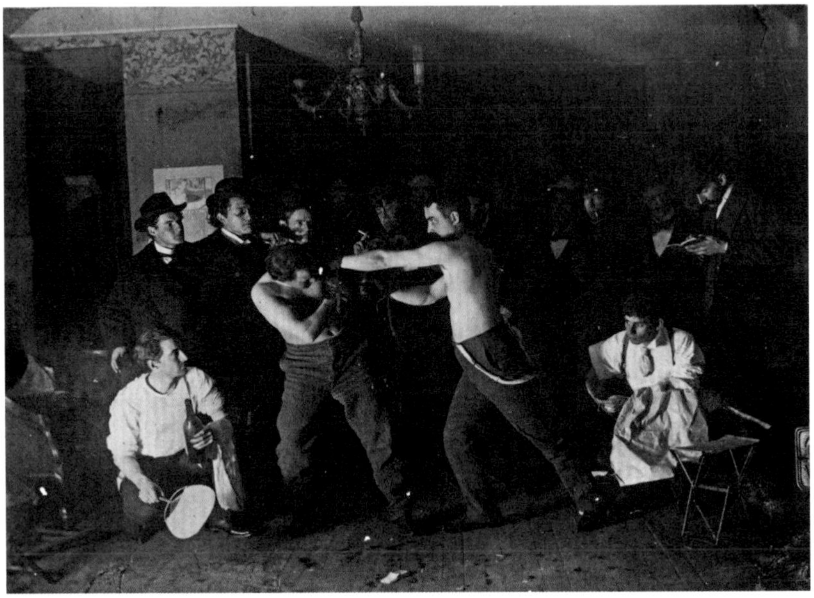

Fig. 121
Mock boxing match at 806 Walnut Street, Philadelphia, c. 1894–95
George Luks is the boxer receiving the punch. Behind Luks, from left to right, stand James Preston, John Sloan, and Everett Shinn.
Archival photograph
Delaware Art Museum, Wilmington; John Sloan Manuscript Collection, Helen Farr Sloan Library & Archives (JS_PhO_23.15)

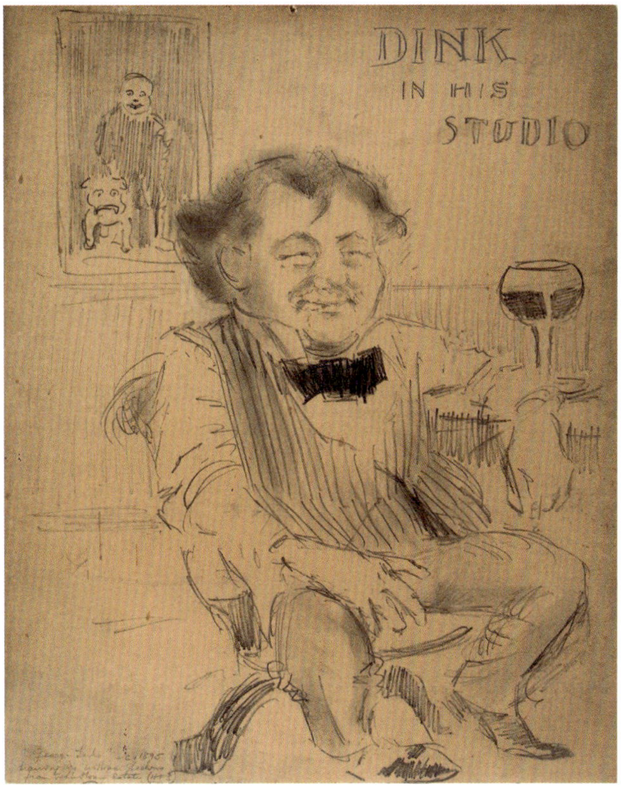

Fig. 122
William Glackens
Dink in His Studio, c. 1895
Graphite and charcoal on illustration board
Sheet: 14 7/16 × 11 5/16 in. (36.7 × 28.7 cm)
Delaware Art Museum, Wilmington; Gift of Helen Farr Sloan, 1978 (1978-547)

a modest man, Luks liked to tell people: "There are only two great artists in the world—Frans Hals and George Luks."[3]

In 1893, Luks returned to Philadelphia, taking a job at *The Press*. While working at various newspapers, he befriended fellow illustrators Everett Shinn, William Glackens, and John Sloan, and, through them, the painter Robert Henri. These young men would gather in their studios to drink, smoke, sketch, and complain about the Philadelphia art scene. They put on comic plays and staged photographs, including one of a boxing match that features Luks as a boxer taking a punch (Fig. 121). Even as a young man, Luks, nicknamed Dink, was known for his flamboyant personality and love of alcohol. Both aspects were captured in a lively caricature by Glackens (Fig. 122). Years later, James Huneker, a New York arts writer, described Luks as larger than life:

> He is Puck. He is Caliban. He is Falstaff. He is a tornado. He is sentimental. He can sigh like a lover, and curse like a trooper. Sometimes you wonder over his versatility; a character actor, a low comedian, even a song-and-dance man, a poet, a profound sympathizer with human misery, and a human orchestra. The vitality of him![4]

"Vigor," "vitality," "independence," and "gusto" were characteristic words often applied to both the artist and his work.

Luks was the first of the group to receive a coveted position as a special correspondent for the *Philadelphia Evening Bulletin*. He was sent to cover the tensions in Cuba late in 1895. His published drawings are signed, and the captions inform readers that they were "sketched by a 'Bulletin' artist now in Cuba."[5] In reality, Luks spent more time in bars than observing battles, but his active strokes and architectural details convey the sense of being on-site. Early the following year, Luks was fired from his position, and by April he had relocated to New York and found work at Joseph Pulitzer's *New York World*, where he illustrated features and drew the comic strip *Hogan's Alley* (already made popular by cartoonist Frederick Opper), which focused on the exploits of children in tenements.

In New York in the early 1900s, Luks was also painting portraits and city scenes, often depicting the residents and markets of the Lower East Side. His focus on the city's immigrant neighborhoods gained him little favor with artists, critics, and collectors steeped in a genteel artistic tradition, but Luks found like-minded members of the art world, especially as his Philadelphia friends, one by one, moved to New York.

In 1907, the rejection of one of Luks's canvases from a juried exhibition at the National Academy of Design spurred the organization of a protest exhibition at Macbeth Galleries in New York. Organized by Luks and his friends, primarily Henri and Sloan, the show brought together eight artists: Luks, Glackens, Henri, Shinn, and Sloan (all formerly of Philadelphia and now living in New York) were joined by Arthur B. Davies, Ernest Lawson, and Maurice Prendergast. They were not an organized group or school, but Huneker gave them the moniker "The Eight" months before their show opened. The Eight differed in styles, subjects, and levels of success. What they shared was a sense of frustration with academic art and the institutions that served it, particularly the National Academy.

The first exhibition of The Eight became a watershed in the history of modern art in the United States. Organized by a group of artists independent of an arts institution, the exhibition reflected an emerging strategy in the American art world. The art, too, was modern, particularly in its subject matter, with Luks, Glackens, Sloan, and Shinn presenting scenes of contemporary urban life.

The artists promoted the exhibition tirelessly, talking it up in the press for nearly a year. In the lead-up to the show, feature articles, written by friendly critics, presented The Eight as insurgents taking on a conservative art establishment. Luks was the subject of a 1907 feature in *The Craftsman*, whose author characterized the painter thus: "Above all Luks is an American. He believes sincerely, passionately in the future of America and American art."[6] The promotional push may have seemed like overkill to Luks, but it was successful. The exhibition of The Eight drew attention across the art and general press, resulting in crowds of visitors and over $4,000 in sales. Luks's *Woman with Goose* (Fig. 123) was one of four paintings sold to Gertrude Vanderbilt Whitney.

Fig. 123
George Luks
Woman with Goose, 1907
Oil on composition board
20 × 16 in. (50.8 × 40.6 cm)
Whitney Museum of American Art, New York; Gift of Gertrude Vanderbilt Whitney 31.288

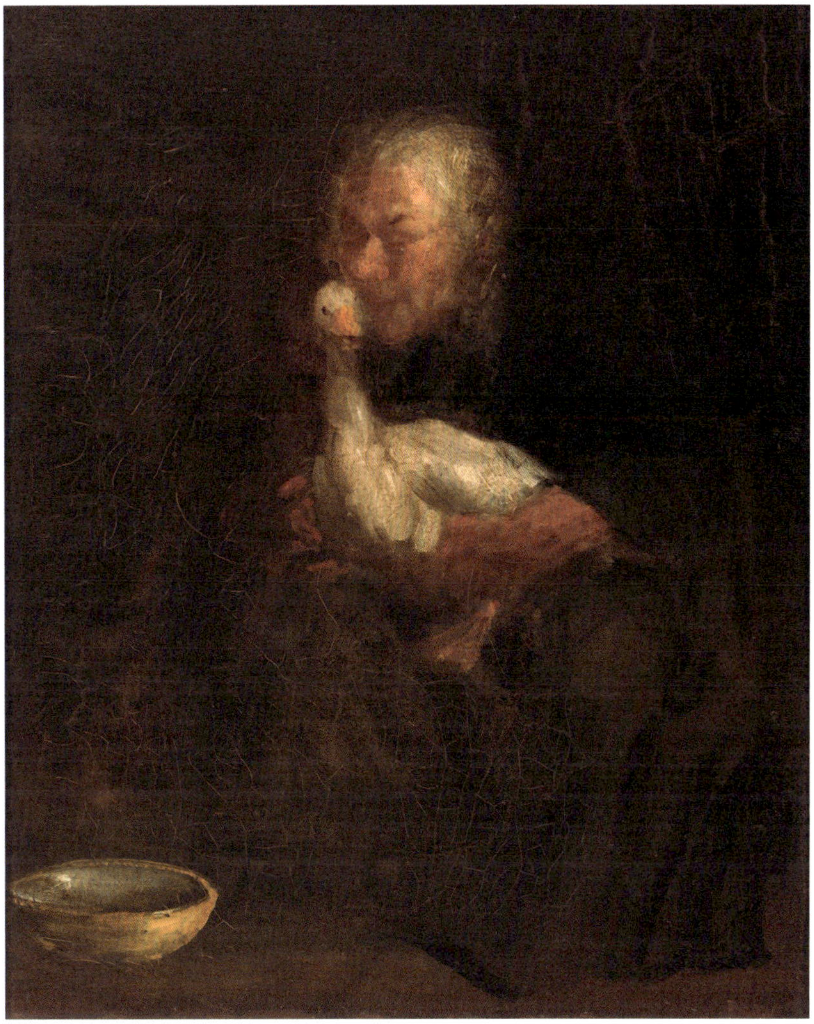

For about five years, The Eight were the revolutionaries of the American art scene, which suited Luks, who enjoyed that designation. Given the opportunity to address the press, he became a vocal proponent of American painting in the early twentieth century, discussing the importance of injecting life and energy into art. In interviews, Luks also boasted about his skills and shared stories (some of them fictional) about his life. In 1910, the artist had his first solo show at Macbeth Galleries, where paintings like *The Wrestlers* (Fig. 124) and *The Spielers* (Fig. 125) earned him praise, including the prediction that his works would eventually "be classed among the 'old masters.'"[7]

The avant-garde status of The Eight ended abruptly in 1913, when the Armory Show introduced broader American audiences to contemporary European modernism, and artists like Matisse, Duchamp, and Brancusi made Luks and his friends seem tame by comparison. In the wake of the Armory Show, American artists explored modernist approaches to form and color. Thanks to the firsthand

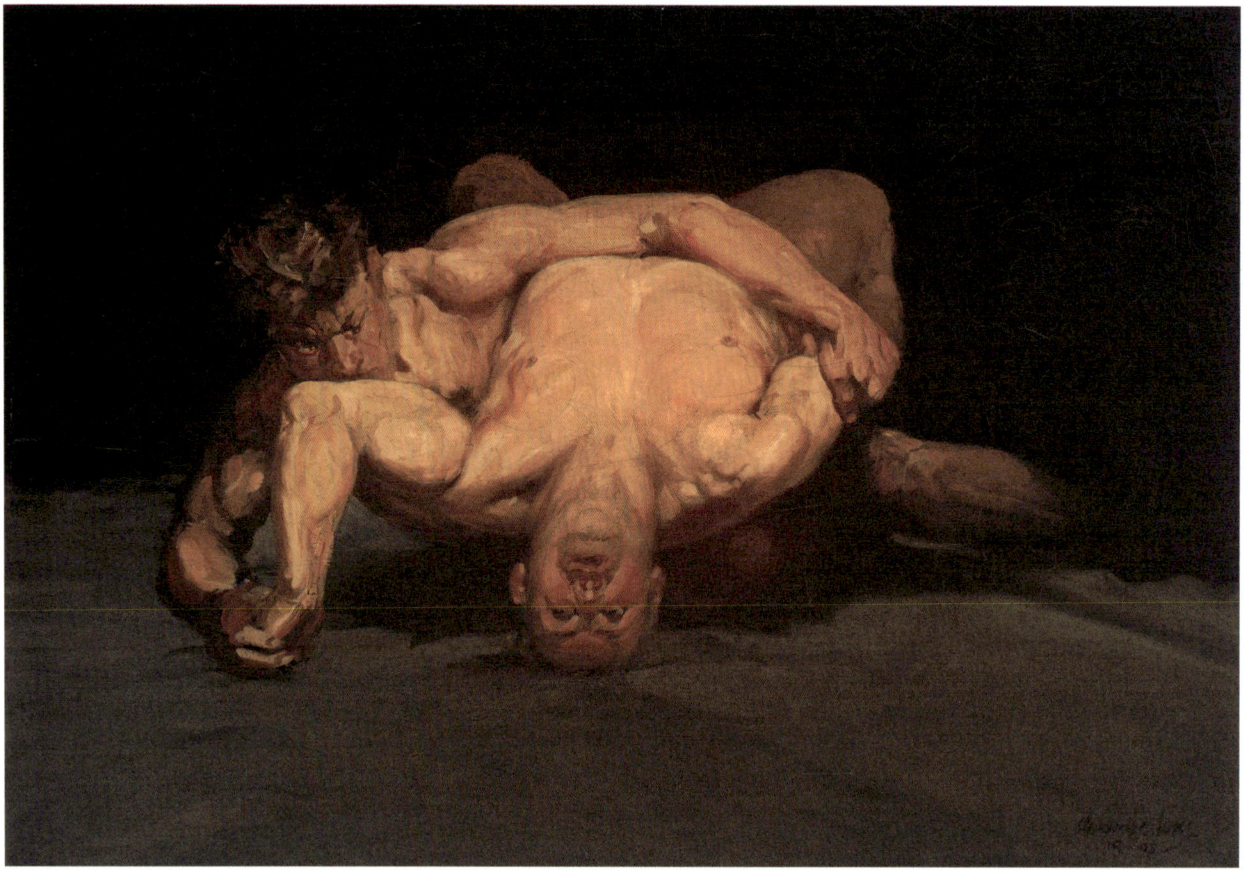

Fig. 124
George Luks
The Wrestlers, 1905
Oil on canvas
48⅜ × 66⅜ in. (122.9 × 168.6 cm)
Museum of Fine Arts, Boston; The Hayden Collection—Charles Henry Hayden Fund, 45.9

knowledge gleaned on his trips to France, Glackens had adopted a Post-Impressionist palette in his paintings by 1910, and after 1913, Henri and Sloan began employing brighter, contrasting hues as they deepened their experiments with color.

Luks, however, continued to paint his urban genre scenes and portraits with colors more or less observed in nature. He was not a man for systems or movements in art. As scholar Robert Gambone noted in his study of Luks, the painter refused even to adopt a singular approach within his own practice. Gambone quotes a writer for the *New York Post* who mused: "He adores paint, plays with it, wrestles with it, scatters it royally upon his canvasses. He makes all methods as he needs them. One picture is brushed in at a jet, the next is glazed and over-touched like an old master."[8] Often, Luks painted street scenes directly with thick impasto, while his most famous portrait subjects emerge from hazy, glazed depths. In the teens, Luks also began to exhibit watercolors, in which the influence of Post-Impressionism—particularly in the pictures of his friend Maurice Prendergast—was more apparent.[9]

Despite his refusal to settle into a signature style, Luks became part of the national art establishment in the years following the Armory

Fig. 125
George Luks
The Spielers, 1905
Oil on canvas
36¹⁄₁₆ × 26¼ in. (91.6 × 66.7 cm)
Addison Gallery of American Art,
Phillips Academy, Andover, MA; Gift of
anonymous donor 1931.9

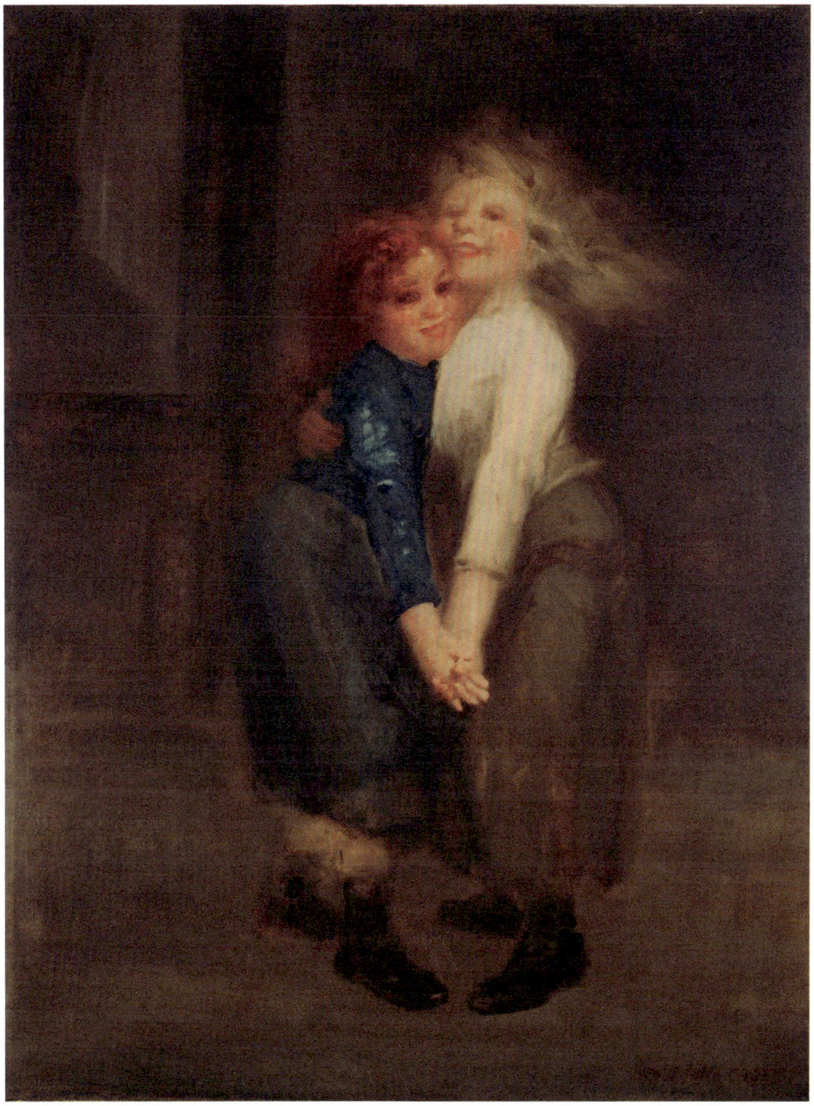

Show. In 1916, he won the Hudnut Prize at the New York Watercolor Club and the William A. Clark Prize from the Corcoran Gallery of Art in Washington, DC. The following year, he had a solo show at the Newark Museum, and in 1918 he won the Temple Gold Medal at the Pennsylvania Academy of the Fine Arts for *Houston Street* (Fig. 126). The same year, critics raved about his portrait of fourteen-year-old Antoinette Kraushaar, completed in a week and exhibited at a solo show at Kraushaar Galleries, where his work was regularly shown in the teens. In 1919, Luks was invited to exhibit at the Pennsylvania Academy, to serve on the jury for their annual exhibition, and to show at the Corcoran. His work was accepted into high-profile juried shows at the Albright Art Gallery in Buffalo and the Toledo Museum of Art.

Going into the summer of 1919, then, Luks was receiving consistent acclaim as a painter of oils and watercolors. Gambone has observed,

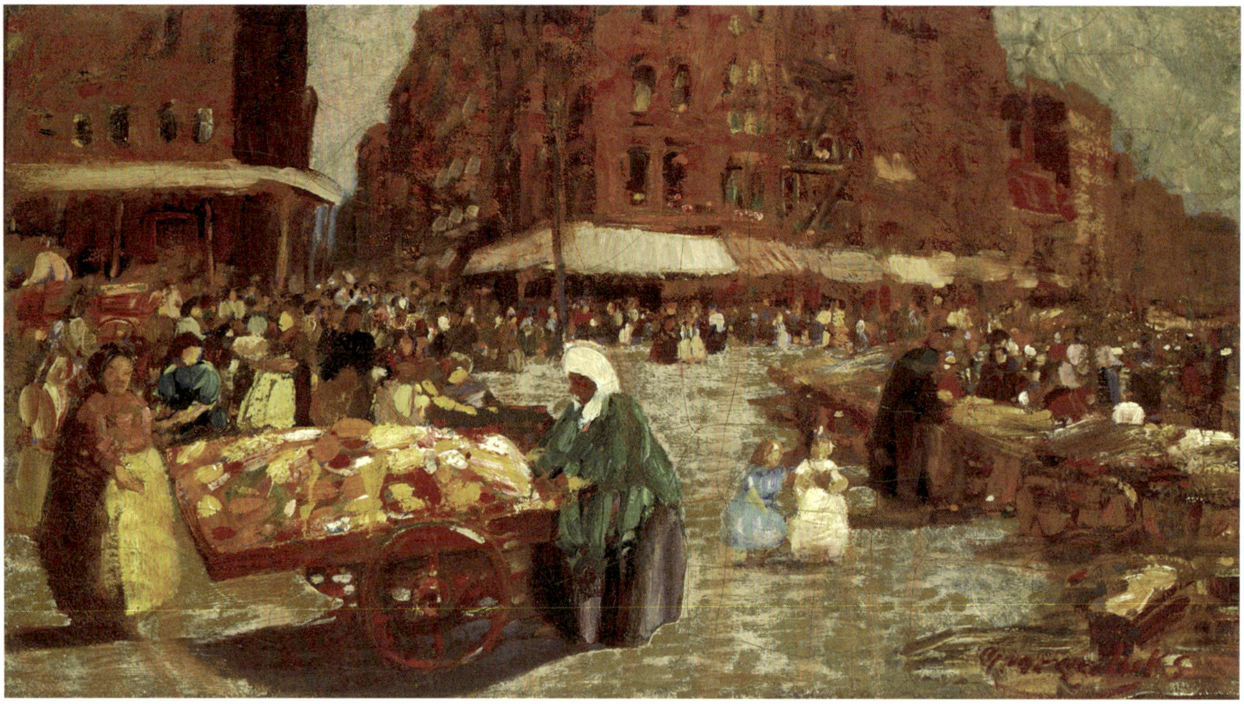

Fig. 126
George Luks
Houston Street, 1917
Oil on canvas mounted on Masonite
23⅞ × 41⅝ in. (60.6 × 105.7 cm)
Saint Louis Art Museum; Bequest of Marie Setz Hertslet 121:1972

"While detesting academia and cultivating the image of art's bad boy, he had become mainstream"—not mainstream enough to be accepted into the National Academy of Design, but no longer on the cutting edge of American painting.[10] For an artist who had developed a persona based on adversity, it was time for a new challenge outside the city with which he was so closely associated.

SUMMER WORK

Leaving New York in the summer of 1919, Luks joined an annual exodus. Summer travel was common among American artists in the early twentieth century. Some went to Europe, while others traveled around the United States. Artists' colonies were growing in coastal and country locations like Gloucester, Massachusetts; Ogunquit, Maine; and Old Lyme, Connecticut.

As they became successful, Luks's friends began regularly spending summers outside of the city. Henri passed several summers in Ireland and others in California and Santa Fe, New Mexico. Wherever he found himself, Henri produced portraits of locals, which provided material for his busy winter exhibition schedule. From 1914 through 1918, Sloan rented a summer home in Gloucester, where he painted lively landscapes outdoors. Beginning in 1919, he spent summers in Santa Fe, eventually buying property and becoming a central member of the growing art scene there. Santa Fe subjects soon replaced New York pictures as Sloan's most heavily exhibited works.

Nova Scotia did not have a burgeoning artist's colony on the scale of Gloucester or Santa Fe in 1919, but it was not unheard-of for artists to find inspiration there, and two of Luks's friends, Ernest Lawson and William Glackens, had firsthand experience in the region.[11] Lawson was born in Halifax and returned regularly; he was in Nova Scotia's capital in June 1919 for a solo show at the art museum. Although there is no evidence of him and Luks crossing paths in Canada, Lawson could have encouraged his friend to plan a trip to the region.[12]

Glackens traveled to coastal locations every summer, including Nova Scotia in 1910. While his family vacationed in the village of Chester on Mahone Bay, Glackens experimented with high-keyed color inspired by Renoir. Canvases like *The Bathing Hour, Chester, Nova Scotia* (Fig. 127 and frontispiece) marked a breakthrough, and Glackens would turn his attention from darkly painted scenes of urban recreation to bright images of beachside resorts for years to come.[13] Luks may have been seeking a similar spark when he headed to Nova Scotia in late summer 1919.

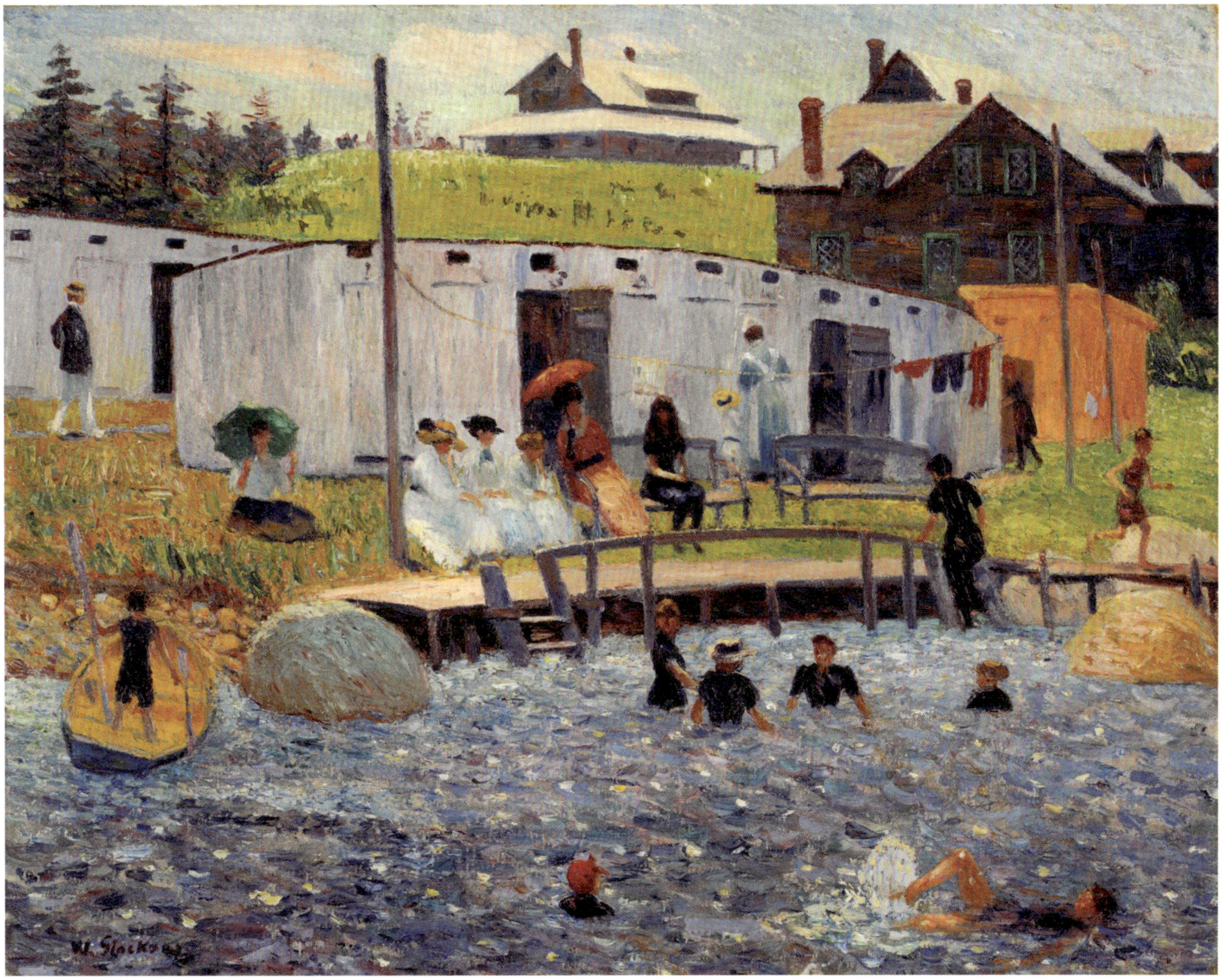

Fig. 127
William Glackens
The Bathing Hour, Chester, Nova Scotia, 1910
Oil on canvas
26 × 32 in. (66 × 81.3 cm)
The Barnes Foundation, Philadelphia; BF149

LUKS AND SPORTING TOURISM

Considering his itinerary, Luks was likely lured to Canada by forces beyond recommendations from artist friends. Nova Scotia was a popular tourist destination by 1900, and advertisements for the island regularly appeared in New York newspapers and national magazines.[14] Entries in the *New York Herald*'s "Resorts" column listed "bungalows, log cabins, hospitable farm-houses," and "comfortable hotels" within an easy journey from New York.[15] A guidebook issued by Canadian National Railways touted the accessibility of Nova Scotia's hunting and fishing grounds, the plentitude of fish and game, and the affordability of the region.[16]

Through the popular press, the sportsman's experience was marketed to American men looking to get back to nature by fishing and hunting in the forests and waterways of Nova Scotia. In the back pages of *Forest and Stream,* a single-column advertisement grabbed readers' attention with a moose head—a trophy sought after for urban clubrooms and suburban studies—and provided information on fishing and hunting licenses.[17] The titles of his paintings place Luks at Lake Rossignol and the Medway River, in areas famed for fishing and moose hunting.[18]

Starting in 1919, the writer Phil H. Moore began peppering American outdoor magazines with humorous anecdotes and practical advice about hunting and fishing in Nova Scotia. A raconteur with urbane roots—he was born in Boston, graduated from Harvard, and made his living as a mining engineer before settling in Nova Scotia—Moore was an ideal interpreter of the sporting experience for American men. He composed articles for *Outing* and *Forest and Stream* in 1919 and would publish books and poems about Nova Scotia in the early 1920s.

Moore's writing made it possible for Americans like Luks to imagine and prepare for a visit to Nova Scotia. He couched practical tips for urbanites in humorous prose ("High-heeled boots are an abomination in a canoe"[19]) and shared specific advice for first-time visitors to Nova Scotia. About purchasing insect repellant, he advised: "Pick out the strongest smelling, greasiest looking mess you can find. Nova Scotia black flies are no epicures."[20] Published in 1922 and entitled *With Gun and Rod in Canada,* Moore's first book anthologized and expanded upon his essays.[21] His writing served promotional as well as informational ends—he was the proprietor of Moore's Camps on Lake Rossignol. Located only twelve miles from the railroad station at Caledonia, the venture allowed Moore to accommodate and outfit visiting sportsmen, or "sports," on fishing and hunting adventures.

In June 1919, when Luks may have been preparing for his trip north, *Forest and Stream* printed Moore's article describing what sportsmen needed to bring to Nova Scotia. He introduced his list by declaring what visitors did not need: "It is usual for any well-equipped guide or sporting camp proprietor to furnish a first-class tent, canoes, paddles, dishes, axes, lantern, blankets, etc." Moore continued, detailing the correct rods, reels, line, and flies, as well as the ideal clothing to pack. His column is echoed in the attire Luks wears in a photograph from Lake Rossignol and in the figure in *Trout Fishing*: long sleeves, high woolen socks, and leather moccasins. The writer listed nearly two dozen necessities, only a handful of which most men would already own. For a city dweller, such a trip required an investment.

Moore went on to warn readers about the "luxuries and inconveniences" that a sporting goods salesman might try to "force upon" them, saving the most ridiculous items for last: "A folding bathtub, a tea basket and a wife are all luxuries that add to the hilarity of the occasion."[22] The author made it clear that sporting vacations were geared toward unmarried men and those willing to leave their wives at home. With his career solidified and his second marriage (to Emma Noble) slowly heading toward divorce, Luks had both the means and the motivation to undertake this particular journey.

LUKS IN NOVA SCOTIA

Luks arrived in Nova Scotia by ferry from Portland, Maine, likely landing in Yarmouth, and made his way inland to Queens County. For most of his visit, the artist's home base was probably Moore's Camps—he made portraits of guides who worked there—and he would have traveled by boat to fish and hunt further afield. The exact dates of his trip are unclear, but Luks inscribed a drawing "Lake Rossignol" in September, and stayed through early October, when moose hunting season started.[23]

Encompassing the traditional hunting and fishing grounds and gathering places of the Mi'kmaq, a First Nations people, the Lake Rossignol watershed is a region of interconnected lakes and rivers.[24] In watercolors and oils, Luks focused primarily on the trout and salmon habitats within this pocket of Canadian wilderness, and the titles of his works asserted sporting bona fides when he name-checked local sites the Screecher and the Medway and characters like Pat Lacey.[25]

Working in watercolor, Luks recorded his response to the natural beauty of the region.[26] In *The Screecher, Lake Rossignol, Nova Scotia*, a man (likely a guide) manages a boat while standing in shallow water near the shore (Fig. 128). He appears to be maneuvering the craft through rocky territory, with the motion of the water and the proximity of rocks adding drama to the situation. Luks filled the foreground, more than half of the composition, with deep blue swirls and S-curves. Lighter passages only accentuate the continuous motion and, near the boat, allow a glimpse of rocks below the surface. The density of the water is exceeded by that of the foliage, which Luks produced by

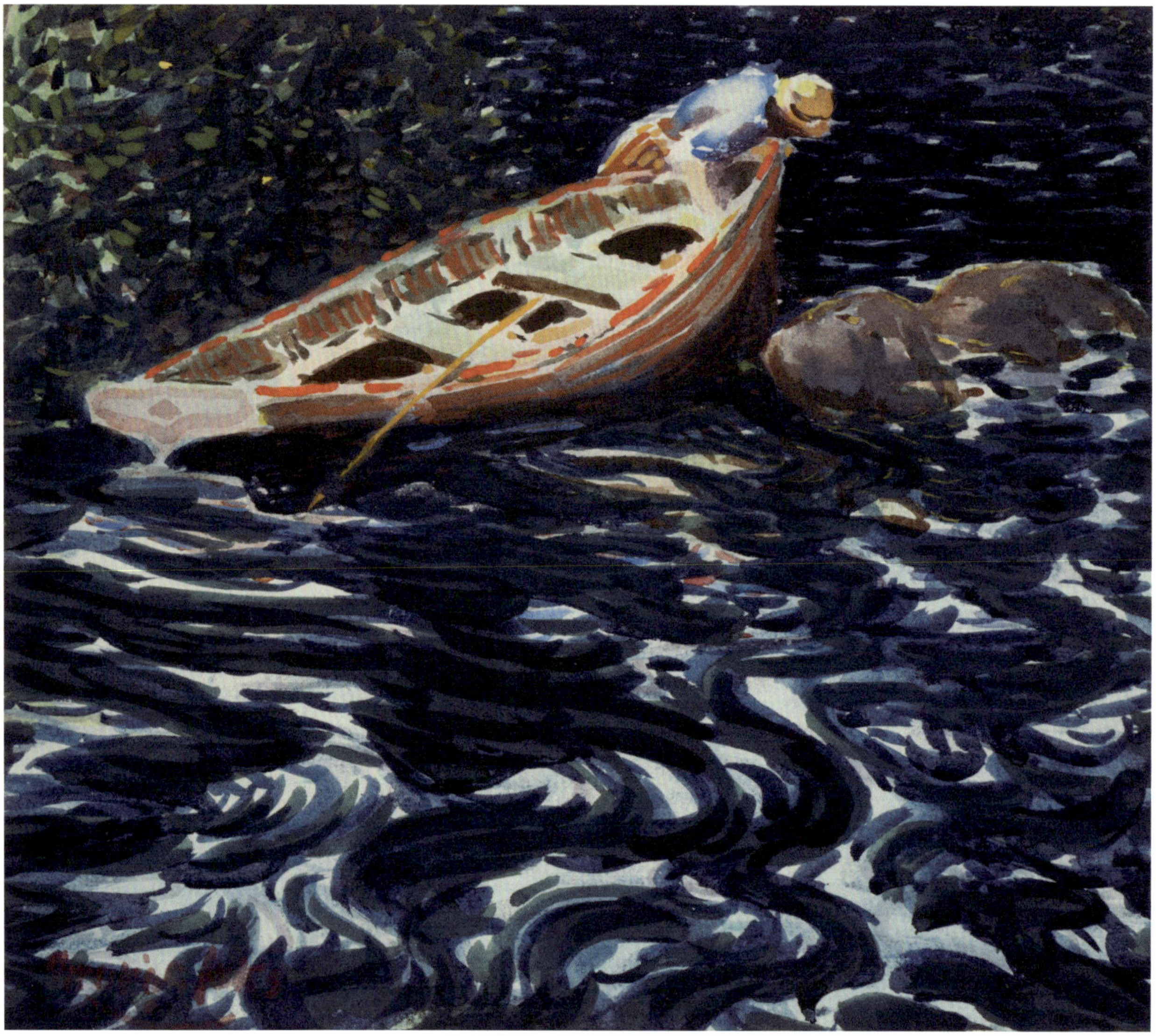

Fig. 128
George Luks
The Screecher, Lake Rossignol, Nova Scotia, 1919
Watercolor on paper
8⅜ × 9⅛ in. (21.3 × 23.2 cm)
Munson Museum, Utica, NY; Purchase 58.159

layering dashes and daubs of greens, blues, and browns in the upper left. Paler and warmer in tone, the figure and his rowboat contrast with the elements that surround them. The slope of the boat pulls the eye toward the man, who seems to be dragging it by the bow, and the long lines of the boat are echoed in the figure's striped trousers. Luks used color and line to set man and boat against nature.

Like *The Screecher*, the large watercolor *The Brook, Nova Scotia* (Fig. 129) features a skyless, asymmetrical composition and energetic mark making. With swaths of white at its center, the composition zooms in on a patch of rocks and water. A cluster of logs, distinctive for their man-made cuts, is the only evidence of human presence. In contrast to the consistent curves of *The Screecher*, here rushing water is rendered with long, short, and looping strokes of blue, teal, lavender, and gray. Darker and denser but still loosely painted, the rocks and branches are formed from strokes, daubs, and washes of black, purple, pink, burgundy, brown, and chartreuse. The result is a delightful cacophony of color and motion that conveys the complex topography of a rushing brook.

Guide Fishing (Fig. 130) and *The Strike* (Fig. 131) each depict a lone fisherman poised atop a boulder, with his rod bending into the water. For *Guide Fishing*, Luks alternated continuous waves of pure blue with shorter curved strokes and empty white paper to give a sense of water moving at various speeds and pooling in different depths. Regular brushstrokes in *The Strike* create a cobalt carpet with only a few spots of white, implying calm, deep water. In both, the figures, rocks, and vegetation are created with short, layered strokes of tan, gold, green, and orange—earthy tones that contrast to the blue. The fishermen appear small, perched on boulders and surrounded by moving water and dense growth.

Seen as a group, the Nova Scotia watercolors play as variations on the theme of man in nature, presenting a range of moods and experiences with a consistent vocabulary of patterned brushwork and dynamic, asymmetrical compositions. Small figures are subsumed by their lush surroundings. Focused on the rhythms of nature, Luks included no lodges or campsites, no sky, and, perhaps most surprisingly, no fish or game.

Fig. 129
George Luks
The Brook, Nova Scotia, 1919
Watercolor and pencil on paper
14 × 20 in. (35.6 × 50.8 cm)
The Metropolitan Museum of Art, New York; The Lesley and Emma Sheafer Collection; Bequest of Emma A. Sheafer, 1973 (1974.356.13)

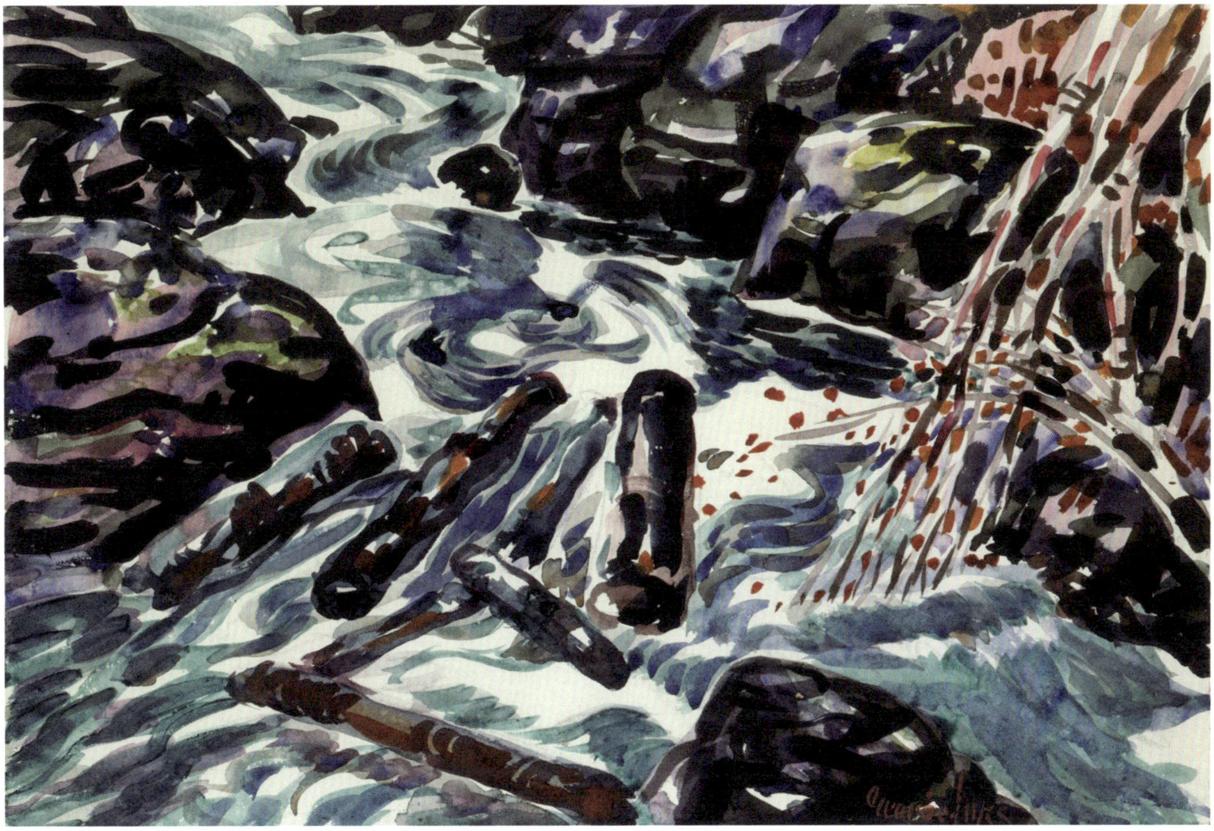

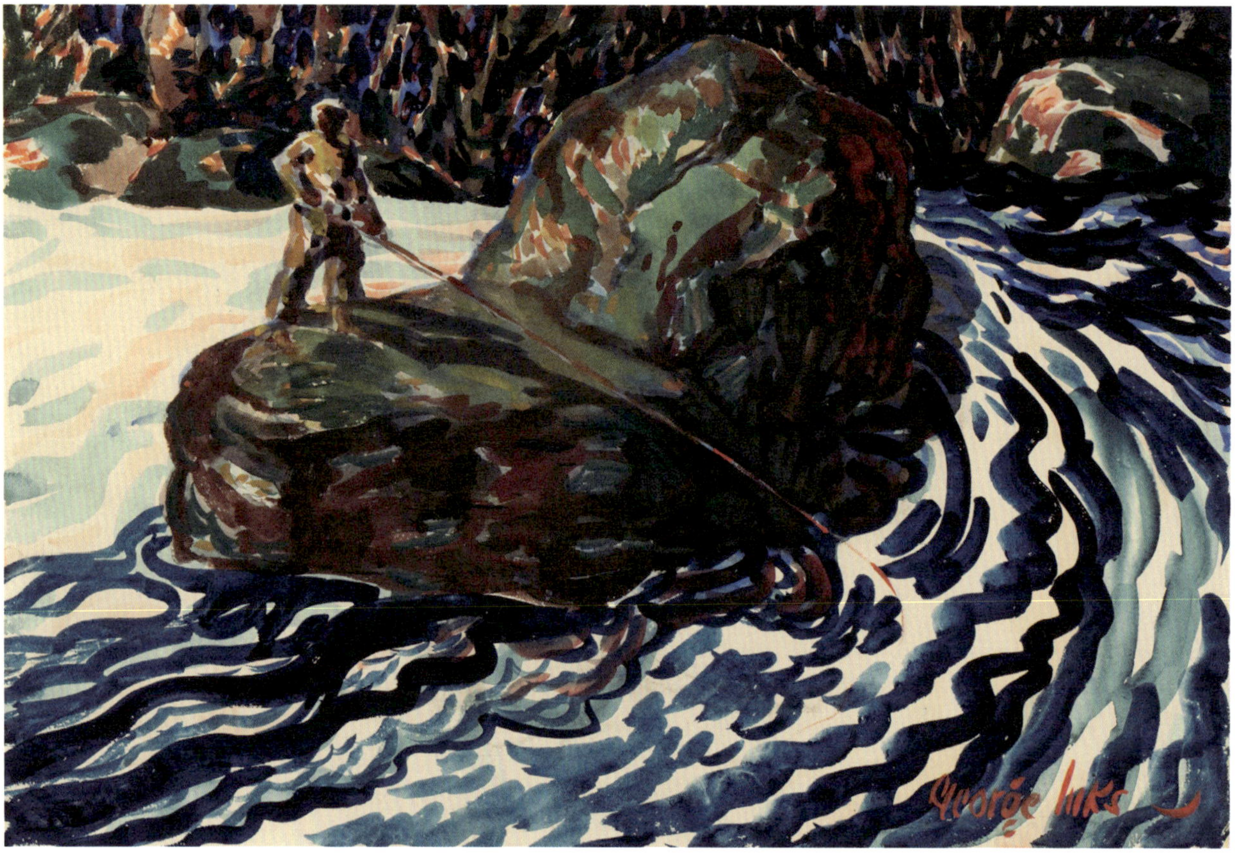

Fig. 130
George Luks
Guide Fishing, 1919
Watercolor on paper
Sheet: 14 1/16 × 20 1/16 in.
(35.7 × 51 cm)
Delaware Art Museum,
Wilmington; Gift of Titus C.
Geesey, 1962 (1962-51)

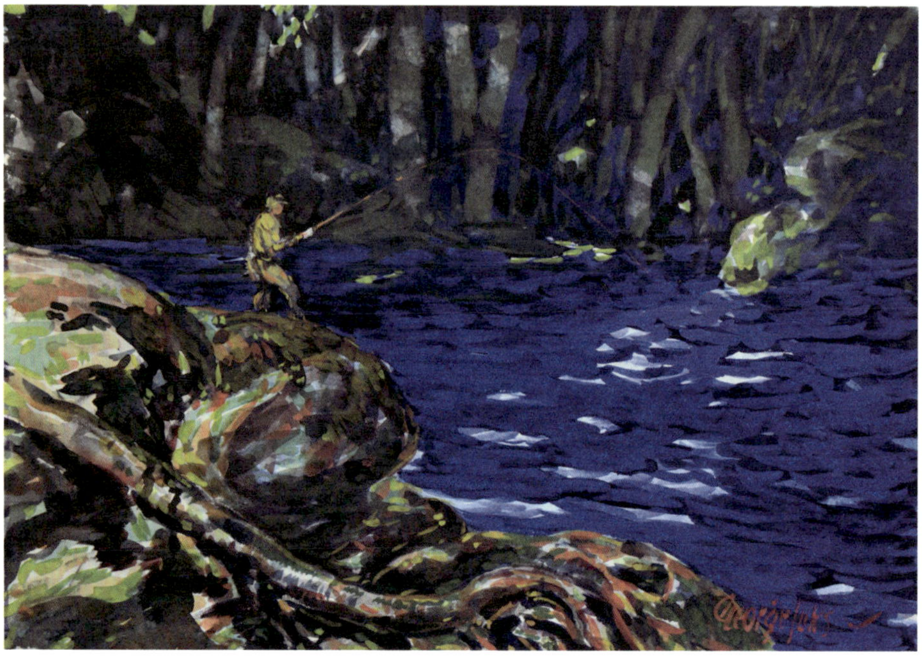

Fig. 131
George Luks
The Strike, c. 1920
Watercolor on paper
13 1/2 × 19 1/2 in. (34.3 ×
49.5 cm)
The Reading Public
Museum, Reading, PA;
Museum Purchase

NOVA SCOTIA IN OIL

In Luks's oil paintings of similar subjects, tight cropping and flashy brushwork carry over across media.[27] Figures are more prominent in paintings like *Trout Fishing*, *"The Screecher," Lake Rossignol, Nova Scotia* (see Fig. 120) and *Salmon Fishing, Medway River, Nova Scotia* (Fig. 132), lending the oils a more narrative and less decorative character. Cutting diagonally across the canvas, the fisherman's line in *Trout Fishing* foreshadows a fresh catch drawn in from the deep water. In *Salmon Fishing*, unruly vegetation spreads across the center and foreground of the canvas, creating a thicket sure to snag any miscast line. The fisherman—clad in striking yellow from shoulders to shins—contrasts sharply to the leaden tones of his surroundings, emphasizing the poor weather conditions, while whitewater churns around him.

Widely reproduced in 1920 but unlocated today, *Salmon Pool, Medway River* (Fig. 133) was the centerpiece of contemporary reviews. Its

Fig. 132
George Luks
Salmon Fishing, Medway River, Nova Scotia, 1919
Oil on canvas
25³⁄₁₆ × 30 in. (64 × 76.2 cm)
Whitney Museum of American Art, New York; Gift of Mr. and Mrs. Herbert R. Steinmann 61.11

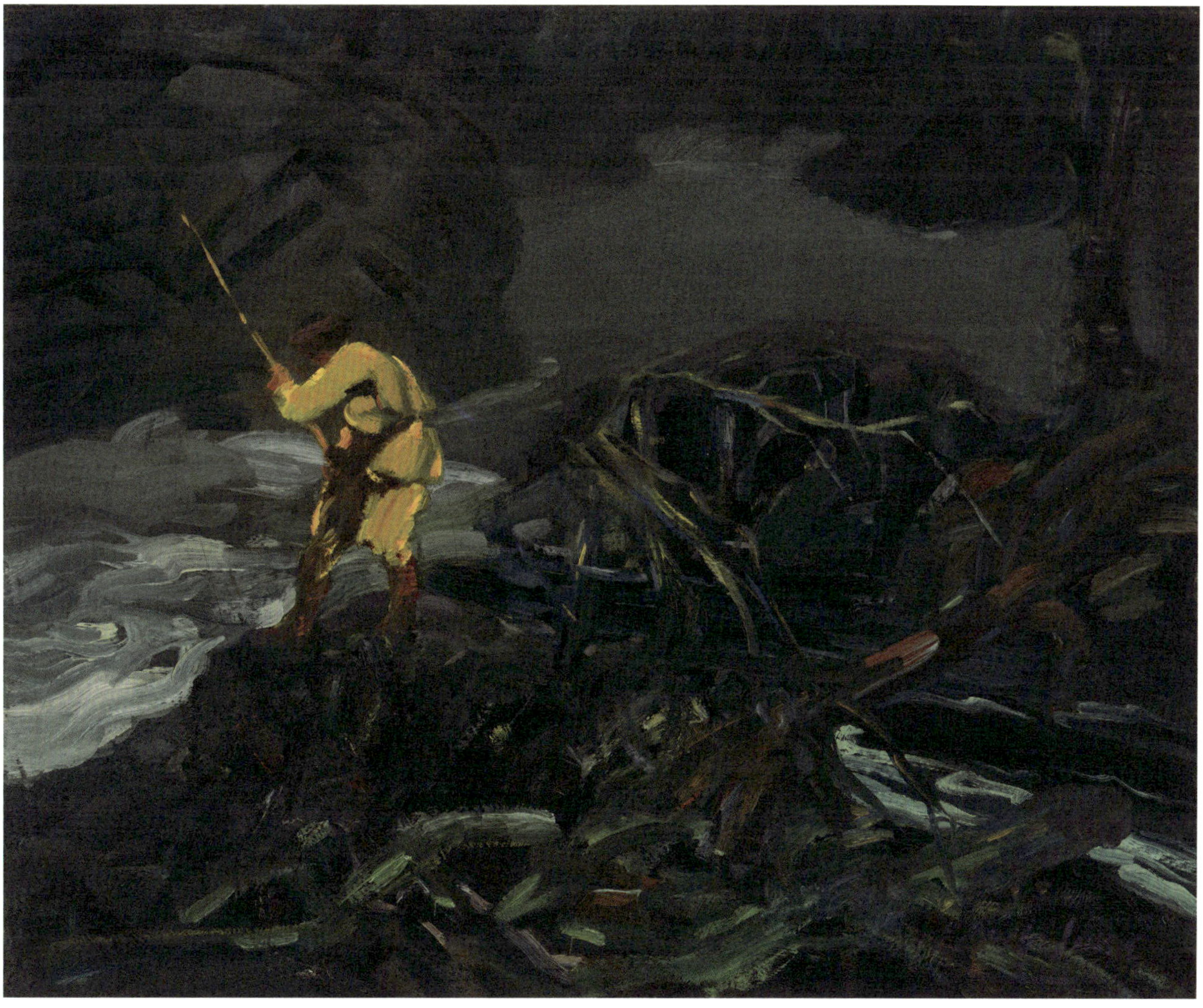

Fig. 133
George Luks
Salmon Pool, Medway River, 1919
Location unknown
In "Wood, Wind and Water (Nova Scotia): Eight Paintings by George B. Luks," *Century* 99, no. 4 (February 1920): 500

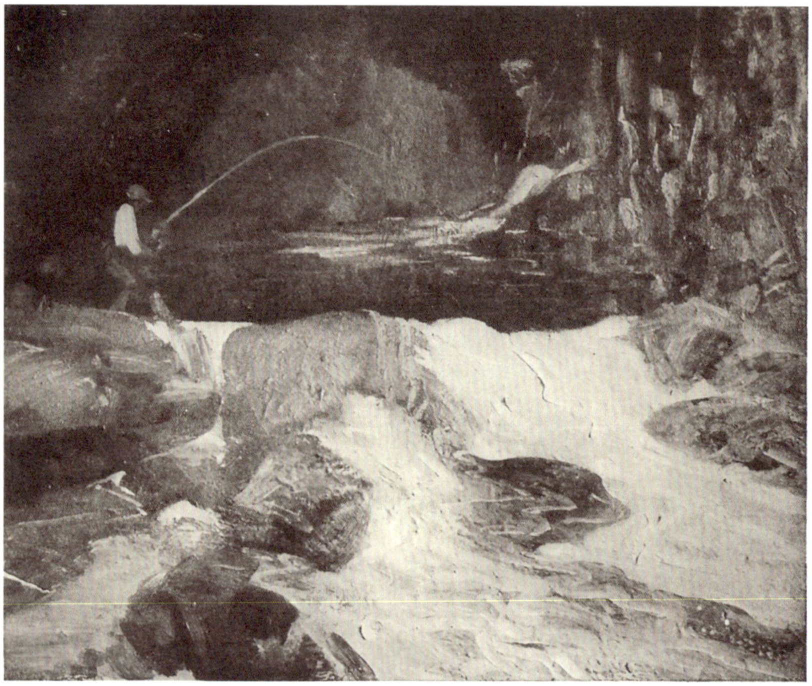

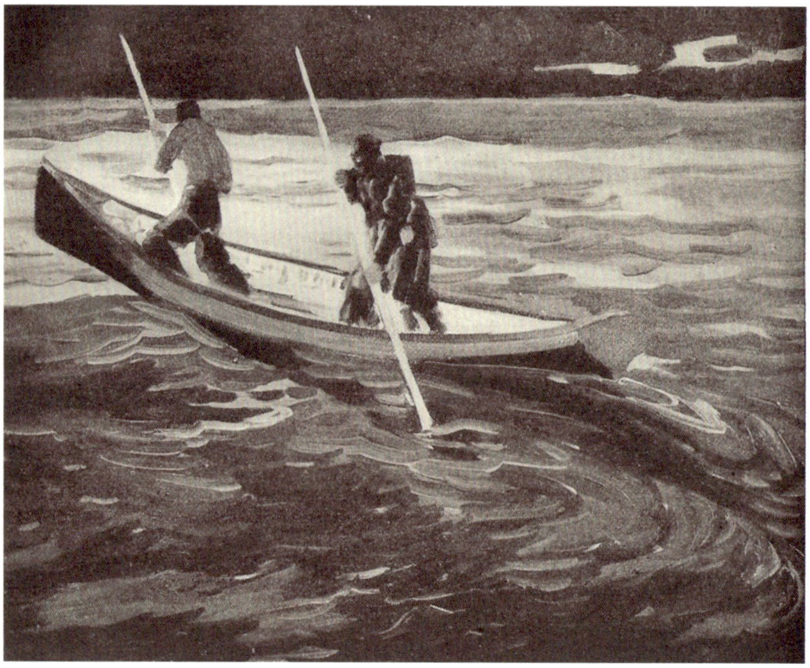

Fig. 134
George Luks
Guides in a Storm on Lake Rossignol, 1919
Location unknown
In "Wood, Wind and Water (Nova Scotia): Eight Paintings by George B. Luks," *Century* 99, no. 4 (February 1920): 502

protagonist is another lone fisherman with a long rod. He is positioned precariously, one leg extending across a rocky waterfall. In the center and foreground, thick paint actualizes the rushing, foaming water. As one critic noted when the painting was first exhibited, "In applying highlights [Luks] loaded his brushes more heavily than Sargent would have done, so the crest of the high lights falls over in scraggy threads."[28] The *New York Tribune*'s art critic Royal Cortissoz praised the "sheer gusto" of this work and its ability to connect with the viewer: "The still pool and the swirling falls above and below it, the eager fisherman masterfully hinted in a few swift stenographic touches, are all bound together in a pictorial unit which makes us at once joyfully at one with the scene."[29] And James Gregg located in this picture "the solidity of Corbett [*sic*] and that great master's command over the mystery of the deep woods," inspiring him to rank Luks "among the most distinguished of our landscape painters."[30]

Another fishing picture to attract high praise from Gregg was *Nova Scotia Guides, Lake Rossignol* (also known as *Guides in a Storm on Lake Rossignol*) (Fig. 134), which recorded a challenging feat performed in poor weather. The action Luks chose to depict is a difficult maneuver, when men use long poles to propel a canoe upstream.[31] In the painting, the canoe rides a swell, elevating the front third of the boat above the water. Employing larger figures placed in the center of the canvas, Luks communicated the physical exertion of his wiry subjects in their bent knees and bowed backs. Their heads incline toward the rolling water, following the lines of their yellow poles, focused on the task at hand. Luks's title informs the viewers that these skilled and determined men are not tourists, but professional guides.

PORTRAITS OF NOVA SCOTIA

As implied in the action of *Nova Scotia Guides, Lake Rossignol*, the artist's sporting trip to Nova Scotia was not the solitary adventure indicated in most of the fishing pictures. Sportsmen visiting Canada were required to be accompanied by professional guides.[32] Nova Scotia's guides were Mi'kmaq, Canadian, and American men, and their employers included the proprietors of camps and lodges. Guides made sure sportsmen did not get lost, endanger wildlife, or exceed catch limitations. They took visitors to the best fishing spots, packed and managed the canoes, set up camp, and cooked meals. As captured in Luks's only hunting scene from Nova Scotia, *Dunraven Bog, Nova Scotia* (published in *Century* magazine in 1920 as *Calling the Moose, The Dunraven Bog*) (Fig. 135), some guides specialized in tracking and calling elusive moose for visiting hunters.[33] By the fire in the evening, guides shared tales of their escapades.

Guides featured heavily in outdoor travel literature from the early twentieth century. Independent, experienced with weapons, and able

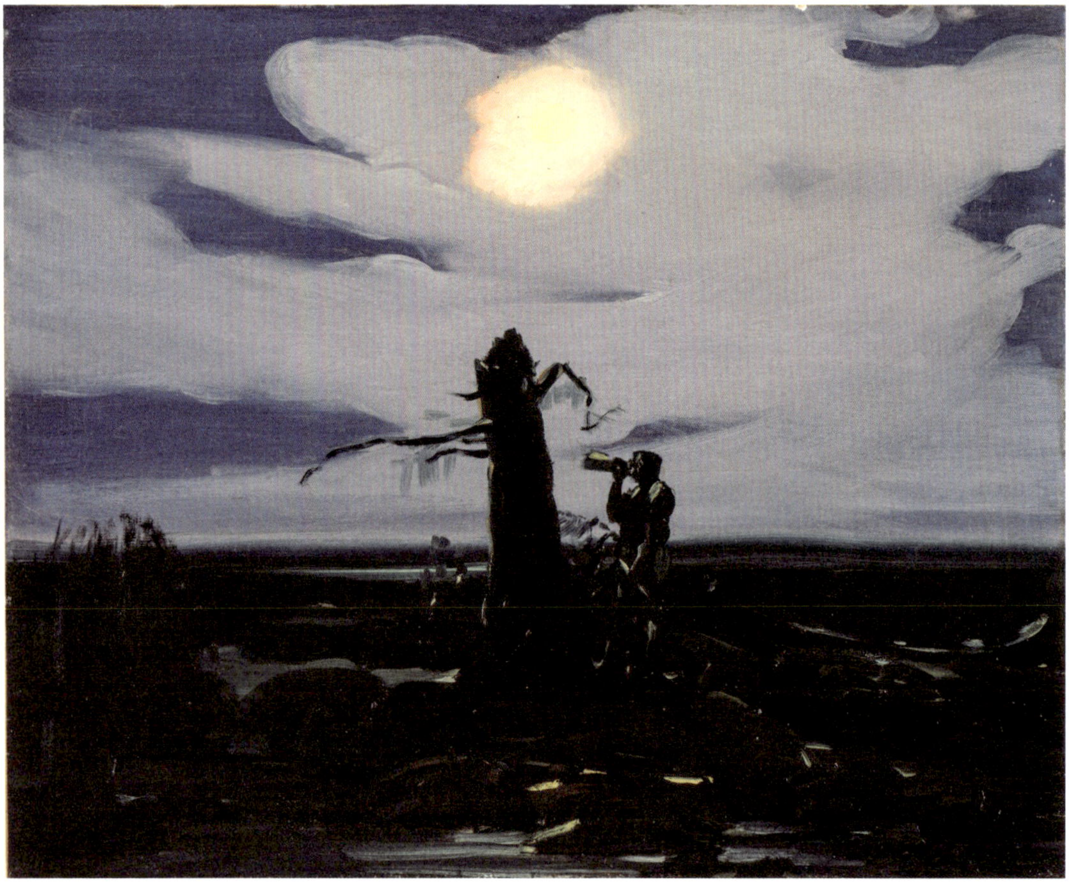

Fig. 135
George Luks
Dunraven Bog, Nova Scotia, 1919
Oil on canvas
25⅛ × 30⅛ in. (63.8 × 76.5 cm)
Hirshhorn Museum and Sculpture Garden, Smithsonian Institution, Washington, DC; Gift of Joseph H. Hirshhorn, 1966

to live off the land, guides served as exemplars of rugged masculinity. Magazine writers detailed the guides' triumphs as hunters and their colorful personalities. As described by author Elon Jessup in *Outing*, one longtime guide, Joe Patterson, claimed to have been employed as a sheriff in Montana. Patterson was skilled with a whittling knife, a Colt revolver, and a birchbark moose call and described himself as "the biggest liar and best guide in Nova Scotia."[34] Canada's guides were so storied that thousands gathered to witness the Guides Meet in Yarmouth in August 1919, an annual competition that tested participants' prowess in canoe races and trapshooting events.[35] Through the many articles published about their exploits, a handful of individual guides gained a modicum of fame, and visiting sportsmen were encouraged to respect the men who were responsible for ensuring their safety and comfort.

The foil to the guide was the visiting "city nimrod." Unfamiliar with firearms, axes, canoes, and tents and perhaps unable to swim, these men were hazards in the wilderness and dependent on their guides for survival.[36] As an artist from New York, Luks might naturally have fallen into this category. However, through his Nova Scotia pictures, with their accurate details and heroic protagonists immersed in nature, the artist placed himself among the initiated.

In a testament to the impression made by his skilled guides, Luks produced significant paintings of Joe Armstrong and Pat Lacey.[37] In these portraits, as in popular outdoor writing, the guides are larger than life and rendered with broad strokes. In *Pat Lacey, Bear-Hunter and Guide* (Fig. 136), Luks depicted his sitter attired in a flat cap and a loose jacket, with unruly facial hair. Lacey featured in the humorous anecdotes of multiple outdoor writers. Described by Moore as "a middle-aged hunter and trapper of great fame," Lacey was known to travel "winter and summer alike" with a repeater rifle for hunting bears, wildcats, and small game.[38]

Luks's initial drawing of the famous guide portrays him hatless and wearing a wool sweater, his mustache tamed, and hair swept back from a high forehead (Fig. 137). His weathered face and high cheekbones are delineated with care, and he is instantly recognizable from photographs published in books and magazines. With its thick, fluid brushstrokes and prominently placed rifle, Luks's painting is more iconic than the pencil drawing, presenting Lacey as the archetype of an outdoorsman. In the *Herald*, Gregg admired the painting, stating that it was "bound to do more for the enduring fame of that hero of the wilds than all the exploits of his life."[39] Sadly, this prediction did not come true, as the painting remains unlocated.

Fig. 136
George Luks
Pat Lacey, Bear-Hunter and Guide, 1919
Oil on canvas
Location unknown
In "Wood, Wind and Water (Nova Scotia): Eight Paintings by George B. Luks," *Century* 99, no. 4 (February 1920): 499

Fig. 137
George Luks
Portrait of Pat Lacey, 1919
Graphite on paper
9¾ × 6⅝ in. (24.8 × 16.8 cm)
Westmoreland Museum of American Art, Greensburg, PA; Gift of Mary Marchand Wood Memorial Fund 1959.70

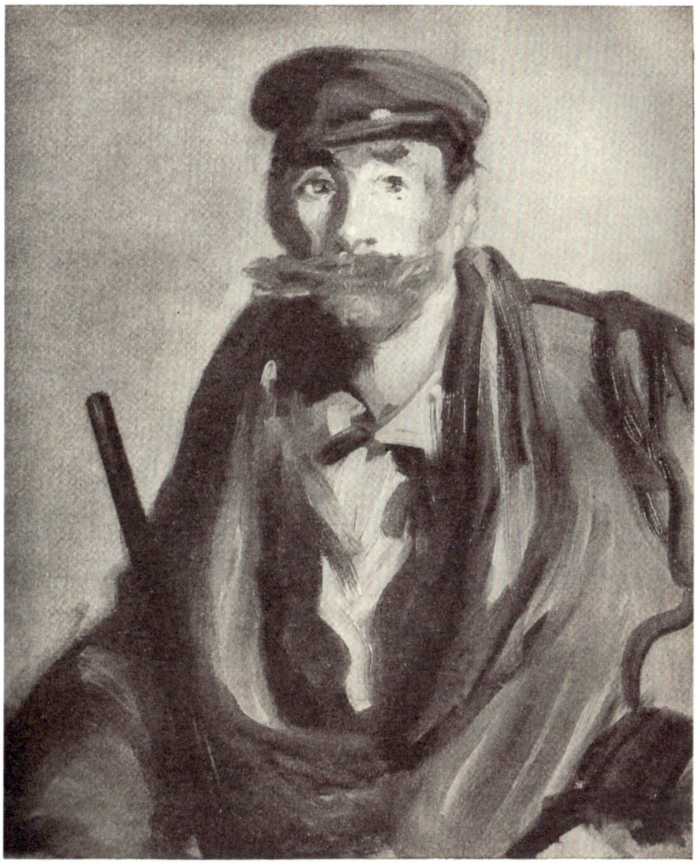

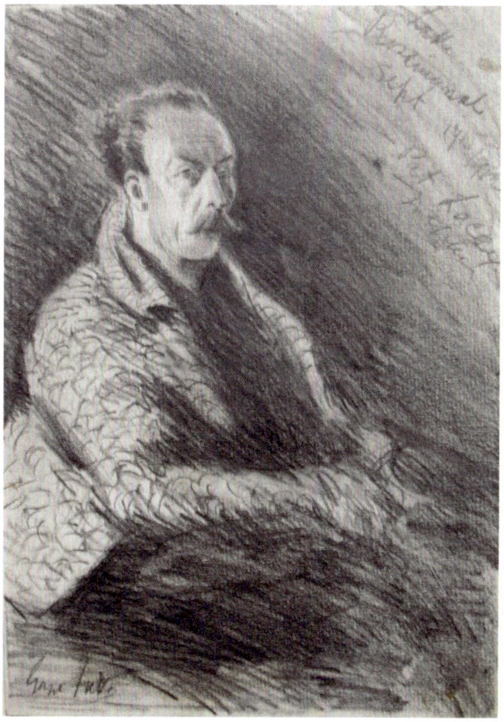

Fig. 138
George Luks
Rosie, 1919
Oil on canvas
30⅟₁₆ × 25⅛ in. (76.4 × 63.8 cm)
Whitney Museum of American Art, New York; Gift of Gertrude Vanderbilt Whitney 31.287

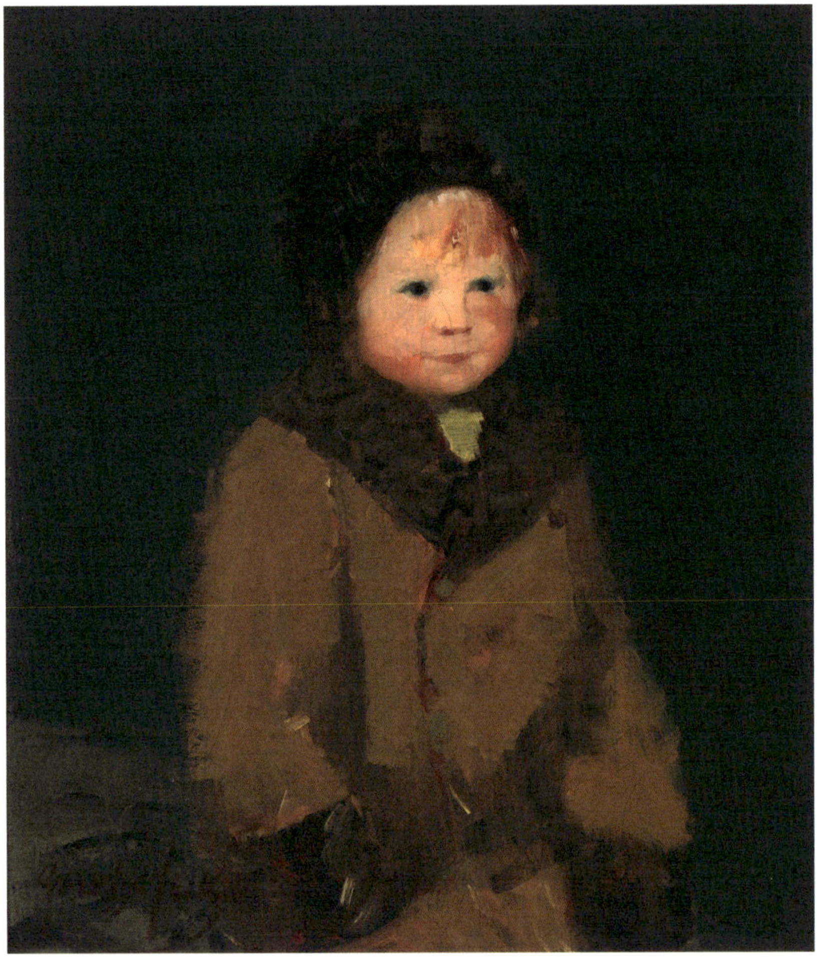

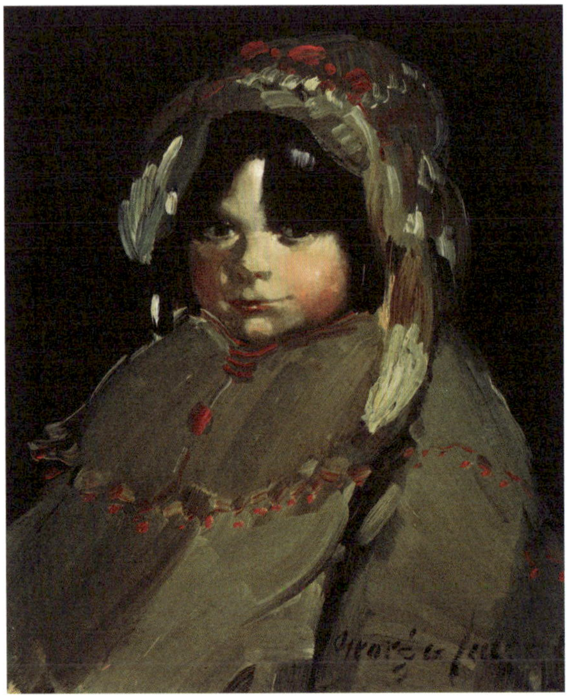

Fig. 139
George Luks
The Trapper's Daughter, c. 1920
Oil on canvas
20 × 16 in. (50.8 × 40.64 cm)
Buffalo AKG Art Museum; James H. Madison Fund, 1930. 1930:5

Inspired by his stay in Nova Scotia, Luks also produced portraits of local children. *Rosie* (Fig. 138) and *The Trapper's Daughter* (Fig. 139) appealed to critics and collectors accustomed to seeing Luks as an expert painter of children in the city. Both have striking eyes and wear distinctive fur jackets and hats that identify them as children from a community shaped by hunting and trapping. Gregg praised the pictures for their lack of sentimentality and their "humor, sympathy and extreme characterization."[40] Unlike most of the Nova Scotia pictures, *Rosie* and *The Trapper's Daughter* entered museum collections during the artist's lifetime.

EXHIBITING NOVA SCOTIA

Upon his return from Canada, Luks must have gone to work immediately on the oil paintings. He completed twelve canvases in about three months, in time for the opening, on January 11, 1920, of a solo show at C. W. Kraushaar's Fifth Avenue gallery. Critics seized on the occasion to weigh in on the latest work and the long-term reputation of an undeniably significant artist.

Under the headline "Self-Determination in American Art," Cortissoz introduced the "ambiguous veracity" on view: "Mr. Luks spills his broad, vigorous notes like so many anecdotes of a fishing trip in which he has taken immense delight." The critic praised Luks for his "unaffected feeling for nature . . . a world of tumbling waters, keen winds, and a sportsman's active life" and admired the "zest" in the subject and the "truth" in the artist's handling. However, Cortissoz was disappointed by Luks's disinterest in beauty: "It is a good thing to see the facts so powerfully stated. But was it impossible, was it undesirable, to endue them with charm, the charm that flows from pigment sensitively handled?" He particularly disliked the portraits, which he found brutal and ugly. Praising the artist's independence, virtuosity, sincerity, and "genuine talent," Cortissoz echoed earlier reviews of Luks's art in lamenting that "the instinct for beauty has been left out of his cosmos."[41]

Gregg, on the other hand, delighted in all he saw at Kraushaar, stating that the exhibition presented Luks's most "vigorous and individual" showing to date.[42] Although he generally promoted The Eight, Gregg was not blind to the "unevenness" of Luks's oeuvre. He compared the 1920 exhibition favorably to previous shows and suggested that the current display proved the artist's mature vitality. Gregg took pains to situate the new work within Luks's career, referencing *The Spielers* and reminding readers of the artist's history of resistance to the National Academy. He informed his readers that Luks's 1907 painting *The Pawnbroker's Daughter* (Fig. 140) was on view at the Metropolitan Museum of Art, on loan from the eminent collector Edward Root. Seemingly unsatisfied with the two-column review on January 11, the *Herald* revisited Luks's exhibition the following day to encourage readers

Fig. 140
George Luks
The Pawnbroker's Daughter, 1907
Oil on canvas
30 × 25⅛ in. (76.2 × 63.8 cm)
Munson Museum, Utica, NY; Purchase
58.43

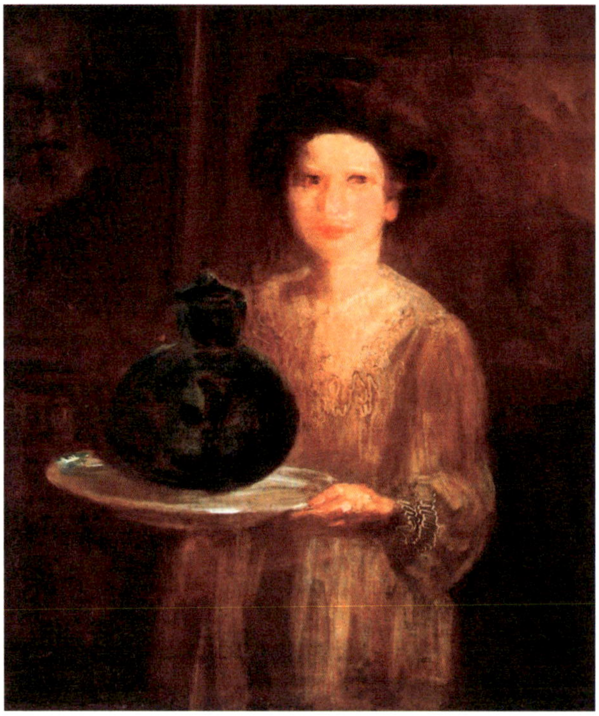

who enjoyed the artist's early work not to assume that his best years were behind him. "When an artist who has achieved pictures that are sure to give him a lasting place on the American records decides to paint in a different manner from that which made him famous there is no need for agitation. An artist cannot go on repeating himself."[43]

In the *Herald*'s positive reviews, the Nova Scotia paintings were compared not only to Luks's own work but also to Winslow Homer, with *Nova Scotia Guides, Lake Rossignol* (*Guides in a Storm on Lake Rossignol*) described as "something which Winslow Homer might have been proud to father."[44] While this comparison to Homer might seem strained today, the idea was sincere and ubiquitous in 1920. A writer for the *New York Times* admired the works at Kraushaar, while admitting that Luks "was not quite so much of a fisherman as Winslow Homer, with whom inevitably he will be compared."[45] Of Luks's portraits, a critic for the *Brooklyn Daily Eagle* stated the case even more vehemently: "Luks has painted them as Homer would have painted them, not perhaps from the standpoint of technique, but Homer's sympathies were the same, his heart was in the same place as Luks's. If Winslow Homer's art lives today in the work of any of our painters it lives in that of George Luks."[46]

As these writers made clear, this inevitable comparison was based not on stylistic similarity but on sensibility and subject matter. Homer's strong association with fishing and hunting subjects, his commitment to realism, and his reputation for artistic independence resonated with critical appraisals of Luks and his Nova Scotia pictures. And although

Luks was famous for denying the influence of other artists and for boldly proclaiming the preeminence of his own work, he may not have resented comparisons to Homer.

Luks became an artist in the years when Homer was being enshrined as *the* American old master.[47] As a young newspaper illustrator in Philadelphia, Luks saw Homer's work enter a museum collection for the first time, when *The Fox Hunt* (1893) was purchased by the Pennsylvania Academy of the Fine Arts in 1894. Homer's fishing and hunting scenes, with their depictions of trout streams and grizzled guides, were exhibited at Knoedler in New York in the late 1890s and early 1900s, as Luks was building his career in that city.[48] Homer's masterful watercolors may well have inspired Luks as he established himself in the medium.[49]

As explicated by Sarah Burns and Bruce Robertson, the praise that swirled around Homer's art reflected turn-of-the-century ideals of masculinity. In Robertson's words: "The terms contemporaries used most often to describe Winslow Homer were *big*, *virile*, *American*, and *real*."[50] This language intensified in the early 1890s, when he began to exhibit hunting and fishing pictures (Fig. 141) and stormy landscapes of Prouts Neck, Maine. Luks witnessed the enduring popularity—with critics, collectors, and general audiences—of Homer's sublime outdoor subjects.

After Homer's death in 1910, encomiums for the painter only increased. In the teens, Homer was in the news for museum acquisitions, a monograph by Kenyon Cox, and achieving record prices for American art. Homer was seen as the prototype for every painterly realist, especially those who, like The Eight, claimed a role in the

Fig. 141
Winslow Homer
The Adirondack Guide, 1894
Watercolor over graphite pencil on paper
Sheet: 15³⁄₁₆ × 21½ in. (38.6 × 54.6 cm)
Museum of Fine Arts, Boston; Bequest of Mrs. Alma H. Wadleigh, 47.268

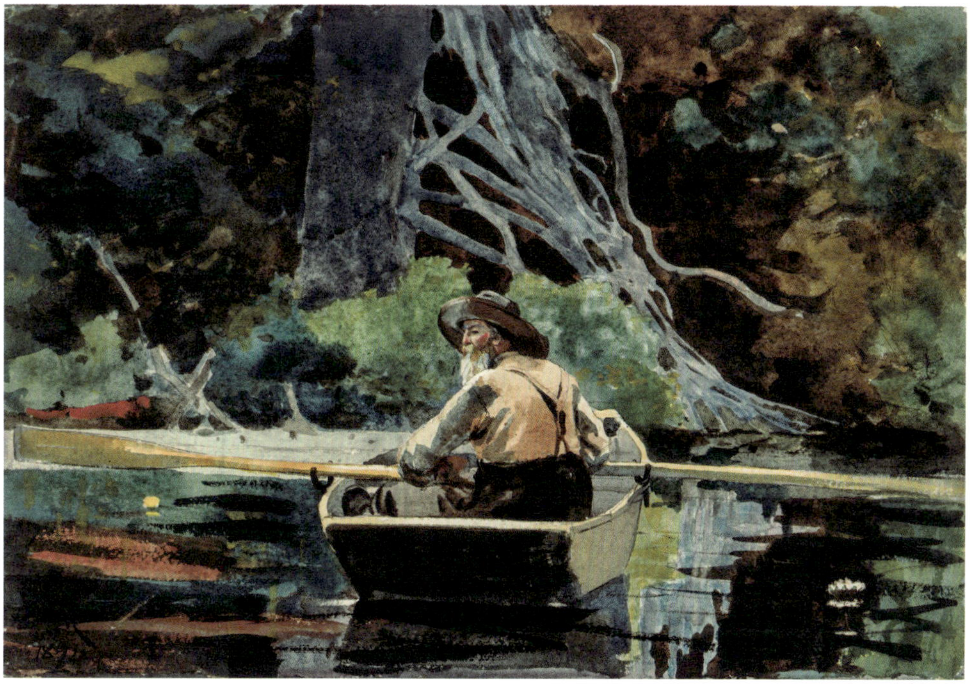

emergence of a distinctly American art.[51] Alongside Henri, Rockwell Kent, and George Bellows, Luks was linked to Homer when he turned his attention to landscape painting, a connection that would only strengthen when he began working in Maine in the 1920s.[52]

Decades passed between Homer's fishing pictures and Luks's foray into the subject, but the appeal of sporting imagery and masculine metaphors remained strong, even as more women began studying and exhibiting art, organizing politically, and participating in outdoor sports. In 1914, a writer for *Forest and Stream* declared: "The day when the woman in the woods was regarded as overstepping the prerogatives of her sex and having entered a domain sacred to mankind has passed forever."[53] Despite this admission and occasional articles penned by women writers, most of the magazine's stories and advertisements depicted the outdoors as populated solely by men and animals.

Luks's Canadian voyage commenced in the shadow of significant cultural changes. The artist arrived in Nova Scotia just a few months after Congress passed the 19th Amendment to the US Constitution, granting women the right to vote. In this moment, Luks constructed an attractive vision of self-sufficient men in nature. Reviews of his Nova Scotia paintings, like the pictures themselves, employed familiar tropes of masculinity. Writers described the works and the artist interchangeably as vigorous, individual, and powerful, and celebrated Luks for his "sheer gusto," "inherent manliness," and independence.[54] Cortissoz went a step further, criticizing Luks's approach in terms of violence, calling his portraits "brutal" and employing metaphors of a fist and a triphammer—not complimentary terms, but manly ones, to be sure.

EPILOGUE

After the exhibition at Kraushaar, Luks's paintings immediately found a national audience, appearing in *Century* magazine in February 1920. Eight paintings were published as a stand-alone portfolio, under the title "Wood, Wind and Water." It was one of a series of pictorial collections by American artists that launched with "Industrial America" by Jonas Lie in November 1919. The other entries were regional groupings by recognized artists: "From Prairie and Desert" by E. Irving Couse, "Through Valley and Hills" by George Gardner Symons, and "The Voice of Wave and Tree" by Cullen Yates. Aside from Luks, all the artists were members of the National Academy of Design.

The critical success and wide circulation of the Nova Scotia paintings may have encouraged Luks's future travels. Painting forays to Maine, Massachusetts, and rural Pennsylvania occupied the artist in his later years. Today, Luks's fame rests on urban scenes and portraits, but the Nova Scotia landscapes appealed to the ambitions of the American art establishment in 1920 and edged the artist closer to old master status.

NOTES

1. The exhibition at Kraushaar Galleries opened by January 11, 1920.
2. My brief description of Luks's biography is based on the detailed research of scholars Judith H. O'Toole, Stanley L. Cuba, and Robert L. Gambone, with specific sources quoted below.
3. Quoted in Stanley L. Cuba, "George Luks (1866–1933)," in *George Luks: An American Artist* (Wilkes-Barre, PA: Sordoni Art Gallery, Wilkes College, 1987), 7.
4. James Huneker, *Bedouins* (New York: Charles Scribner's Sons, 1920), 108. Quoted in Cuba, "George Luks (1866–1933)," 7.
5. "Sacking of the Town of Jaruco, Cuba," *Philadelphia Evening Bulletin*, March 2, 1896, 1. See also Fig. 40 in the present volume.
6. John Spargo, "George Luks, An American Painter of Great Originality and Force, Whose Art Relates to all the Experiences and Interests of Life," *The Craftsman* 12, no. 6 (September 1907): 599–607.
7. Joseph Edgar Chamberlain, "Good Art Exhibitions, A Splendid Picture by George Luks," *New York Evening Mail*, April 18, 1910, 9.
8. "Paintings by George Luks," *New York Evening Post*, April 16, 1910; Kraushaar Galleries records, clipping file, microfilm reel NKR-2, frame 64, Archives of American Art, Smithsonian Institution. Quoted in Robert L. Gambone, *Lusty Luks: The Art, Life and Times of George Benjamin Luks* (San Bernardino, CA: Robert L. Gambone, 2015), 77.
9. My understanding of Luks's career as a watercolorist relies on Judith Hansen O'Toole's excellent essay in *George Luks: Expressionist Master of Color: The Watercolors Rediscovered* (Canton, OH: The Canton Museum of Art, 1994).
10. Gambone, *Lusty Luks*, 93.
11. In the teens, Nova Scotia was gaining steam as an artist's destination. In 1917, Jonas Lie made some sketches that he showed at Montross. See *New York Herald*, February 4, 1917, 56. In February 1918, Milch Galleries in New York hosted an exhibition of "the Nova Scotia Group," which featured Canadian subjects by six New York painters, including Charles Basing, Eliot Clark, and George Macrum. The show of sixty pictures received only minor notice in the New York newspapers, but it inspired an illustrated feature that was picked up for national syndication. It read: "A new Mecca is beckoning to devotees of art and religion. Its name is Nova Scotia. Already the artists have made a pilgrimage and brought back charming pictures. . . . These pioneers have blazed a trail over which a brush and palette laden army will follow in seasons to come." See "Evangeline's Land Will Soon Have a New Shrine; French Acadians Building Chapel at Grand Pre," *Belleville Daily Advocate*, May 9, 1918, 3.
12. It is worth noting that Lawson, Glackens, and Luks were in very different parts of Nova Scotia. Lawson was in the city of Halifax, while Glackens was on the southern coast at Mahone Bay. Luks headed inland to lake country, over one hundred miles from Halifax. Lawson was in Halifax in June, and Luks was in the lake district in September–October.
13. Entry on Glackens, *Mahone Bay*, 1910, on the website of the Sheldon Museum, University of Nebraska–Lincoln, https://sheldonartmuseum.org/work/glackens-mahone.
14. In the late nineteenth and early twentieth centuries, railroads and hotels invoked Longfellow's romantic poem *Evangeline: A Tale of Acadie* to inspire scenic and cultural tourism in Nova Scotia. The epic poem set around Halifax was first published in 1847 but remained part of the American curriculum and popular culture into the 1930s.
15. See advertisement for Dominion Atlantic Railway under the heading "Resorts. Canada," *New York Herald*, May 27, 1920, 18.

16. *Hunting in Canada* (Canadian National Railways, c. 1924), 8.
17. Advertisement for Dominion Atlantic Railway. A moose head called attention to an advertisement from the chief game commissioner of Nova Scotia in *Forest and Stream* 89 (May 1919): 238.
18. Photographs depict Luks with a moose head and a giant salmon. The originals of these photographs are unlocated. The photograph of Luks with the moose head appears in Cuba, "George Luks (1866–1933)," 37. A photocopy of the photograph of Luks with a large salmon is in a letter from Cuba to O'Toole in the John Sloan Manuscript Collection, Delaware Art Museum, box 131.
19. Phil H. Moore, "Nova Scotian Outfit: The Essentials for a Spring and Summer Fishing Trip in the Land of Many Lakes and Streams," *Forest and Stream* 89 (June 1919): 319.
20. Moore, "Nova Scotian Outfit," 319.
21. Phil H. Moore, *With Gun and Rod in Canada* (New York: Houghton Mifflin, 1922).
22. Moore, "Nova Scotian Outfit," 319.
23. The inscription on Luks's drawing of Pat Lacey (Fig. 137) reads: "Lake Rossignol Sept 14th [or 17th] 1919 Pat Lacey." According to *Hunting in Canada*, moose hunting season commenced October 1. The artist is pictured with a moose head in a photograph from the trip.
24. In 1919, Mi'kmaq people remained in the area, where some men worked as professional guides. I am grateful to Roger Lewis of the Nova Scotia Museum for helping me understand this region and its Mi'kmaq roots, as well as Phil Moore's investment in the area.
25. Lake Rossignol's watershed has changed radically since Luks's visit, due to the construction of a dam in the late 1920s. Places like Moore's Camps, the Screecher, and Lowes Landing no longer exist.
26. It is not clear whether all of Luks's Nova Scotia watercolors were produced on-site. There are smaller, less composed works (like the small, unsigned sketch *Fishing, Nova Scotia*, reproduced in *George Luks, Expressionist Master of Color: The Watercolors Rediscovered*, 36) that were almost certainly made *in situ*, but some of the larger, more carefully composed works may have been made in the studio after his return. While some of the smaller watercolors remained in the artist's family, the large, signed sheets, like *The Brook*, *Guide Fishing*, and *The Strike* (all approximately fourteen by twenty inches), were exhibited and sold. Invited to submit six watercolors to an exhibition at the Memorial Art Gallery in 1921, Luks selected at least four Nova Scotia subjects: *Fifth Lake Carry, Nova Scotia*; *Guides in a Storm on Lake Rossignol*; *The Screecher*; and *Trout Fishing*.
27. Some of the oils are directly related to watercolors, though it is not clear if the watercolors were studies for the oils or independent works.
28. [James Gregg?], "Remington Works to Open Galleries," *New York Herald*, January 12, 1920, 9.
29. Royal Cortissoz, "Self-Determination in American Painting," *New York Tribune*, January 11, 1920, 37.
30. James Gregg, "George Luks Shows Work of a Year," *New York Herald*, January 11, 1920, 63.
31. Moore explained the skill required to pole a canoe upstream and suggested that nonprofessionals kneel rather than stand for this maneuver. Moore illustrated his discussion with photographs that convey the mechanics of poling a canoe, but not the challenge that he describes in the text and Luks captures in his painting. Moore, *With Gun and Rod in Canada*, 142–69.
32. Wildlife conservation was already a concern in Canada. Hunting seasons were in effect, and regulations limited the number of fish and game sportsmen could kill.

33. On moose hunting, see Phil H. Moore, "Hunting the Moose," *Forest and Stream* 89 (September 1919): 490.
34. Elon Jessup, "While the Gods Laughed," *Outing* 77, no. 2 (November 1920): 98.
35. "Guides Sports at Yarmouth Two Days," *Evening Mail* (Halifax, Nova Scotia), August 26, 1919, 12.
36. Moore, *With Gun and Rod in Canada,* 46–58.
37. Armstrong's portrait was published in Luks's portfolio in *Century* magazine. His dark clothing is sketchily executed, bringing focus to his expressive eyes, surrounded by wrinkles that reflect his age. Armstrong turned 47 in 1919. A true local professional, he lived most of his life in Queens County near Lake Rossignol, where he worked as a guide for more than forty years. Details on Armstrong come from census records and his death certificate preserved and digitized by the Public Archives of Nova Scotia. I deeply appreciate the assistance of Michelle MacCrea at the DeBrisay Museum in locating these documents for me. *Hunting in Canada* (11) lists J. Armstrong among the guides employed by Moore's Camps.
38. Moore, *With Gun and Rod in Canada*, 219; M. B. Miller, "From Rossignol to Tusket—II," in *Forest and Stream* 77, no. 11 (September 9, 1911): 408.
39. Gregg, "George Luks Shows Work of a Year," 63.
40. Gregg, "George Luks Shows Work of a Year," 63.
41. Cortissoz, "Self-Determination in American Painting," 37.
42. Gregg, "George Luks Shows Work of a Year," 63.
43. [Gregg?], "Remington Works to Open Galleries," 9.
44. Gregg, "George Luks Shows Work of a Year," 63.
45. "At the Kraushaar Galleries," *New York Times*, January 11, 1920, 54.
46. "The Paintings of George Luks," *Brooklyn Daily Eagle,* January 25, 1920, 69.
47. See Sarah Burns, *Inventing the Modern Artist: Art and Culture in Gilded Age America* (New Haven, CT: Yale University Press, 1996), 187–217.
48. On Homer's fishing scenes, see Patricia Junker and Sarah Burns, *Winslow Homer: Artist and Angler* (New York: Thames & Hudson, 2002). For his work in the Adirondacks, see Randall C. Griffin, *Winslow Homer: An American Vision* (New York: Phaidon, 2006), 147–67. For a broader consideration of American hunting scenes, see Kevin Sharp, ed., *Wild Spaces, Open Seasons: Hunting and Fishing in American Art* (Norman: University of Oklahoma Press, 2016).
49. It is worth noting that the Kraushaar exhibition in 1920, which inspired all the talk of Winslow Homer, did not include Luks's Nova Scotia watercolors. Although there are parallels in subject matter, Luks's composition and handling have little in common with Homer's fishing watercolors.
50. Bruce Robertson, *Reckoning with Winslow Homer: His Late Paintings and Their Influence* (Cleveland, OH: Cleveland Museum of Art, 1990), 63.
51. On Luks as a proponent of a distinctly American art, see Spargo, "George Luks, An American Painter of Great Originality and Force," 601.
52. Robertson, *Reckoning with Winslow Homer*, 101–36.
53. "Milady in the Woods," *Forest and Stream* 82, no. 9 (February 28, 1914): 9.
54. "Sheer gusto" is quoted from Cortissoz, "Self-Determination in American Painting," 37. "Inherent manliness" is from "The Paintings of George Luks," *Brooklyn Daily Eagle*, January 25, 1920, 69.

Contributors

Avis Berman is an independent writer and art historian. In 2014 she organized *William Glackens*, the first comprehensive survey of the artist's work in nearly fifty years, and is the author or co-author of numerous books, including *Rebels on Eighth Street: Juliana Force and the Whitney Museum of American Art* (1990), *Edward Hopper's New York* (2005), *My Love Affair with Modern Art: Behind the Scenes with a Legendary Curator* (2006), *Roy Lichtenstein: Sea and Sky* (2015), and *Roy Lichtenstein: The Impossible Collection* (2019). She has also sustained a parallel career as an oral historian in the visual arts. To date, she has interviewed more than five hundred artists, curators, critics, dealers, collectors, and other figures in the art world for museums, archives, and artist's foundations.

Heather Campbell Coyle is Curator of American Art at the Delaware Art Museum. She lectures and researches primarily on American art, illustration, and photography from the late nineteenth and early twentieth centuries. She is the editor and lead author of *Jazz Age Illustration* (2024), *An American Journey: The Art of John Sloan* (2017), *Fashion, Circus, Spectacle: Photographs by Scott Heiser* (2014), and *Howard Pyle: American Master Rediscovered* (2011), and co-editor and co-author of *John Sloan's New York* (2007). She has also published essays and curated exhibitions on Helen Farr Sloan, William Glackens, Robert Henri, Gertrude Käsebier, Everett Shinn, and the Society of Independent Artists.

David B. Dearinger graduated from the University of Kentucky in 1972, after which he moved to New York City to work for TWA as one of the first men hired by the airline industry into the previously all-female ranks of flight attendants. He was promoted to the rank of Flight Service Manager and was a founding member of the Independent Federation of Flight Attendants. While continuing to work domestic and international flights for TWA, he earned an MA and a PhD in art history from the Graduate Center of the City University of New York. He has been a tenured adjunct professor at the State University of New York's FIT, Chief Curator at the National Academy of Design, and Hilles Curator of Paintings & Sculpture at the Boston Athenaeum. His work has been recognized by grants from the National Endowment for the Arts, the National Endowment for the Humanities, the Luce Foundation, and others.

Kathleen A. Foster is The Robert L. McNeil, Jr., Senior Curator of American Art and Director of the Center for American Art at the Philadelphia Museum of Art. With degrees from Wellesley College (BA) and Yale University (MA, MPhil, PhD), she has held curatorial posts at the Pennsylvania Academy of the Fine Arts and the Indiana University Art Museum, and taught at Williams College, Temple University, Indiana University, and the University of Pennsylvania, where she currently serves as an adjunct professor in the History of Art. She has published work on topics in American art from the late eighteenth century to the present, with an emphasis on the work of Thomas Eakins. Long-running study yielded *American Watercolor in the Age of Homer and Sargent* (2017), with an affiliated exhibition and research website. She led the Philadelphia Museum of Art's team in the installation of new Early American Galleries, which opened in 2021.

Carol Troyen, Kristin and Roger Servison Curator Emerita of American Paintings at the Museum of Fine Arts (MFA), Boston, is an independent scholar. While at the MFA, she organized many exhibitions, including *Charles Sheeler: Paintings and Drawings* (1987), *Awash in Color: Homer, Sargent, and the Great American Watercolor* (1993), and *Edward Hopper* (2007). She has lectured at museums across the country and has served as interim chief curator at the Wadsworth Atheneum. Her recent publications include essays on American still-life painting, on Charles Sheeler's last works, and on Thomas Cole's *Garden of Eden*.

Index

NOTE
Page numbers in italic type refer to illustrations.

L

M

S

T

PHOTOGRAPHY CREDITS

Every effort has been made to locate the copyright holders for the works of art illustrated. Unless otherwise noted, photography was supplied by the owners or custodians of the works as indicated in the captions and are reproduced by their permission; their courtesy is gratefully acknowledged. Additional credits are listed here.

Addison Gallery of American Art, Phillips Academy, Andover, MA/Art Resource, NY (Fig. 125)
Joseph M. Arseneau/Shutterstock.com (Fig. 98)
The Art Institute of Chicago/Art Resource, NY (Figs. 20, 35, 64, 86)
Courtesy of The Barnes Foundation (Frontispiece, and Figs. 81, 127)
Courtesy of Bowdoin College Museum, Brunswick, ME. © 2024 Delaware Art Museum/Artists Rights Society (ARS), New York (Fig. 25)
Bridgeman Images (Figs. 75, 126)
Courtesy of Brooklyn Museum, NY (Figs. 63, 78, 84, 92, 115)
Buffalo AKG Art Museum/Art Resource, NY (Fig. 139)
Carnegie Museum of Art/Art Resource, NY (Fig. 8)
Chapin Library, Williams College, Williamstown, MA (Figs. 109, 112)
© Christie's Images/Bridgeman Images (Figs. 79, 118)
© Cincinnati Art Museum/Bridgeman Images (Fig. 68)
Courtesy of Cleveland Museum of Art, OH (Fig. 18)
Courtesy of Colby College Museum of Art, Waterville, ME (Fig. 82)
Courtesy of Columbus Museum of Art, OH (Fig. 31)
Courtesy of Concord Free Public Library, William Munroe Special Collections, MA (Fig. 106)
Courtesy of Conner-Rosenkranz, New York (Fig. 100)
Courtesy of Crystal Bridges Museum of American Art, Bentonville, AR (Fig. 113)
Daderot, 2008/CC BY-SA-3.0 (Fig. 108)
Courtesy of Delaware Art Museum (Figs. 120, 121, 122, 130)
Image courtesy of Delaware Art Museum. © 2024 Delaware Art Museum/Artists Rights Society (ARS), New York (Fig. 13)
Courtesy of Frederic Remington Art Museum, Ogdensburg, NY (Figs. 49, 54, 59)
Hathi Digital Library Collection (Fig. 41)
Courtesy of Helen Farr Sloan Library & Archives, Delaware Art Museum (Fig. 23)
Heritage Images, Hulton Archive/Getty Images (Fig. 107)
History and Art Collection/Alamy Stock Photo (Fig. 111)
Courtesy of Hood Museum of Art, Dartmouth College, Hanover, NH (Fig. 17)
Internet Archive: Digital Library (Figs. 39, 53)
© Peter A. Juley & Son Collection, Smithsonian American Art Museum, Washington, DC (Fig. 105)
Courtesy of Kraushaar Galleries, New York (Fig. 7)
Photography by Mike Lalich, 2008. © 2024 Delaware Art Museum/Artists Rights Society (ARS), New York (Fig. 24)
Photography by Robert LaPrelle (Fig. 28)
Courtesy of the Library of Congress, Washington, DC (Figs. 2, 33, 34, 43, 45, 48, 50, 51, 52, 55, 58)
Library of Congress Prints and Photographs Division, Washington, DC, Detroit Publishing Company Photograph Collection (Fig. 110)
The Loomis Chaffee Archives; Loomis Chaffee School, Windsor, CT (Fig. 94)
Patti McConville/Alamy Stock Photo (Fig. 44)
Image © The Metropolitan Museum of Art. Image source: Art Resource, NY (Cover, Figs. 10, 16, 60, 62, 80, 93, 95, 96, 99, 101, 103, 129)
Image © The Metropolitan Museum of Art, Image source: Art Resource, NY. © 2024 Delaware Art Museum/Artists Rights Society (ARS), New York (Figs. 11, 12)
Munson Museum, Utica, NY/Art Resource, NY (Figs. 128, 140)
Courtesy of Museum of Fine Arts, Boston (Fig. 124)
Photograph © 2025 Museum of Fine Arts, Boston (Fig. 141)
National Academy of Design/Bridgeman Images (Fig. 114)
Courtesy of National Gallery of Art, Washington, DC (Figs. 19, 29, 69)
Courtesy of Nelson-Atkins Media Services, Gabe Hopkins (Fig. 65)
Collection of Newark Museum of Art/ Art Resource, NY (Fig. 85)
Courtesy of NSU Art Museum, Fort Lauderdale, FL (Figs. 4, 6, 22, 57)
Courtesy of Pennsylvania Academy of Fine Arts (Fig. 5)
Courtesy of Philadelphia Museum of Art (Figs. 3, 32, 66, 83)
Photograph: Allen Phillips/Wadsworth Atheneum. © 2024 Georgia O'Keeffe Museum/Artists Rights Society (ARS), New York (Fig. 88)
Courtesy of The Phillips Collection, Washington, DC (Fig. 15)
Courtesy of The Phillips Collection, Washington, DC. © 2024 Delaware Art Museum/Artists Rights Society (ARS), New York (Fig. 26)
Photograph © President and Fellows of Harvard College (Fig. 67)
Courtesy of The Reading Public Museum, PA (Fig. 131)
Courtesy of Research and Scholars Center, Smithsonian American Art Museum, Washington, DC (Fig. 116)
Rhododendrites, CC BY-SA 4.0 (Fig. 104)
Courtesy of The San Diego Museum of Art, CA (Fig. 119)
Courtesy of Sheldon Museum of Art, University of Nebraska, Lincoln, NE (Fig. 21)
Courtesy of Smithsonian American Art Museum, Washington, DC (Figs. 71, 90, 117)
Photograph courtesy of Smithsonian American Art Museum, Washington, DC. © 2024 Georgia O'Keeffe Museum/Artists Rights Society (ARS), New York
Photography by Lee Stalsworth, Hirshhorn Museum and Sculpture Garden (Figs. 9, 76, 135)
The Stapleton Collection/Bridgeman Images (Fig. 36)
Courtesy of Sullivan Goss, Santa Barbara, CA (Fig. 77)
© Tate Images Tate Enterprises, Ltd, London, UK (Figs. 1, 30)
Courtesy of Terra Foundation for American Art, Chicago (Fig. 61)
Photography © Terra Foundation for American Art, Chicago (Fig. 14)
Photography by Jerry L. Thompson. Image © The Metropolitan Museum of Art. Image source: Art Resource, NY (Figs. 89, 91, 102)
Courtesy of Carol Troyen (Fig. 47)
USAPhoto © Detroit Institute of Arts/ Bridgeman Images (Fig. 37)
Courtesy of Westmoreland Museum of Art, Greensburg, PA (Fig. 137)
Courtesy of Whitney Museum of American Art, New York (Figs. 27, 123, 132, 138)
Photograph: Wikimedia Commons, https://en.m.wikipedia.org/wiki/File:Judge-2-6-1897.jpg (Fig. 46)